MW00714281

IBM

International Technical Support Organization

Enterprise Business Portals with IBM Tivoli Access Manager

August 2002

SG24-6556-00

Take Note! Before using this information and the product it supports, be sure to read the general information in "Notices" on page xxi.

First Edition (August 2002)

This edition applies to IBM Tivoli Access Manager Version 3.9.

Comments may be addressed to:
IBM Corporation, International Technical Support Organization
Dept. OSJB Building 003 Internal Zip 2834
11400 Burnet Road
Austin, Texas 78758-3493

When you send information to IBM, you grant IBM a non-exclusive right to use or distribute the information in any way it believes appropriate without incurring any obligation to you.

Contents

Figures

Tables

Notices

This information was developed for products and services offered in the U.S.A.

IBM may not offer the products, services, or features discussed in this document in other countries. Consult your local IBM representative for information on the products and services currently available in your area. Any reference to an IBM product, program, or service is not intended to state or imply that only that IBM product, program, or service may be used. Any functionally equivalent product, program, or service that does not infringe any IBM intellectual property right may be used instead. However, it is the user's responsibility to evaluate and verify the operation of any non-IBM product, program, or service.

IBM may have patents or pending patent applications covering subject matter described in this document. The furnishing of this document does not give you any license to these patents. You can send license inquiries, in writing, to:
IBM Director of Licensing, IBM Corporation, North Castle Drive Armonk, NY 10504-1785 U.S.A.

The following paragraph does not apply to the United Kingdom or any other country where such provisions are inconsistent with local law: INTERNATIONAL BUSINESS MACHINES CORPORATION PROVIDES THIS PUBLICATION "AS IS" WITHOUT WARRANTY OF ANY KIND, EITHER EXPRESS OR IMPLIED, INCLUDING, BUT NOT LIMITED TO, THE IMPLIED WARRANTIES OF NON-INFRINGEMENT, MERCHANTABILITY OR FITNESS FOR A PARTICULAR PURPOSE. Some states do not allow disclaimer of express or implied warranties in certain transactions, therefore, this statement may not apply to you.

This information could include technical inaccuracies or typographical errors. Changes are periodically made to the information herein; these changes will be incorporated in new editions of the publication. IBM may make improvements and/or changes in the product(s) and/or the program(s) described in this publication at any time without notice.

Any references in this information to non-IBM Web sites are provided for convenience only and do not in any manner serve as an endorsement of those Web sites. The materials at those Web sites are not part of the materials for this IBM product and use of those Web sites is at your own risk.

IBM may use or distribute any of the information you supply in any way it believes appropriate without incurring any obligation to you.

Information concerning non-IBM products was obtained from the suppliers of those products, their published announcements or other publicly available sources. IBM has not tested those products and cannot confirm the accuracy of performance, compatibility or any other claims related to non-IBM products. Questions on the capabilities of non-IBM products should be addressed to the suppliers of those products.

This information contains examples of data and reports used in daily business operations. To illustrate them as completely as possible, the examples include the names of individuals, companies, brands, and products. All of these names are fictitious and any similarity to the names and addresses used by an actual business enterprise is entirely coincidental.

COPYRIGHT LICENSE:
This information contains sample application programs in source language, which illustrates programming techniques on various operating platforms. You may copy, modify, and distribute these sample programs in any form without payment to IBM, for the purposes of developing, using, marketing or distributing application programs conforming to the application programming interface for the operating platform for which the sample programs are written. These examples have not been thoroughly tested under all conditions. IBM, therefore, cannot guarantee or imply reliability, serviceability, or function of these programs. You may copy, modify, and distribute these sample programs in any form without payment to IBM for the purposes of developing, using, marketing, or distributing application programs conforming to IBM's application programming interfaces.

Trademarks

The following terms are trademarks of the International Business Machines Corporation in the United States, other countries, or both:

AIX®	MQSeries®	S/390®
AS/400®	OS/390®	SecureWay®
Balance®	PAL®	SP™
CICS®	Perform™	SP2®
DB2®	RACF®	Tivoli®
DirectTalk®	Redbooks™	WebSphere®
Everyplace™	Redbooks(logo)™	z/OS™
IBM®	RS/6000®	3890™

The following terms are trademarks of International Business Machines Corporation and Lotus Development Corporation in the United States, other countries, or both:

Approach®	Lotus Notes®	Sametime®
Domino™	Lotus Sametime™	Word Pro®
Lotus®	Notes®	

The following terms are trademarks of other companies:

ActionMedia, LANDesk, MMX, Pentium and ProShare are trademarks of Intel Corporation in the United States, other countries, or both.

Microsoft, Windows, Windows NT, and the Windows logo are trademarks of Microsoft Corporation in the United States, other countries, or both.

Java and all Java-based trademarks and logos are trademarks or registered trademarks of Sun Microsystems, Inc. in the United States, other countries, or both.

C-bus is a trademark of Corollary, Inc. in the United States, other countries, or both.

UNIX is a registered trademark of The Open Group in the United States and other countries.

SET, SET Secure Electronic Transaction, and the SET Logo are trademarks owned by SET Secure Electronic Transaction LLC.

Other company, product, and service names may be trademarks or service marks of others.

Preface

IBM Tivoli Access Manager for e-business is one of the most robust and secure access control management solutions for e-business and legacy applications on the market today. It uniquely addresses the top challenges of e-business security, such as escalating costs, growing complexity, and the inability to implement security policies across an entire environment, and helps lower the total cost of secure computing. By providing highly-available, centralized authentication and authorization services, Tivoli Access Manager enables you to better manage your business-critical, distributed information. It provides simple, secure access to critical information, and enhances communications with customers, business partners, and others, therefore enabling your e-business to thrive. This IBM Redbook will help you understand and design some of the major Tivoli Access Manager strong points:

► Centrally define and manage security policy for your e-business applications.

► Transparently enforce authorization policy through access control rights to Web applications.

► Support virtually any client device, including browsers and pervasive devices.

► Use a multitude of authentication and delegation mechanisms to access existing Web-based applications without rewriting or modifying them.

► Provide single sign-on to Web-based applications.

The team that wrote this redbook

This redbook was produced by a team of specialists from around the world working at the International Technical Support Organization, Austin Center.

Left to right: Armando, Axel, Chris, Jani, Dieter, Andreas

Axel Bücker is a Certified Consulting Software IT Specialist at the International Technical Support Organization, Austin Center. He writes extensively and teaches IBM classes worldwide on areas of Software Security Architecture. He holds a degree in Computer Science from the University of Bremen, Germany. He has 16 years of experience in a variety of areas related to Workstation and Systems Management, Network Computing, and e-Business Solutions. Before joining the ITSO in March 2000, Axel was working for IBM in Germany as a Senior IT Specialist in Software Security Architecture.

Chris Eric Friell is a Consulting IT Specialist with IBM Norway. He has worked with IBM for 16 years and has spent the last three years on customer security projects. He holds a degree in Telecommunications from East London University. He also is a member of the Nordic Certification Board. His areas of expertise include AIX, Catia, Computer Integrated Telephony, and Tivoli Policy Director.

Armando Lemos is the Information Security Officer at Maxblue Brazil (http://www.maxblue.com.br). He is a Certified Information Systems Security Professional (CISSP) with 14 years of experience in the data processing field, including IBM Mainframe and Midrange systems. He holds a degree in Computer Science from Pontificia Universidade Catolica in Sao Paulo. His areas of expertise include Hypertext Technology, Computer Security, Operating Systems, and Disaster Recovery.

Rick McCarty is a Senior Security Architect and Practice Lead for Security with IBM Tivoli Services. Based in Austin, Texas, his current work focuses on Policy Director/Access Manager Architecture. In addition to security, Rick's background extends across a broad range of computing areas, including operating systems, artificial intelligence, TCP/IP networking, e-mail gateway systems, directory services, and high-availability. His software development experience spans approximately 17 years at IBM, Tandem Computers, and Texas Instruments. Rick received his Bachelors Degree from the University of Texas at Austin.

Jani Perttilä is an Advisory IT Specialist with IBM Finland and has been working at IBM for six years. He is MCSE and PSE certified and used to work with Microsoft software and IBM hardware. He moved to the Tivoli field about four years ago with the Tivoli IT Director. In February 2000 he was part of a team writing the redbook *Managing AS/400 with Tivoli IT Director*, SG24-6003, in Austin. For the last two years he has almost exclusively been working with Tivoli Policy Director. While doing this, he gained experience with LDAP, IT Security, DCE, and various other fields that relate to the product.

Dieter Riexinger is a Security Architect in IBM Germany. He has 10 years of experience mainly in Networking, Java Development, and IT Security. He holds a degree in Computer Science from University Mannheim. His areas of expertise include IBM Tivoli Policy Director, LDAP, Identrus, Electronic Bill Presentment and Payment (EBPP), and User Management.

Andreas J. Schmengler is a Certified Consulting IT Architect in IBM Germany. He holds a degree in Computer Science from the University of Bonn, Germany. He has more than 16 years of experience, mainly in Networking and IT Security disciplines and has led design and architecture engagements for complex IT infrastructures. He is a member of the IBM Technical Expert Council (TEC) and lectures at the University of Applied Sciences, Cologne, Germany.

We would like to thank all the people involved in developing Tivoli Access Manager and for the outstanding product, support, and documentation as an invaluable contribution to this project. Additionally, we want to thank the people that directly shared their knowledge and time with our team:

International Technical Support Organization, Austin Center
Julie Czubik

IBM Tivoli Security Team US

Mark Vandenwauver, Paul Ashley, Heather Hinton, Neil Readshaw, Ivan Milman, Sridhar Muppidi, Mark Simpson, Michael Campbell, Patrick Wardrop, Venkat Raghavan, Rich Caponigro, Jim Wade, Anthony Moran, Kellie LeCompte, Tim Ledwith, Peter Spicer

IBM WebSphere Team US

Tony Cowan

IBM Tivoli Security Team Australia

Vernon Murdoch, Robert Fyfe, Mike Thomas, Charles Chan

IBM UK

Jon Harry and Avery Salmon for their outstanding deliverables and class material on Policy Director/Access Manager, Vincent Cassidy, Joanna Hodgson

IBM Switzerland

Daniel Kipfer

MaxBlue Information Security

Hai Ngo, Manager, for his management support in releasing Armando Lemos to participate in this exciting residency

Notice

This publication is intended to help security officers, administrators and architects to understand how to build a secure business portal solution using the IBM Tivoli Access Manager for e-business. It will provide information on the integration with different e-business application platforms in order to better design security aspects in heterogeneous IT environments. The information in this publication is not intended as the specification of any programming interfaces that are provided by any Tivoli branded security product. See the individual product documentation section of the Tivoli security applications for a more detailed description.

Comments welcome

Your comments are important to us!

We want our Redbooks to be as helpful as possible. Send us your comments about this or other Redbooks in one of the following ways:

► Use the online **Contact us** review redbook form found at:

`ibm.com`/redbooks

► Send your comments in an Internet note to:

    redbook@us.ibm.com

► Mail your comments to the address on page ii.

Part 1

Tivoli Access Manager introduction

In this part we introduce the general components of the IBM Tivoli Access Manager for e-business and what it has to offer in the access control area of the overall security architecture. Access Manager handles a multitude of integration aspects with all sorts of IT infrastructures and application environments, which are detailed throughout this part of the book. After talking about general considerations and architectures, Part 2, "Insurance environment" on page 213, and Part 3, "Banking environment" on page 317, provide a much more detailed scenario based approach.

Introduction to Access Manager components

In this chapter we introduce the components of Access Manager. We will discuss three types of components:

► Base components, which are generally common to all Access Manager installations

► Blades, which support authorization for specific application classes

► Interface components, which permit application programs to directly interact with Access Manager functions

Discussion of these components provides the foundation for introducing the elements of the Access Manager architecture.

Note: Due to the latest IBM Tivoli changes in naming and branding you will be confronted with the new name for Tivoli Policy Director: IBM Tivoli Access Manager for e-business. On some occasions, when we are referring to older versions of the product, we still use Policy Director Version 3.8 or Version 3.7. All references to Tivoli Access Manager are based on the current Version 3.9, which became available in April 2002.

1.1 Base components

Access Manager provides several components that support basic product functionality. The Access Manager "base" consists of a small set of architecturally "core" components and management facilities that are generally required to support and administer the environment.

1.1.1 Overview

Access Manager's base functions are provided through a set of core components and various management components.

Core components

Access Manager is fundamentally based on two components:

► A user registry

► An Authorization Service, consisting of an authorization database and an authorization engine

These components support the core functionality that must exist for Access Manager to perform its fundamental operations, which are:

► Knowing the identity of who is performing a particular operation (users)

► Knowing the roles associated with a particular identity (groups)

► Knowing what application entities a particular identity may access (objects)

► Knowing the authorization rules associated with application objects (policies)

► Using the above to make access decisions on behalf of applications (authorization)

► Auditing and logging all activity related to authentication and authorization

In summary, a user registry and an Authorization Service are the fundamental building blocks upon which Access Manager builds to provide its security capabilities. All other Access Manager services and components are built upon this base.

Management components

The Access Manager environment requires certain basic capabilities for administrative control of its functions. Management facilities are provided through the following base components:

► The Policy Server, which supports the management of the authorization database and its distribution to Authorization Services

- The pdadmin utility, which provides a command line capability for performing administrative functions, such as adding users or groups
- The Web Portal Manager, which provides an Web browser based capability for performing most of the same functions provided by the pdadmin utility

1.1.2 User registry

Access Manager requires a user registry to support the operation of its authorization functions. Specifically, it provides:

- A database of the user identities that are known to Access Manager
- A representation of groups in Access Manager (roles) that may be associated with users
- A data store of other metadata required to support authorization functions

Identity mapping

While it can be used in authenticating users, this is not the primary purpose of the user registry. An application can authenticate a user via any mechanism it chooses (ID/password, certificate, and so on), and then map the authenticated identity to one defined in the user registry. For example, consider a user John who authenticates himself to an application using a certificate. The application then maps the DN in John's certificate to the Access Manager user named john123. When making subsequent authorization decisions, the internal Access Manager user is john123, and this identity is passed between the application and other components using various mechanisms, including a special credential known as an Extended Privilege Attribute Certificate (EPAC).

Note: One of the primary goals of the authentication process is to acquire credential information describing the client user. The user credential is one of the key requirements for participating in the secure domain.

Access Manager distinguishes the authentication of the user from the acquisition of credentials. A user's identity is always constant. However, credentials, which define the groups or roles in which a user participates, are variable. Context-specific credentials can change over time. For example, when a person is promoted, credentials must reflect the new responsibility level.

The authentication process results in method-specific user identity information. This information is checked against user account information that resides in the Access Manager user registry. WebSEAL maps the user name and group information to a common domain-wide representation and format known as the Extended Privilege Attribute Certificate (EPAC).

Method-specific identity information, such as passwords, tokens, and certificates, represent physical identity properties of the user. This information can be used to establish a secure session with the server.

The resulting credential, which represents a user's privileges in the secure domain, describes the user in a specific context and is only valid for the lifetime of that session.

Access Manager credentials contain the user identity and groups where this user has membership.

User registry structure

The user registry contains three types of objects:

► User objects, which contain basic user attributes.

► Group objects, which represent roles that may be associated with user objects.

► Access Manager metadata objects, which contain special Access Manager attributes that are associated with user and group objects. The metadata includes information that allows an Access Manager user ID to be linked to its corresponding user object.

The default user registry is LDAP-based and Access Manager 3.9 consolidates its registry support around a number of LDAP directory products.

Access Manager is capable of using the following directory products for its user registry:

- ► IBM Directory Server
- ► Critical Path LiveContent Directory
- ► Netscape iPlanet Directory
- ► Microsoft Active Directory (Windows 2000 advanced Server only)
- ► Lotus Domino Name Address Book (Access Manager on Windows only)
- ► OS/390 Security Server
- ► z/OS Security Server

The IBM Directory Server is included with Access Manager and is the default LDAP directory for implementing the user registry.

Access Manager components support the use of directory replicas, and in production installations, it is generally advantageous to use replicas for scalability and availability purposes.

Directory schema

To support its critical and private registry data, Access Manager requires certain support in the directory schema. There are certain object classes and attributes that are specific to Access Manager and are configured as needed during product installation. Access Manager, however, only adds new subclasses to existing directory entries, for example, inetOrgPerson.

Attention: While it might seem relevant to inquire about the details of the directory schema that Access Manager uses, such information is not necessarily useful (and may in fact be somewhat "dangerous" to have). It is important to keep in mind that Access Manager components are the exclusive users of these special object classes and attributes. The schema definitions and their usage can change from release to release. As such, application components should not assume any knowledge of Access Manager-specific schema definitions or how they are used. Instead, application interaction with registry information or functions should only be performed using published Access Manager interfaces.

1.1.3 Authorization database

Separately from the user registry, for its authorization functions, Access Manager uses a special database containing a virtual representation of resources it protects. Called the "protected object space", it uses a proprietary format and contains object definitions that may represent logical or actual physical resources. Objects for different application types may be contained in different sections of the object space, and the object space may be extended to support new application types as required.

The security policy for these resources is implemented by applying appropriate security mechanisms to the objects requiring protection. Security mechanisms are also defined in the authorization database, and include:

► Access control list (ACL) policy templates

ACLs are special Access Manager objects that define policies identifying user types that can be considered for access, and specify permitted operations. In the Access Manager model, ACLs are defined separately from and then attached to one or more protected objects. So an ACL has no effect on authorization until it becomes associated with a protected object.

Access Manager uses an inheritance model in which an ACL attached to a protected object applies to all other objects below it in the tree until another ACL is encountered.

► Protected object policy (POP) templates

A POP specifies additional conditions governing the access to the protected object, such as privacy, integrity, auditing, and time-of-day access.

POPs are attached to protected objects in the same manner as ACLs.

► Extended attributes

Extended attributes are additional values placed on an object, ACL, or POP that can be read and interpreted by third-party applications (such as an external Authorization Service).

Figure 1-1 on page 9 depicts the relationships between the protected object space, ACLs, and POPs.

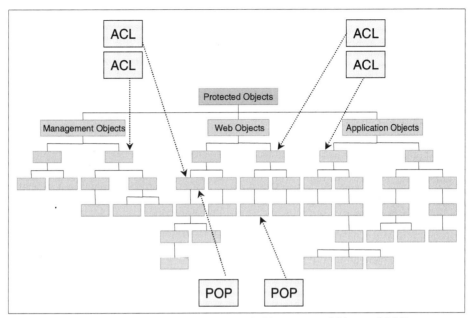

Figure 1-1   Relationship between the protected object space, ACLs, and POPs

Successful implementation of a security policy requires that the different content types are logically organized (and the appropriate ACL and POP policies applied). Access control management is simplified by structuring the protected resources in such a way as to minimize the number of ACL and POP attachments required to implement the security policy, and thus gaining maximum benefit from the sparse ACL model that we implement.

1.1.4 Policy Server

The Access Manager Policy Server maintains the master authorization database for the secure domain. This server is key to the processing of access control, authentication, and authorization requests. It also is responsible for distributing and updating all authorization database replicas and maintains location information about other Access Manager servers in the secure domain.

There can only be a single Policy Server in an Access Manager domain. For availability purposes, a standby server can be configured to take over Policy Server functions in the event of a system failure. This can be supported via manually executed recovery actions, or automatically, using an appropriate high-availability product (for example, HACMP on AIX platforms). This is further discussed in 4.2, "Availability" on page 81.

1.1.5 Authorization Service

The foundation of Access Manager is its Authorization Service, which permits or denies access to protected objects (resources) based on the user's credentials and the access controls placed on the objects.

The Policy Server provides an Authorization Service that may be leveraged by applications and other Access Manager components that use the Authorization Application Programming Interface (aznAPI) (described in 1.3.1, "aznAPI" on page 29). Optionally, additional Authorization Servers may be installed to offload these authorization decisions from the Policy Server and provide for higher availability of authorization functions. The Policy Server provides updates for authorization database replicas maintained on each Authorization Server.

The Access Manager Authorization Service can also be directly embedded within an application. In this case, the functions of an Authorization Server are contained in the application itself.

1.1.6 The pdadmin utility

pdadmin is a command-line utility that supports Access Manager administrative functions. In Policy Director versions prior to 3.8, multiple, specialized command line utilities supported various administrative needs. These functions (including management of WebSEAL junctions) have now been combined within pdadmin.

1.1.7 Web Portal Manager

The Access Manager Web Portal Manager (WPM) provides a Web browser-based graphical user interface (GUI) for Access Manager administration. It replaces the Management Console used in earlier releases of Access Manager.

A key advantage of the Web Portal Manager over the pdadmin command and the earlier Management Console is the fact that it is a browser-based application that can be accessed without installing any Access Manager-specific client components, or requiring special network configuration to permit remote administrator access. In fact, the authorization capabilities of WebSEAL (described in 1.2.1, "WebSEAL" on page 14) can be used to control access to the Web Portal Manager. This allows greater flexibility in where administrators are located with respect to the physical systems they are managing.

The Web Portal Manager was designed to be an alternative to the pdadmin command line interface (CLI) for many administrative functions. However, not all pdadmin functions are supported (for example, managing WebSEAL junctions must be done using pdadmin), and the command line interface will still be required in certain cases.

The Web Portal Manager also provides a delegated user administration capability. This allows an Access Manager administrator to create delegated user domains and assign delegate administrators to these domains, as shown in Figure 1-2.

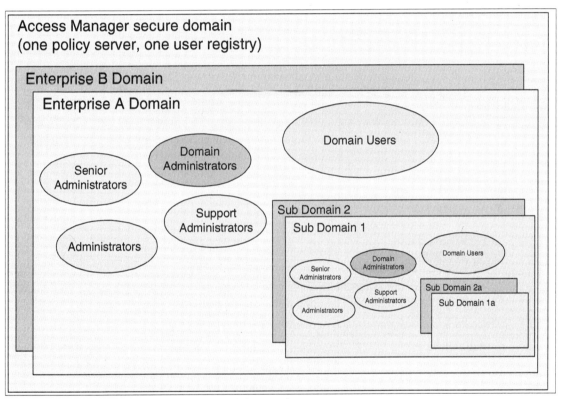

Figure 1-2   Access Manager delegation model example

The initial aim of the Web Portal Manager is to allow multiple independent enterprises to manage their own user population in a single Access Manager secure domain. This functionality could be used where a service provider that is using Access Manager to provide access control to Web resources wants to allow its customers to define and manage their own user population.

Note: The Web Portal Manager Version 3.9 has been aligned with Tivoli's Identity Manager user interface for better administrative usability.

The WPM provides a simple Web-based interface to the existing delegated administration function of Access Manager. It allows a super user (for example, sec_master) to define a number of Enterprise domains, each with one or more domain administrators that are the super users in that domain. WPM is supported on Windows NT SP6a, Windows 2000 Advanced Server SP2, AIX Version 4.3.3. and 5.1.0, and Solaris 7 and 8 platforms.

A Domain Administrator can create, modify, and delete domain users within the domain and can delegate administration within the domain. Domain administrators can also create sub-domains inside the domain they control.

All administrative users in a domain (including the Domain Administrators) can be limited so they can only view and/or modify the users within their domain.

Depending on their assigned roles, the delegate administrators can perform a subset of the administration functions aligning the security administration with different organization and business relationships, such as:

► Departments
► Dealerships
► Branch offices
► Partnerships
► Suppliers
► Distributors

There are four different levels of administration in Access Manager with the basic fields of action shown in Table 1-1.

Table 1-1   Delegated administration roles in Access Manager

Action/role	Domain admin	Senior admin	Admin	Support	Any other
View user	X	X	X	X	X
Reset password	X	X	X	X	
Add existing Access Manager user as an administrator	X	X	X		
Create domain user	X	X			
Remove user	X	X			
Domain control	X				

Architecture

The Web Portal Manager is built using Java Server Pages (JSP), which support the various administrative functions. It uses a Web application server servlet engine; WebSphere Application Server 3.5 is provided with Access Manager to support this capability. Figure 1-3 provides an architectural view of how the Web Portal Manager works.

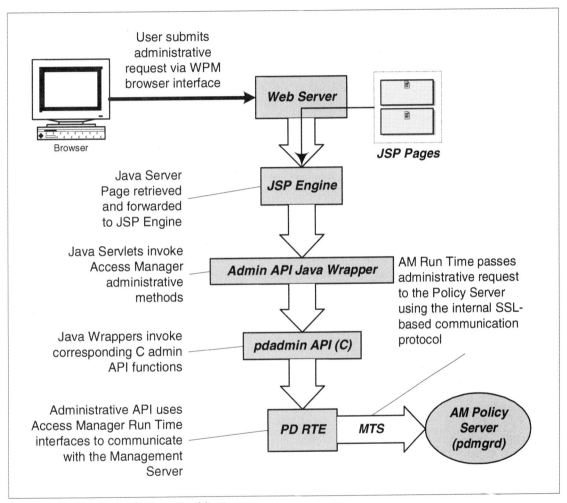

Figure 1-3 Web Portal Manager architecture

Other issues

There are a number of other issues that should be kept in mind when deploying the Web Portal Manager:

► There is no limit to the number of Web Portal Manager instances that may be deployed.

► It is possible to provide access to the Web Portal Manager via a WebSEAL junction (discussed below); however, transparent sign-on is not supported in the current (3.9) release. In other words, a user logged on to WebSEAL must also log on to the Web Portal Manager.

1.2 Blades

Blades are components that provide Access Manager authorization support for specific application types.

1.2.1 WebSEAL

WebSEAL is a high-performance, multi-threaded reverse proxy, front-ending back-end Web services that applies a security policy to a protected object space (which is defined in the authorization database, described in 1.1.3, "Authorization database" on page 7). WebSEAL can provide single sign-on solutions and incorporate back-end Web application server resources into its security policy. Being implemented on an HTTP server foundation, it listens to the typical HTTP- and HTTPS ports.

More details on an architectural discussion on positioning Access Manager components, especially WebSEAL, within an Internet-centric environment can be found in Chapter 2, "Access Manager Web-based architecture" on page 33.

Platforms

WebSEAL is supported on all Access Manager platforms except Intel-based Linux systems.

Junctions

The back-end services to which WebSEAL can proxy are defined via *junctions*, which define a set of one or more back-end Web servers that are associated with a particular URL.

For example, suppose a junction on the WebSEAL host www.abc.com is defined such that a request for any URL specifying the path /content/xyz (relative to the Web space root, of course) is to be proxied to the back-end Web server def.internal.abc.com. /content/xyz is the *junction point*, which can be thought of in a loose sense as being similar in concept to a file system mount point.

A user at a browser then makes a request for http://www.abc.com/content/xyz/myhtmlfiles/test.html; WebSEAL will examine the URL and determine whether the request falls within the Web space for the /content/xyz junction point. It will then proxy the request to def.internal.abc.com and forward the resulting response back to the browser.

From the perspective of the browser, the request is processed by www.abc.com. The fact that it is actually handled by the target server def.internal.abc.com is not known to the user. To support this, WebSEAL performs various transformations on the response sent to the browser to assure that the back-end server names are not exposed. This exemplifies one of the powerful capabilities provided by WebSEAL junctions, that is, the "virtualization of the Web space." Junctions may be defined to the individual Web spaces on various back-end servers, yet from the browser's point of view, there is only one single Web space.

It was hinted above that more than one target server may be defined for a particular junction point. For example, the server ghi.internal.abc.com could be defined as an additional target for the /content/xyz junction point. In this case, WebSEAL can load-balance among the servers, and should a back-end server be unavailable, WebSEAL can continue forwarding requests to the remaining servers for the junction. For situations where it is important that subsequent requests for a particular user continue going to the same back-end server, WebSEAL is capable of supporting this via what are called *stateful junctions*.

The above assumes that processing a request does not involve any security considerations. While WebSEAL is capable of doing a fine job of simply managing access to Web-based content and applications via simple junctions, this, of course, leaves out a primary purpose of utilizing WebSEAL. Its integration with the base Access Manager services to provide access control and flexible authentication services for Web resources is its main reason for existence.

WebSEAL security functions

One of WebSEAL's key functions is to protect access to Web content and applications. To do this, it uses Access Manager's Authorization Services. The Authorization Service must know which Web objects (that is, URLs) require protection, and what level(s) of access to these objects is permitted for the Access Manager users and groups defined in the user registry.

The protected object space is defined in the Access Manager authorization database. It is populated using a special CGI program that runs on each back-end junctioned Web server. This program, named query_contents, is run by the Web Portal Manager and scans the Web directory hierarchy on the server. It populates the authorization database with representations of the various objects it finds. ACLs and POPs can be "attached" to these objects, and WebSEAL can then use Access Manager's authorization engine to make access decisions on requests for various URLs.

Of course, the authorization engine cannot make access decisions without being told something about the identity of the user. WebSEAL supports the ability to authenticate a user and assign an Access Manager identity for use when making authorization decisions. Whenever a URL is requested that is not accessible by an unauthenticated user, WebSEAL will attempt to authenticate the user by issuing an HTTP authentication challenge to the browser (it supports multiple authentication mechanisms, which are discussed in 5.4, "Supported WebSEAL authentication mechanisms" on page 108). Upon establishment of an authenticated "session," the authorization engine is then consulted to determine whether the user may access the content specified by the requested URL. This WebSEAL session is maintained until the user exits the browser or explicitly logs off, or until the session times out from inactivity. Subsequent URL requests for this session continue to be checked to see if access is permitted. In this manner, WebSEAL provides single sign-on capabilities for Web-based content and applications.

The access control granularity provided can be anywhere from a coarse-grained protection of particular directories (containers) in the Web space to specific, fine-grained protection of individual Web objects, for example, an individual HTML file. Additionally, URL "patterns" may be defined that represents dynamic URLs. For example, application parameters are often defined in URLs, and may differ across invocations. By defining a pattern to Access Manager's Web object space that matches such a URL, it is possible to accommodate these situations.

Authentication to back-end servers

Often it is necessary to provide special authentication information to junctioned Web servers, for the purpose of verifying the identity of the WebSEAL server, providing the identity of the logged-in user, or both. WebSEAL provides a number of mechanisms to support such authentication requirements.

WebSEAL authentication

If necessary, WebSEAL can authenticate itself to a junctioned server using either server certificates, forms-based authentication, or HTTP basic authentication. When using an SSL communication channel for this junction, WebSEAL and the junctioned server can also mutually authenticate each other. This is very important in order to establish the trust relationships between WebSEAL and back-end Web application servers.

As an added functionality, WebSEAL supports *forced login* and *switch user* functions. Forced login is used to force a user to log in again, based on a policy setting or a session time-out. Switch user allows administrators to log on to Access Manager as a user without having to supply their password. This will aid help desk administrators with customer support issues. It can also be used by administrators to easily troubleshoot and verify the correct functionality of access control lists without the need to create test users.

Delegated user authentication

WebSEAL supports a number of mechanisms to supply a junctioned server with the identity of the logged-in user, including:

► Providing the user's identity via HTTP header values, which can be read and interpreted by the junctioned server.

► Insertion of an HTTP basic authentication header to provide the junctioned server with login information for the user, including a password. This basic authentication header can optionally permit login to the junctioned server with a different identity than the one for the user who is logged in to WebSEAL.

► For junctions that support it (for example, WebSphere Application Server and Domino), insert an Lightweight Third-Party Authentication (LTPA) cookie identifying the user into the HTTP stream that is passed to the junctioned server.

WebSEAL-delegated authentication capabilities are discussed more fully in 5.5, "WebSEAL delegation mechanisms" on page 114.

Replicated WebSEALs

It is possible to replicate WebSEAL servers for availability and scalability purposes. There are specific configuration requirements to create WebSEAL replicas, and a front-end load balancing capability must be used to distribute incoming requests among the replicas. Also, because each WebSEAL replica maintains active session states for its own authenticated users, the load balancing mechanism used must support a "sticky" capability to route subsequent requests to the same replica (in other words, users log on to a specific WebSEAL server). The use of WebSEAL replicas will be discussed and illustrated in Chapter 4, "Increasing availability and scalability" on page 79.

Virtual hosting

Multiple instances of WebSEAL can be created on a single machine using the WebSEAL configuration/unconfiguration utility. Each WebSEAL will require its own unique IP/port combination. This approach enables a something like a virtual hosting solution by running multiple WebSEALs with unique URL identifiers. True virtual hosting would require WebSEAL to use the host HTTP Header information in order to distinguish between the different domains, which it does not do.

Communication protocols

WebSEAL can communicate with the clients and back-end servers with both encrypted (SSL) and unencrypted (TCP) protocols. The supported encryption types are SSLv1, SSLv2, SSLv3, and TLSv1.

Secure Sockets Layer (SSL) hardware acceleration support

For performance improvement, WebSEAL supports SSL hardware acceleration. Utilizing the functionality of GSKit5, hardware acceleration can minimize the CPU impact of SSL communications, improving the overall performance of the system.

The nCipher nForce 300 card will be supported for the AIX, Solaris, and Windows platforms. Please refer to the product documentation for the complete description of all the cards we will support when the product is generally available.

This support applies to any SSL session that WebSEAL is involved in, but the performance impact that the users see is exclusive to the browser/WebSEAL session. The performance advantage the SSL hardware acceleration card can give us is the initial SSL handshaking between two communicating parties. Once an SSL tunnel is set up, the card does not help any more. In other words, the card provides benefits only for the RSA public key authentication part (happening in the initial SSL handshaking), but not for the DES encryption part used in normal data transmission afterwards. Most SSL sessions are built during the configuration time or the junction setup time and will be reused, so we will not get performance improvement from SSL hardware acceleration. The browser-to-WebSEAL SSL session is built whenever a user with a browser tries to communicate with WebSEAL. The customer value is the improved performance in browser-WebSEAL SSL session setups, and the higher numbers of users that can be supported due to the offloading of work from the WebSEAL host's processor to the card.

There is no Access Manager-specific documentation to cover this enhancement; the support of the card is simply a function of GSKit, and so the card's documentation is all that is needed.

Other WebSEAL functionality

WebSEAL supports an e-community single sign-on functionality that allows Web users to perform a single sign-on and move seamlessly between WebSEAL servers in two separate secure domains. We take a closer look at e-community single sign-on in Chapter 7, "Access control in a distributed environment" on page 151.

WebSEAL also supports a capability that permits failover of logged on users to another replica in the same domain in the event that their assigned WebSEAL server becomes unavailable. This fail-over cookie feature is also supported by the Plug-In for Edge Server, which is discussed in 1.2.2, "Plug-In for Edge Server" on page 20.

Architecture

The WebSEAL architecture is summarized in Figure 1-4 on page 20. The WebSEAL server directly interacts with the browser and proxies requests to junctioned Web servers, determining which junction to pass the request to by examining the URL.

Before passing the request, WebSEAL also uses the authorization engine to check the URL against the Web objects. If the URL is not protected, the request is simply proxied to the appropriate junction. If the URL is protected, an access control check must first be made. If the user is not yet authenticated, an authentication challenge is sent to the browser, and WebSEAL uses its authentication services to validate the user's claimed identity and map it to an appropriate Access Manager identity in the user registry. Access to the object is then checked against this identity, and if allowed, the request is proxied.

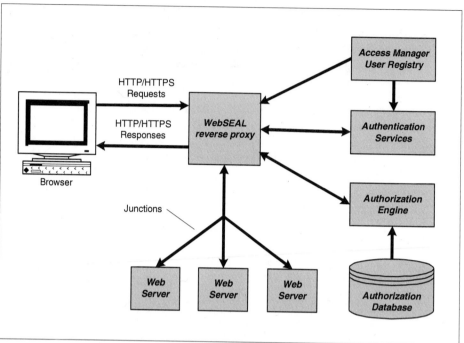

Figure 1-4   WebSEAL architecture

1.2.2 Plug-In for Edge Server

The Access Manager Plug-In for Edge Server is a plug-in for the Edge Server Caching Proxy component of the IBM WebSphere Edge Server. It adds Access Manager authentication and authorization capabilities to the proxy, and in certain scenarios it provides an alternative to WebSEAL for managing access to Web content and applications.

While the Plug-In for Edge Server shares many of the same capabilities as WebSEAL, its configuration is different. However, architecturally, it fits into most Access Manager scenarios in the same manner as WebSEAL.

While there are other differences, two key differentiators between the plug-in and WebSEAL are:

► Use of the plug-in with the Edge Server Caching Proxy provides direct support for virtual hosting.

► The plug-in can be used in both forward and reverse proxy configurations (WebSEAL only supports a reverse proxy).

The plug-in also integrates with the WebSphere Everyplace Suite, and supports forms-based login, and Access Manager WebSEAL fail-over cookies.

Architecture

Figure 1-5 provides a simplified view of the Plug-In for Edge Server architecture used as a reverse proxy (a forward proxy scenario is virtually identical, except that the proxy operations are to the outside rather than back-end servers). It should be noted that while this architecture is similar to that for WebSEAL (Figure 1-4 on page 20), the specific functionality and configuration of various components does differ.

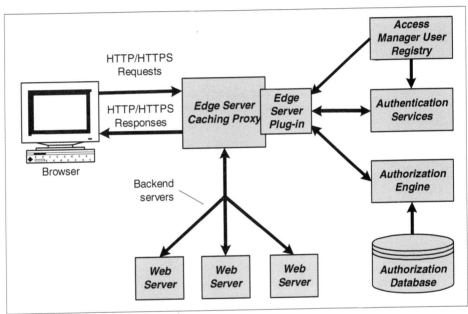

Figure 1-5   Plug-In for Edge Server architecture

1.2.3 Plug-In for Web servers

In Access Manager 3.9 we have full capability for Web server plug-ins. This Web Server Plug-In architecture provides a solution where the customer has decided on deploying a Web plug-in architecture for his solution architecture rather than a reverse proxy approach.

Table 1-2 summarizes the capabilities that are provided by this implementation based on a WebSEAL comparison.

Table 1-2   Plug-In for Web server functionalities

Authentication support	
Authentication based on client IP address	Supported
User name/password (basic authentication and forms-based), certificate, and SecureID authentication	Supported
Step-up authentication	Supported
Cross Domain Authentication Service (CDAS)	Supported
Interoperability with WebSEAL fail-over cookies	Supported
Web SSO (basic authentication and forms-based authentication)	Supported
SSO from plug-in Web server to back-end BEA WebLogic Server (BEA WLS) or WebSphere Application Server	Supported
e-community SSO (requires a WebSEAL Master Authentication Server (MAS)	Supported
SSO from WebSEAL to plug-in	Supported
Forms-based SSO	Supported
Password policy support, including password strength, password expiration, extensible password policy native implementation of "N strikes out password policy"	Supported
Junction from WebSEAL to plug-in	Supported; will accept WebSEAL-to-WebSEAL junctions
Authorization support	
ACL and POP policies	Supported
Tag/value support	Supported
PD_PORTAL support	Supported
Pass user/groups/creds in HTTP header	Supported
Failover (same as authentication failover)	Supported

Authentication support	
Platform support	
Note: One Web server per host is assumed.	
IIS on Windows 2000	▶ IIS 5.0 (need to clarify service packs and security fixes) ▶ Windows 2000 Server and Windows 2000 Advanced Server
IPlanet on Solaris	▶ IPlanet 6.0 ▶ Solaris 7 (Sparc) ▶ Solaris 8 (Sparc) - "run at"
Apache	▶ Apache 1.3.20 ▶ Red Hat Linux 7.1 (x86) ▶ Mod_ssl 2.8.4
Other	
Directory support: IBM Directory Server, Netscape iPlanet Directory, MS Active Directory, and Domino NAB Registry	Supported
Virtual hosting	Provided by the host Web server
Install/configure/uninstall	Simple and intuitive
URL and HTTP protocol transparency	Supported
Globalization-languages supported	Same as Access Manager Base, except bi-directional languages will not be supported

For an architectural overview of the Web server plug-in implementation, look at Figure 1-6 on page 24.

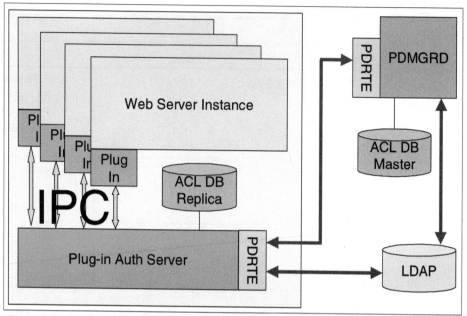

Figure 1-6   Access Manager Web server plug-in architecture

In most Web server environments, there are multiple server threads in operation on the machine. These might be different threads of the same Web server instance or threads of different Web server instances. Having a distinct authorization engine for each thread would be inefficient, but would also mean that session information would have to be shared between them somehow.

The architecture used contains two parts:

► Interceptor

This is the real *plug-in* part of the solution. Each Web server thread has a plug-in running in it that gets to see and handle each request/response that the thread deals with. The interceptor does not authorize the decisions itself; it sends details of each request (via an inter-process communication interface) to the Plug-In Authorization Server.

► Plug-In Authorization Server

This is where authorization decisions are made and the action to be taken is decided. There is a single Plug-In Authorization Server on each machine and it can handle requests from all plug-in types. The Plug-In Authorization Server is a local aznAPI application that handles authentication and authorization for the plug-ins. The Authorization Server receives intercepted requests from the plug-ins and responds with a set of commands that tell the plug-in how to handle the request.

1.2.4 Access Manager for Business Integration

Tivoli Access Manager for Business Integration provides comprehensive security services for IBM MQSeries. It extends the MQSeries environment to support end-to-end security across queues, and includes the following capabilities:

► User identity based upon Access Manager (standard MQSeries uses the local process user identity and is platform/OS-specific)

► Centralized management of access control to application messages on queues (using the Access Manager authorization engine)

► End-to-end message encryption for confidentiality and data integrity (messages are encrypted when placed on a queue and then decrypted when received from a queue)

These services are provided transparently to MQSeries, meaning that existing applications are supported without requiring any changes to them. Access Manager actually exchanges the original MQ.DLL with one that provides an interceptor to Access Manager.

Architecture

Access Manager for Business Integration provides an "interceptor" process that sits between an MQSeries application and MQSeries itself. Calls made by the application to MQSeries for services are captured by this interceptor, which determines:

► Whether the request for MQSeries services is authorized, based upon an authorization check against an Access Manager object representing the resource

► Whether the data in the transaction should be encrypted and/or digitally signed before being placed in the queue requested

Access Manager for Business Integration can also provide access control services for local applications attempting to access remote queues on servers running on platforms that its interceptor does not run on today. For example, Access Manager for Business Integration can prevent an application running on Solaris or NT from getting or putting messages onto a local queue that maps to a remote queue actually on a mainframe or AS/400.

Encryption and digital signing of messages requires that the Access Manager for Business Integration interceptor be running on both sides of the transaction. If services are needed to a mainframe or other platform the interceptor does run on today, a customer can set up a proxy system running the interceptor. A typical environment is a remote network of distributed servers running MQSeries transactions across public networks to a central IT center. With Access Manager for Business Integration, transaction flows across the public network can be protected.

User/application authentication for Access Manager for Business Integration employs PKI credentials. PKI client services are required to provide the S/MIME encryption services used to protect MQSeries message data integrity.

Figure 1-7 illustrates the flow of messages within the Access Manager for Business Integration architecture.

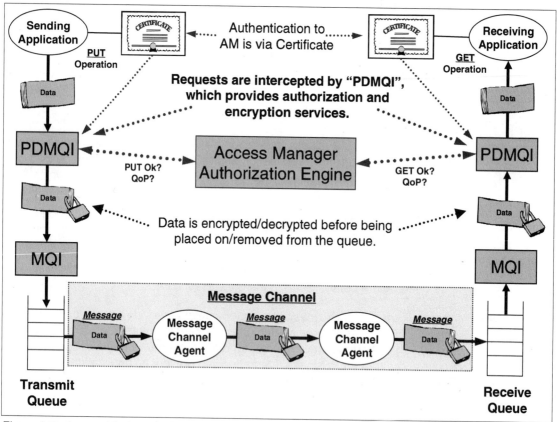

Figure 1-7   Access Manager for Business Integration architecture

1.2.5 Other blades

There are several other blades available for Access Manager, some of which are targeted at a system-level integration and others at an application-level integration.

Access Manager for Operating Systems

Access Manager for Operating Systems provides the security engine for Tivoli Security Manager (TSM) and Tivoli Identity Manager (TIM) on UNIX platforms. It is composed of a security engine that intercepts certain operating system calls requiring authorization checks, such as for file access. The native operating system authorization checks are supplanted by checks against Access Manager objects that represent the system resources for which access is requested. In this way, Access Manager for Operating Systems provides an operating system-independent view of security for these resources.

Access Manager for WebSphere Application Server

Access Manager 3.9 provides the industry's first Java 2 Platform Enterprise Edition (J2EE) container-level integration with WebSphere Application Server 4.0.2.

Access Manager for WebSphere Application Server consists of the WebSphere 4.0.2 Authorization Plug-In and an associated migration utility. This J2EE integration provides an Access Manager-compatible implementation of the WebSphere Version 4.0.2 authorization table interface for most *workstation* platforms supported by WebSphere Advanced Edition. In addition, a J2EE-to-Access Manager user/role migration utility will be provided to assist customers in populating the Access Manager policy database with users and roles.

This enables enterprises to leverage a common security model across WebSphere and non-WebSphere resources leveraging common user identity and profiles, Access Manager-based authorization, and using Access Manager's Web Portal Manager to leverage a single point of security management across J2EE and non-J2EE resources.

The integration is transparent to the J2EE applications because no coding or deployment changes are needed at the application level. More details can be obtained in Chapter 6, "WebSphere application integration" on page 123.

Access Manager for BEA WebLogic Server

Access Manager for WebLogic Server is an Access Manager 3.9-based implementation of a BEA WebLogic Server 6.1 *Custom Realm*, which supports single sign-on via WebSEAL, as well as a common, Access Manager-administered user registry. SSO is achieved when WebSEAL acts as a front-end authentication server that establishes a trust relationship with the Access Manager Custom Realm. WebSEAL authenticates the external user and vouches for the user to the Access Manager realm. Internal users can still authenticate themselves to the WebLogic Server in the usual way. The Access Manager Custom Realm distinguishes between those users that are vouched for by WebSEAL and those that need to be authenticated in Access Manager.

The advantages of the Access Manager Custom Realm support include:

▶ Providing common user registry administration across many different protected resources.

▶ Supporting Web single sign-on when used in conjunction with WebSEAL. This allows many authentication mechanisms to be used, including certificates, without any impact to the target application.

▶ Providing centralized access control of WebLogic resources in two ways:

   − Changing a user's group memberships alters her access privileges to WebLogic's J2EE resources in accordance with the group-to-role mappings contained in each application's deployment descriptors.

   − WebSEAL controls access to URLs that correspond to objects in the Access Manager policy database. These can be static URL strings or be represented by pattern matching.

> **Note:** The WebLogic Server does not expose authorization interfaces, so centralized control of user access to WebLogic's J2EE resources is limited to moving users between groups that have been assigned to roles in application deployment descriptors.

1.3 Interfaces

Access Manager supports a number of programming interfaces that permit direct application interaction with its components. While these interfaces support a rich set of functionality and are useful in many situations, it is important to point out that there is substantial product function that does not require their use. Initially, many organizations do not need to utilize these interfaces, allowing rapid deployment of security components such as WebSEAL. However, as the needs of the organization evolve, these interfaces allow for a high level of security integration and customization.

1.3.1 aznAPI

The Access Manager aznAPI provides a standard programming and management model for integrating authorization requests and decisions with applications. Use of the aznAPI allows applications to utilize fined-grained access control for application-controlled resources.

Application-specific resources may be individually defined and added to the protected object space and maintained in the authorization database in the same manner that WebSEAL and other standard Access Manager blades define their respective resources. ACLs and POPs may be attached to these application objects, and aznAPI calls may then be used to access the Access Manager Authorization Service to obtain authorization decisions.

1.3.2 Java API for Access Manager-based authorization

A powerful feature is to use Access Manager as an authentication and authorization back-end inside the Java 2 security model.

The Access Manager Authorization Java Classes provide an implementation of Java security code that is fully compliant with the Java 2 security model and the Java Authentication and Authorization Services (JAAS) extensions. More detailed information on this topic can be found in 6.4, "Access Manager and WebSphere integration" on page 132.

1.3.3 Management API

Also known as the pdadmin API, the Management API provides C language bindings and Java admin classes to the same functions supported by the pdadmin command line utility. It may be used by custom applications to perform various Access Manager administrative functions.

1.3.4 External Authorization Service

The External Authorization Service (EAS) interface provides support for application-specific extensions to the authorization engine. This allows system designers to supplement Access Manager authorization with their own authorization models.

An EAS is accessed via an authorization "callout," which is triggered by the presence of a particular bit in the ACL that is attached to a protected object. The callout is made directly by the Authorization Service.

In the current release of Access Manager, the EAS interface is supported via a simple Authorization Service plug-in capability. This allows an EAS to be constructed as a loadable shared library.

The EAS architecture is summarized in Figure 1-8.

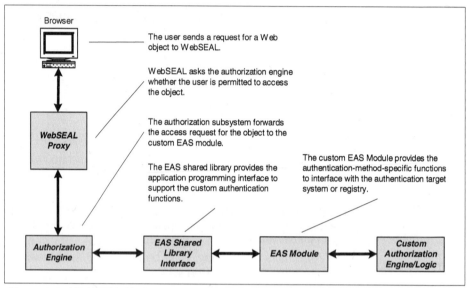

Figure 1-8   WebSEAL EAS architecture

1.3.5 Cross Domain Authentication Service

The Cross Domain Authentication Service (CDAS) is specific to WebSEAL. It provides a shared library mechanism that allows you to substitute the default WebSEAL authentication mechanisms with a custom process that ultimately returns an Access Manager identity to WebSEAL.

When WebSEAL determines that it must authenticate a user, an installation-specific CDAS can be invoked that performs the authentication using whatever mechanism is desired (for example, the user could be authenticated against a "foreign" user registry). Upon authenticating the user, the CDAS then "maps" the user to an identity defined in the Access Manager user registry (for example, one could log on via a foreign registry as joe and then be mapped by a CDAS to the Access Manager user fred).

An overview of the CDAS architecture is show in Figure 1-9 on page 31.

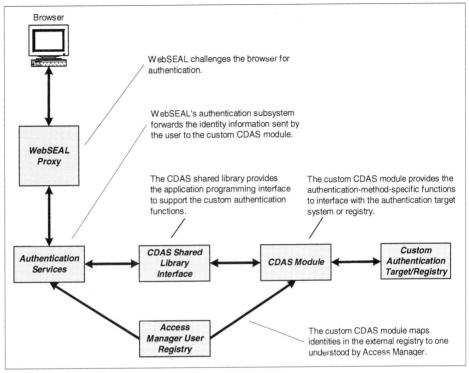

Figure 1-9   CDAS architecture

1.3.6 Cross Domain Mapping Framework

The Cross Domain Mapping Framework (CDMF) is a programming interface that may be used in conjunction with WebSEAL e-community SSO and Cross Domain Single Sign-On (CDSSO). It allows a developer to customize the mapping of user identities and the handling of user attributes when e-community SSO functions are used.

Conceptually, the mapping in a CDMF function works in a similar manner to a CDAS, except that it is used to map an Access Manager user in one secure domain to an Access Manager user defined in a different secure domain.

2

Access Manager Web-based architecture

Today, a Web presence has become a key consideration for the majority of businesses and other organizations. Almost all organizations see the Web as an essential information delivery tool. Increasingly, however, the Web is being seen as an extension of the organization itself, directly integrated with its operating processes. As this transformation takes place, security grows in importance.

This chapter introduces the elements of the Access Manager architecture in a Web-centric environment. While it focuses on the use of WebSEAL, it covers key architectural issues associated with any Access Manager deployment, and provides a foundation for the architectural discussions in later chapters.

2.1 Typical Internet Web server security characteristics

Perhaps the best place to begin the discussion of Access Manager architecture is with the issues typically encountered by organizations as they begin to address Web security requirements.

It is a generally accepted practice for organizations to place Internet-facing Web servers in a protected zone [also known as a demilitarized zone (DMZ)], which is generally firewalled and separated from the Internet. There are many ways of doing this, depending on the needs of the business. For example, many organizations do not even maintain their Web servers in-house; instead they rely on hosting services to provide the appropriate network infrastructure to support their Web content. Other organizations, especially large ones with significant Web content and application infrastructure, maintain protected zones within the context of their own network infrastructure. In any case, it is generally recognized that it is not a good idea to place Web servers in an organization's internal network directly on the Internet. A typical Internet Web server architecture is shown in Figure 2-1.

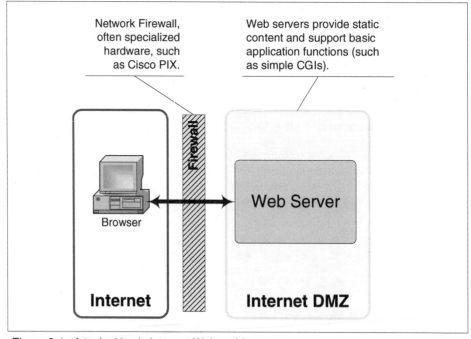

Figure 2-1   A typical basic Internet Web architecture

In Figure 2-1 on page 34, note that the Web server(s) directly serves content and may perform substantial application processing. Obviously, there is some level of security risk, depending on the sensitivity of the content and applications provided by the Web server.

In more advanced scenarios, where content is increasingly driven by complex applications, there are usually back-end components in the environment. For example, an application may rely on a large mainframe database, or substantial portions of the application may execute on back-end systems.

Direct Internet access to such components may present a significant security risk. Even assuming the Internet-facing firewall uses appropriate filtering to prevent access, compromise of the firewall could prove disastrous. For this reason, back-end components may be placed in an internal network, firewalled from the Internet DMZ, leaving only the Web server component exposed to direct browser access, as illustrated in Figure 2-2. This "double firewall" architecture has become common, not only for Internet application access, but increasingly for internal organization access to critical computing resources as well.

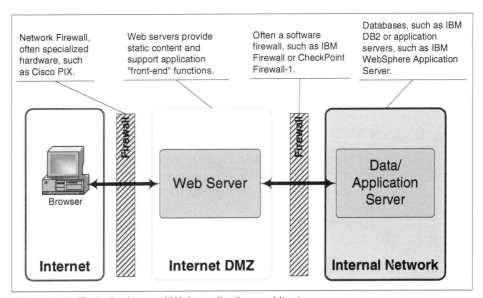

Figure 2-2   Typical advanced Web application architecture

While such architectures successfully address security from a network perspective, they do not address a larger set of concerns, including:

► Security-sensitive information may reside in the static content of Web servers (for example, human resources, sales, and personal information).

► Authentication/authorization may be driven by platform-specific mechanisms.

- ► Authentication, authorization, and audit functions may not be centralized.

- ► Managed security policies may be inconsistent and vary from server to server (access policies controlled by many different individuals or groups).

In such environments there may be sensitive functions and content which, if compromised, could represent a significant business risk.

Access Manager is capable of addressing the above issues. Combined with an appropriate network architecture, an organization can deploy Web content and applications with a high degree of assurance that the environment is secure, and that the security functions and policies may be consistently applied.

In the following sections, we will introduce the elements of Access Manager architecture, using the deployment of WebSEAL as a focal point.

2.2 Access control of Web content and applications

While most Web servers contain basic mechanisms to provide authentication and authorization, such capabilities prove woefully insufficient to deal with the access management requirements being encountered today.

Many organizations want to enable a single sign-on capability to Web applications. This can prove difficult, as most organizations have a diverse set of components, each with their own authentication requirements. It is also often important that the authentication capability is directly tied into the authorization functions that control access to specific resources.

WebSEAL allows organizations to tie authentication and authorization for Web resources together under a common umbrella. Users need only log on once, and WebSEAL's back-end authentication capabilities "mask" authentication to individual back-end components. Because WebSEAL also directly controls access to Web resources, authorization may be controlled using a common, platform-independent model.

For some organizations, in conjunction with WebSEAL's URL-level authorization capabilities, it may be necessary to control access to Web-based content and applications at an even more granular level—for applications, even down to specific functions or data values. With appropriate integration, Access Manager is capable of supporting such fine-grained access control in the context of a common security model. This is a significant advantage over other security products. Let us take a closer look at the architectural component layer using the IBM Method for Architecting Secure Solutions (MASS). You can obtain basic information on MASS in *Enterprise Security Architecture using IBM Tivoli Security Solutions*, SG24-6014.

2.3 Access control subsystem

An access control subsystem is responsible for data and component protection by providing mechanisms for identification and authentication as well as authorizing component access. In addition to these major functions, it also provides security management and cryptographic support.

Figure 2-3 on page 38 shows a user case model of an access control subsystem. The physical view shows the systems involved in the transaction. The component view depicts the information flow control function that will examine messages being sent and, based upon a set of rules, allow valid messages to flow. Invalid messages are rejected and recorded. The logical view breaks down the access control process into distinct functions.

The *access policy evaluator* is the major component that gets involved when it comes to an access control decision. Since it is positioned between two security domain boundaries, every transaction or information request has to be routed through this component.

If the sending component has not yet been authenticated, the access policy evaluator involves the *credential validator* service in order to verify the requester and issue a credential package that will be returned to the access policy evaluator. If the requester could not be successfully authenticated, the *error handler* will be involved, and the *audit generator* writes an entry into the error log.

If the sending component has already been authenticated, the access policy evaluator involves the *state manager* to verify the current status of the session.

If the session is still active and everything proves valid, the access policy evaluator proceeds with the evaluation of the request by applying access control rules from the policy rules database.

If access is granted, the access policy evaluator updates the information in the state manager and hands the task over to the *binding enabler*. If configured, the binding enabler might ask the audit generator to write a positive log entry. It also configures the requester's HTTP headers according to the active configuration and allows the reverse proxy to handle the requested information flow.

If access is not granted, the access policy evaluator updates the information in the state manager and hands the task over to the error handler, which will write a log entry. It then informs the binding enabler of the negative decision, which in return will inform the requester of the denied access.

This example user case flow demonstrates that we can easily depict the functions necessary for an access control subsystem. There are several other possible user cases for the access control subsystem, but for our purpose, this will remain the only example.

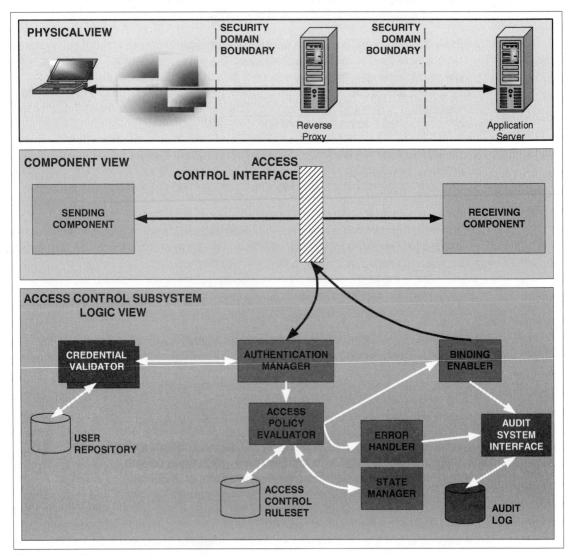

Figure 2-3   Access control subsystem

The remaining sections of this chapter discuss the fundamental architecture issues associated with deploying Web single sign-on and URL-based authorization with WebSEAL.

2.4 Web-based requirement issues

As discussed in 1.2.1, "WebSEAL" on page 14, WebSEAL junctions provide powerful capabilities for managing access to multiple Web servers through a common access portal. The use of WebSEAL often is driven by key business requirements, which are reflected in specific design objectives, or technical requirements as particularly lined out in the IBM MASS approach.

2.4.1 Typical business requirements

There are a number of commonly encountered business requirements that tend to drive Web security solutions such as those using WebSEAL:

► Different back-end and Web content hosting systems require users to authenticate multiple times, which generates a negative user experience.

 In order to improve customer satisfaction, a method for single-user authentication has to be implemented.

► The Web-based functions of the business are extending into content and applications, which increasingly require sophisticated security management.

 Almost all businesses that are on the Web are encountering this. The moment one goes beyond basic, static informative content, the inadequacies in the simple security mechanisms typically present in many Web servers become clear. The enforcement of Web security across the enterprise cannot be successful without something more sophisticated and manageable at the enterprise level.

► Web security policies must be consistently applied across the business.

 Without a common security infrastructure, Web content and application security policies tend to be applied differently by various parts of the business. This results in a hodge-podge of differing security mechanisms that enforce policy in different ways, often to the point where one cannot easily understand what the organization's overall security policies are.

► The costs of Web security management must be predictable.

 Security requirements will evolve with the business. Ultimately, the costs of a commonly leveraged solution that is reliable and scalable to the needs of the business will be far more predictable than other approaches.

► Threats of inadvertent security compromises or hacker attacks represent significant risks to business operations and company goodwill.

 The direct costs of investigation and recovery after a security incident may be significant, but the indirect costs may be even greater. Especially when doing business on the Web, a perception that security is inconsistent and may be compromised can cause substantial revenue loss.

▶ Competitors are leveraging security solutions to explicitly generate user trust.

This is related to the above. Even if threats are minimal, it still may be essential to maximize the trust that users have in the business' ability to protect itself from compromise. Competitors that can successfully present a "rock-solid" image may often have an advantage over a business that can not.

2.4.2 Typical design objectives (technical requirements)

In conjunction with the business requirements that drive the need for a Web security solution, the following design objectives (technical requirements) are often encountered:

▶ There is a need to apply security policy independent of application logic.

▶ A common security control point for Web infrastructure is needed.

▶ Security policy management must be operating system platform independent.

▶ Single-sign-on for access to Web content and applications is needed.

▶ Authorization policy management and enforcement mechanisms must be consistent across applications.

▶ Exposure of Web content and applications to potential attack must be minimized.

▶ There must be a common audit trail of accesses to all Web applications.

These are only examples of some of the possible design objectives that might drive Web security solutions, such as those utilizing WebSEAL. Applying MASS to individual scenarios will generate fine-grained design objectives that can be applied within the solution.

2.5 WebSEAL architectural principles

The most common Access Manager scenarios involve management of access to Web content using WebSEAL. Our approach to WebSEAL architecture is based on three principles, consistently applied.

2.5.1 Principle 1

Web security must begin at the front gate.

First, this means that there should in fact be a logical Web "front gate" to your content and applications. Side and back gates create vulnerabilities. Second, you must control access at this point, because once someone gets inside, there are many more available channels through which vulnerabilities may be exploited. Your Web front gate is also the initial checkpoint for auditing access attempts.

WebSEAL is the Access Manager component that provides this logical Web front gate. Its authentication capabilities and integration with the Access Manager Authorization Services allow us to know who a user is and make appropriate access decisions before exposing any additional Web infrastructure.

2.5.2 Principle 2

Minimize the number of direct paths to each component.

Ideally, we should have only one HTTP/HTTPS path to our Web server(s) from a browser. To enforce this, we can utilize the stateful packet filtering capabilities of firewalls to allow/disallow certain traffic.

This is fine to protect us from certain types of attack—unless the firewall itself is compromised. The attacker then may be able to launch a multitude of direct attacks on the Web server in an attempt to gain direct access to sensitive content and control of applications. By interposing a reverse proxy such as WebSEAL, the range of possible attack scenarios in the event of a firewall compromise is lessened.

2.5.3 Principle 3

Keep critical content and application functions away from hosts that directly interface to Web clients (that is, browsers).

The further away components are from a potential attacker, the easier it is to minimize the number of available direct paths to exploit them.

2.6 Basic WebSEAL component interactions

As discussed in Chapter 1, "Introduction to Access Manager components" on page 3, all Access Manager architectures share a common set of base components. Specifically, all Access Manager deployments have a user registry and a Policy Server. WebSEAL interacts with these components to provide its security functions, as shown in Figure 2-4.

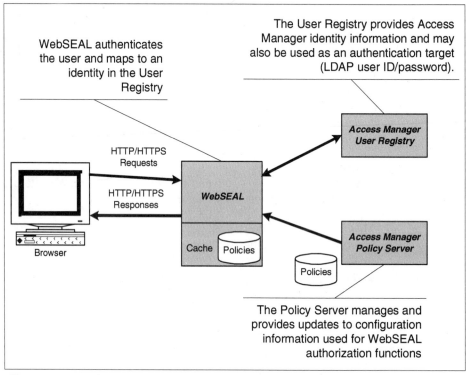

Figure 2-4   WebSEAL interaction with other Access Manager components

In the most basic of WebSEAL architectures, as shown in Figure 2-5 on page 43, a user at a Web browser contacts WebSEAL with a URL request, and then WebSEAL directly serves the content itself (recall that while it functions as a reverse proxy, WebSEAL is also a Web server with the ability to use locally stored content).

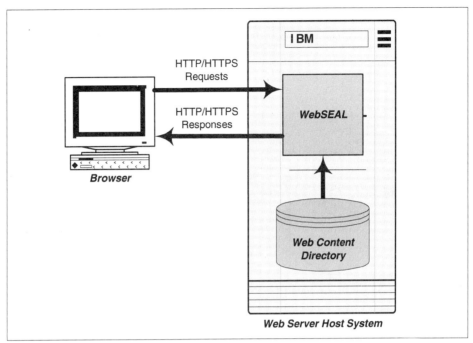

Figure 2-5   Direct serving of Web content from WebSEAL

While illustrative of WebSEAL capabilities, such a scenario may not be terribly interesting, given the evolution of Web-based application architectures that employ significant back-end infrastructure. Also, while directly serving non-sensitive content may be acceptable, when sensitive content is involved, it is generally better to serve it via proxy. Such environments are, in fact, ones where WebSEAL proves to be an ideal solution.

Web applications may involve significant back-end infrastructure, and there are advanced Access Manager scenarios in which direct security integration with such components is important. However, even in complex scenarios, the basic elements of Access Manager architecture still apply. In the current discussion, we will only address applications in the context of back-end Web servers that are junctioned to WebSEAL.

With WebSEAL junctions, a browser user does not directly interact with the target Web server. Instead, WebSEAL takes care of initial user authentication as required and performs appropriate authorization checks on URL requests. Authorized requests are then proxied via the appropriate junction. Figure 2-6 on page 44 shows the basic flow involved in processing such a request.

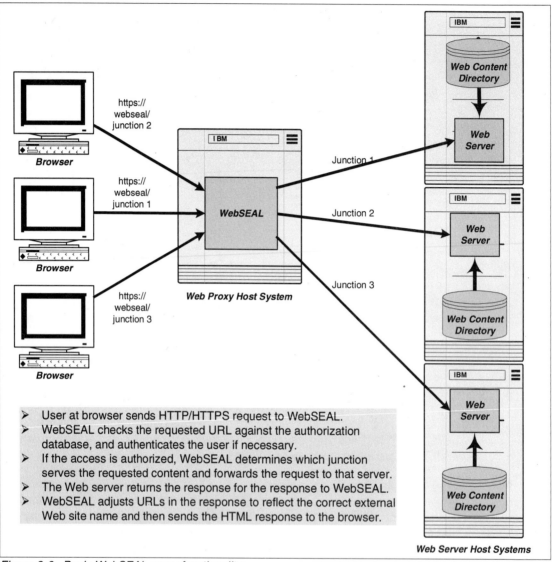

Figure 2-6   Basic WebSEAL proxy functionality

The flow in Figure 2-6 represents the common architecture for all WebSEAL deployments. The differences that come into play include such things as how components may be combined or distributed among host systems, junction configuration, and back-end authentication issues. However, WebSEAL deployments are built from the same basic architectural elements.

At this point we have not yet introduced the role of the network into an Access Manager WebSEAL architecture. Obviously, as we discussed earlier in 2.1, "Typical Internet Web server security characteristics" on page 34, network configuration does play a role, and it is important to understand how WebSEAL and other Access Manager components fit into typical secure network infrastructures.

2.7 Component configuration and placement

Obviously, it is possible to deploy Access Manager components within a single network. While this kind of architecture may be reasonable for a lab or development environment, it is generally not for a production setting. Most Access Manager deployments must fit within the context of network security requirements.

We now discuss how various Access Manager components relate to the network configuration, and provide recommendations for how they should be distributed in a typical architecture. While much of what is in this section may be applied to Access Manager generally, the focus is on deployment of a WebSEAL architecture.

2.7.1 Network zones

At this point we will discuss different network zones in the specific context of Access Manager architecture.

We have to consider four types of network zones in our discussion of Access Manager component placement:

► Uncontrolled (the Internet)
► Controlled (an Internet-facing DMZ)
► Restricted (a production or management network)
► Trusted (an intranet)

Since we will not place any components in an uncontrolled zone, we take a closer look at the remaining three zones.

Internet DMZ (controlled zone)
The Internet DMZ is generally a controlled zone that contains components with which clients may directly communicate. It provides a buffer between the uncontrolled Internet and internal networks.

Because this DMZ is typically bounded by two firewalls, there is an opportunity to control traffic at multiple levels:

- Incoming traffic from the Internet to hosts in the DMZ
- Outgoing traffic from hosts in the DMZ to the Internet
- Incoming traffic from internal networks to hosts in the DMZ
- Outgoing traffic from hosts in the DMZ to internal networks

WebSEAL fits nicely into such a zone, and in conjunction with the available network traffic controls provided by the bounding firewalls, it provides the ability to deploy a highly secure Web presence without directly exposing components that may be subject to attack by network clients.

Production or management DMZ(s) (restricted zone)

One or more network zones may be designated as *restricted*, that is, they support functions to which access must be strictly controlled, and of course, direct access from an uncontrolled network should not be permitted. As with an Internet DMZ, a restricted network is typically bounded by one or more firewalls and incoming/outgoing traffic may be filtered as appropriate.

These zones typically would contain *back-end* Access Manager components that do not directly interact with users.

Intranet (trusted zone)

A trusted zone is one that is generally not heavily restricted in use, but an appropriate span of control exists to assure that network traffic does not compromise operation of critical business functions. Corporate intranets may be examples of such zones.

Depending on the specific level of trust existing in a trusted zone, it may be appropriate to place certain Access Manager components within it.

Other networks

Keep in mind that the network examples we are using do not necessarily include all possible situations. There are organizations that extensively segment functions into various networks. Some do not consider the intranet a trusted zone and treat it much like the Internet, placing a DMZ buffer between it and critical systems infrastructure contained in other zones. However, in general, the principles discussed here may be easily translated into appropriate architectures for such environments.

Placement of various Access Manager components within network zones is, on the one hand, a reflection of the security requirements in play, and on the other, a choice based upon existing/planned network infrastructure and levels of trust among the computing components within the organization. While requirement issues may often be complex, especially with regard to the specific behavior of certain applications, determination of an Access Manager architecture that appropriately places key components is generally not difficult. With a bit of knowledge about the organization's network environment and its security policies, reasonable component placements are usually easily identifiable.

Figure 2-7 summarizes the general Access Manager component type relationships to the network zones discussed above.

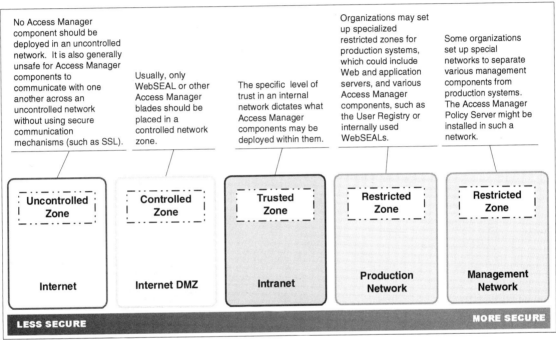

Figure 2-7   Network zones

2.7.2 Secure communication issues

All communication among Access Manager components is, or is configurable to be as needed, secure, using SSL. Given this, one might assume that it is fine to simply place all components within an Internet DMZ and rely on SSL to deal with protecting the communication among them. However, if it were that simple, there would only be a single Access Manager architecture pattern, and this part of the book would be quite short.

SSL only addresses the issues of privacy and integrity of communication among components. It does not deal with other types of security exposures that are inherent in the physical placement of those components within the network infrastructure. The choice to use SSL among certain components should be primarily based upon the trust relationships that exist *within* the network zones in which they operate. While trust may influence the placement of various Access Manager components within different network zones, the use of SSL itself does not necessarily govern such placements.

2.7.3 Specific Access Manager component placement guidelines

Now that we have discussed the basic issues involved in component placement, we can go into greater detail regarding specific components typically found in an Access Manager WebSEAL architecture.

Policy Server

The Access Manager Policy Server should always be placed in a restricted (or at least a trusted) zone. Figure 2-8 summarizes the guidelines for placement.

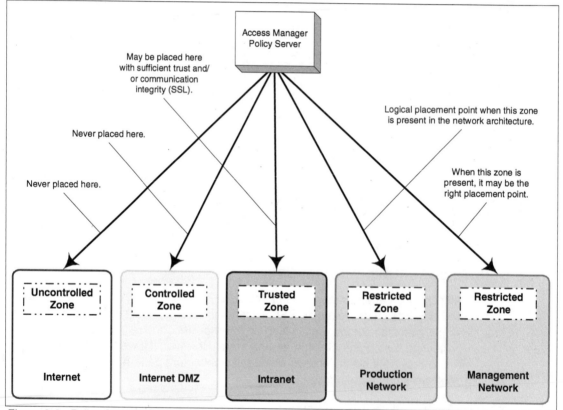

Figure 2-8   Policy Server placement guidelines

User registry

As we have discussed previously, WebSEAL interacts with the Access Manager user registry to perform some of its functions. This means that the registry must be accessible to WebSEAL. However, it probably should not be accessible to general users, especially from the Internet.

The registry should be in a restricted zone to which access may be strictly controlled, or at least a trusted network. Firewall configurations should disallow any possibility of access to the user registry from the uncontrolled zones such as the Internet (for example, port 389 access might be disallowed by an Internet-facing firewall, and outgoing port 389 accesses only allowed to pass from the Internet DMZ to another zone if initiated by a WebSEAL server).

Figure 2-9 summarizes network zone placement guidelines for the user registry.

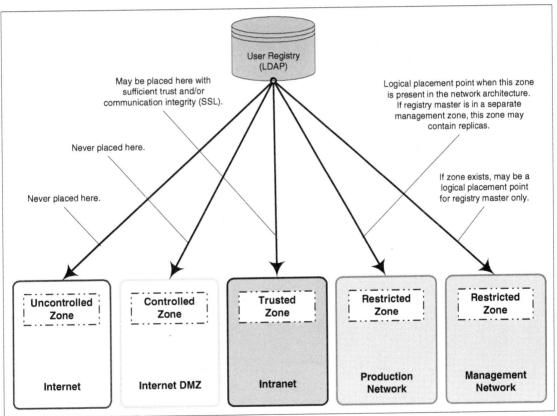

Figure 2-9   User registry placement guidelines

An example user registry placement using network filtering rules to limit access is shown in Figure 2-10 on page 50.

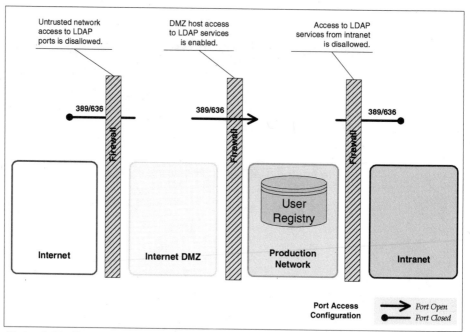

Figure 2-10   Restricting network access to user registry

Additionally, it may make sense to separate the *read* functions of the registry that are needed by WebSEAL from the *write* functions that are required by Access Manager management components. This can be done by creating a registry replica used for *read only* access (such as authentication) and leaving the registry master only for making updates. If there is a special *management DMZ* into which all management components must be placed, such a configuration may be appropriate. An example of doing this is shown in Figure 2-11 on page 51.

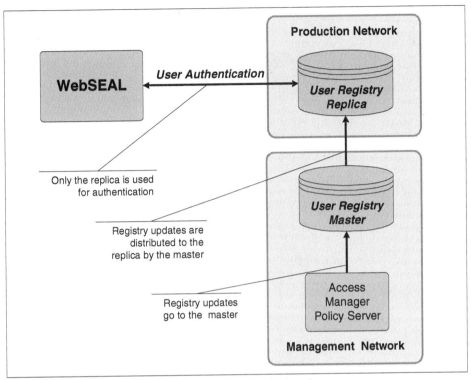

Figure 2-11   Separating user registry read and write functions

Web Portal Manager

The Web Portal Manager should always be placed in a restricted (or at least a trusted) zone. If a separate management DMZ is used, there may be issues in how to best structure the configuration of the Web Portal Manager in such an environment.

Because the Web Portal Manager's functions are accessed via HTTP/HTTPS, access to it can be configured via a WebSEAL junction. If this is done, special consideration should be given to its placement and how access should be controlled.

Figure 2-12 on page 52 summarizes placement guidelines for the Web Portal Manager.

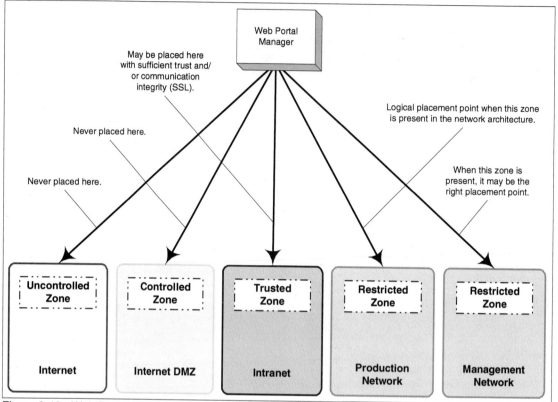

Figure 2-12   Web Portal Manager placement guidelines

WebSEAL

WebSEAL should always be the sole HTTP/HTTPS contact point for a Web server from an Internet client. When using WebSEAL in an intranet setting, this is usually desirable as well.

Internet

Based on our discussion so far, it should be clear that WebSEAL servers accessible via the Internet should be placed in a DMZ. WebSEAL in such a setting should generally be in a network zone separate from those that contain other Access Manager components upon which it relies, and from the Web servers to which it is junctioned.

The DMZ network boundaries are generally best secured through firewalls, and appropriate traffic filters are used to strictly control the flows into and among components. In this case, the Internet-facing firewall should be configured to make ports 80/443 only accessible through WebSEAL by using a firewall rule for a *destination host:port* combination. This is shown in Figure 2-13.

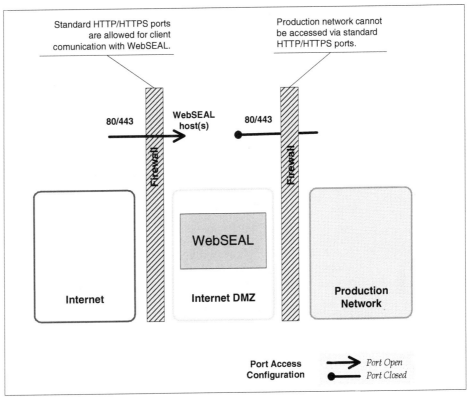

Figure 2-13   Restricting HTTP/HTTPS network traffic paths

This approach has several advantages:

► It focuses all Web traffic through a single path.

► Secured Web content is not directly accessible.

► Compromise of the Internet-facing firewall results in a limited security exposure.

This points out one of WebSEAL's key strengths: As a reverse proxy, it provides security capabilities that cannot be supported by any other approaches, such as plug-ins.

WebSEAL minimizes the numbers of hosts that must be placed in an Internet DMZ. In addition to the security benefits, for businesses that utilize hosting services to support their DMZs, this may allow them to reduce costs by moving substantial amounts of Web infrastructure back into their internal networks, leaving WebSEAL hosts as the key component in their hosted environments.

Intranet user access via WebSEAL

WebSEAL may also be used to serve Web content to internal clients. There are some specific issues that must be addressed when using it in this manner.

It may seem reasonable to simply force internal clients to use the same WebSEAL hosts that are serving Internet clients. However, such an approach may not be the best, because a security compromise of the Internet DMZ could create direct attack paths to internal clients.

An alternative approach is to dedicate a separate WebSEAL server for internal uses, and place it in an appropriate internal network zone. Depending on the level of trust and other configuration factors, the following choices exist for placement of an internal WebSEAL server:

▶ Place the WebSEAL server in the same network zone as other Access Manager components.

▶ Place the WebSEAL server in an internal DMZ that is separated from other Access Manager components—essentially, mirror the Internet DMZ scenario internally.

Given a sufficient level of trust internally, it may be reasonable to choose the first approach and put the internal WebSEAL in the same zone as other components. This is quite often the approach chosen when architecting WebSEAL solutions for internal user access.

For environments in which the internal trust is insufficient to justify placing WebSEAL into a common zone with other components, the second approach may be more appropriate.

WebSEAL placement summary

Figure 2-14 on page 55 summarizes the guidelines for WebSEAL placement.

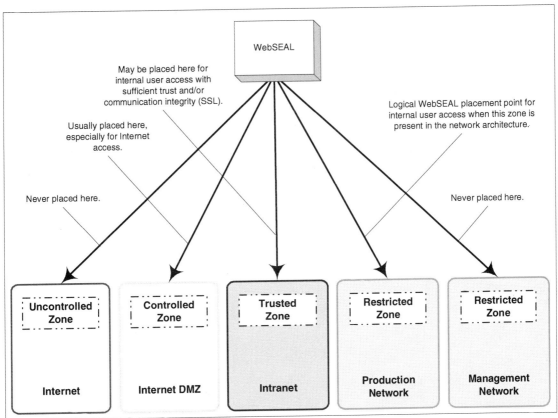

Figure 2-14   WebSEAL placement guidelines

Junctioned Web servers

In a WebSEAL configuration, it is recommended that junctioned Web servers not reside in an Internet DMZ. While WebSEAL does not restrict Web server placement in any way, the further away one can move critical resources from uncontrolled zones, the better.

Ideally, Web servers should be in a special, restricted zone, but could also be placed in a more open, yet trusted, network zone if appropriate configuration steps are taken (such as utilizing SSL for communication with WebSEAL and configuring the Web server so that it will only accept connections from a WebSEAL host). Figure 2-15 on page 56 summarizes the zone placement guidelines for Web servers that are junctioned via WebSEAL.

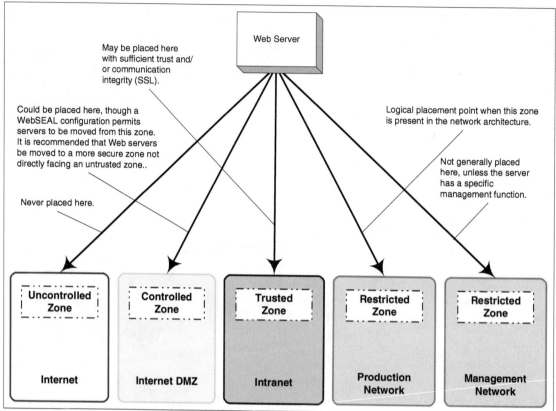

Figure 2-15   Web server placement guidelines

It may be a good idea to configure junctioned Web servers to use ports other than 80/443 (for example, 81/1443). This permits the Internet DMZ firewall configuration to be structured such that port 80/443 accesses can only be made to the Internet DMZ, and the internal-facing firewall to be configured to disallow ports 80/443 and only allow these alternate ports into the restricted/trusted zone. Such a configuration is exemplified in Figure 2-16 on page 57.

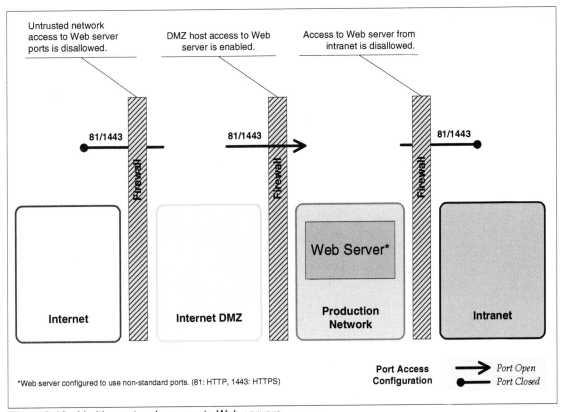

Figure 2-16   Limiting network access to Web servers

Putting it all together

Now that we have discussed the placement of the various components in a WebSEAL configuration, let us put it all together in a typical architecture. Assume that the following network zones exist:

- ► An uncontrolled Internet zone
- ► A controlled Internet DMZ zone
- ► A restricted production network zone

Without discussing the specific requirements of the organization, let us assume a basic WebSEAL configuration for both Internet and internal user access. One possible architecture could be as depicted in Figure 2-17 on page 58.

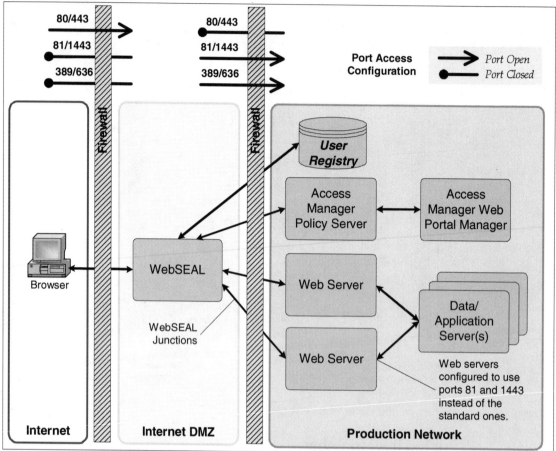

Figure 2-17   An example Access Manager WebSEAL architecture

It should be clear that by simply following the guidelines, many Access Manager WebSEAL architectures are relatively straightforward. The real complexities often come into play when addressing things other than the overall architecture itself, which are normal issues involved in enterprise systems deployment. This includes such things as configuration, deployment plans, capacity requirements, operational policies and procedures, and specific application integration issues.

2.7.4 Summarizing Access Manager component placement issues

In the above discussion, it must be emphasized that, to a large extent, the placement of Access Manager components represents a set of choices. Nothing in Access Manager itself dictates what kind of network configuration is required. The above component placement guidelines are actually related more to overall security principles than any particular need Access Manager has. In fact, in a WebSEAL deployment such as we have discussed in this chapter, Access Manager actually offers greater component placement flexibility than many other approaches to Web security.

This said, keep in mind that you cannot simply separate network configuration issues from Access Manager. While Access Manager components perform their duties extremely well, good sense dictates that they must operate in an environment that prevents them from being bypassed and protects them from undue exposure to other forms of attack. With *any* security solution, not just Access Manager, this must be kept in mind.

2.8 Physical architecture considerations

In our discussion of WebSEAL architecture above, we have focused primarily on the logical relationships among software components, and not necessarily on specific system configurations upon which they are installed.

2.8.1 Access Manager components

It should be clear from our earlier discussion that, at least for Internet scenarios, WebSEAL should reside on a separate host from other Access Manager components.

However, where other (back-end) components should go is not as clear. Honestly, there are no rules regarding this. Where these components should be placed is dependent on a number of factors, including:

► The specific network configuration within which Access Manager is installed

► The capacity/capability (that is, "horsepower") of the host systems upon which these components are installed

► The amount of flexibility required for future expansion of the security infrastructure

► Specific security or operational policies that may dictate certain Access Manager configurations

It is certainly possible to place all required back-end Access Manager components on a single host system. However, other than in a very simple WebSEAL deployment or a lab setting, this may not be the best approach. For example, a common way of breaking things out would be to place the management functions on one host and the user registry on another. Figure 2-18 on page 60 shows a physical system layout mapping of the example architecture shown previously in Figure 2-17 on page 58. Keep in mind that this is simply an example and it does not represent the only way in which components may be combined on host systems.

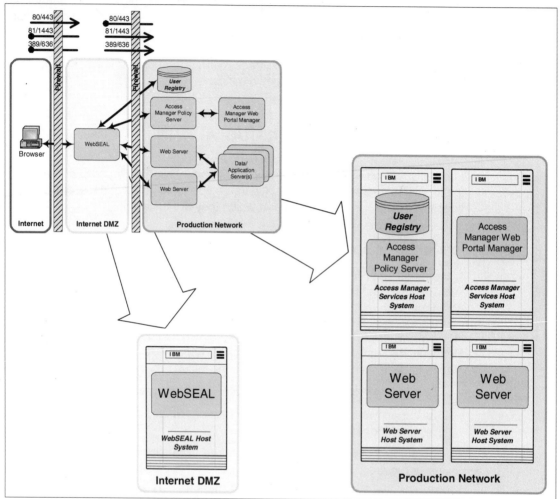

Figure 2-18   An example physical component layout

2.8.2 Other infrastructure components

In addition to Access Manager components themselves, there are other components that are a natural part of the infrastructure in most typical environments, including:

► Domain name service (DNS) or other, similar naming services

- ▶ Time services, such as Network Time Protocol (NTP)
- ▶ Host configuration services, such as Dynamic Host Configuration Protocol (DHCP)
- ▶ Mail transport agents (MTAs), such as sendmail
- ▶ File transfer services, such as FTP

Domain name service

In general, Access Manager components themselves should avoid the use of naming services for address resolution. It is usually best to directly configure host addresses locally, both for availability and security reasons.

In cases where access to a name service is needed by an Access Manager host, consideration should be given to installing a DNS secondary on the host itself or in close proximity to the host in an appropriately protected network zone. In no case should the security infrastructure share DNS services with the general user community, either internal or external.

Another note regarding the use of DNS in an Internet WebSEAL setting. It is recommended that a "split-level" DNS configuration or other approach be employed to assure that external clients have no IP address resolution visibility beyond the WebSEAL hosts themselves.

Time services

Time services are useful to ensure that logs can be aligned across multiple machines in the enterprise environment. The Network Time Protocol (NTP) is one of the recommended choices for time synchronization and an appropriate implementation should be available on all platforms upon which Access Manager runs.

Host configuration services

Host configuration services, such as DHCP, should never be used by any host running Access Manager components. IP addresses should be statically configured. It is also recommended that DHCP services not be provided by hosts that are running Access Manager components.

Mail transport agents

Mail transport agents, such as sendmail, are often present within the network infrastructure to route mail both internally and externally. Such mail gateways should not be configured on Access Manager hosts, as their use may substantially affect the performance characteristics of the system and diminish performance predictability.

Additionally, a WebSEAL host, especially one that is accessible via the Internet, should not respond to SMTP (port 25) connection requests.

File transfer services

File transfer services, such as anonymous FTP, are often present within the network infrastructure to support access to program archives or other information. It is recommended that such services should not be configured on Access Manager hosts, as their use may substantially affect the performance characteristics of the system and diminish performance predictability.

Additionally, a WebSEAL host, especially one that is accessible via the Internet, should not respond to FTP (port 20) connection requests.

2.8.3 General host "hardening" considerations

In addition to the recommendations above, it may make sense to "harden" certain hosts that participate in an Access Manager configuration. This may be especially true for Internet-facing WebSEAL hosts.

While the specifics of hardening an operating system are beyond the scope of this book, the following items are representative of the types of issues addressed:

► The number of incoming paths through which it may be accessed is minimized (for example, turning off certain network services that are not necessary for system operation).

► The number of outgoing paths from the system to other hosts is minimized (for example, limiting the system's knowledge of other hosts to those absolutely necessary for proper operation).

► Appropriate system auditing functions are enabled to assure traceability of accesses.

► The set of users that may access the system is minimized to a level that is necessary for system operation, and clear roles and responsibilities are defined for those users (and where possible, enforced).

Additionally, certain network firewall configurations may be employed to enforce the restrictions of a hardened environment.

2.9 WebSEAL in an overall security solution

It would be a mistake to assume that deployment of WebSEAL alone is sufficient to fully address all security requirements. WebSEAL provides key functionality, which is essential for Web security, but it is not a "silver bullet." As should be evident from the discussion of other topics within this book, there are other security considerations that should be addressed in conjunction with WebSEAL.

3

A basic WebSEAL scenario

Our earlier discussion of Access Manager has been helpful in describing the basic elements of architecture for deployment. At this point, we will apply those guidelines to a simple Web scenario for an example organization with a typical set of requirements.

In our discussion we will deliberately avoid certain issues, including availability considerations and specific issues relating to application integration. These areas are discussed in later chapters.

Also, while host machine configuration and capacity is touched on in this chapter, we deliberately avoid providing much in the way of specifics. This is because without appropriate capacity planning activities, which consider simulated/real loads of the actual application, it can be difficult to make accurate determinations.

3.1 Company profile

Stocks-4u.com is a wholly owned subsidiary of a major brokerage company, Medvin, Lasser & Jenkins (ML&J). ML&J's online presence has, to this point, been limited, consisting mainly of informational Web content. Online trading has not been a priority. The clientele has traditionally been major accounts with assets greater than $5 million, and transactions are almost exclusively done via direct contact with a broker. While the company, a privately held corporation, has maintained solid profitability over the past several years, largely due to a stable client base, the company's growth has stagnated, remaining at approximately the same revenue levels since 1995.

Market trends have forced a rethinking of ML&J's approach to business. The individual investor community has increased substantially in recent years, and the company has not shared in that growth. Consequently, the company's market share has eroded. Also, the rise of online trading has begun to affect a portion of ML&J's client base. In the last year, there has been a net outflow of investment funds cutting across approximately ten percent of all client accounts. Research has shown that 95 percent of these outflows are being redirected to online brokerages. This trend, if it continues, threatens to affect the long-term viability of the business.

An online component to complement ML&J operations has been judged a necessity. Stocks-4u.com was started with assets recently acquired from a failed Internet startup, and additional capital has been provided to fund completion of the company, which recently began full production operation ramp-up, and services the online trading requirements of ML&J's current clients, while focusing on developing additional clients who are primarily online traders with trading capital in excess of $250,000.

> **Attention:** As of April 2002, our fictitious domain name Stocks-4u.com was not reserved by anyone.

3.1.1 Technology background

Stocks-4u.com has been deployed as a Web-based online trading system with capabilities similar to those found at other online trading sites. This software is composed of a number of underlying applications, all of which perform functions based upon each user's privileges. For example, only users who have paid for level II quotes may access that application.

In concert with the ongoing application development activities, the company has been examining alternatives for providing secure access to their Web site. Originally, a "master" application was developed, which provided a single access point for providing user authentication and authorization utilizing the underlying capabilities of the operating system.

Following initial deployment, additional requirements became apparent. It became clear that the level of effort required to fully address all functional requirements was cost-prohibitive. The tie-in to the operating system security mechanisms began to limit certain deployment options. The CIO felt that this approach was locking them in architecturally to an in-house solution that would require long-term sustaining and support services. After examining marketplace alternatives in a proof-of-concept (POC) setting, a decision was made to deploy an Access Manager security capability, leading with Web security.

The company wants to transition its user base from the in-house Web security system to a WebSEAL-based one over the next several months. They initially wish to deploy adequate capacity to address their anticipated loading over the six months, and then incrementally add more as needed.

3.1.2 IT infrastructure

The Stocks-4u.com concerns on becoming an integral part of the ML&J IT infrastructure are partitioned into three major categories:

- ▶ Data centers
- ▶ Network
- ▶ Operational plans

A closer look at these individual aspects is provided in the following sections.

Data centers

Stocks-4u.com has two major data centers. One is located in San Diego, California, and the other is in Savannah, Georgia. At this time, all Internet application access and key internal application access is provided through the San Diego center, in which the company's IT Operations (OPS) group is based. The Savannah center is currently supporting a few other internally used applications and houses the company's IT Architecture, Development, and Deployment Support (ADDS) business unit.

While Stocks-4u.com did consider hosting its Web servers through a third-party provider, it was decided that all subsidiaries deploy their servers in-house. However, they have not ruled out migrating certain Web operations to a hosting provider in the future. This could bring additional data centers into play.

Network

The data centers are connected by redundant T3 (45 mbps) access. At this time Internet connectivity is provided through the San Diego center, with multiple T3 lines from three different providers. The diagram depicted in Figure 3-1 shows the national Stocks-4u.com network.

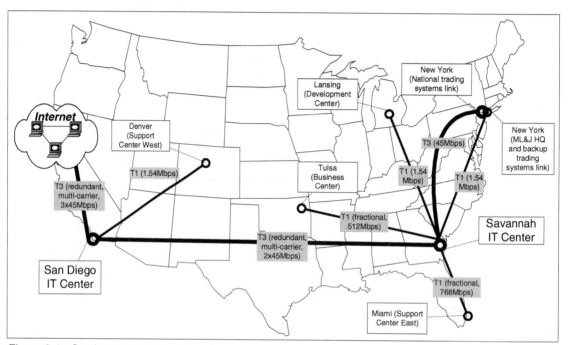

Figure 3-1   Stocks-4u.com data network

Within the San Diego center, all Internet access is channeled through Web servers residing in a demilitarized zone (DMZ). These Web servers provide front-end application logic, including presentation services. Back-end application logic is hosted on systems residing behind the DMZ in an internal production network.

The Savannah center has no direct Internet access. It has a production network for internal application systems.

In addition to the specific network capabilities at each of the sites, there is also a general company intranet shared across all corporate locations. This network is not considered secure, and is not authorized for hosting production systems.

Operational plans

Early plans are in the development stage for future expansion of Internet operations into the Savannah center to provide for a redundant access capability with load-balancing for customers on the US East and West coasts. At this time there is no requirement to actually support this. However, the Stocks-4u.com chief architect wants to be certain that the security solution they deploy is capable of meeting such a requirement. During the Access Manager proof-of-concept, it was determined that this should not be a problem.

3.1.3 Business requirements

The CIO has provided input on the business drivers for the targeted solution:

► Provide an enabler for consistent application of security policy across the business. The business cannot afford to create multiple, competing security infrastructures.

► Assure client confidence by offering a flexible, yet perceptively secure solution. It is essential that the security system not get in the way, while at the same time protecting client information and assuring that financial transactions are conducted securely.

► Competitively position the business to react quickly in deploying secure premium services and content. Quickly deploying value-add capabilities is important to gaining and maintaining market share.

Allow for the integration of special premium applications capabilities to Medvin Lasser's "select" clients. Medvin Lasser is very focused on maintaining their existing high-income client base by providing them with special capabilities that are not available through any other online service. For example, additional bond management capabilities within the portfolio management application are being developed specifically for these clients.

► Provide for expansion of services with minimal incremental investment. It is essential that, once in place, the security solution grow with the company. It is unacceptable to require extensive and continuing re-engineering efforts for the security infrastructure as the company expands its operations.

► Meet applicable US Securities and Exchange Commission (SEC) requirements. There are certain legal requirements for assurance that client assets and transactions are handled properly. The security infrastructure should be supportive of these requirements.

3.1.4 Security design objectives

Based upon initial discussions and a security workshop, it has been determined that the following key technical requirements exist:

- ► Provide a single sign-on capability for all Web-based applications. A user should only need to log in one time to one entity to obtain access to all authorized applications and content that may reside on various servers.

- ► Remove the need for application developers to authenticate users. The company does not wish to invest in developing any authentication capabilities within its new applications.

- ► Provide a cross-platform security solution. Previous experience with the in-house security application clarified the need to maintain operating system independence for Web-based application security.

- ► Provide the ability to control access to Web applications and content, which may be hosted through multiple Web servers, at the URL-level.

- ► Provide the ability to make fine-grained authorization decisions within applications. While this is not an immediate deployment requirement, the solution must allow for this capability to be added.

- ► Support browser-based access to applications from both employees and customers. From their desks, internal users may access both Internet-hosted applications and internal applications. At this time, there is no requirement for employees to have access to internal applications from the Internet.

- ► For the first six months following deployment, load requirements are for up to 40,000 Internet users, with an annual growth rate of 50 percent over the next five years. In five years, the online client base is expected to exceed 300,000 users. Approximately 25 percent of all clients are expected to conduct at least one transaction on any given day.

- ► The internal employee user base is currently around 250, and is expected to be approximately 1000 in the next five years. Approximately 80 percent of employees are expected to conduct at least ten transactions on any given day.

3.1.5 Requirements analysis

The requirements for this access control subsystem are typical of those found in many Web application environments. Also, Stocks-4u.com's experience with home-grown security is not unique. With today's Web-centric application focus, many organizations approach the security issue from that perspective, yet they often utilize existing host-based security systems that prove inadequate in addressing key requirements. The fact is that, while some host-based security capabilities are extensive, they are tied to a specific platform. This is inconsistent with the reality of today's Web-based applications. These applications often run on several different machines on several different platforms, and on various Web server implementations.

An Access Manager WebSEAL capability is an obvious fit for Stocks-4u.com's current needs. In fact, most Access Manager deployments start with a Web focus. However, there are clear requirement statements that discuss future infrastructure expansion, and the same Access Manager environment that supports WebSEAL will also be capable of addressing those needs.

For example, it is clear that the company has a future need to support a tighter application level integration with security, using Authorization Application Programming Interface (aznAPI) or JAVA2 security-based functionality to allow very detailed authorization for application components. The inherent architecture of Access Manager allows these requirements to easily be met.

In this example, we will address the immediate requirements of Stock4.com with a WebSEAL solution. However, in a later chapter of this book, we may introduce additional requirements or revisit some of the remaining issues to illustrate how they may be addressed as the company expands its use of Access Manager.

To summarize from the requirements discussion above, we know the following:

► We need to have a WebSEAL capability covering both internal and external users.

► There is a relatively small number of users initially, but this will dramatically grow.

We also know that:

► All Internet access will go through a single site (San Diego).
► All Web servers we need to access are housed at a single site (San Diego).
► Web servers reside in an Internet DMZ network.
► Production systems reside in a special production network.
► All internal users share a common intranet across company site locations.

From this we can easily address an initial WebSEAL-based Access Manager architecture for Stocks-4u.com.

3.1.6 Access control architecture

As we know it today, the diagram in Figure 3-2 on page 72 summarizes the existing security architecture deployed by Stocks-4u.com with multiple Web server host systems deployed in the Internet DMZ.

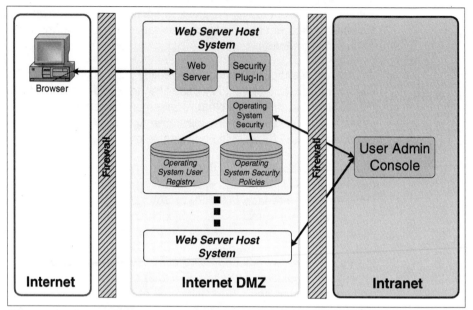

Figure 3-2   Current Stocks-4u.com architecture

The following are the most pressing issues:

- ▶ The operating system security model is too centric.
- ▶ Key components are exposed within the DMZ.
- ▶ It is difficult to apply a uniform security model.
- ▶ Long-term maintenance staffing is required.
- ▶ It is difficult keeping up with evolving standards.
- ▶ Authentication is not flexible for requirements.

This is our starting point for developing an Access Manager architecture to meet current requirements, which, as we shall see, is actually simple and straightforward.

Initial architecture approach

Recalling the discussions in Chapter 1, "Introduction to Access Manager components" on page 3, and Chapter 2, "Access Manager Web-based architecture" on page 33, we obviously know that we will place a WebSEAL server in the DMZ, which will provide for Internet user access. We also know that the user registry, Policy Server, and Web Portal Manager (WPM) should not reside in the DMZ, and we will place those components in the San Diego center internal production network.

As you will recall, the company currently has its Web servers in the DMZ. With WebSEAL, there is obviously no longer a need to do that, and these Web servers may be migrated to the production network. This is a good thing, as it enhances the security of the overall solution by moving the front-end application logic out of the DMZ.

Our initial architectural diagram is displayed in Figure 3-3.

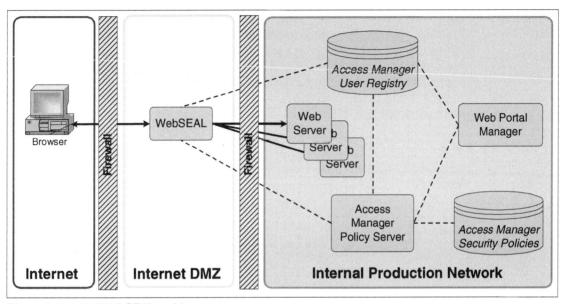

Figure 3-3   Initial WebSEAL architecture

This initial architecture provides us with the following benefits:

- The security model is independent of the operating system.
- We have a limited component exposure within DMZ.
- It is architecturally consistent and we have a uniform security model.
- It is not dependent on internal resources to support core security component code.
- As standards evolve, the security infrastructure may be readily upgraded.

Internal user access

Now let us discuss the internal user access. There are potentially many issues here, but to keep things simple for the moment, we know that we only need to support employee access to internal applications from inside the company. In other words, Internet application access is currently only being provided for client applications and content.

We could route browser traffic to internal applications through the same WebSEAL that resides in the Internet DMZ. However, this is not a recommended approach, partly for security reasons, and partly for manageability and performance reasons. So in this case, we will go with another WebSEAL server that is dedicated solely to internal access. This allows us to create a different set of junctions for the internal and external WebSEAL servers, which permits better segregation of content between the two access classes.

> **Tip:** There is an interesting issue here that we will touch on briefly, but not dwell on. That is, there may be scenarios where it makes sense to have different user name spaces for employees and clients. This can easily be accomplished by creating a second Access Manager secure domain. However, in this scenario, such requirements do not exist. In this architecture, we will keep it simple and use a single Access Manager user registry covering both employee and client users in a common user ID name space.

Where should this internal WebSEAL server reside? In our case, based upon the Stocks-4u.com network structure, the logical place for this is in the production network. The updated architecture diagram is depicted in Figure 3-4.

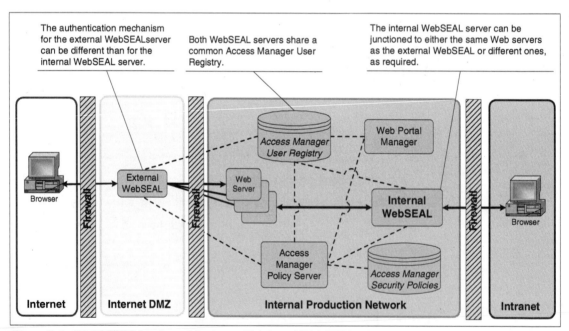

Figure 3-4   WebSEAL security architecture with internal WebSEAL

Connecting the pieces

Now that we have placed the key components in this scenario, let us discuss how they will all interact with one another.

The Internet-facing WebSEAL will be listening on ports 80 and 443 (SSL). We will also modify the configuration of the Web servers slightly to have them listen on alternate ports—in our case, we use ports 81 and 1443. This will permit us to close ports 80 and 443 on the firewall between the DMZ and production networks in the manner described previously in Chapter 2, "Access Manager Web-based architecture" on page 33. We will also disallow LDAP port (389/636) access from the Internet, because WebSEAL is the only entity that needs to communicate from the DMZ to the user registry.

There is also the question of whether the junctions between the Internet-facing WebSEAL and the Web servers require the use of SSL. Because, in this case, the Web servers are in a controlled zone, it is not strictly necessary to do so. If the Web servers were in the open corporate intranet, SSL should probably be used. The choice to use SSL may be made based upon the specific risk associated with the content involved. The answer is similar with respect to communication with the user registry.

The internal WebSEAL in the production network, unlike the Internet-facing WebSEAL, will be co-located with the Web servers it is junctioned to. It will listen on ports 80 and 443 and the firewall between the intranet and production network will be configured to disallow access via these ports. If for some reason it is not possible to disable these ports (for example, there could be Web servers that are separate from the Access Manager infrastructure), the junctioned Web servers may be configured to only accept connections from the WebSEAL server. This would allow both WebSEAL and non-WebSEAL controlled resources to coexist in the same network while maintaining the integrity of the back-end Web servers.

Another general comment is that the Internet-facing firewall should be configured to make ports 80/443 only accessible through WebSEAL by using a firewall rule for a *destination host:port* combination and not allowing the ports in general. This way you can enforce all incoming HTTP/HTTPS traffic to go through WebSEAL components.

Important: If you place a production Web server under WebSEAL access control, it is recommended that you do not allow access to it via non-WebSEAL channels without careful consideration. Prior experience has shown that this can lead to confusion, manageability issues, and most important, security breaches.

Generally, co-locating internal WebSEALs with Web servers is acceptable to many organizations; however, groups that may wish to impose an internal DMZ in front of a production network may do so in the same manner as is done for the Internet-facing WebSEAL. This is a legitimate architecture and may make sense in some cases. However, in the current scenario, the requirements may be satisfied as we have described.

Now that we have addressed the communication among the components, our new architecture is shown in Figure 3-5.

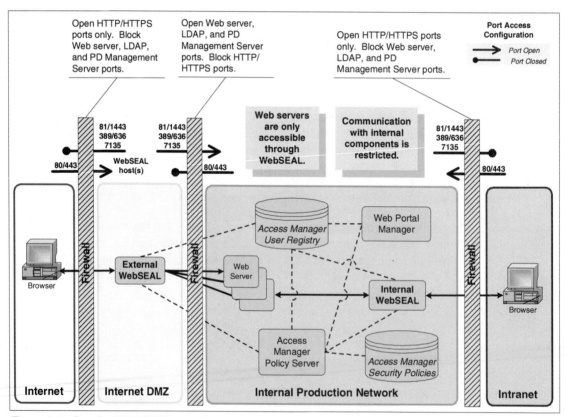

Figure 3-5   Detailed WebSEAL security architecture with internal WebSEAL

3.1.7 Building the physical architecture

With the locations of the pieces decided, now we need to know how many machines we need and what parts have to be configured on what systems.

Internet DMZ

Obviously, because the Internet-facing WebSEAL is in the DMZ by itself, it will need to be on a separate machine. This is typical for most WebSEAL scenarios. While technically this machine could support other applications or services along with WebSEAL, such configurations are not generally recommended, especially in an Internet-facing scenario.

A single WebSEAL host, appropriately configured, should be able to handle the expected client load over the next six months.

Production network

In the production network, things get a little more complicated, although not by much.

An obvious place to consolidate components would be to put the Access Manager Policy Server and the user registry on the same machine, provided it has sufficient capacity. The Policy Server uses little overhead in a basic deployment such as this one, which has a relatively small number of components and users. The major user of memory and processor capacity will be the user registry. We will place these components on a single machine.

> **Tip:** It is important to point out that, as the company expands its operations, it may make sense to eventually split these functions out onto separate machines. This should be easy to do when the time comes.

The WPM component can run on a Windows NT or Windows 2000 platform as well as on AIX and Solaris. One thing to keep in mind is that a midrange desktop system that meets minimum WebSphere memory requirements will generally work well to host WPM.

The internal WebSEAL is the remaining issue. Unlike the Internet-facing WebSEAL, we have more flexibility here. First, we know the number of users is relatively small. However, they are each performing several transactions a day. It may be possible to consolidate this WebSEAL onto the same host running the user registry and Policy Server. However, in this case, we will opt to place the WebSEAL on a separate machine to avoid any potential performance effects due to component interactions.

The final physical architecture for this initial deployment is depicted below in Figure 3-6.

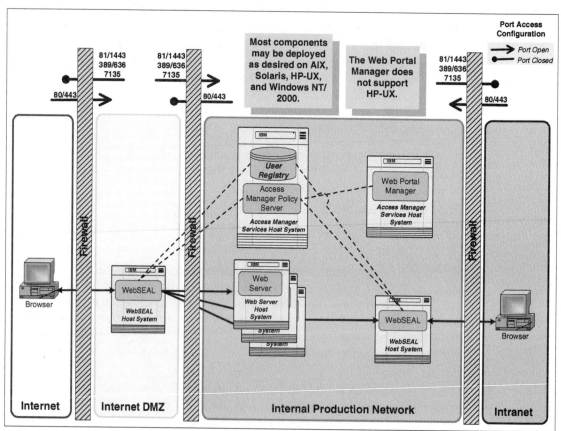

Figure 3-6   WebSEAL physical architecture

3.1.8 Architectural summary

In this chapter, we have used the guidelines discussed previously in this book to illustrate the thought process involved in developing a typical WebSEAL solution architecture. You can easily understand that a Web security solution with Access Manager is often straightforward.

With this as a base, we can easily extend any Access Manager architecture to add additional capability and capacity, as we will see in later chapters.

## 4

Increasing availability and scalability

In this chapter we continue the discussion from the previous section with our customer Stocks-4U.com. Previously, the concern was access control and user and account integration, as well as systems and network integration. Now the focus has shifted slightly and the need to address additional requirements of a growing business have come to the forefront. This growth and the increased expectations pose new challenges to the architecture.

Availability is the major concern that a failing part within the infrastructure will cause the overall solution to languish. This will eventually lead to unsatisfied customers and decreasing business success.

Scalability describes the capacity to be able to instantaneously change and adapt the IT infrastructure in order to handle an increased number of information and transaction requests without reducing the quality of the online experience for customers.

4.1 Further evolution

Stocks-4U.com has seen steady growth of their business. This growth, and the continued success of the business, has introduced new business requirements that mirror the evolving business. Based on these new requirements, we have to alter the security design objectives.

You, as the architect, now face the added design objectives of availability and scalability. Content, access control, and centralized audit and policy enforcement, as well as a single entry point into the site, are still very much a part of the scenario and must be included with the new requirements.

4.1.1 Business requirements

After the initial Web presence approach, the Web-based functions have functionally extended into content and applications and the security management becomes more viable. With the successful reception by the public, and an increasing client base, the availability of the Stocks-4U.com Web site is crucial. E-businesses have no set hours of operation and must be reachable and operational twenty-four hours a day, seven days a week (24x7).

At this stage, the CIO is looking for a way to guarantee the availability of the business application around the clock. Customers are entrusting their financial investments more and more to Stocks-4U.com, and they have to be rewarded with a reliable e-business application infrastructure that is always there for them.

After some serious downtime of the WebSEAL portal (due to some operating system problems and some issues with the back-end Web server availability, due to security vulnerabilities), the CIO demands some protection measures in the availability and portability of the corresponding systems be taken.

A second concern of his is the constantly increasing number of customers visiting the Web site. The CIO asks for future flexibility and ways to dynamically add functional empowerment of the single systems to better cope with new e-business opportunities.

4.1.2 Security design objectives

The major design objectives of these business requirements target two areas of the e-business implementation:

▶ The access control infrastructure

Embracing the internal and external WebSEAL portals, as well as the underlying security base, with the Access Manager Policy Server and the LDAP user registry

- ► The e-business application

  Consisting of the HTTP Web servers and the applications running on those servers

Basically we have to consider two different approaches, as outlined by the CIO:

- ► Availability

  Allowing systems to be available on a 24x7 schedule by providing enough resources in additional, duplicated systems or other fail-over mechanisms.

- ► Scalability

  Allowing the e-business solution to scale to any number of future capacities by adding additional components of the same sort and providing smart load balancing mechanisms to perfectly utilize these new components. In a second viewpoint, this can also imply moving a current functional implementation to a new, more powerful operating platform.

Let us take a closer look at how to approach these design objectives.

4.2 Availability

The Internet has changed forever the idea of fixed hours of operation. Suddenly there is the need to have your customers access your site at any time, day or night, increasing your visibility and profitability. The IT systems must be reliable and offer consistent content in a timely fashion to the client at any time. In our initial architecture, there are different points of failure in the infrastructure.

Each element in a configuration must be analyzed for failure points, including the hardware. Most hardware appliances, such as routers or switches, can be configured for fail over or alternate paths, and cold standbys can be kept available, should a hardware failure occur.

The discussion in this section will focus on the availability of all components that are part of the Web application; we will not consider infrastructure elements, such as firewalls and routers.

4.2.1 Failure situations

Web servers and applications can and do fail. The reasons for failure vary: Program code, "bleeding" edge technologies, disk failures, and even human error. In Figure 4-1 on page 82, the instance of only one WebSEAL user registry Access Manager Policy Server with its authorization master database, Web Portal Manager, and each individual Web server are in themselves single points of failure.

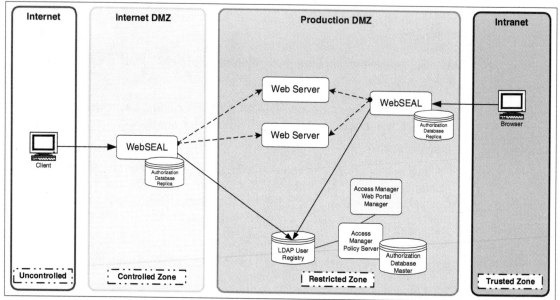

Figure 4-1   Initial Web architecture

What happens if the WebSEAL server fails? What happens if a Web server fails? What happens if the user registry server stops working? Let us take a closer look at the individual components.

WebSEAL failure

If the WebSEAL portal to either the Internet or the intranet fails, and there is no operational replacement, the client attempting access will be denied access to the site. While the content and the application might be fully functional behind WebSEAL, the failure of the WebSEAL server leads the user to perceive that the site is down.

Web server failure

If a Web server stops operating, the applications and/or services that reside on it are no longer available. While other applications are still working, the client that tries to access offerings on this particular machine perceives the site or the application as down.

User registry failure

If the user registry is down, WebSEAL will no longer be able to authenticate incoming users in order to access Web content and applications that are protected and require user authentication. While WebSEAL and the Web servers may still be operational, the client is unable to gain access and thus perceives the site is down.

Access Manager Policy Server failure

Although it is definitely not funny if your Policy Server fails, at least it will not affect the availability of your Web site. WebSEAL can still perform all necessary authorization operations because it uses the local cache mode, which means that the Authorization Service running on the WebSEAL machine uses a local authorization database replica. You only lose the ability to administer your Access Manager secure domain while your Policy Server is down.

The same is valid for the Web Portal Manager, which provides the administration graphical user interface Web application for the Access Manager administrators. The Web application will not be affected if WPM is not available. The only impact is that the administration of the Access Manager secure domain has to be postponed until the service is available again.

In addition to problems or failures of these components, sheer volumes can affect availability as well. With the growth of the Internet and your business, the ability to handle the traffic to your site has changed the scope and appearance of the architecture. Internet sites can become unstable or even fail under severe load conditions.

Tip: Besides adding multiple replicas for increasing availability and performance, you should also consider that your Web environment can scale on different operating system platforms with different availability characteristics. If you are stuck with only one supported platform, you might lose the ability to grow your business later.

The best example is the Web server itself. The IBM HTTP Server or the Apache Web Server can scale from entry platforms like Windows NT or Windows 2000 to other powerful platforms like Solaris, HP-UX, AIX, or even OS/390 or z/OS. As a side effect, you also have to consider developing your Web applications supporting only open standards like basic HTML, JAVA, Java Server Pages (JSP), or Enterprise JavaBeans (EJB); otherwise, you might get stuck with one particular platform.

4.2.2 Providing high availability

Adding replicas of crucial servers increases your site's availability. After depicting an overview of this configuration in Figure 4-2, we describe the different areas with their solutions.

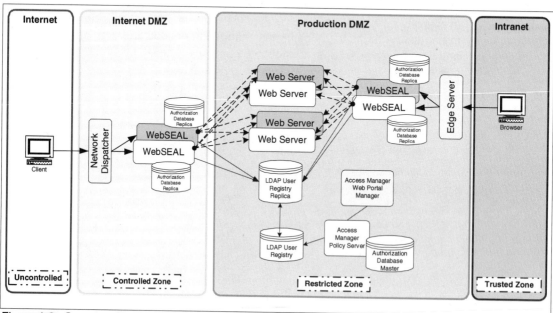

Figure 4-2   Server replication to increase availability

WebSEAL availability

Increasing the availability of your WebSEAL-controlled Web site starts with at least two front-end WebSEAL servers. Replicated front-end WebSEAL servers provide the site with load balancing during periods of heavy demand as well as fail-over capability—if a server fails for some reason, the remaining replica server(s) will continue to provide access to the site. Successful load balancing and fail-over capability results in high availability for users of the site. The load balancing mechanism is handled by a mechanism such as the Network Dispatcher component of the IBM WebSphere Edge Server or Cisco Local Director.

In a redundant WebSEAL configuration environment, as depicted in Figure 4-3, there are several places where the configuration must be duplicated.

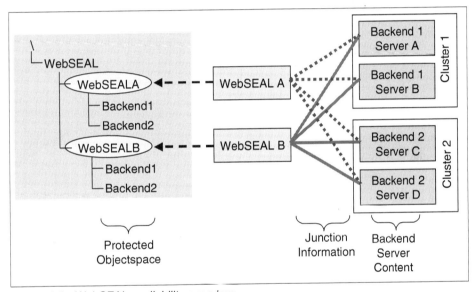

Figure 4-3   WebSEAL availability overview

Configuration must be duplicated:

► Back-end server content

   This must be the same on every server in the same cluster. Maintaining this is the responsibility of the individual system's administrator for the corresponding servers. More information can be found in "Web server availability" on page 87.

► Junction information

Each duplicated WebSEAL server must have the same junction information. This is made easy in Access Manager because all that is required is copying the junction database from one WebSEAL to another. All the junction information is kept in XML formatted files.

► Protected object space

Both WebSEALs must have the same ACLs attached to the same places in their object space. In a normal configuration, both WebSEALs have their own object space, so work must be duplicated. However, it is possible to make WebSEAL servers share a single object space, as shown in Figure 4-4.

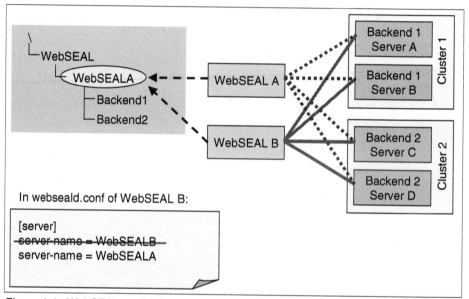

Figure 4-4   WebSEAL availability configuration

Configuring a WebSEAL cluster

In order to make two WebSEAL servers share the same object space, we need to change the part of the object space that one of the WebSEAL servers uses when making authorization decisions.

Normally, when WebSEALB checks permissions on /index.html, the object checked is /WebSEAL/WEBSEALB/index.html. However, if the server-name parameter in webseald.conf is changed to WEBSEALA, WEBSEALB will now check the object /WebSEAL/WEBSEALA/index.html.

The portion of the object space under /WebSEAL/WebSEALB is now redundant; all checks are done against the objects under /WebSEAL/WEBSEALA. As long as the file space of both servers is identical (which means they have the same junctions and the same back-end servers), then this will be fine, and will remove the need to duplicate work. You have to ensure that a copy of the XML junction information gets distributed to all clustered WebSEAL servers if new Web server junctions are being configured.

After renaming the server name value WebSEALB to WebSEALA in the webseald.conf file on WebSEALB, the server object in the name space is now meaningless and can be removed:

```
pdadmin>object delete /WebSEAL/WebSEALB
```

WebSEAL fail-over cookies

Fail-over cookies are used in Access Manager to allow a user to access a redundant WebSEAL server (in case of failure) without having to re-authenticate. Access Manager supports the use of fail-over cookies over HTTP or HTTPS.

The failover-cookies-keyfile entry in the webseald.conf file points to a file containing a triple DES key created using the cdsso_key_gen utility. This keyfile must be shared by all WebSEAL servers in the Access Manager secure domain that the user might be redirected to in the event of a failure.

Note: The processing of fail-over cookies is processor-intensive, and should only be used for failure recovery. They should not be used for load balancing.

More information on this configuration can be obtained in the section "Replicating Front-end WebSEAL Servers" in the *Tivoli SecureWay Policy Director WebSEAL Administration Guide*, GC32-0684.

Web server availability

In order to increase the availability of your Web server space you have to exactly duplicate your servers. The Web administrator has to ensure that the content of the Web root directories on the duplicated servers are kept in-sync. After you have created an initial WebSEAL junction for your first Web server, you can add your replicated Web servers to the same junction.

By default, Access Manager WebSEAL balances back-end server load by distributing requests across all available replicated servers when the replicated servers use the same junction point, as depicted in Figure 4-3 on page 85. Access Manager uses a "least-busy" algorithm for this task. This algorithm directs each new request to the server with the fewest connections already in progress.

For static Web content this approach is very easy to implement. However, there are some other considerations you have to regard.

Maintaining a stateful junction

Most Web-enabled applications maintain a "state" for a sequence of HTTP requests from a client. This state is used, for example, to:

► Track a user's progress through the fields in a data entry form generated by a CGI program.

► Maintain a user's context when performing a series of database inquiries.

► Maintain a list of items in an online shopping cart application where a user randomly browses and selects items to purchase.

Servers that run Web-enabled applications can be replicated in order to improve availability through load sharing. When the WebSEAL server provides a junction to these replicated back-end servers, it must ensure that all the requests contained within a client session are forwarded to the correct server, and not distributed among the replicated back-end servers according to the load balancing rules.

Authorization Server availability

Although not initially depicted in the basic scenario in Figure 4-2 on page 84, let us assume we have extended our Web application using some fine-grained Authorization Application Programming Interface authorization calls. This authorization information is provided by Access Manager and the application servers can be configured to request this information from a specific Access Manager Authorization Server if the applications run in remote cache mode configuration. This scenario is shown in Figure 4-5 on page 89.

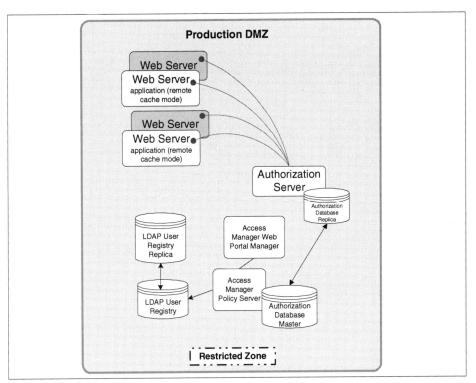

Figure 4-5   Authorization Server scenario for Stocks-4U.com

However, when this Authorization Server fails, the application cannot perform its fine-grained authorization calls and will therefore fail. In order to provide high availability of the application Authorization Services, the scenario configuration would result as shown in Figure 4-6 on page 90.

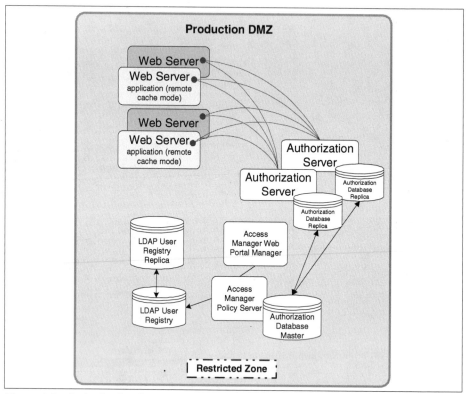

Figure 4-6   Authorization Server scenario with high availability

After implementing a second Authorization Server, you would only need to configure your aznAPI applications to be aware of the new replica. This is done by executing the `bassslcfg - add_replicas` command.

Another way of implementing this particular scenario could be by configuring the applications to run in local cache mode, shown in Figure 4-7 on page 91. By doing this, the aznAPI calls would not go out to a remote Authorization Server for access control checks, but use the local authorization database replica instead.

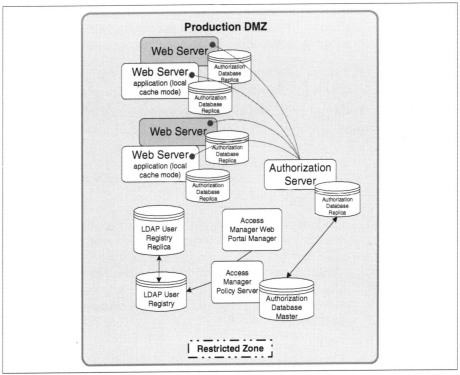

Figure 4-7   Authorization Server scenario on local cache mode

User registry availability

The IBM Directory Server supports the concept of master and replica LDAP servers.

A master server contains the master directory from which updates are propagated to replicas. All changes are made and occur on the master server, and the master is responsible for propagating these changes to the replicas.

A replica is an additional server that contains a database replica. The replicas must be exact copies of the master. The replicas do not allow updates to them (except from replication from the master). The replica provides a backup to the master server. If the master server crashes, or is unreadable, the replica is still able to fulfill search requests and provide access to the data.

Access Manager configuration for multiple LDAP directories

Access Manager connects to the LDAP master server when it starts up. If the LDAP master server is down for any reason, the Access Manager server must be able to connect to an available LDAP replica server for any read operations.

Many operations, especially those from regular users, are read operations. These include such operations as user authentication and sign-on to back-end junctioned Web servers. After proper configuration, Access Manager will fail over to a replica server when it cannot connect to the master server.

You can find the configuration parameters for LDAP fail over in the [ldap] stanza of the ldap.conf configuration file:

UNIX   /opt/PolicyDirector/etc/ldap.conf

Windows   *install-path*\etc \ldap.conf

In order to configure Access Manager for the use of multiple LDAP directories, you have to define the master and replica LDAP servers to be used:

1. Master Server configuration

   IBM Directory Server (LDAP) supports the existence of a single read-write master LDAP server. iPlanet Directory Server supports multiple read-write LDAP servers. Access Manager treats the iPlanet "supplier" server as the master server for configuration purposes. The active configuration lines in the ldap.conf file represent the parameters and values for this master LDAP server. You determine these values during Access Manager configuration. For example:

   ```
   [ldap ]
   enabled =yes
   host =outback
   port =389
   ssl-port =636
   max-search-size =2048
   ```

   If you make a change to the LDAP database, such as adding a new user account through the WPM, Access Manager always uses the read-write (master) LDAP server.

2. Replica Server Configuration

   IBM Directory Server (LDAP) supports the existence of one or more read-only replica LDAP servers. iPlanet Directory Server (LDAP) supports the existence of one or more read-only replica LDAP servers referred to as "consumers."

   You must add lines to the [ldap] stanza that identify any replica servers available to Access Manager. Use the following syntax for each replica:

   ```
   replica =ldap-server,port,type,preference
   ```

   Changes to the ldap.conf file do not take effect until you restart Access Manager. Further details on configuration can be found in the *IBM Tivoli Access Manager for e-Business Version 3.9 Base Administration Guide,* GC23-4684.

Access Manager Policy Server availability

The only portion of Access Manager that cannot be replicated within the same secure domain is the Policy Server. You can, however, have a second server in stand-by to provide manual fail-over capabilities as a first aid response. If you want to assure a 24x7 availability of your Access Manager Policy Server you would need to implement a high availability cluster solution like HACMP for AIX. For further details check the *HACMP Enhanced Scalability Handbook*, SG24-5328.

> **Note:** The purpose of the Policy Server is to maintain the master authorization database that contains the protected object space with the access control information (ACLs and POPs). The Policy Server replicates the authorization database to all other Access Manager Authorization Servers in the secure domain. Every application, configured in local cache mode, that uses this Authorization Service (like WebSEAL and third party utilization of the aznAPI) has its own local copy (replication) of the master authorization database and can therefore provide authentication and Authorization Services, even if the Policy Server is not available for a brief period of time.

Web Portal Manager availability

Again, the same is valid for the Web Portal Manager, which provides the administration GUI Web application for the Access Manager administrators. If the implementation requires a 24x7 availability of the Web administration interface, more than one Web Portal Manager should be deployed. This can very well be the case if you have delegated administration for your business partners to external domain administrators or if you are in the ASP business.

Since WPM runs on a WebSphere Application Server base, you would need to deploy the application using another WebSphere Edge Server dispatcher unit in front of your multiple WPM or set up a WebSEAL junction for the WPM application in order to use the Edge Server/WebSEAL deployment as a frontage for high available access.

Conclusion

Again, this point is clear: The Internet has changed the rules of how business is conducted. It has also changed the rules or concepts concerning customer loyalty. When users are experiencing slow response times or refused connections, they are having what is considered an unsatisfactory experience, which may cause them to never visit your site again and instead prefer one of your competitors. This line of thought leads us to the next discussion about scalability and performance.

4.3 Adding scalability

Scalability means that your systems have the capability to adapt readily to the intensity of use, volume, or demand. Designing scalability into your architecture also allows for fail over of critical systems and continuous operation at the same time. A lot of the availability discussion can be applied to the scalability issue as well; the topics are all very similar. Let us take a closer look at some specific viewpoints concerning scalability.

Access Manager component scalability

Access Manager automatically replicates the primary authorization policy database that contains the policy rules and credentials when a new application component, configured in local cache mode, or an Access Manager blade (like WebSEAL or an Authorization Server) is configured. This capability provides the foundation of Access Manager's scalable architecture. After you have designed and installed your Access Manager secure domain and your Policy Server, you can easily extend and configure this IT security landscape.

WebSEAL scalability

In order to add another WebSEAL machine to your existing cluster you would need to execute the following tasks:

► Install and configure a new WebSEAL server; an initial copy of the authorization database gets copied from the Policy Server.

► Edit the [server] stanza in the webseald.conf file, as shown in Figure 4-4 on page 86.

► Copy the existing junction definitions (XML files) to the new server.

► Add the new WebSEAL IP address to the load balancing table of your IBM Network Dispatcher or Cisco Local Director.

► Install and configure the necessary certificate information if you are using SSL communication, mutual authentication with your back-end Web servers, or fail-over cookies.

► Start the new WebSEAL.

The new WebSEAL will immediately receive browser requests that are routed from the load balancer product. This way, you can easily extend or change your WebSEAL infrastructure.

Tip: If you have installed WebSEAL multi-processor machines, then they scale best if you put one WebSEAL per two CPUs, and lock them to use the specific CPUs only. Next configure the WebSEAL instances into the load balancer.

Authorization Server scalability

In order to add another Authorization Server component to your infrastructure, you will need to execute the following tasks:

1. Install a new Authorization Server; an initial copy of the authorization database gets copied from the Policy Server.

2. Define this server as a new Authorization Server replica to your applications by using the `bassslcfg - add_replicas` command.

3. Install and configure the necessary certificate information if you are using SSL communication.

The new Authorization Server will immediately be available to receive authorization requests from your applications. This way, you can easily extend your application infrastructure.

Infrastructure component scalability

In order to achieve overall scalability, we need to take a closer look at the other infrastructure components.

Web server scalability

When your current Web server-installed base is not capable anymore of handling incoming requests, it is time to add a new server, maybe on a different, more powerful hardware and operating system platform. In order to get the new system incorporated into your existing Web server infrastructure, you need to apply the following tasks:

1. Install a new HTTP server on a new machine and create an exact mirror of your published root directory structure from your existing Web server.

2. Add a WebSEAL junction to the same junction point as your existing Web server.

3. If you were previously using only one Web server at this particular junction, you have to consider defining a stateful junction at this time, if your Web application is relying on session states.

4. If you require SSL connections between WebSEAL and your Web server, you have to configure the junction appropriately.

Using WebSEAL as a mechanism for Web server load balancing and high availability makes it a simple task to scale your Web server environment to your individual demands. You could even replace a grown Web server cluster of multiple Intel machines with a new high power server platform by reconfiguring your WebSEAL junction information without losing one second worth of business or redefining any of your security access control information.

User registry scalability

In order to enhance the overall scalability of the implementation, LDAP replica servers can be added at will to improve the response time for user applications relying on LDAP access. In conjunction with using preference values, you can place LDAP replica servers close to the application functionalities—logically or location dependant.

Preference values for replica LDAP servers

Each replica LDAP server must have a preference value (1–10) that determines its priority for selection as:

▶ The primary read-only access server
▶ A backup read-only server during a failover

The higher the number, the higher the priority. If the primary read-only server fails for any reason, the server with the next highest preference value is used. If two or more servers have the same preference value, a least-busy load balancing algorithm determines which one is selected.

Remember that the master LDAP server can function as both a read-only and a read-write server. For read-only access, the master server has a hard-coded default preference setting of 5. This allows you to set replica servers at values higher or lower than the master to obtain the required performance. For example, with appropriate preference settings, you could prevent the master server from handling everyday read operations.

You can set hierarchical preference values to allow access to a single LDAP server (with failover to the other servers), or set equal preferences for all servers and allow load balancing to dictate server selection. Further details on configuration can be found in the *IBM Tivoli Access Manager for e-Business Base Administration Guide Version 3.9*, GC23-4684.

For further capacity and availability discussion, refer to the *IBM Tivoli Access Manager for e-Business Maintenance and Troubleshooting Guide Version 3.9*, GC32-0846, and the *IBM Tivoli Access Manager for e-Business Capacity Planning Guide Version 3.9*, GC32-0847.

5

Authentication and delegation with Access Manager

This chapter describes the flexibility of user authentication mechanisms with Access Manager. It presents several mechanisms for the identification of users and shows how they can be used in various Web-based scenarios. It also introduces the basic concepts of achieving single sign-on solutions in Web-based environments.

This chapter does not look into any particular customer scenario, but rather presents the technological groundwork for the scenario in Chapter 6, "WebSphere application integration" on page 123.

Different approaches are needed to provide different types of user access, for example, unrestricted access or restricted access with passwords, SecurID tokens, or PKI certificates, to a variety of back-end applications. This flexibility should be provided within one security solution, and the maintenance of this security solution has to be done by a centralized security staff, while maintenance of the Web applications can be done by other individual groups.

The goal of this security solution is to enforce user authentication and to perform target-based, coarse- or fine-grained authorization before forwarding a user's request alongside with his credentials to any of the Web application servers. This way, the Web application developers can stay free of maintaining any security infrastructures.

The security solution is implemented as a reverse proxy Access Manager WebSEAL, which is located in the Internet demilitarized zone (DMZ). In order to serve as the single point of access control, it has to be used as the only access point for all incoming HTTP and HTTPS connections. Its major task will be to initially authenticate the user and to forward the user's request together with sufficient information about the user's identity to a Web server in a more secured network.

There are several issues we have to look out for:

► We have to make sure that WebSEAL does not allow any bypassing of the access control system. All internal and external access to Web-based resources should be channeled through WebSEAL.

► When using SSL connectivity to and from WebSEAL, you have to administer a private key for each WebSEAL and Web server participating in the SSL traffic flow. You should carefully control and document the usage of the private keys.

► You have to protect WebSEAL against unauthorized physical access. Because the reverse proxy has to terminate incoming SSL connections, all connection data will be unencrypted on WebSEAL. Although the data will be encrypted again when using an SSL connection to a back-end application server, physical access to WebSEAL or its memory might allow you to listen to communications even if the data is not being held in a cache.

► It is recommended that you use a hardened operating system for WebSEAL. Do not use the machine for any other purposes. Restrict physical and logical access and use intrusion detection tools to monitor any type of unauthorized connection attempts.

> **Note:** You can perfectly integrate this and other intrusion detection tools with the IBM Tivoli Risk Manager centralized auditing infrastructure. To learn more about this solution read the redbook *Enterprise Security Architecture using IBM Tivoli Security Solutions*, SG24-6014.

We have already focused on general WebSEAL architecture issues in 1.2.1, "WebSEAL" on page 14, as well as throughout Chapter 2, "Access Manager Web-based architecture" on page 33, and Chapter 3, "A basic WebSEAL scenario" on page 65. In this specific chapter, we will concentrate on the different authentication and delegation mechanisms that can be utilized with WebSEAL.

5.1 Typical business requirements

In addition to the typical business requirements described in 2.4.1, "Typical business requirements" on page 39, which were driven by an overall Web security approach, we want to add the following concerns from the authentication aspect:

► The business application developers should only focus on business functions and not on security in order to eliminate hidden security management costs.

Today a lot of applications use their own authentication and authorization mechanisms as well as security information repositories. There are also a lot of fields where basic operating system security is being used to achieve authentication. These approaches are forcing applications to be constantly maintained when changes to either security policy or operating system have to be implemented.

► Increase authentication flexibility without the need to change any application logic.

Separate user registries for internal and external applications are used, as well as separate security administration for inside and outside applications.

Another flexibility requirement is to allow different authentication methods for certain applications. A basic Web order system might be sufficiently protected with user ID and password authentication, while access to the same ordering system by business partners with high volume orders has to be controlled by providing a certificate- or token-based authentication.

► Increase authentication strength within one session without the need of changing any application logic.

Sometimes it is necessary to process a step-up authentication when an already authenticated user tries to access data that is identified as critical. This would result in the user being prompted for an additional authentication after he already signed in.

5.2 Typical security design objectives

In addition to the typical security design requirements described in 2.4.2, "Typical design objectives (technical requirements)" on page 40, which were driven by an overall Web security approach, we want to add the following concerns from the authentication aspect.

Here are some of the technical requirements for authentication that WebSEAL has to address:

► Authentication

Enforce authentication of users, where the type of authentication depends on the resources they want to access. Sometimes all users need to be authenticated, sometimes only users that want to access some protected URLs or applications need to identity themselves.

► User-based authorization

Perform an initial user-based authorization check, for example, decide if a user should be allowed to initially contact any of the Web applications. This step prevents certain users from accessing the system at all.

► Target-based authorization

Perform a resource-based authorization by deciding if a user should be allowed to contact a certain Web application.

► Delegation

If user authentication and authorization was successful, forward the user's request and user's credentials to a certain Web application server for further processing. This aspect of forwarding a user's credential is also referred to as single sign-on.

► Allow usage of a separate component for authentication

It might be necessary to allow a separate and already existing authentication application and repository to perform the initial user authentication. These additional authentication methods should be usable without having to rewrite any of the applications.

5.3 Solution architecture with WebSEAL

The best way to achieve the design objectives is by using a reverse Web proxy with sufficient security functions in front of the existing Web application servers. Figure 5-1 on page 101 shows a basic architecture for protecting Web applications.

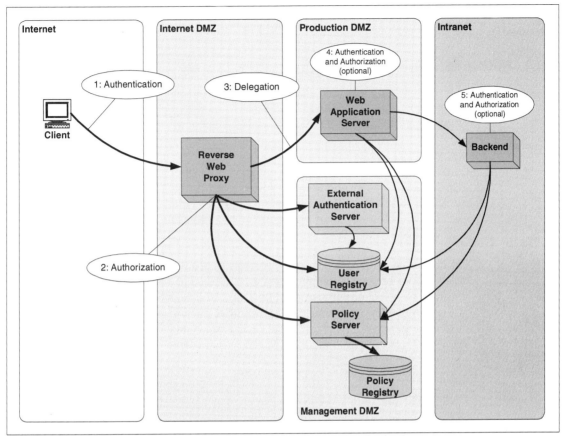

Figure 5-1   Reverse proxy flow for authentication, delegation, and authorization

The reverse proxy is used as a mediator between the end user and the Web application servers. The functions of the reverse proxy have to provide the following details:

► Accept either HTTP or HTTPS connections.

► If needed, gather user credentials.

► If needed, perform user authentication (locally or by using an external authentication service).

► Gather authorization information and make an authorization decision.

► Proxy the user's connection together with user credentials to the applicable Web application server.

Because this is a pure architectural discussion on functionality, the placement of additional components like load balancers or high-availability mechanisms are described in Chapter 4, "Increasing availability and scalability" on page 79.

5.3.1 Authentication and delegation mechanisms

This section presents the basic principles of authentication and delegation mechanisms that are used by WebSEAL to enforce protected access when a user tries to connect to a certain Web application from its Web browser.

Authentication describes the process of exchanging credentials to identify the communication partners. Authentication can be directional or mutual. Delegation is the process of forwarding information about a user's identity in a secure way to another system. WebSEAL can enforce certain types of user authentication and can use several delegation mechanisms to forward user requests together with user information to a Web application server.

Figure 5-2 on page 103 gives an overview of the various authentication and delegation mechanisms supported by WebSEAL. It depicts the available authentication schema between a user and WebSEAL, as well as the authentication between WebSEAL and other back-end application servers. The different mechanisms are discussed in greater detail in 5.4, "Supported WebSEAL authentication mechanisms" on page 108.

> **Note:** All authentication methods, except for the certificate-based authentication, can be used with HTTP or HTTPS. This was not possible with earlier Policy Director versions, where HTTP sessions were not supported and some mechanisms were only available for HTTPS.

Let us take another look at Figure 5-1 on page 101 in order to describe the steps during the authentication process:

1. The user contacts the Web site by entering the HTTP address of a Web page or Web application. His first point of contact is the WebSEAL server. Because WebSEAL works as a reverse proxy, the user does not realize that there is another system involved in the communication between him and the Web server he tries to contact.

   If access to the requested information is restricted, WebSEAL requests authentication information and authenticates the user. After successful authentication, WebSEAL generates user credential information.

2. Once authenticated, WebSEAL achieves an authorization decision based on the user credentials and the policy information that protects the information. WebSEAL decides whether the user is allowed to contact the system at all.

3. WebSEAL selects the junction for the user's requests and forwards the user credentials and user request to the Web application server.

4. Based on the forwarded user credentials, the Web application server can proceed with further, more fine-grained authorization decisions.

5. Based on the forwarded user credentials, the back-end application server can proceed with further, more fine-grained authorization decisions.

WebSEAL provides enough flexibility to support multiple authentication and delegation mechanisms to act as a reverse Web proxy between different user groups and different types of Web application servers in a secure way.

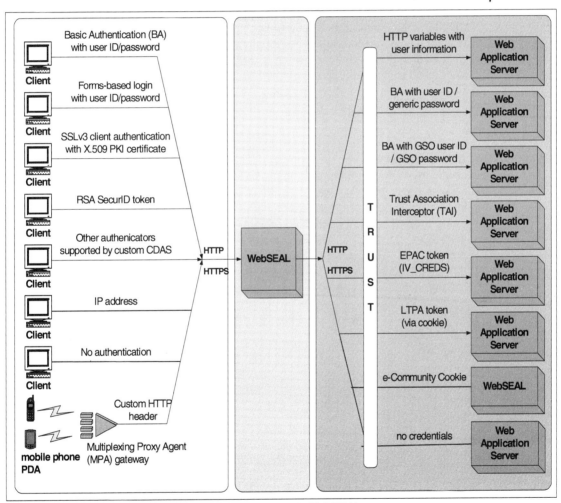

Figure 5-2 Access Manager authentication methods with WebSEAL

The left portion in Figure 5-2 on page 103 lists all authentication mechanisms available between a user and WebSEAL. The right side lists all delegation or single sign-on mechanisms between WebSEAL and another Web application server.

Some of those mechanisms can be combined, for example, access to a certain URL can be restricted to require a certain IP source address and the correct user ID/password combination. It is also possible to combine any authentication mechanism with any delegation mechanisms.

A single WebSEAL server may be configured for three different levels of authentication, of which unauthenticated is the first. Usually the next one is the user ID and password, but it can be any of the supported authentication mechanisms. Moving up to authenticated access happens when access control lists on the requested object do not allow access for unauthenticated users. The next level of authentication, which is usually a token (but can be any of the supported authentication mechanisms), is required when a protected object policy requiring it is set on an object.

5.3.2 Trust

An important factor for a centralized security portal solution is trust. If you configure all information requests to be routed through your central WebSEAL reverse proxy, you only want to authenticate the user once. This approach would imply that all back-end application servers trust all incoming user requests as being properly authenticated and authorized by a preliminary authority like WebSEAL. This solution is very useful if WebSEAL can do all necessary authorization. Figure 5-3 on page 105 shows a list of Web server products that can be protected with Access Manager's WebSEAL using some of the mechanisms listed above.

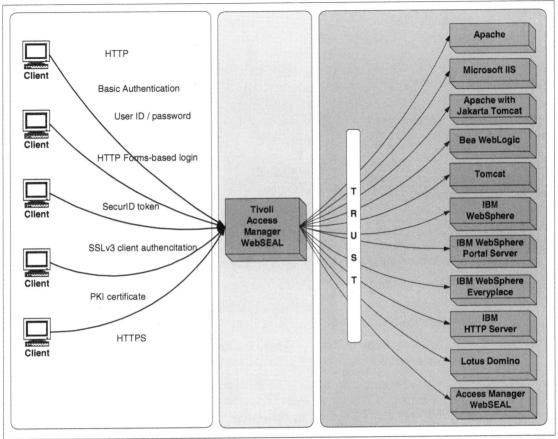

Figure 5-3   Overview of Web server products protected with WebSEAL

In order to fully implement a secure trust relationship, you would also have to configure each and every back-end application server to only accept incoming requests from WebSEAL on the specified port. No other direct connections, internal or external, are to be allowed to any of the servers. In cases where this is not yet practical or possible to achieve, you would have to specify the junctions to forward the user credentials in a way for the back-end servers to re-authenticate the user principal. This discussion has also been addressed in Chapter 2, "Access Manager Web-based architecture" on page 33.

5.3.3 Generic authentication mechanism with WebSEAL

Before going into the specific authentication model details, let us use Figure 5-4 on page 106 to take a look at a generic picture of the WebSEAL authentication model.

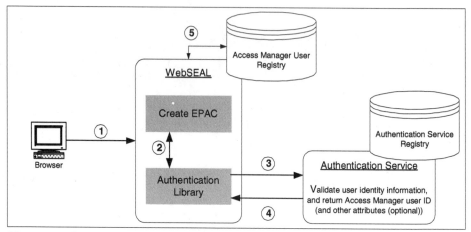

Figure 5-4   Generic WebSEAL authentication model

The following steps explain Figure 5-4.

1. The user presents his identity information to WebSEAL.

2. WebSEAL invokes the configured authentication library (password, token, certificate, or custom).

3. The authentication library passes the user identity information to the Authentication Service to perform user validation.

4. After validating the user, the Authentication Service maps the information according to its configuration and returns an Access Manager user ID. The Authentication Service may return the same individual user information that it received on input or it may use a mapped-to ID if each input user is also the output user that is referred to one-to-one mapping, and if many input users are mapped to the same output user that is referred to as many-to-one. In both cases, the returned user must be defined to the Access Manager's user registry.

5. WebSEAL now uses the Access Manager user registry to create the Access Manager credential—Extended Privilege Attribute Certificate (EPAC)—that is cached for the duration of the session and used for any authorization decisions.

Note: The EPAC is a token that details the user's identity and the roles that he can use. It can also contain additional attributes if required. EPACs are often misunderstood, are not encrypted or signed, and do not time out. They should only be trusted from within the Access Manager secure domain.

5.3.4 Generic delegation mechanism with WebSEAL

As discussed in 1.2.1, "WebSEAL" on page 14, WebSEAL junctions provide powerful capabilities for managing access to multiple Web application servers through a common access portal. Figure 5-3 on page 105 shows the different junctions WebSEAL can establish.

If you want to delegate further authentication and/or authorization tasks to the back-end application, you have to provide information about the user and the session. In order to pass on that kind of information, you have to define your junctions accordingly. You can actually provide the following information for your junctioned servers.

Supplying client identity in HTTP headers

You can insert Access Manager-specific client identity and group membership information into the HTTP headers of requests destined for junctioned third-party servers. The Access Manager HTTP header information enables applications on junctioned third-party servers to perform user-specific actions based on the client's Access Manager identity.

Supplying client IP addresses in HTTP headers

You can insert the client IP address information into the HTTP headers of requests destined for junctioned application servers. The Access Manager HTTP header information enables applications on junctioned third-party servers to perform actions based on this IP address information.

Passing session cookies to junctioned portal servers

A Web portal is a server that offers a broad array of personalized resources and services. You can send the Access Manager session cookie (originally established between the client and WebSEAL) to a back-end portal server. This option currently exists to directly support the integration of WebSEAL with different vendors' portal solutions. Note that the passing of session cookies is for downstream SSO from the portal to applications, not for WebSEAL to portal.

Global sign-on solution

Access Manager supports a flexible single sign-on solution that features the ability to provide alternative user names and passwords to the back-end Web application server.

Dynamic business entitlements

Access Manager offers a dynamic business entitlement functionality for passing information to back-end Web applications. This is implemented with two steps:

1. It is now possible to insert any field from an Access Manager user's LDAP record into her credential at login time. These values can be extracted by an application using the Authorization Application Programming Interface accessing the delegated client identity information.

2. Being able to insert arbitrary values from LDAP into the credential (without writing new authentication code) is a useful addition to Access Manager; however, the next step goes one step further, allowing back-end Web applications to access the information without the need to use aznAPI.

   WebSEAL can extract the values from the credential and pass them to the back-end Web server as fields in the HTTP request header. This allows most Web applications to access them without using any special code.

5.4 Supported WebSEAL authentication mechanisms

This section shows the authentication mechanisms that are supported by WebSEAL to protect access to a Web environment. All mechanisms in this section can be combined with any of the delegation mechanisms in the next chapter to make the connection between a user and a Web application.

WebSEAL uses the concept of Plug-on Authentication Modules (PAMs) to use different authentication methods. The programming interface is now available so users can write their own modules.

The following Plug-on Authentication Modules exist in Access Manager:

- ► passwd-ldap: Password authentication (Forms/BasicAuth)
- ► token-cdas: Token authentication (SecureID)
- ► cert-ldap: SSL client certificate authentication
- ► http-request: HTTP header authentication
- ► cdsso: e-Community single sign-on

5.4.1 Basic authentication with user ID/password

Basic authentication (BA) is part of the HTTP standard and defines a standardized way in which user ID/password information is passed to a Web server. When WebSEAL sends a BA challenge to the browser, the browser pops up a dialog panel requesting user name and password from the user. Once this information is entered, the browser sends its original request again, but this time with the user name and password included in the BA header of the HTTP request. WebSEAL extracts this information from the header and uses it to verify the user's identity. In this case, a specific library shipped with Access Manager implements a built-in authentication service and performs a check against the Access Manager user registry. If successful, an EPAC is created and cached.

Once a user has authenticated an ID and password through the browser, the browser caches this information in memory and sends it with each subsequent request to the same server. Even by configuring a session log out parameter, which is possible for HTTPS sessions, the user will automatically log on to WebSEAL with each new requests he sends. The only way to clear this cache (and log the current user out) is to close all browser panels.

5.4.2 Forms-based login with user ID/password

The alternative to using basic authentication is to use forms-based login. Rather than sending a basic authentication challenge in response to a client request, WebSEAL responds with a sign-in form in HTML format. The client browser displays this and the user fills in his user ID and password. When the user clicks on the send or logon button, the form is returned to WebSEAL using an HTTP POST request. WebSEAL extracts the information and uses it to verify the user's identity by using the Access Manager authentication service, where it performs a check against the Access Manager user registry.

As the user ID and password information is not cached on the browser, it becomes possible to perform a programmatic log out for the user. On a client request, WebSEAL presents a customizable logout form to a user. After the user confirms the logout, the session is considered closed and the EPAC is deleted from the WebSEAL cache.

Another benefit to using the forms-based login process is that you can enforce a time-based logout for authenticated sessions. The time values can be customized in the WebSEAL configuration files.

5.4.3 Authentication with X.509 client certificates

In response to a certificate request from WebSEAL, as part of the SSL Version 3 tunnel negotiation, the browser prompts the user to select a certificate from the local certificate store or smartcard. The user is asked for a password before he can access the private key. Once the user has chosen a certificate, it is passed to WebSEAL, which passes it on to the certificate authentication library, where the signature of the client certificate using the Certificate Authority (CA) certificates that it trusts is checked. It also checks the validity period to ensure the certificate has not expired. Assuming the certificate is OK, the identity in the certificate is mapped (one-to-one) to an Access Manager identity. Once the Access Manager identity is passed back to WebSEAL, WebSEAL pulls the user information from the Access Manager user registry and builds the EPAC.

If you configure Access Manager to use X.509 client certificates for authentication, but the user does not have a certificate available, WebSEAL can fall back to basic authentication, if required.

5.4.4 Authentication with RSA SecurID token

Access Manager includes a Cross Domain Authentication Service (CDAS) that supports authentication of clients using user name/token pass code information from an RSA SecurID token authenticator (TAR), a physical device that stores and dynamically generates a piece of authentication data (a token).

The TAR is used in tandem with an authentication server (the RSA ACE/Server), which actually performs the authentication. During authentication to WebSEAL, the client enters a user name and pass code. The pass code consists of:

► The unique PIN number associated with the client's SecurID TAR
► The current number sequence generated by the SecurID TAR

The Ace/Server uses its own registry database to determine the PIN that the user should be using, checks it, and strips it off of the pass code. It then checks the remaining number sequence against its own internally generated number sequence. A matching number sequence completes the authentication.

At this point, the role of the token CDAS is complete. The CDAS does not perform identity mapping, but simply returns to WebSEAL an Access Manager identity containing the user name of the client. This user name must match a user ID stored in the Access Manager user registry.

5.4.5 Custom authentication using CDAS

All the authentication mechanisms described above assume that the user identity validation information is held in the Access Manager user registry or can be verified locally on WebSEAL. Of course, there are situations where this is not the case, and user authentication has to be performed outside the Access Manager trusted domain: One-time password servers (for example, RSA SecureID), RADIUS, Resource Access Control Facility (RACF), and so on. On the other side, depending on the requirements, it may become necessary to extend or enrich the capabilities provided by built-in authentication libraries.

WebSEAL provides a capability referred to as *Cross Domain Authentication Service (CDAS)* in order to meet these requirements.

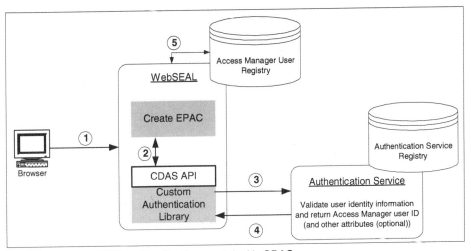

Figure 5-5   WebSEAL authentication model with CDAS

As shown in Figure 5-5, the CDAS allows you to substitute the default built-in WebSEAL authentication mechanism with a highly flexible shared library mechanism that allows custom handling and processing of client authentication information. The CDAS application programming interface (API) is available for download by registered customers.

You can customize the CDAS shared library to handle authentication data according to your security requirements given the following options.

The custom CDAS can process authentication data internally and return an Access Manager identity. This is especially useful if it is desired to have enriched authentication mechanisms in comparison to built-in ones, for example, checking client certificate validity via Online Certificate Status Protocol (OCSP). The user identity validation information may reside in the user registry and not be used for authentication by default, for example, providing a customer number along with user ID and password in B2B scenarios.

Extending the built-in capabilities of authentication mechanisms provided by Access Manager is another reason to built a custom CDAS. This method allows you to authenticate clients who are not direct members of the Access Manager security domain. In that case, the custom CDAS can direct authentication data to be processed by an external authentication mechanism and third-party registry (for example, RACF, One-Time Password Server, or authentication via personal question). Ultimately, the CDAS returns an Access Manager identity to WebSEAL for querying the Access Manager user registry and creating an EPAC.

5.4.6 Authentication using customized HTTP headers

Access Manager supports authentication via customized HTTP header information supplied by the client or a proxy agent.

This mechanism requires a mapping function (a shared library) that maps the trusted (pre-authenticated) header data to an Access Manager identity. WebSEAL can take this identity and create a credential for the user.

WebSEAL assumes custom HTTP header data has been previously authenticated. For this reason, it is recommended that you implement this method exclusively with no other authentication methods enabled. It is possible to impersonate custom HTTP header data.

By default, this shared library is built to map data from entrust proxy headers.

5.4.7 Authentication based on IP address

Access Manager supports authentication via an IP address supplied by the client.

This mechanism is best used in combination with other mechanisms. For example, you can use IP network addresses to identity a certain group of users, give them access to a certain application, and then use additional authentication mechanisms to give access to more protected applications.

Such a configuration can be used to implement a two-factor authentication as well. It will possibly be more secure than plain password authentication.

5.4.8 No authentication

Any user that can reach WebSEAL belongs to the group of unauthenticated users. This group can also get certain permissions.

This group of unauthenticated users generally is used to define public Web access. WebSEAL can force unauthenticated users to use another authentication method when selecting certain protected URLs.

All users that can reach WebSEAL might already have enough permissions to contact certain junctioned Web servers. For example, if WebSEAL is connected to a VPN gateway, only authorized VPN users will be able to reach that server and additional authentication might not be needed. In this situation, it might be OK to treat unauthenticated users similarly to a group of password-authenticated Internet users.

5.4.9 MPA authentication

Access Manager provides an authentication mechanism for clients using a Multiplexing Proxy Agent (MPA). This is a special variation of the authentication with customized HTTP headers, often used for mobile phones and PDAs today, but not limited to these.

Multiplexing Proxy Agents are gateways that accommodate multiple client access. IBM Everyplace Wireless Gateway (EWG) is an integrated part of the IBM WebSphere Everyplace Suite that provides security-rich wired and wireless connectivity between the IT network and the communications network; for example

► Cellular networks, including GSM, CDMA, TDMA, PDC, PHS, iDEN, and AMPS

► Packet radio networks, including GPRS, CDPD, DatatTAC, and Mobitex

► Satellite and Wireline environments, including DSL, cable modems, Internet service providers, ISDN, Dial, and LAN

In addition, the Everyplace Wireless Gateway provides protocol translation as a Wireless Application Protocol (WAP) gateway, information push as a WAP push proxy gateway, and support for short messaging services (SMS). EWG establishes a single SSL channel to the origin server and "tunnels" all client requests and responses through this channel.

To WebSEAL, the information across this channel initially appears as multiple requests from one client. WebSEAL must distinguish between the authentication of the MPA server over SSL and the additional authentication requests for each individual client.

Because WebSEAL maintains an SSL session state for the MPA, it cannot use SSL session IDs for each client simultaneously. WebSEAL instead authenticates the clients using HTTP authentication techniques over SSL.

If the user is authenticated at the EWG, for example, to a RADIUS Server, then WebSEAL can be configured to receive an "authenticated ID" from the gateway and not re-authenticate the user.

Today, WebSEAL support for the Entrust Proxy and the Nokia WAP gateway exists.

5.5 WebSEAL delegation mechanisms

After a user has been authenticated by WebSEAL and an authorization decision has been made, WebSEAL has to forward the user's request to a back-end Web application server. If needed, WebSEAL can include information about the user, for example, X.509 distinguished name, group memberships, or any other value.

The mechanisms to forward that information can vary. It is possible to use standard protocols, for example, the HTTP basic authentication header, or to use proprietary mechanisms when talking to specific server products. WebSEAL supports several mechanisms for forwarding requests to Web application servers.

This section presents alternatives on how to pass information about the user and the user's request to the back-end application.

When a protected resource is located on a junctioned Web application server, a client requesting that resource can be required to perform multiple logins—one for the WebSEAL server and one for the back-end server. Each login may require different login identities. The problem of administering and maintaining multiple login identities can often be solved with a single sign-on mechanism.

The Open Group defines single sign-on as a "mechanism whereby a single action of user authentication and authorization can permit a user to access all computers and systems where that user has access permission, without the need to enter multiple passwords"[1]. While Tivoli Global Sign-On addresses the authentication issues on various applications running on different operation systems, WebSEAL's realm is to provide the single sign-on functionalities for Web infrastructures. Acting as a Web reverse proxy to the company's Web

---

[1] Taken from the security section of the Open Group Web site (http://www.opengroup.org/security/topics.htm).

environment, WebSEAL communicates with the junctioned servers on behalf of the users. It allows the user to access a resource, regardless of the resource's location, using only one initial login. Any further login requirements from back-end application servers are handled so they are transparent to the user.

Depending on integration requirements, different data should be sent to the WebSEAL-secured Web application using different formats. However, most of the Web applications support standard HTTP-based mechanisms for the user identification, which are exploited by WebSEAL.

5.5.1 Tivoli Global Sign-On (TGSO) lockbox

Most Web applications support basic authentication for checking authenticity and obtaining a user's identity information. When using this support, an application or the server the application is running on maintains a database with user IDs and passwords (in the most simple case). In our initial example in Chapter 3, "A basic WebSEAL scenario" on page 65, it was operating system-based user management on multiple Web servers, containing lists of user IDs and passwords. After challenging a user and obtaining user ID and password, an application would look up the matching entry and, if one was found, the user was considered authenticated and his or her identity was associated with the provided user ID. In more sophisticated environments relational databases, legacy applications or LDAP-based repositories are targeting that scope.

Access Manager supports a flexible single sign-on solution that features the ability to provide alternative user IDs and passwords to the Web application servers.

The integration is achieved by creating "SSO-aware" junctions between WebSEAL and Web servers hosting the applications. TGSO resources and TGSO resource groups must first be created in Access Manager for every application. When WebSEAL receives a request for a resource located on the "SSO-junctioned" server, WebSEAL queries the Access Manager user registry for the appropriate authentication information. The user registry contains a database of mappings for each user registered for using that application, which provides alternative user IDs and passwords for specific resources. Evidently, that information has to be in the repository prior to initial using. The values (user IDs and passwords) should match those stored in the application "home" registry.

Note: Although junctions are set up on a Web server basis, it is possible to provide different SSO data to different applications hosted on the same server. In order to achieve this, multiple TGSO junctions to the same Web server are created. However, using access control lists, the access to the resources is defined that way, so that only appropriate URLs can be requested through a specified junction.

The visible advantage of the solution is that no changes are supposed to be made on the application side. However, the following issues should be considered:

▶ Synchronization of the user IDs and passwords in the application's home user registry and Access Manager user registry

▶ Storage of SSO passwords in the Access Manager user registry in the clear, as they should be passed through to the application in the clear (they could be protected from the disallowed access, for example, LDAP ACLs)

A special situation emerges if Access Manager and the secured application are sharing the same repository for storing user data, as shown in Figure 5-6 on page 117. An LDAP directory is the most suitable platform for maintaining application-specific information about users and groups. Given compatible LDAP schemas[2], many applications may share the same LDAP directory. LDAP provides a standardized way of authenticating users based on user ID and password stored as user attributes. However, it provides no flexibility in defining object classes to be used for authenticating a user, rather than performing a call based on primary identification attributes of a user (user ID and password). While using an Access Manager TGSO-junction, Access Manager uses specific LDAP attributes for storing TGSO-information for every TGSO user. As a result, the TGSO user ID and password provided for a specific junction are not necessary the same as primary ones. However, a junctioned application sharing the same LDAP repository would then try to authenticate a user using these values against primary ones (by doing LDAP bind or compare). The need to keep the values of primary user IDs and passwords as TGSO ones arise.

---

[2] LDAP schema describes the way of storing the information in a LDAP directory in terms of object classes and attributes.

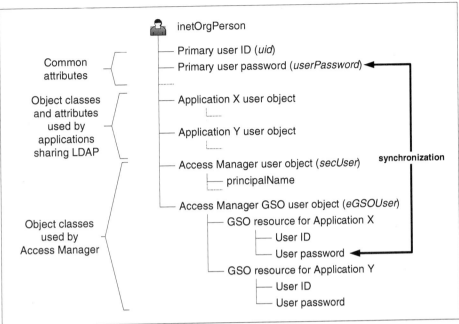

Figure 5-6   LDAP shared by Access Manager and other applications

The following issues should be considered while looking for solutions for integrating Access Manager and Web applications using the same LDAP repository:

► Main user passwords are allowed to be in the clear (keep in mind, Access Manager TGSO passwords are always in clear). The possibility of protecting LDAP data based on ACLs always exists.

► Changing the main password should be reflected in the change of the TGSO password for a particular user. This can happen immediately, for example after a user changes his password[3], or in a batch run on a regular basis. The last situation presumes that main passwords are in clear.

---

[3] Note that a custom Web application should be developed in order to achieve the "on-the-fly" synchronization of main and TGSO passwords. All password changes should be handled by users through that application that will subsequently carry out the changes for main and TGSO passwords. This would allow main user passwords to be encrypted. However, the Access Manager mechanisms for setting up and maintaining password policies may not be in place any longer. Otherwise, the Access Manager native interface for changing passwords, and not the custom application, would be invoked, for example, in the case of password expiration.

Another way to resolve the LDAP "bind-issue" while sharing the same LDAP repository between Access Manager and secured Web applications is maintaining separate user entries. For example, a different subset of users is defined and maintained for Access Manager and its secured application. A user may have the DN=CN=Jon Doe,O=IBM,C=US and DN=CN=Jon Doe,OU=Access Manager,O=IBM,C=US for use by applications and Access Manager respectively, as shown in Figure 5-7.

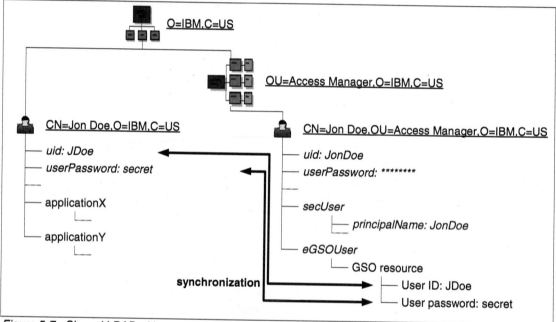

Figure 5-7   Shared LDAP with separate user entries

As a result, while performing authentication, the application will try to bind using its own user IDs and passwords. The TGSO user IDs and passwords could be more easily kept in-sync with those maintained by an application. The trade-offs of this solution are:

▶ The need to maintain the user information sets per application sharing is the same LDAP.

▶ As the same user identity would exist multiple times, it would raise the direct cost if the licensing of the LDAP software is on a per-user base.

5.5.2 Passing an unchanged basic authentication header

WebSEAL can be configured to pass the received basic authentication data unchanged to the junctioned application. If Access Manager and the application share the same LDAP registry, Access Manager authenticates a user against the same LDAP attributes as an application performing a regular LDAP bind, that is, using a main user ID and password. In this case, there is no need to maintain the TGSO attributes of a user and the main password may be encrypted. However, basic authentication is the only available authentication method used by WebSEAL, as WebSEAL has to obtain the BA header values in order to pass them through.

5.5.3 Junction without authentication

This may be useful if WebSEAL does all the authentication and authorization and there is no need to forward any information to the back-end servers.

This scenario seems applicable for either servers without any reliable security functions or where there is no need of extra back-end authentication and authorization, for example, providing only static Web pages. Nevertheless, this approach requires full trust towards WebSEAL, and the back-end servers should be configured to only accept incoming requests from WebSEAL proxies.

5.5.4 Providing a generic password

At this point, the following sections are based on the assumption that trust between WebSEAL and the back-end application server is established.

Given a Web application that may be contacted through WebSEAL only, an integration solution based on providing a user ID along with a uniform generic password and shared by WebSEAL and the application can be considered. As the process of authenticating a user is performed by WebSEAL, and given WebSEAL is the only gateway into the application, there is no need to carry out the authenticity check again. Although no changes have to be made in the application, it still could perform authentication in its obvious manner. However, its scope should only be the gaining of user identity. There should be no other possibilities available to contact the application avoiding WebSEAL.

The application can maintain its own user repository or share that of Access Manager (LDAP-based). In the second case, however, the LDAP-bind issue discussed before (see 5.5.1, "Tivoli Global Sign-On (TGSO) lockbox" on page 115) has to be considered. That leads to the necessity of maintaining separate entries for a single user for Access Manager and the secured application.

5.5.5 Supplying user and group information

WebSEAL can be configured to provide information about user ID, groups, and resources the user has access to, to a junctioned application. That is accomplished by supplying the values of defined HTTP variables:

iv_user　　　　　For user ID

iv_user_l　　　　For user's LDAP distinguished name

iv_groups　　　　For groups a particular user belongs to

iv_creds　　　　For the user's credentials

The variables supplied in the HTTP stream can be easily mapped to the CGI environment variables that can be interpreted by a Web application. As no password information can be supplied this way, no authentication can be performed by the junctioned Web application. However, it is possible to combine this option with any previously described.

Secure credential exchange

We would like to briefly introduce the notion of secure credentials and how they could be exchanged between Web applications.

Credentials are basically created as a result of a successful authentication. Credentials created by a WebSEAL reverse proxy can be understood by other WebSEALs in the same Access Manager security domain and even beyond (see Chapter 7, "Access control in a distributed environment" on page 151). However, the credential exchange with the junctioned Web server is not necessarily trivial mainly due to the lack of standardization. Kerberos, PKI, DCE, and Active Directory (with related products) are the most well-known security technologies, providing security interoperability for different platforms and applications, including Web-based environments; however, the applications have to be enabled for that. Not less important is the fact that these technologies do not interoperate seamlessly with each other; neither do the applications.

In order to support the interoperability of Web applications, WebSEAL today uses a generic HTTP-based interface as described in the previous sections.

5.5.6 Using LTPA authentication with WebSEAL

WebSEAL can provide authentication and authorization services and protection to an IBM WebSphere or Lotus Domino environment. When WebSEAL is positioned as a protective front end to WebSphere or Lotus Domino, accessing clients are faced with two potential login points. Therefore, WebSEAL supports a single sign-on solution to one or more IBM WebSphere or Lotus Domino servers across WebSEAL junctions.

WebSphere provides the cookie-based lightweight third party authentication mechanism (LTPA). You can configure WebSEAL junctions to support LTPA and provide a single sign-on solution for clients.

When a user makes a request for a WebSphere or Lotus Domino resource, the user must first authenticate to WebSEAL. Upon successful authentication, WebSEAL generates an LTPA cookie on behalf of the user. The LTPA cookie, which serves as an authentication token for WebSphere or Lotus Domino, contains user identity and password information. This information is encrypted using a password-protected secret key shared between WebSEAL and the WebSphere or Lotus Domino server.

WebSEAL inserts the cookie in the HTTP header of the request that is sent across the junction to WebSphere or Lotus Domino. The back-end WebSphere or Lotus Domino server receives the request, decrypts the cookie, and authenticates the user based on the identity information supplied in the cookie.

To improve performance, WebSEAL can store the LTPA cookie in a cache and use the cached LTPA cookie for subsequent requests during the same user session. You can configure lifetime timeout and idle (inactivity) timeout values for the cached cookie.

The creation, encryption, and decryption of LTPA cookies basically introduces processing overhead. The LTPA cache functionality allows you to improve the performance of LTPA junctions in a high load environment. By default, the LTPA cache is enabled. Without the enhancement of the cache, a new LTPA cookie is created and encrypted for each subsequent user request.

Note: With previous versions of WebSphere you needed to enable SSO for the Access Manager LTPA authentication to work correctly. This meant that WebSphere sent a cookie containing an LTPA token back to the browser with the HTTP response. This cookie was not used or required for Access Manager LTPA to work. However, because this cookie contained the LTPA token and is sent back to the browser, there was an exposure. The LTPA keys could be cracked in an off-line attack. This meant it was important to periodically regenerate the LTPA keys within WebSphere and redistribute them to Access Manager.

With WebSphere Version 4 SSO and WebSEAL, it is no longer required for Access Manager LTPA authentication to work. Even if it is enabled, the LTPA token is no longer sent to the browser, eliminating this exposure.

Having the LTPA cookie enabled is independent of the basic authentication header. This means that with the LTPA cookie inserted into the request header, it is still possible to have the BA header to carry any authentication information to the back-end server depending on the -b option specified during the junction creation. The usage of the BA header depends on the configuration of the back-end WebSphere or Lotus Domino server. Figure 5-8 shows the available usage scenarios with the LTPA authentication.

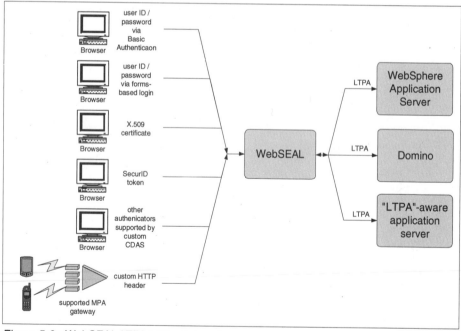

Figure 5-8 WebSEAL LTPA token delegation

## 6

WebSphere application integration

One of the nightmares in IT security management is application-managed security. When different applications on different platforms driven by different project groups are implementing their own view of security functionalities, the result is an expensive, unmanageable turmoil that opens security holes instead of providing a strong access control solution. In developing new Java-based e-business Web applications, we can start to build a solution that lets us distinguish and differentiate between security and application functions.

Looking at application development platforms within today's e-business environments, we have to take a closer look at Java 2 Platform Enterprise Edition (J2EE)-based Web application servers. Two major products have already been integrated with Access Manager to some extent: BEA's WebLogic Application Server and IBM's WebSphere Application Server. This chapter examines the details of integration between Access Manager and WebSphere Application Server.

6.1 Business requirements

Security is such a fundamental enabler of e-business that in the emerging B2C and B2B markets, effective security can make the difference between owning the market and becoming an "also ran." The promise of e-business and its ability to create new revenue streams is predicated upon the ability of these new business processes to reach these new markets and customers. But that promise evaporates if security issues are not addressed properly.

In this world of e-business, WebSphere has become a Web application server market leader. A growing number of customers are deploying WebSphere and WebSphere-based solutions as their core e-business software platform. Few, if any, customers will put their WebSphere-based applications and solutions into production without the assurance that their business processes and data will be protected from malicious and inadvertent loss. More importantly, as enterprises extend their business applications to reach new markets and customers, security and trust issues become of paramount importance. This has always been true in core, mission-critical, intranet-based applications. This is even more true as these applications are leveraging the Internet's Web-based computing model for B2C and B2B.

As customers have moved to a Web-based computing model, some have found it very difficult to implement security on an application-by-application basis. And with disparate applications that require disparate security approaches, it becomes clear very quickly that there is no security policy when there are numerous *islands of security* that cloud the picture. There is nothing nefarious about the islands of security approach; in fact, it can be a natural evolution for customers because many products, including IBM's WebSphere, come with some form of security built in. But when the islands begin to diminish, the ability to clearly manage security according to policy for your organization decreases, so there is tremendous value in securing applications in a way that is consistent and compatible with securing applications and application components running on other middleware and platforms in the enterprise.

For this scenario we define the following business requirements for existing as well as new e-business applications based on WebSphere family products:

► Reduce the costs of implementing and maintaining proprietary Web security solutions (islands of security)

► Fast time-to-production

► Reduce cost and complexity of application development

► Consistently manage end-to-end security (from browser to Web application) in order to mitigate risks of fraud

► Develop applications according to standards and standard architectures in order to achieve independence of specific vendor solutions

6.2 Security design objectives

Based on business requirements, we define the following security design objectives to be achieved by integrated solutions:

► Simplification of application development and off-loading the security policy of the application

► Simplification of system administration by maintaining a consistent security model across Web applications and related systems

Regarding the implementation of an access control subsystem, the systems fall into one of three categories.

Category 1

Category 1 systems implement their own authorization decision processes based on security policies, defined in proprietary formats, as well as enforcement of those policies, as shown in Figure 6-1.

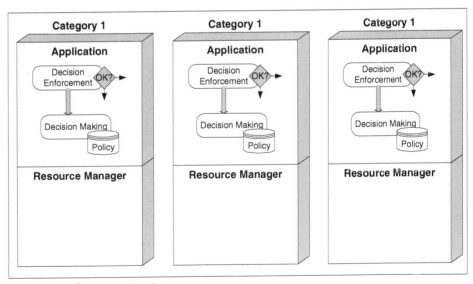

Figure 6-1   Category 1 systems

Obviously, these are home-grown applications that may even precisely reflect the existing security policies. However, the risk is rather high that such implementations go outside the designed limits in rapidly extending and changing IT environments. As security decision making, as well as its enforcement, is implemented inside the application, any change in the policies requires reflection in the application code. Moreover, it becomes difficult to ensure that all category 1 systems enforce the same policy. As an outcome in category 1 systems, maintenance cost for updating security in the applications are rising, and the valuable development time is spent on writing security, not business functions.

Category 2

Systems of category 2 address this issue by off-loading the authorization decision-making process out of the application to a resource manager, as shown in Figure 6-2. The resource manager takes over the role of providing the requested resources to the application and decision-making process. If a resource is requested by the application, it calls the authorization decision-making process residing in the resource manager. The resource manager consults its policy database and provides the application with a simple yes or no decision. It is then up to the application to enforce the received decision and provide information on the user's request or decline it. A series of subsequent authorization decision calls may be necessary to come to the final go or no go decision.

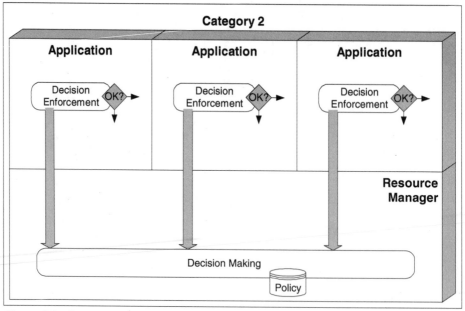

Figure 6-2   Category 2 systems

By separating the two functions (decision making and decision enforcement), it is much easier to achieve reusability of the decision-making processes and consistency of the policies. The Tivoli Access Manager software architecture supports this category, providing a uniform framework for authorization decisions and Open Group's Authorization application programming interface (API) for its querying. Decision enforcement takes place on the blades in order to meet the needs of distributed applications acting in disparate environments with different security requirements. However, an application based on a system of category 2 has to implement its own decision enforcement and, if not standardized (for example, based on Authorization API provided by Open Group), the decision requester as well, which may be considered to be more error-prone.

Category 3

To avoid this problem, systems of category 3 rely on mechanisms provided by a resource manager and have no need to even maintain decision enforcement, as shown in Figure 6-3.

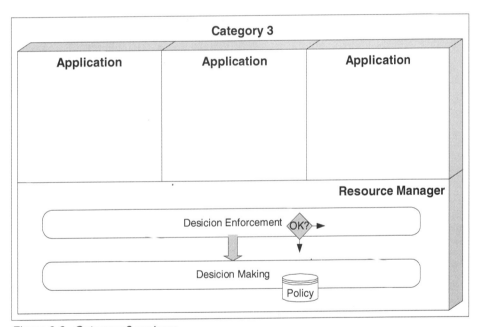

Figure 6-3   Category 3 systems

A Web server providing access to files in a defined directory is an application that falls in this category. In a simple case, it uses security mechanisms of the operating system that act as a resource manager. If a user is requesting an HTML document, the operating system's file permissions are decisive for granting access. The application (Web server) requests a resource (file), managed by the operating system. While serving the request, the operating system makes a decision, based on the permission attributes (policy) of the requested file, and, if allowed, provides access to the file (decision enforcement) by the Web server. WebSphere Enterprise JavaBean (EJB)-based applications work in a similar fashion.

This approach works just fine as long as applications reside together with the resource manager on the same system. But it becomes much more difficult to manage if multiple applications of the same kind are distributed through the IT environment and communicate with the same resource manager. Moreover, as soon as a need arises to establish security policies throughout applications based on different resource managers of different kinds, a new consolidation layer is required. As shown in Figure 6-4, Access Manager provides that uniform authorization framework, which allows you to consolidate the decision-making process based on a consistent policy database.

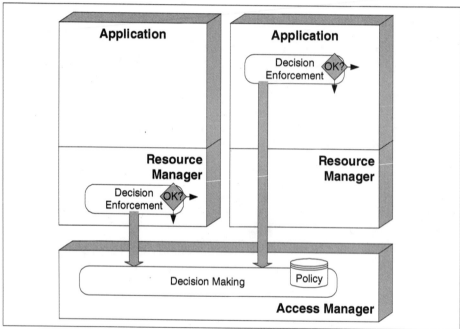

Figure 6-4   Policy enforcement based on consistent decision making

6.3 WebSphere Application Server Version 4.0 security

WebSphere Application Server Version 4 is a Java 2 Enterprise Edition, or J2EE 1.2 compliant Java application server. It implements the required services as they are specified. There have been a number of changes in the architecture and functionality of WebSphere Application Server Version 4.0 in order to become compliant with J2EE 1.2. Probably the most noticeable change is the structure of the artifacts that make up an application and are installed into WebSphere. All components intended to run in WebSphere are now packaged as Enterprise Archive (EAR) files. Another change is the addition of a major new tool, the Application Assembly Tool (AAT). The AAT is used to build an EAR from component modules, and configure all the deployment descriptors. In this chapter we concentrate on the J2EE security features implemented in WebSphere Version 4.0:

► Role-based security
► Declarative security
► Programmatic security

Role-based security

One of the goals of the EJB 1.1 specification was to lessen the burden of application security on application developers. Previously, if a portion of code could only be executed by particular types of users, the code itself had to handle the authorization, often right within the business logic. For example, if only managers were allowed to execute a function, then each user attempting to call that function would have to be identifiable as a manager. This might require a lookup in an employee database to determine the user's employee type or group type. This leads to the development of category 1 systems, as described in Figure 6-1 on page 125.

EJB 1.1 and J2EE 1.2 attempt to move this security burden to the application *assemblers* and *deployers*. This allows them to define security roles, sets of permissions for access to Web resources, and specific EJB methods. The use of roles provide a level of indirection that allows the subsequent assignment of those roles to users and groups to be done at application installation time, rather than during development. It also allows security constraints within modules developed by different teams to be resolved at assembly, deployment, or installation time.

The J2EE specification defines a security role as a logical grouping of users that is defined by an application component provider or assembler. It is then mapped by a deployer to security identities, for example, principals or groups, in the operational environment. A security role can be used either with declarative security or with programmatic security. Thus, WebSphere's security model has changed from permission-based to role-based.

Declarative security

The declarative security mechanisms, as part of J2EE, are stored in a document called deployment descriptor using a declarative syntax. Global security roles for a WebSphere application are stored in the XML deployment descriptor. Security roles for WebSphere components are stored in their corresponding deployment descriptors inside the EAR, Java archives (JARs), and WARs.

WebSphere uses method permissions, introduced in the EJB 1.1 specification, to describe security roles for EJBs. For a particular EJB resource, method permissions are the association of role names with the sets of methods, based on what types of permissions should be required to invoke the methods. Example 6-1 demonstrates a slightly abbreviated sample role description for EJB methods within an ejb-jar.xml deployment descriptor. Only a user that can be mapped to the security role teller and is allowed access to the methods getBalance and getLastTransaction of the bean AccountBean.

Example 6-1   Method permissions in the ejb-jar.xml deployment descriptor

```
<method-permission>
      <role-name>Teller</role-name>
      <method>
         <ejb-name>AccountBean</ejb-name>
         <method-name>getBalance</method-name>
      </method>
      <method>
         <ejb-name>AccountBean</ejb-name>
      <method-name>getLastTransactions</method-name>
      </method>
</method-permission>
```

If WebSphere security is enabled and EJBs have no method at all configured with security, then the default is to grant access to the EJB methods. If WebSphere security is enabled and at least one method has a security constraint, then the request to the EJBs is denied. This kind of behavior is different compared to the Web modules' components. By default, access is allowed to all Web resources. Parts of the Web resources can be protected using security constraints.

For a particular Web resource (servlet, JSP, and URL), security constraints are the association of role names with the sets of HTTP methods, based on what types of permissions should be required to access the resource. These are defined in the WAR's deployment descriptor. Example 6-2 on page 131 shows a WAR deployment descriptor that restricts access to any URL containing the URL-pattern /sales/ to the methods HTTP-POST and HTTP-GET and to users that can be mapped during runtime to a security role called SalesPerson.

Example 6-2   Security constraints and permissions in a WAR deployment descriptor

```
<web-app>
      <display-name>Retail Application</display-name>
      <security-constraint>
         <web-resource-collection>
            <web-resource-name>SalesInfo</web-resource-name>
            <url-pattern>/sales/*</url-pattern>
            <http-method>POST</http-method>
            <http-method>GET</http-method>
<         /web-resource-collection>
         <auth-constraint>
            <role-name>SalesPerson</role-name>
         </auth-constraint>
      </security-constraint>
</web-app>
```

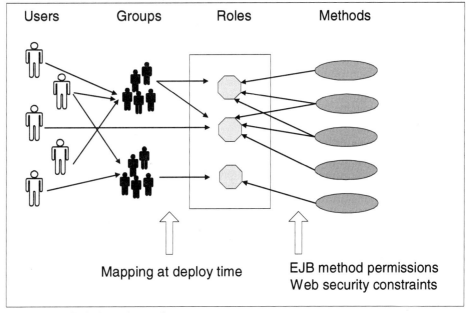

Figure 6-5   Role-based security

Figure 6-5 depicts declarative security based on security roles. The objects (EJB methods, static Web pages, servlets, and JSPs) are protected by method permissions or security constraints. Permissions and constraints are mapped to security roles. The deployer grants access to roles for users and groups. So far there is no need for a developer to implement a single line of code to achieve security.

Programmatic security

Declarative security is not always sufficient to express the security model of the application. Let us look at the example of a payment transaction. A customer has to have access to a bean method in order to transfer money. If he is granted access, he can perform any transaction he wants. In order to limit the amount of money that can be transferred by this user, the application needs to have knowledge about the role of the customer.

Developers can check security constraints programmatically using the name of the role. The API for programmatic security in J2EE 1.2 consists of two methods of the EJB EJBContext interface and two methods of the servlet HttpServletRequest interface:

► isCallerInRole (EJBContext)
► getCallerPrincipal (EJBContext)
► isUserInRole (HttpServletRequest)
► getUserPrincipal (HttpServletRequest)

These methods allow components to make business logic decisions based on the security role of the caller or remote user. In our example, the application may use the method isUserInRole to verify if the user is allowed to transfer the amount of a given sum. Another possibility would be to use the method getUserPrincipal to use the user's principal name as a key to get more authorization information stored elsewhere.

To summarize, WebSphere Application Server 4.0 authorization uses a role-based model rather than the permission-based model of previous versions. WebSphere Application Server 4.0 treats a role as a set of permissions to access particular resources.

6.4 Access Manager and WebSphere integration

Providing a standard-based authorization framework for WebSphere applications, Tivoli Access Manager supports the Java 2 security model as well as the Java Authentication and Authorization Services (JAAS) and Java 2 Enterprise Extensions (J2EE).

Integrating WebSphere and Access Manager adds WebSphere resources to the significant list of elements that can be managed via Tivoli Access Manager's consistent authorization policy, and it also adds to WebSphere applications the benefits that accrue in an Access Manager-protected environment. The examples of this discussed in the previous chapters include URI-based access control, availability and scalability characteristics inherent in Access Manager implementations, and the ability to support many authentication mechanisms without any impact to the target application and Web single sign-on, which are fully applicable for WebSphere Application Server.

The integration of WebSphere Application Server and Access Manager offers the following additional options/possibilities:

► Shared user registry

► Web single sign-on using:

- Tivoli Global Sign-On (TGSO) junctions
- Web Trust Association Interceptor (TAI)
- WebSEAL LTPA cookie support

► Application integration utilizing:

- Authorization Application Programming Interface (aznAPI)
- JAAS
- PDPermission
- J2EE security

6.4.1 Shared user registry

Both WebSphere and Access Manager need a user registry to store user information, such as IDs and passwords. The first area of integration is for both products to use the same user registry, and so have a single, common set of users defined to both WebSphere and Access Manager. They each support a number of Lightweight Directory Access Protocol (LDAP) servers for this purpose. Obviously, to share the same user registry you must choose a server that both products support. Table 6-1 provides an overview of supported user registrys for WebSphere 4.0.2 and Access Manager 3.9.

Table 6-1   LDAP directories supported by WebSphere and Access Manager

LDAP directory	WebSphere 4.0.2 support	Access Manager 3.9 support
Netscape iPlanet Directory Server 5.0	X (not on AIX 5.x)	X
Lotus Domino Enterprise Server 5.0.5	X	Access Manager for Windows
IBM SecureWay Directory 3.2.1	X	X
Windows 2000 Active Directory 2000	X	X

LDAP directory	WebSphere 4.0.2 support	Access Manager 3.9 support
Critical Path InJoin Directory		X

For the newest information about LDAP support in WebSphere 4.0.2 refer to:

`http://www-3.ibm.com/software/webservers/appserv/doc/v40/prereqs/ae_v402.htm`

Information for WebSphere 3.5.3 can be found at:

`http://www-3.ibm.com/software/webservers/appserv/doc/v35/idx_aas.htm`

Administration considerations

WebSphere has no interface for administering users in an LDAP server, so you have to use the tools that are provided with the LDAP server product. Access Manager, on the other hand, does have tools: The pdadmin command and the WPM Administrator Console.

WebSphere never changes the default installation of the LDAP server, but Access Manager does. WebSphere and the LDAP server need additional configuration after Access Manager has been installed to allow them all to work together. The changes to be aware of are:

► Anonymous access to LDAP is no longer permitted. WebSphere must be configured with a bind distinguished name.

► Schema is modified. The default WebSphere group filter defined for the particular LDAP server must be updated.

► LDAP access control lists are modified. You require a special privilege to be able to perform a directory-search. WebSphere needs to be able to perform directory-searchs to retrieve users and groups and populate user and group-selection lists, so the WebSphere administration ID must be added to the LDAP's security group.

6.4.2 Single sign-on

Single sign-on between Access Manager and WebSphere can be achieved using three different mechanisms:

► Trust Association Interceptor
► TGSO junctions
► LTPA cookies

Web Trust Association Interceptor (TAI)

In a customer's corporate distributed environment, the Access Manager security architecture utilizes a reverse proxy security server, WebSEAL, as an entry point to all service requests. The intent of this implementation is to have WebSEAL as the only exposed entry point. As such, it authenticates all requests that come in and provides course-granularity junction point authorization.

When WebSphere is used as a back-end server it further exploits its fine-grained access control. WebSEAL can pass to WebSphere an HTTP request that includes credentials of the authenticated user. WebSphere can then use these credentials to authorize the request.

Former versions of WebSphere did not understand the format of the credential information passed by WebSEAL. WebSphere 3.5.3 and its later versions include a new execution mode in its security framework, the Trust Association Interceptor mode, in which it can interface with third-party objects that intercept requests issued by trusted proxy servers, such as WebSEAL. These objects are collectively known as *Trust Association Interceptors* or simply *interceptors*.

TAI implies that WebSphere's security application recognizes and processes HTTP requests received from WebSEAL. WebSphere and WebSEAL engage in a contract in which the former will give its full trust to the latter, which means that WebSEAL will apply its authentication policies on every Web request that is dispatched to WebSphere.

This trust is validated by the interceptors that reside in the WebSphere environment for every request received. The method of validation is agreed upon by WebSEAL and the interceptor. Setting values for parameters defined in the webseal.properties file that resides on the WebSphere Application Server will determine the method of validation for the interceptors.

The TAI version that ships with Access Manager 3.9 can be configured in three different ways:

- ► Trust association with -b supply option
- ► Trust association without -b supply option (improved version)
- ► Trust association using mutually authenticated SSL

In the following sections we describe the different options and requirements.

Using TAI with a -b supply junction

In order to get TAI to work there must be a WebSEAL junction to the WebSphere Application Server. In the earlier version of TAI, the only available authentication of WebSEAL was to secure the junction with the -b supply option, which has an associated risk for security attacks. The WebSEAL user ID/password used in TAI is not authenticated by WebSEAL, but is used by WebSphere to authenticate the traffic coming from WebSEAL. The following steps, as depicted in Figure 6-6, explain this in more detail:

► When a user requests access to a WebSphere-protected resource through his browser, WebSEAL authenticates the user, generates the Extended Privilege Attribute Certificate (EPAC) (based on userid=John) and obtains his own WebSEAL user ID/password (ws_itso/chuy5) from the pd.conf file located on the WebSEAL server.

► WebSEAL sends this WebSEAL user ID/password in the BA header along with the authenticated user credentials in the iv-user, iv-groups, and iv-creds fields.

► WebSphere extracts the WebSEAL user ID/password in the BA header to bind to LDAP in order to authenticate the traffic from WebSEAL.

► The user ID in the iv-user header is extracted by WebSphere and used to authorize the request to access the protected resource.

► Because WebSphere trusts the TAI authentication over the junction (-b supply), the password for the user requesting access is not required or used by WebSphere.

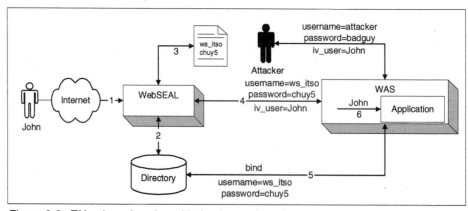

Figure 6-6 TAI using a junction with the -b supply option

Suppose now that we have an attacker who is a legitimate user of some other part of the system. This attacker can impersonate any other user by creating a packet with his own user ID and password in the BA header and any other user's ID in the iv-user header. WebSphere will bind to LDAP and use the attacker's ID to authenticate the traffic. The user ID in the iv-user header is used to authorize access to a protected WebSphere resource. This is not a good situation if the protected resource is, for example, a payroll system.

Using TAI without a -b supply junction

The new and current version of TAI provides better security. Only WebSEAL's password is sent in the BA header, which is being defined as the basic-dummy-passwd value in the pd.conf file located on the WebSEAL server. WebSphere uses the password sent in the BA header and then extracts WebSEAL's user ID value from the webseal.properties file located on the WebSphere server to authenticate the traffic from WebSEAL.

> **Note:** The com.ibm.websphere.security.WebSEAL.user name value in the webseal.prpoperties file contains the WebSEAL user ID.

Attackers who are legitimate users of some other part of the system would no longer be able to use their own user ID and password to impersonate a valid user. They would need access to the WebSEAL password. This version of TAI is shown in Figure 6-7.

Where an internal network is defined as secure, TAI without the -b supply option can be used without SSL.

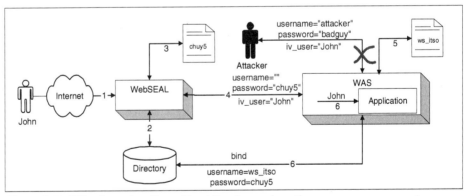

Figure 6-7   TAI using a junction without the -b supply option

Using TAI with mutually authenticated SSL junction

This approach improves the performance by eliminating the necessity of WebSphere calling LDAP for authentication of each WebSEAL connection. The webseal.propeties file is located on the WebSphere Application Server, and by setting the value of the com.ibm.websphere.security.WebSEAL.mutualSSL to yes, we can eliminate a BIND to LDAP to validate WebSEAL's identity. It can only be used when the junction between WebSEAL and WebSphere is a *mutually authenticated* SSL junction, as described in the section "Mutually Authenticated SSL Junctions" in the *IBM Tivoli Access Manager for e-Business WebSEAL Administration Guide Version 3.9, GC23-4682*. WebSphere will *trust* this junction and no additional mechanism is used to authenticate WebSEAL. This situation is depicted in Figure 6-8.

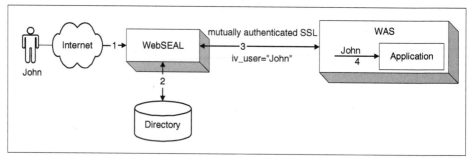

Figure 6-8   TAI using a mutually authenticated SSL junction

Summary of how TAI works

Let us see how trust association works using the WebSphere Administration Applications:

1. The browser requests a URL that WebSEAL recognizes to be a protected resource.

2. WebSEAL prompts the user to provide a user ID and password (this can either be via a basic authentication challenge or a custom form).

3. WebSEAL authenticates the user.

4. Once properly authenticated, WebSEAL forwards a modified HTTP request to the back-end WebSphere server.

5. Depending on the configuration:

   - If the junction has been defined without -b supply, the modified HTTP request contains the basic-dummy-passwd value in the BA header field that is only used between WebSEAL and WebSphere. This password and the value of the com.ibm.websphere.security.WebSEAL.username property is used to bind to LDAP. If this bind is successful, WebSphere will trust this session and the values sent with the http headers (this is done in method: validateEstablishedTrust()).

     Note: WebSphere uses the method validateEstablishedTrust to extract the WebSEAL user ID and password from the BA header and binds to LDAP to authenticate WebSEAL. If this fails, an exception is thrown, and WebSphere denies access.

   - If the junction has been defined with -b supply, the modified HTTP request contains the user ID and password value of WebSEAL in the BA header field and the requestor's user ID in the iv-user field. WebSphere binds to LDAP using the user ID and password specified in the BA header.

   - Alternatively, if the junction between WebSEAL and WebSphere is a mutually authenticated SSL junction and the property value of com.ibm.websphere.security.WebSEAL.mutualSSL is yes, WebSphere trusts the session and does not need to bind to LDAP.

6. TAI then extracts the value of the iv-user http header and returns this as the authenticated user that should be used by WebSphere authorization (this is done in method getAuthenticatedUsername()).

TGSO junctions

Access Manager's Global-Sign-On provides a mapping between the primary user identity (used for login to WebSEAL) and another user ID/password that exists in another user registry.

In a pure WebSphere environment, accessing a protected URL will cause an HTTP 401 challenge to the browser. The end user enters their authentication details (user ID and password) and this information is passed in a basic authentication header back to WebSphere. WebSphere Application Server then uses the authentication information to perform an LDAP-bind to authenticate the user.

The different TGSO options and capabilities are described in detail in 5.5.1, "Tivoli Global Sign-On (TGSO) lockbox" on page 115.

WebSEAL LTPA cookie support

WebSphere Application Server uses an LTPA token (a cookie by another name) to provide single sign-on across multiple WebSphere servers. After the user has been authenticated by WebSphere, an LTPA cookie is created and sent to the browser. The browser will return this cookie on subsequent requests, allowing the origin WebSphere Application Server (or other WebSphere Application Server within the same TCP domain) to recognize the user. The LTPA cookie is protected by a 3DES key, which also proves that it was created by a trusted source.

Access Manager WebSEAL can generate an LTPA cookie that will be accepted by the WebSphere server. The WebSphere server will trust this LTPA cookie because it is encrypted with the correct shared key.

Figure 6-9 shows a WebSEAL junction that is configured for LTPA. An LTPA key is generated on the WebSphere machine and then exported to a keyfile (protected by a password). This keyfile must then be manually copied to the WebSEAL machine. When the junction to the WebSphere server is configured, it is specified as an LTPA junction, and the keyfile and password are given as parameters.

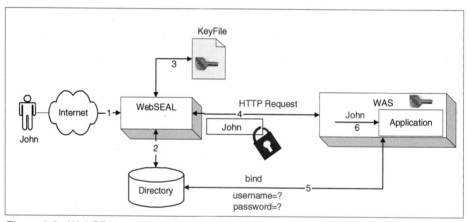

Figure 6-9   WebSEAL creates LTPA cookies for authenticated users

When a user authenticates to WebSEAL and requests a resource on this junction, WebSEAL creates an LTPA cookie using the key from the keyfile. This encrypted cookie contains the Access Manager user ID of the user and is included in the HTTP request sent to the WebSphere server. When WebSphere receives the HTTP request, it extracts the user ID from the LTPA cookie and uses it to build WebSphere's credential for the user. It would be usual for WebSEAL and WebSphere to share a registry to avoid synchronization problems. WebSphere then applies its own authorization decision to the request. A general description of LTPA is provided in 5.5.6, "Using LTPA authentication with WebSEAL" on page 120.

How to select the SSO option

In fact, if you assume that Access Manager and WebSphere share a user registry, then TGSO would be the last choice for SSO. Instead, using either the Trust Association Interceptor or the LTPA support would be the preferred solution. TGSO is only an option for the following scenarios:

► WebSEAL and WebSphere rely on different user registries. Under this circumstance, you may need to supply a different user ID and password combination for the user to WebSphere that is meaningful to WebSphere's user registry.

► There might be situations, even in the case of a shared user registry, where -b gso might be useful. For example, if internal users should be able to connect to WebSphere directly using basic authentication, and then they should have indirect access through WebSEAL with WebSEAL being configured to provide forms based login.

Otherwise, we recommend the TAI option, because it is easy to configure and maintain. There is no key distribution or periodic update required. TAI is also the method used when WebSphere supports integration with third party reverse proxy security servers in general.

6.4.3 Application integration

If we want to integrate WebSphere applications with Tivoli Access Manager we have to distinguish between:

► Integration of new applications that are to be developed or existing applications that will be changed

► Integration of existing applications without any changes

Access Manager provides a C version of the Authorization API and pure Java classes: *PDPermission*, *PDPrincipal,* and *PDLoginModule*. PDPermission is usable in both a Java Authentication and Authorization Services (JAAS) and non-JAAS environments. These methods can be used for securing new applications or to adjust existing applications. We provide an overview of these methods in "aznAPI" on page 142 and "PDPermission and JAAS" on page 142.

Often there are already existing J2EE applications secured by WebSphere declarative security and/or using J2EE security methods. Tivoli Access Manager for WebSphere Application Server offers the possibility of importing WebSphere security definitions into Access Manager's object space. The function that determines if a user is granted any permitted roles is now handled by Access Manager. We describe Tivoli Access Manager for WebSphere Application Server in "Access Manager for WebSphere Application Server" on page 143.

aznAPI

aznAPI is an API specifically designed for Access Manager. It has been approved by the Open Group as the standard implementation of the Authorization Model. Access Manager provides a C version of the API, and Java Wrappers are available as Open Source. WebSphere applications may use the aznAPI to retrieve fine-grained authorization information about a user.

PDPermission and JAAS

The original Java security model dealt almost exclusively with the needs of the Java environment's first major user, the Web browser. It focused on the complexities of secure usage of mobile code, so it worried about the origins of code and its authors, as indicated by digital signatures. The Java 2 environment generalizes that model to concern itself with all code, not just that loaded from remote locations. The Java 2 architecture also restructures the internals of the Java Runtime Environment to accommodate a very fine-grained usage of security. JAAS, a standard extension of the Java 2 environment, adds in the concept of who the user is that is running the code and factors this information into its security decisions.

All levels of Java security have been policy based. This means that authorization to perform an action is not hard coded into the Java runtime or executables. Instead, the Java environment consults policy external to the code to make security decisions, and therefore maps to systems of category 2 or 3, as described previously in 6.2, "Security design objectives" on page 125. In the simplest case, this policy is implemented in a flat file, which somewhat limits its scalability and also adds administrative overhead.

To overcome the flat file implementation of Java 2 policy, and to converge to a single security model, the authorization framework provided by Access Manager can be leveraged from inside a normal Java security check. As mentioned earlier, the most natural and architecturally pleasing implementation of this support is inside a JAAS framework. Support for this standard provides the flexibility for Java developers to leverage fine-grained usage of security and Authorization Services as an integral component of their application and platform software.

With the Java 2 and JAAS support delivered in Tivoli Access Manager, Java applications can:

► Invoke the Tivoli Access Manager-supplied JAAS LoginModule to acquire authentication/authorization credentials from Access Manager.

► Use the PDPermission class to request authorization decisions.

This offers Java application developers the advantages that:

► The security of Java applications that use PDPermission is managed using the same consistent model as the rest of the enterprise.

► Java developers do not need to learn anything additional beyond Java 2 and JAAS.

► Updates to security policy involve Tivoli Access Manager-based administrator actions, rather than any code updates.

Today, JSPs, servlets, and EJBs can take direct advantages of these services. When WebSphere containers support Java 2 security, EJB developers can avoid the need to make security calls by having the containers handle security while they focus on business logic.

There are two options for implementing fine-grained authorization (at the level of actions on objects) within servlets and EJBs today:

► Given the Access Manager credential information (EPAC) passed in the HTTP header, the servlet or the EJB would have to use the PDPermission class extensions directly to query Access Manager for access decisions. The access enforcement is still the responsibility of the application (servlet or EJB).

► Develop a proxy bean (a session bean) within an EJB. This proxy bean will intercept all method invocations and communicate with Access Manager (using the PDPermission class) to obtain the access decision and enforce it.

Access Manager for WebSphere Application Server

If the application is designed as a J2EE application, it would rely on the J2EE security methods to get a user ID and role. Tivoli Access Manager for WebSphere Application Server provides container-based authorization and centralized policy management for WebSphere Application Server Version 4.0.2. Tivoli Access Manager for WebSphere Application Server is implemented as an Access Manager aznAPI application running on the WebSphere Application Server instance.

A graphical user interface utility, the Access Manager Web Portal Manager, and the pdadmin command provide a single point for security management of common identities, user profiles, and authorization mechanisms.

Access Manager for WebSphere Application Server supports applications that use the J2EE Security Classes without requiring any coding or deployment changes to the applications.

Tivoli Access Manager for WebSphere Application Server is used to evaluate access requests from a user to protected resources based on the following tasks:

► Authentication of the user.

► Determination if the user has been granted the required role by examining the WebSphere deployment descriptor.

► The WebSphere container will use Access Manager to perform role membership checks for security code added directly into an application (programmatic security).

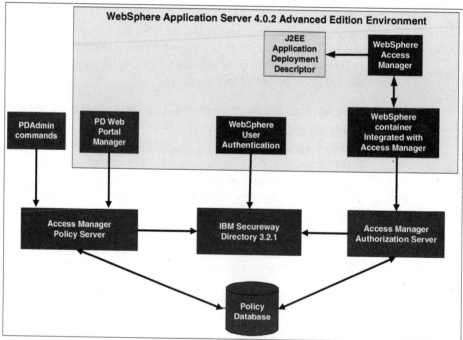

Figure 6-10   Access Manager integration with WebSphere Application Server

Figure 6-10 shows the integration of Access Manager with WebSphere Application Server Advanced Edition Version 4.0.2.

When a user tries to access a protected resource by running an application with J2EE security, the following sequence of events occur:

1. WebSphere Application Server authenticates the user. For WebSphere Advanced Edition, the authentication is against the SecureWay Directory Version 3.2.1 LDAP user registry. This LDAP user registry is shared with Access Manager.

2. WebSphere container collects information from the application deployment descriptor to determine the required role membership for the protected resource.

3. The WebSphere container uses the integrated Access Manager module to request an authorization decision from the Access Manager Authorization Server.

4. The Authorization Server obtains the user credentials from the SecureWay 3.2.1 LDAP users registry and checks the users permissions for a specified role. The Access Manager security model uses the definitions stored in the protected object name space to build a hierarchy of resources to which ACLs can be attached. These ACLs define the mapping of roles in the J2EE application deployment descriptor to users and/or groups defined in the SecureWay LDAP 3.2.1 user registry.

5. The Authorization Server returns the access decision to the WebSphere container, which either grants or denies access to the protected resource.

Migration of roles to principals and groups

Tivoli Access Manager for WebSphere Application Server has a migration utility that maps the roles in WebSphere Application Server to Access Manager principals and groups.

The *IBM Tivoli Access Manager for e-Business WebSphere Application Server User's Guide Version 3.9,* GC32-0850, provides a fully detailed chapter on this migration utility and is recommend for further study. In this chapter we will give a brief description of the migration utility.

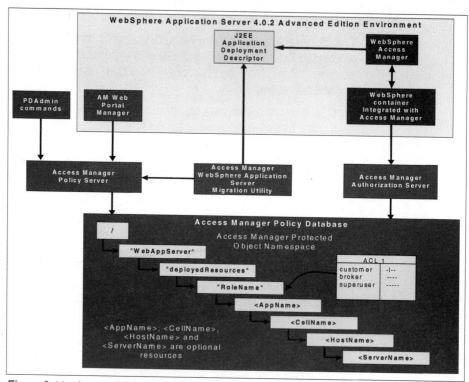

Figure 6-11   Access Manager utility to map roles to principals and groups

Figure 6-11 depicts the single steps executed by the migration utility. This utility extracts information on roles from the J2EE deployment descriptor and maps them to group/principal information in Access Manager.

This information is converted into Access Manager format and it is passed to the Access Manager Policy Server using the PDAdmin API, which is used to add entries to the protected object name space to represent roles defined for the application. The appropriate principals and groups are added to the ACLs that are attached to the new objects. This migration utility is executed on the machine that has access to the J2EE application deployment descriptors (EAR files).

After migration, the system administrator can use the pdadmin commands or the Access Manager Web Portal Manager to modify the ACLs and add new roles and users.

Attention: The migration utility is executed only once, prior to application runtime. It must not be used as a maintenance tool for roles. Use either the pdadmin command or the Access Manager Web Portal Manager to manage roles.

Central policy management for multiple WebSphere servers

Tivoli Access Manager can manage security policy across multiple WebSphere servers.

After using the migration utility as described earlier, the Access Manager Web Portal Manager can be used to manage changes in security definitions related to the mapping of roles to principals and groups.

Important: Changes to role mapping made through the WebSphere console will not be visible in the Access Manager security model.

The Access Manager security model may also be managed using the pdadmin commands. Access Manager also provides a programmatic interface to administration tasks accomplished by pdadmin and the Web Portal Manager. The APIs can be used by programmers to develop tasks specific to an application.

In our security architecture, we have chosen to use multiple WebSphere servers to host a new Internet application. This is a high availability consideration; server 2 is a mirror copy of server 1. Each server accepts Web traffic simultaneously routed to it through the load balancing capabilities of WebSeal. Central administration of the security policy is required to achieve this.

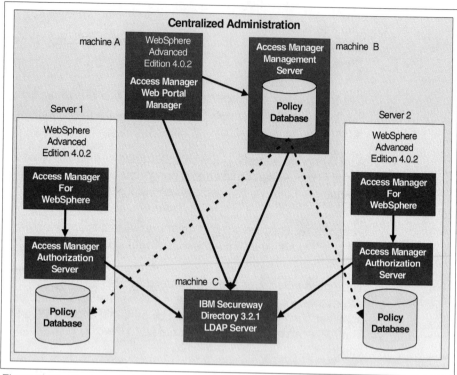

Figure 6-12   Central administration for multiple WebSphere servers

Figure 6-12 illustrates central administration of two WebSphere servers. The Access Manager Web Portal Manager has been installed on *machine A*. Access Manager Policy Server with the master policy database is installed on *machine B*. The Web Portal Manager uses the Access Manager Policy Server to administer the security policy.

Two WebSphere Advanced Edition Version 4.0.2 machines are shown, *server 1* and *server 2*. Access Manager Authorization Server is also installed on these machines. Co-location of Access Manager Authorization Server with WebSphere Application Server optimizes performance when making authorization decisions. This is because Tivoli Access Manager for WebSphere Application Server is an aznAPI application, and it communicates with the Authorization Server. Therefore, placing the Authorization Server on the same machine as the WebSphere Application Server application eliminates network connection overhead. This configuration is recommended.

The Access Manager policy databases on *server 1* and *server 2* are replicated from machine B, which improves performance and fail-over capability.

Access Manager servers and the WebSphere servers share the same LDAP user registry, in this case, IBM SecureWay Directory Version 3.2.1.

Access Manager provides a powerful command line-based utility (pdadmin) for the management of the Access Manager security domain. Administrators can also use this utility within scripts or programs to automate the administrations tasks.

Access Manager also provides a programmatic interface to the administration tasks accomplished by pdadmin and the Web Portal Manager. Application developers can use this API to perform administration tasks that are specific to the application.

For more information, see the *Tivoli Access Manager Administration API Developer Reference*, GC32-0843, and the *Tivoli Access Manager Administration for e-Business Java Classes Developer's Reference*, SC32-0842.

## 7

Access control in a distributed environment

To this point our discussions of Access Manager have focused primarily on WebSEAL scenarios in which all components are typically deployed in a relatively contained single security domain deployment environment at a single site. This chapter addresses key issues relating to situations where components of both single and multiple Access Manager secure domains may be distributed among multiple sites. We also touch on the use of Access Manager for Business Integration as a component of a distributed application.

> **Note:** Due to the latest IBM Tivoli changes in naming and branding, you will be confronted with the new name for Tivoli Policy Director for MQSeries: IBM Tivoli Access Manager for Business Integration. On some occasions when we are referring to older versions of the product, we still use Policy Director Version 3.8 or Version 3.7. All references to Tivoli Access Manager are based on the current Version 3.9, which became available in April 2002.

7.1 Cross-site distribution of a single security domain

In order to introduce the aspects of multiple security domains, let us take a closer look at the distributed Web security requirements at Stocks-4u.com.

Earlier, in Chapter 3, "A basic WebSEAL scenario" on page 65, we introduced Stocks-4u.com's key Web security requirements. Our scenario discussion focused on supporting a Web security infrastructure at a single site—the San Diego IT Center. We mentioned the need for future expansion of Internet operations into the Savannah center to provide for a redundant access capability with load-balancing for customers on the US East and West coasts. After the initial Access Manager deployment in San Diego, Stocks-4u.com management has initiated planning for an extension of the security infrastructure to the Savannah IT Center, starting with a review of key business and technical requirements.

7.1.1 Business requirements

The need to distribute Web security is related to some key business issues:

► The growth rate of the customer base will require Internet application capacity to double over the coming year, and double again the following year. The San Diego site will require expansion to support this growth. However, Savannah has substantial additional space which, if utilized, could reduce the San Diego expansion need by 70 percent.

► Stocks-4u.com competitors have been promoting higher service availability levels. Competitive pressures require the company support equivalent capability. A recent partial site power failure at the San Diego IT center demonstrated that expected availability levels cannot be achieved by simply replicating Access Manager servers at a single site.

► Related to the above, as part of its premium service offering, Stocks-4u.com has recently established service level agreements in place with a number of its key customers. Should it fail to achieve service level targets, these customers are entitled to substantial levels of compensation.

► The majority of internal applications are deployed in Savannah. To utilize Access Manager security capabilities, internal user browser access must be routed through a WebSEAL server in San Diego. However, 68 percent of company employees are connected to the company intranet through the Savannah IT Center. A consultant has found that 15 percent of the company's total long-haul Telecom cost is associated with routing internal HTTP/HTTPS traffic through San Diego.

From the above, the following business requirements have been proposed by management:

► Savannah facilities be fully utilized to minimize the San Diego expansion requirement.

► Internet customer application access must be immune to a San Diego site failure.

► Management has directed that cross-site Telecom costs for internal applications be reduced by 25 percent and the savings be used to expand network support for customer applications.

7.1.2 Technical requirements

An analysis of Stocks-4u.com business requirements has established the following key technical requirements:

► Internet users must be able to securely access applications via a Web browser through either San Diego or Savannah.

► In the event of a site failure or shutdown, all security functions must be provided through the surviving site.

► Internal HTTP/HTTPS application traffic must be routed through the closest IT center (San Diego or Savannah).

► The Stocks-4u.com network must provide direct network linkages from San Diego to New York trading systems.

If these technical requirements are met, the business requirements will be easily satisfied, and Stocks-4u.com will also be well-positioned for future expansion.

Security architecture changes

Currently, Access Manager components are deployed only in San Diego. The updated architecture will add new Access Manager components in the Savannah IT Center. There will be a single security domain sharing a common user registry, as shown in Figure 7-1 on page 154.

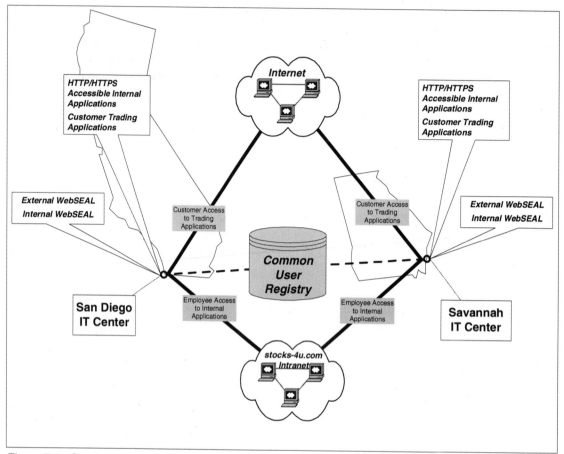

Figure 7-1   Stocks-4u.com security domain

Network changes

To support a distributed environment, the company has planned some changes
to their network. Previously, customer trade transactions required routing through
Savannah and ML&J in New York. A new T3 link is planned, which will directly
connect San Diego to New York trading systems. Another link from the Internet to
Savannah is planned to support direct access as customer application Web
servers are deployed there. Figure 7-2 on page 155 shows the new
Stocks-4u.com corporate network connectivity.

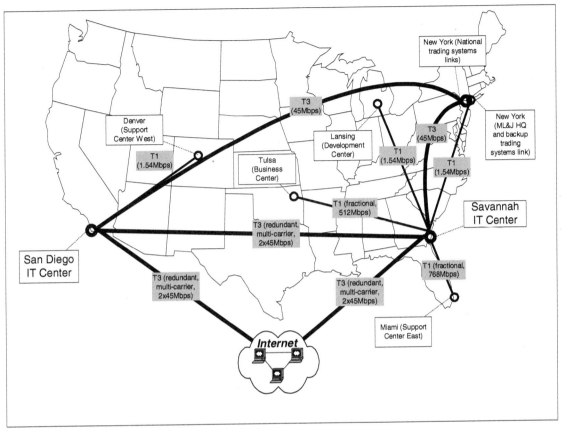

Figure 7-2   Stocks-4u.com updated data network

Within the Savannah IT Center, the internal network configuration will also change to support the new requirements. The new configuration will add an Internet demilitarized zone (DMZ), providing both IT centers with similar zone structure, as shown in Figure 7-3 on page 156.

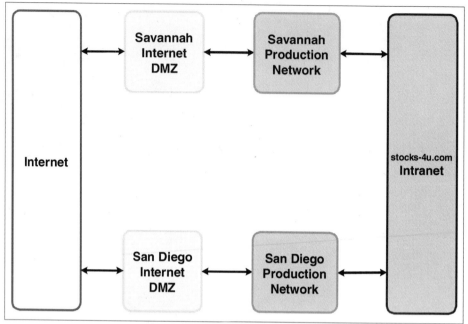

Figure 7-3   IT center network zones

It is important to note that communication between the IT center production zones must go through the corporate intranet.

7.1.3 Access Manager architecture discussion

In the initial WebSEAL deployment, all Access Manager components were installed in San Diego. In the distributed architecture, new Access Manager components must be deployed in Savannah. The question is, which components? In this scenario, we must be concerned about:

- ▶ WebSEAL servers
- ▶ The Access Manager Policy Server
- ▶ The user registry
- ▶ The Web Portal Manager

WebSEAL servers

Certainly, we know that we will need to put WebSEAL servers in Savannah to avoid rerouting requests unnecessarily through San Diego. There will be both internal and external WebSEAL servers at each IT center. As in the existing Access Manager deployment, shown in Figure 3-4 on page 74, the external WebSEAL servers will go into the Internet DMZs, and the internal WebSEAL servers will go in the production networks.

WebSEAL junctions

WebSEAL junctions may be cross-site (that is, WebSEAL servers in San Diego may be junctioned to back-end Web servers in Savannah and vice versa). This is not a problem as long as the cross-site communication between WebSEAL and the junctions is appropriately secured.

For external (Internet-facing) WebSEAL servers, there is another issue that must be addressed when junctioning cross-site; that is, an appropriate network configuration must be created to permit them to pass traffic from their respective DMZs into the production network at the remote site. This obviously is a more complex network scenario than the local site case. We will discuss some of these networking issues below.

As an alternative, Stocks-4u.com may choose to replicate all Web servers between sites so that all WebSEAL junctions are local. Figure 7-4 on page 158 below illustrates both approaches.

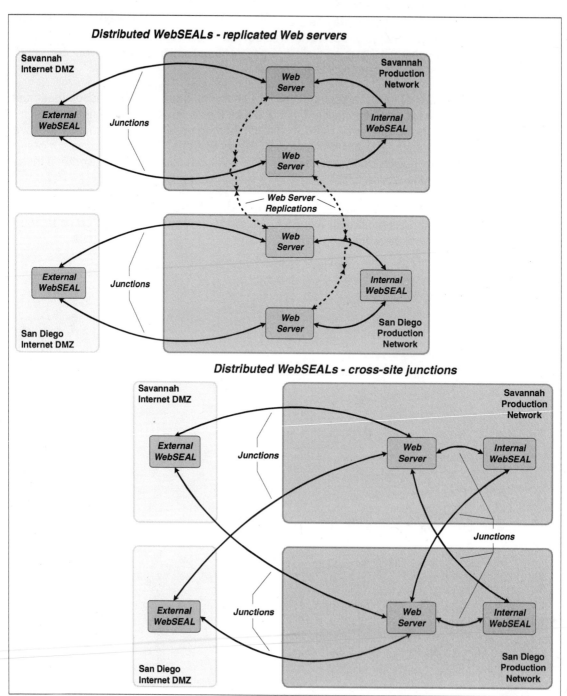

Figure 7-4   Distributed WebSEALs - Replicated Web servers

Access Manager Policy Server

Because there currently can be only one Access Manager Policy Server for a security domain, the current server in San Diego will remain in place and will support both sites.

In the event of a San Diego site outage, Savannah WebSEAL servers will continue to operate. However, configuration changes cannot be made. To address an extended site outage situation, a backup system will be available to take over the Policy Server function. Configuration of a replacement Policy Server involves special considerations.

Cross-site backup takeover considerations

Availability issues are often more involved when dealing with migration of functions across site locations. In a local fail-over situation it is much easier to utilize specialized high-availability software (such as HACMP or Microsoft Cluster Server) to provide an automated recovery capability. Such products generally utilize special network/device connectivity and *heartbeating* to determine failure conditions and initiate a service takeover. Generally, a shared disk is used to assure data consistency

Consider that in a cross-site fail-over scenario, the network subnet addressing, depending on the particular network architecture, may be different between the sites. This means that a simple IP address takeover may not be sufficient to bring a backup system online.

In the case where the backup has a different IP address, services that access it will need to be told of the new address, either by reconfiguration or via domain name server (DNS) changes (and to successfully accomplish an address change via DNS, services must not be caching the old address).

In the alternative, a *shadow* standby network may be created at each site. These shadow networks are configured to the same subnet as the peer site, and are kept offline unless a takeover is required. The backup systems reside in this network. Another twist to this, which would permit the shadow network to be accessible at all times, would be to use Network Address Translation (NAT) in front of the shadow network during normal operation. This would permit network traffic to flow to the backup systems (for example, capturing of configuration updates, and so on). Then, should a takeover be required, the router would have to be removed in order for the backup systems to appear on the local network under the peer site subnet. This approach, of course, assumes a total peer site network failure or loss of communication, because the peer network cannot be accessible simultaneously with the shadow using the same subnet address.

Another problem is that of replicating the existing configuration. Generally for Access Manager, this can be sufficiently handled by doing a periodic backup of critical files and replicating them to the backup site (There are also more sophisticated mechanisms, which can capture updates at the device level and replicate changes across sites).

Perhaps the most difficult issue of all, however, is that of how to deal with the following:

► How can a failure of the primary server be reliably determined across site locations?

► If a backup server takes over, what happens when the primary comes back up?

The reason these issues are so important is because there are unpleasant scenarios that can occur should a backup takeover occur by mistake or without appropriate advance process planning—especially if it occurs when the primary is still actually active (which creates what is known as a *split-brain* scenario).

A communication failure across sites is not sufficient to determine with certainty that the primary has failed. And once a backup takes over Policy Server functionality, the primary cannot be permitted to return to full operation without assurances that updates that may have occurred in the interim have been reconciled.

In addition to a manual process that may be executed to bring a backup server online in a cross-site situation, there are products that provide sophisticated cross-site fail-over capabilities. They are beyond the scope of this book.

The user registry

In the existing San Diego configuration, there is a master LDAP server for the user registry, and an LDAP replica of the registry that is used by WebSEAL for authentication. In our distributed configuration, we will place an additional replica in the Savannah production network. This replica will be used by the Savannah WebSEAL servers for user authentication, with the San Diego replica as a backup. The master will remain in San Diego.

In this configuration, if the San Diego site goes down, the Savannah WebSEAL servers will still have registry services available for authentication. However, updates go through the San Diego master. In the event of an extended San Diego outage, a backup replica server will be *promoted* to a new master.

LDAP master promotion considerations: As with the Access Manager Policy Server, migrating a key function across site locations has special considerations. See "Cross-site backup takeover considerations" on page 159 for further details.

Web Portal Manager

An additional instance of the Web Portal Manager will be installed in Savannah.

Distributed server configuration

Figure 7-5 shows the distributed Access Manager server configuration.

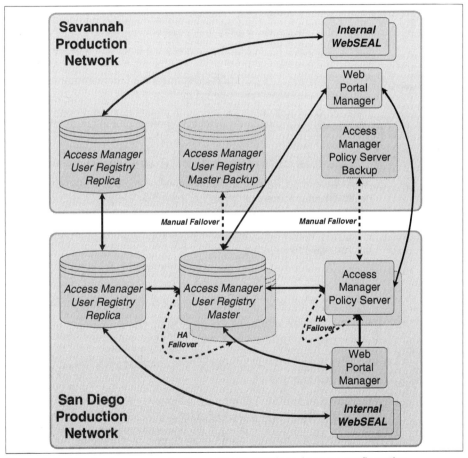

Figure 7-5   Stocks-4u.com production network distributed server configuration

7.1.4 Communication between distributed components

While we have established where Access Manager components will be placed, we have not yet addressed cross-site network communication issues.

Cross-site component interactions

WebSEAL servers will generally communicate with a local user registry instance for authentication. Cross-site communication issues occur with managing and updating configuration data. The master LDAP server and the Policy Server in San Diego must communicate with WebSEAL servers in the Savannah Internet DMZ and Production networks.

The LDAP master in San Diego must communicate with its Savannah replica(s), and must also be accessible from the Savannah Web Portal Manager.

The Policy Server in San Diego must communicate with the WebSEAL servers in Savannah, and must also be accessible from the Savannah Web Portal Manager.

In the network configuration described earlier, communication between production network hosts must go through the Stocks-4u.com intranet. Clearly, it may not be acceptable for security server communications to cross through the Stocks-4u.com intranet unprotected. This requires special considerations.

Cross-site communication alternatives

To assure the integrity and privacy of cross-site traffic between security components, there are three approaches we will consider:

▶ Using SSL across the open Stocks-4u.com intranet
▶ Using VPN capabilities to tunnel between network zones
▶ Bridging of network zones

SSL

All Access Manager components support the ability to interact via SSL:

▶ The Access Manager Policy Server communicates with WebSEAL and other blades via SSL.

▶ The Web Portal Manager communicates with the Access Manager Policy Server via SSL.

▶ The SecureWay LDAP user registry can be configured to communicate via SSL. (Other supported LDAP servers may support SSL as well.)

▶ WebSEAL may be configured to communicate with junctioned servers via SSL, provided the servers support it.

If all components can be configured to use SSL, then Stocks-4u.com cross-site communication may be securely implemented using the company intranet. This may be a viable approach, especially in situations where the amount of cross-site communication is relatively small, and the SSL overhead remains low.

Figure 7-6 shows the use of SSL between Stocks-4u.com IT centers.

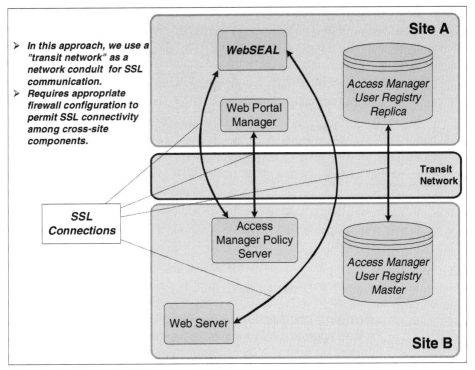

Figure 7-6   Cross-site SSL communication

A VPN approach

An alternative approach to cross-site communication involves the use of VPN technology to *tunnel* between the production networks. For example, a VPN tunnel can be created through the company intranet, which effectively permits unrestricted communication among the cross-site components without additional measures. The VPN traffic may be encrypted, providing for the integrity and privacy of communication between San Diego and Savannah without using SSL.

This approach has the advantage that local communication among Access Manager components does not have to incur encryption overhead as it may if SSL were used. Also, because the hardware/software cost of VPN technology has lowered, it is no longer cost-prohibitive in many cases. Figure 7-7 illustrates the use of a VPN for Stocks-4u.com cross-site Access Manager traffic.

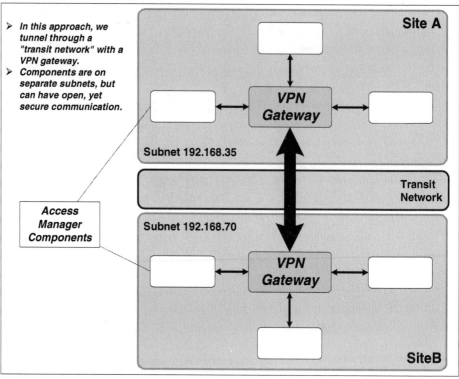

Figure 7-7   Cross-site VPN communication

Bridging production networks

A third approach may be to effectively *merge* the San Diego and Savannah production networks by *bridging* them. The two production networks may then coexist within a single IP subnet. Current network hardware capabilities and costs may make this an attractive approach, especially because it may provide for cross-site IP address takeover when bringing up a backup Policy Server or LDAP master.

> **Note:** The ability to migrate IP addresses across sites does not eliminate the *split-brain* issue mentioned earlier. What it does do, however, is eliminate the need to reconfigure other systems to use alternate IP addresses for backup servers, or to create a *shadow* backup network at the site. In any case, caution and proper planning is still necessary in implementing any availability solution.

Figure 7-8 illustrates the use of a bridged approach to distributing Access Manager components between San Diego and Savannah.

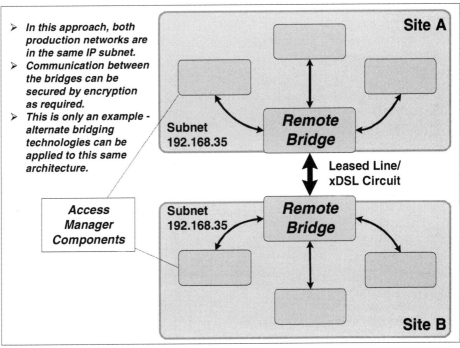

> ➤ In this approach, both production networks are in the same IP subnet.
> ➤ Communication between the bridges can be secured by encryption as required.
> ➤ This is only an example - alternate bridging technologies can be applied to this same architecture.

Access Manager Components

Subnet 192.168.35

Subnet 192.168.35

Remote Bridge

Remote Bridge

Leased Line/ xDSL Circuit

Site A

Site B

Figure 7-8   Bridged cross-site communication

7.1.5 Stocks-4u.com distributed architecture

Summarizing the above architecture discussion, the Stocks-4u.com distributed Access Manager architecture will include the following:

► An architectural choice has been made to utilize a VPN tunnel to connect the Stocks-4u.com production networks together.

► WebSEAL hosts will junction across sites for internal applications. For external (customer) applications, Web servers will be replicated across sites and WebSEAL junctions will be local.

► Within the San Diego site, a standard high-availability configuration using HACMP will be used with the Access Manager Policy Server and the LDAP master. This will assure availability of services as long as the San Diego site remains operational.

► In the event of a communication disruption between San Diego and Savannah, operation will continue without configuration update capability at the Savannah IT Center.

► In the event of a confirmed San Diego site outage lasting more than eight hours, a backup Access Manager Policy Server and a new LDAP master will be brought online in Savannah. (Strict procedures must be in place for this and for bringing the old servers back online upon site recovery.)

Figure 7-9 summarizes the Stocks-4u.com distributed Access Manager architecture.

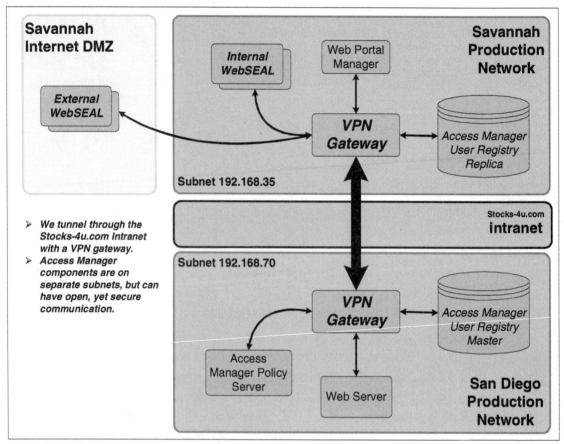

Figure 7-9   Stocks-4u.com distributed WebSEAL architecture summary

7.2 Distributed security domains

Another type of distributed scenario involves single sign-on for access to resources in multiple security domains (that is, each domain has its own user registry and security policy definitions). Consider two divisions of a company, each offering Web-based services to Internet customers. Each division has deployed WebSEAL in separate security domains. However, there is a requirement for certain users in one domain to access resources in the other domain without needing to authenticate twice. WebSEAL supports two different types of cross-domain authentication to address such scenarios: Cross Domain Single Sign-On (CDSSO) and e-community single sign-on.

7.2.1 CDSSO

WebSEAL supports the ability to forward an authenticated identity from a user in one security domain to a WebSEAL server in another security domain. The *receiving* WebSEAL then maps the identity provided by the *sending* WebSEAL to an identity that is valid in its security domain. CDSSO can also be viewed as a *push* model with respect to authentication.

This functionality is known as Cross Domain Single Sign-On. In CDSSO, the user makes a request to a special link on a WebSEAL server, which then initiates the process to forward the request, along with credential information to a WebSEAL server in a different Access Manager domain. If the user were to instead directly access the link in the target domain, he would have to authenticate to that domain.

The CDSSO process contains the following steps:

1. A user initially logs on to a WebSEAL server in one security domain.
2. At some point the user accesses a link controlled by the user's WebSEAL, which contains a special directive (pkmscdsso). This directive results in redirecting the user to a URL controlled by a WebSEAL server in another security domain and passing encrypted credential information to the new WebSEAL.
3. The user is redirected to the other WebSEAL and this server decrypts the credential information passed to it, maps the identity to one defined in its own user registry, and then creates a secure session with the browser.
4. At this point the user has established secure sessions with two WebSEAL servers in different domains, but has only had to log in once.

Another way of looking at CDSSO is that it provides a mechanism by which a WebSEAL server in one security domain can send something analogous to a *letter of introduction* to a WebSEAL server in another security domain.

Figure 7-10 summarizes a typical CDSSO flow.

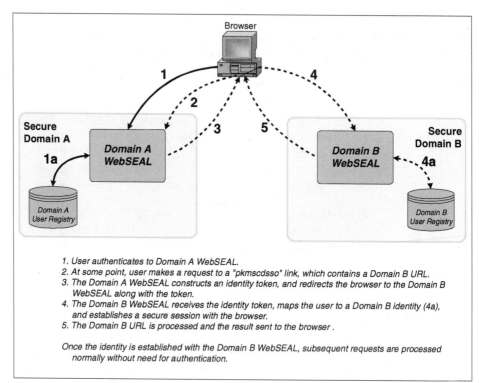

1. User authenticates to Domain A WebSEAL.
2. At some point, user makes a request to a "pkmscdsso" link, which contains a Domain B URL.
3. The Domain A WebSEAL constructs an identity token, and redirects the browser to the Domain B WebSEAL along with the token.
4. The Domain B WebSEAL receives the identity token, maps the user to a Domain B identity (4a), and establishes a secure session with the browser.
5. The Domain B URL is processed and the result sent to the browser.

Once the identity is established with the Domain B WebSEAL, subsequent requests are processed normally without need for authentication.

Figure 7-10   CDSSO identity determination process

The only significant CDSSO implication for a given security domain involves the mapping of user identities. How this mapping is done is not really an architectural issue *per se*—it is more a detailed-design/implementation concern. The important thing to remember is that the mapping must make sense for the specific situation.

It is possible (using the CDMF) interfaces discussed in 1.3.6, "Cross Domain Mapping Framework" on page 31) to map from an ID in one domain to a different ID in another. However, if the IDs in both domains are the same, a direct mapping may be done—this is the default and does not require the use of any special programming interfaces.

Using CDSSO at Stocks-4u.com

Let us briefly examine a possible CDSSO scenario at Stocks-4u.com.

Assume that ML&J has installed Access Manager in its New York offices to manage security for a new set of Web-based tools. This Access Manager domain is separate from the Stocks-4u.com domain, and has its own user registry. Stocks-4u.com wants to make these tools available to certain ML&J customers without requiring them to log in twice (once to a Stocks-4u.com WebSEAL and then to an ML&J WebSEAL).

By setting up CDSSO between the Stocks-4u.com and ML&J Access Manager domains, these users are required to authenticate only once. Also with CDSSO, things can be set up to allow initial authentication in either domain—users initially authenticating to an ML&J WebSEAL server can access their Stocks-4u.com account and vice versa.

Another thing to point out is that with CDSSO, an authorization decision can be made at the Stocks-4u.com WebSEAL to control participation in cross-domain single-sign-on. The ability to do this may be important for business reasons.

Figure 7-11 on page 170 illustrates the above CDSSO scenario.

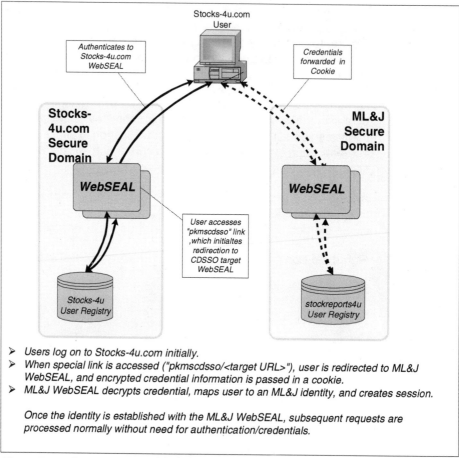

Figure 7-11   Stocks-4u.com CDSSO scenario

7.2.2 e-Community single sign-on

e-Community single sign-on supports a cross-domain authentication capability. However, it differs from CDSSO in a few key respects. Recall that in CDSSO, authenticated identities are *forwarded*. In an e-community scenario, identities are instead retrieved—it is a *pull* model. The use of e-communities has certain advantages over CDSSO, yet have architectural impacts that are not encountered in a CDSSO environment.

In this model, multiple Access Manager domains are defined to be part of a single e-community. While each participating domain has its own user registry, one of the domains is designated to be the *home domain*. Users requesting protected resources in any of the participating domains initially authenticate to a

Master Authentication Server (MAS) in the home domain. Once the initial authentication has taken place, the user has an e-community identity based upon the home domain's user registry. A user's e-community identity may subsequently be mapped, as required, to local identities by WebSEAL servers in other domains within the e-community.

The e-community model is shown in Figure 7-12.

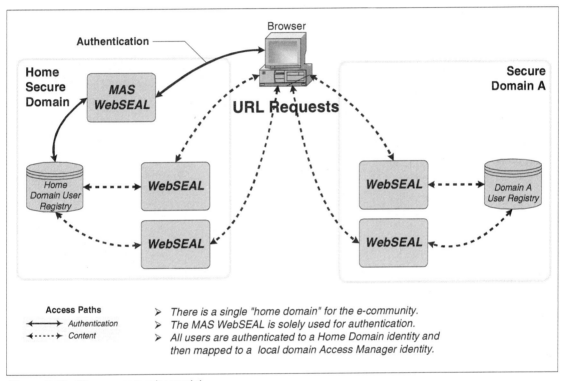

Figure 7-12   The e-community model

The e-community mechanism involves the following steps, generally:

1. A user makes a request for a protected resource controlled by a WebSEAL server in one of the e-community domains. This WebSEAL does not yet have an established secure session with this user.

2. The WebSEAL server redirects the user to the MAS and sends with the request a special directive (pkmsvouchfor), which requests that the MAS provide identity information for the user.

3. The MAS checks to see if the user has already been authenticated to the e-community, and if not, the MAS then authenticates the user.

4. The MAS then sends a token back to the original WebSEAL server that contains credential information that vouches for the user's identity.

5. The WebSEAL server then maps the identity provided to it by the MAS to an appropriate Access Manager within its local domain and establishes a secure session with the browser.

Figure 7-13 summarizes the flow of an initial e-community user authentication.

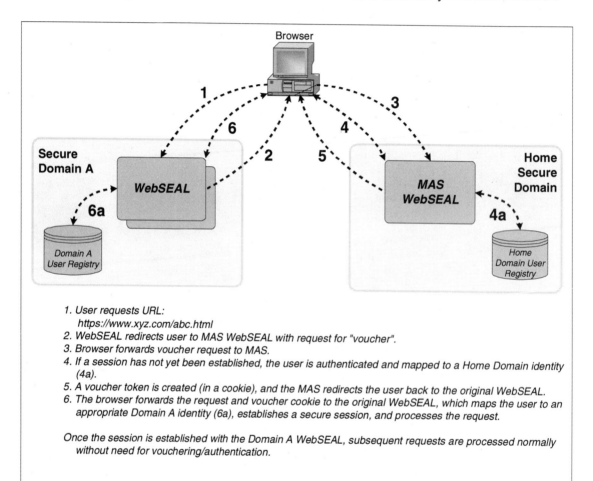

1. User requests URL:
   https://www.xyz.com/abc.html
2. WebSEAL redirects user to MAS WebSEAL with request for "voucher".
3. Browser forwards voucher request to MAS.
4. If a session has not yet been established, the user is authenticated and mapped to a Home Domain identity (4a).
5. A voucher token is created (in a cookie), and the MAS redirects the user back to the original WebSEAL.
6. The browser forwards the request and voucher cookie to the original WebSEAL, which maps the user to an appropriate Domain A identity (6a), establishes a secure session, and processes the request.

Once the session is established with the Domain A WebSEAL, subsequent requests are processed normally without need for vouchering/authentication.

Figure 7-13   e-Community initial identity determination process

Within the *home domain*, unauthenticated requests are always vouched for via the MAS. In other participating domains, once the user has initially logged in to the MAS, subsequent authentication activities to other WebSEAL servers in those domains are handled locally—the first WebSEAL in the domain that validates the user's identity against the MAS then vouches for that user's identity within the local domain. This is depicted in Figure 7-14.

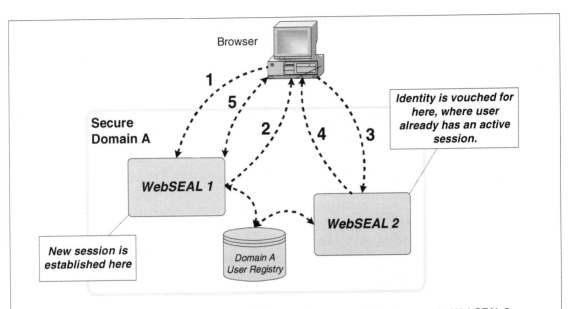

(User has authenticated to an e-community MAS in a previous request to WebSEAL 2. WebSEAL 2 now will vouch for subsequent identity "voucher" requests by other WebSEALs for this user in this domain.)

1. User requests URL from WebSEAL 1:
   https://www.xyz.com/abc.html
2. WebSEAL 1 redirects user to WebSEAL 2 with request for "voucher".
3. Browser forwards voucher request to WebSEAL 2.
4. WebSEAL 2 provides a voucher cookie token, and redirects the user back to WebSEAL 1.
5. The browser forwards the request and voucher cookie to WebSEAL 1, which maps the user to the correct Domain A identity, establishes a secure session, and processes the request.

Once the session is established with the WebSEAL 1, subsequent requests are processed normally without need for vouchering/authentication.

Figure 7-14   e-Community subsequent identity determination process

The key advantage of e-community single sign-on over CDSSO is that the initial URL request can be made directly to the target WebSEAL server. Recall that with CDSSO, the URL request must go through the WebSEAL to which the user is currently authenticated. In an e-community configuration, the target WebSEAL is specifically configured to *retrieve* credential information through the vouching mechanism, and the URL request itself need not be accompanied by special processing or contain special characteristics, as in the CDSSO case.

There are many detailed issues regarding the operation of e-community single sign-on, but they are not architecturally important. The main architectural impact of e-community single sign-on involves the role of the MAS. The key issue is, with all user authentication for the e-community going through a single domain, where should the MAS server(s) be located?

In a geographically distributed situation, this question is especially important. For example, let us look at the Stocks-4u.com distributed scenario.

Applying e-community single sign-on at Stocks-4u.com

Let us assume that Stocks-4u.com has just signed an agreement with a company that provides stock analysis reports via the Web. This company, stockreports4u.com, has an existing client base to which they charge individual usage fees. The Stocks-4u.com agreement allows all Stocks-4u.com users to have access to stockreports4u.com through a special Web site for a flat fee (no individual usage charges).

Stockreports4u.com does not want to manage a user registry of valid Stocks-4u.com users. Instead, they wish to allow users to log in to their site against the Stocks-4u.com user registry, and then map those IDs to a small set of special IDs at their Web site.

Further, they wish to permit direct access to this site without a requirement to link to it through Stocks-4u.com first (that is, it may be directly *bookmarked*). This is a scenario, depicted in Figure 7-15 on page 175, where an e-community approach may be useful.

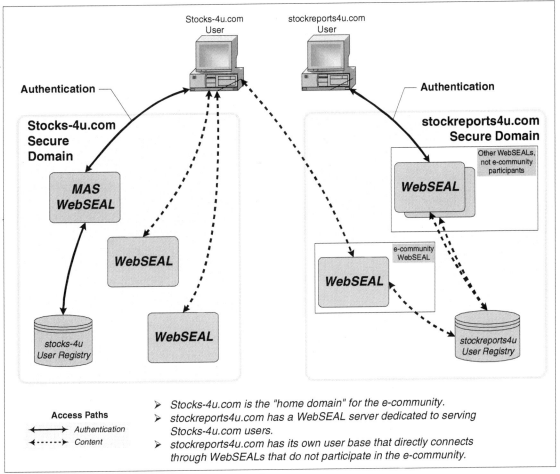

Figure 7-15   Stocks-4u.com e-community scenario

7.2.3 Comparing CDSSO and e-community single sign-on

It is difficult to state hard-and-fast rules regarding when it is best to use an e-community versus a CDSSO approach. Certainly one factor is the desired degree of control over the users.

In an e-community scenario, one site gets to control the users—business models that are focused on profiling, branding, or other factors as mechanisms for revenue generation may be well-served by this approach.

Also, with e-Communities, if authentication at the MAS fails, users may have the option of authenticating directly to the local domain.

7.3 Distributed messaging applications

Application-level messaging with products such as IBM MQSeries is often an important component of distributed applications. In a Web application scenario, MQSeries may be used between back-end application components. Consider a case where a message queue is used between systems located at two sites. How can the message queue traffic be protected appropriately?

While WebSEAL can provide secure communication with a browser, there are sometimes requirements for secure communication between back-end components.

Consider financial transactions that must traverse across unsecured networks. It is essential that the privacy and integrity of such data be maintained—yet it may also be important to remove the need for the application components themselves to worry about providing the appropriate security functions.

In an MQSeries environment, Access Manager for Business Integration can transparently provide security for messages. It can control the ability to enqueue or dequeue messages, and it can transparently encrypt in-transit messages without requiring any application changes.

Consider the case where an organization wishes to exchange application data with another organization using MQSeries over the Internet to eliminate the cost of maintaining a special secure communication link. Access Manager for Business Integration can securely support this capability without requiring any application changes.

7.3.1 An MQSeries distributed application at Stocks-4u.com

Let us briefly take a look at the use of Access Manager in a distributed situation, with IBM MQSeries as a solution component.

Expanding on our current scenario, Stocks-4u.com intends to deploy a new stock transaction record application that uses MQSeries for data exchange between front-end and a back-end application components. In this case, the front-end application component is deployed in the San Diego IT Center and the back-end component is deployed in Savannah on a corporate mainframe host. The front-end application component is embedded within a servlet running on an IBM WebSphere Application Server platform. Clients may access the application via WebSEAL. Figure 7-16 on page 177 illustrates these components.

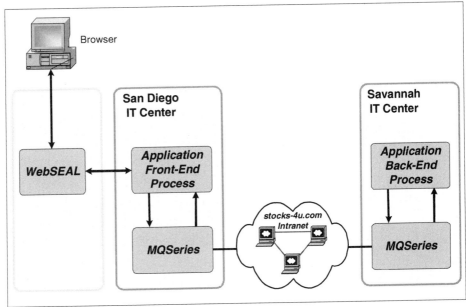

Figure 7-16   A Stocks-4u.com MQSeries application

In this case, the MQSeries channels represent a cross-site communication component that, depending on the specific network configuration, might not be secure. In this case let us assume that the MQSeries communication occurs across the Stocks-4u.com intranet, leaving the traffic largely unsecured. The question is, how can we use Access Manager to secure this communication and assure data privacy and integrity?

Access Manager for Business Integration is specifically designed to address such situations. As mentioned earlier, it provides queue security and transparently applies encryption to message channel traffic, permitting highly secure use of MQSeries over otherwise insecure channels.

Access Manager for Business Integration provides two key functions:

► It provides access control for enqueue and dequeue (put/get) operations using Access Manager's authorization engine.

► It can encrypt individual messages to protect their integrity and privacy. It does this transparently to the application.

Refer to Figure 7-17 on page 178, which depicts Access Manager for Business Integration components and interactions.

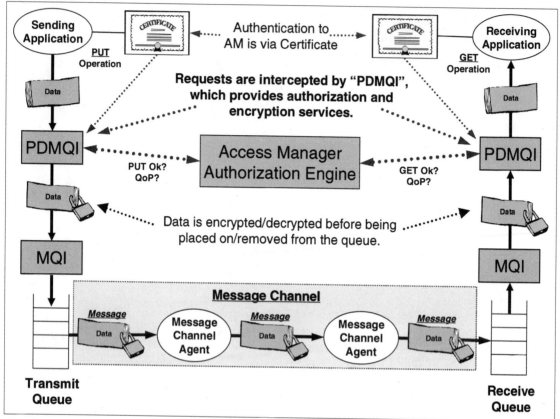

Figure 7-17   Access Manager for Business Integration architecture

Access Manager for Business Integration places a runtime library *shim* in the path between the application and MQSeries. The application continues to call the standard MQSeries runtime functions. These calls are intercepted transparently, where authorization checks and message encryption/decryption is done. Neither MQSeries itself nor the application are aware of Access Manager for Business Integration functions. Architecturally, this permits Access Manager for Business Integration to be deployed in existing MQSeries environments with minimal changes.

In the stock4.com environment, Access Manager for Business Integration can be *overlaid* on top of the MQSeries components used by the stock transaction application. Transaction records queued as MQ messages in San Diego are encrypted while in transit.

Finally, because queue access can now be managed, it is easier to leverage a single queue for multiple applications securely. Stocks-4u.com can deploy a common set of messaging channels used by all of its MQSeries applications, as shown in Figure 7-18.

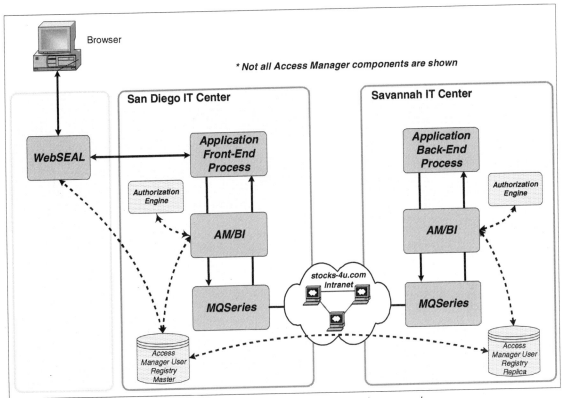

Figure 7-18   A Stocks-4u.com Access Manager for Business Integration scenario

Combining this with a WebSEAL front end, which is interfaced to the application front-end process, one can see how Access Manager components may be utilized at multiple levels within the application framework to meet various security requirements.

7.4 Conclusion

In this chapter, we have focused on more advanced Access Manager architectural issues that relate to its use in distributed environments. As you can see, there are a number of choices that may be required to complete an operational architecture in a distributed scenario.

This said, however, this chapter has hopefully shown that distributed architectures with Access Manager are actually not terribly complex. By following some simple guidelines, and asking the correct questions up-front to determine the requirements, even advanced architectures may be straight-forward.

## 8

Wireless e-business

Wireless e-business is not tomorrow, it is today. Advanced thinking companies have already deployed wireless solutions to expand their traditional business and to reach out for the mobile opportunities to attract additional customers with mobile devices to access their Web sites and do mobile business.

Users' expectations are increasing: They want to receive information wherever they go and, most importantly, on whatever device they are using—Personal Digital Assistants (PDA), cellphones with Wireless Application Protocol (WAP) support, within their automotive systems, even on their home appliances, and of course their traditional dial-in laptop environment.

All this needs to be delivered in a secure way. And that is what is most important in implementing secure wireless e-business solutions today: *Closing the gap between mobile secure access and the user's convenience.*

Only this guarantees that users trust companies and will lead to a highly accepted wireless e-business model.

As well as the wireless-specific security controls, the technologies and processes used in the wired e-business environment for protecting the perimeter networks, systems, and applications are equally vital in wireless solutions.

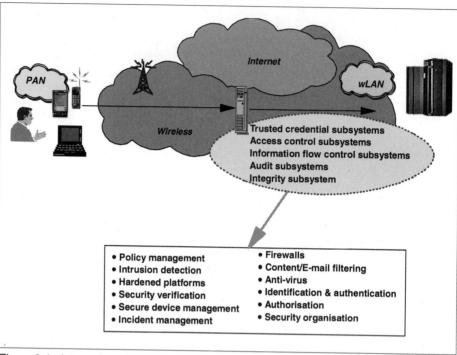

Figure 8-1   Integration of mobile devices: Security issues

The focus of this book is to show the use of IBM Tivoli Access Manager as a central security enterprise business portal and, after giving a short introduction to wireless security issues, we will have a closer look at a flexible architecture build on Access Manager and its integration capabilities for mobile devices.

8.1 Understanding the risks in wireless security

Integrating mobile users into your business means understanding the basic requirements, especially in the area of wireless security. While this book will focus on E2E security in the application space, you should also be familiar with the threats in "lower" layers like transmission or device security. The next section gives a brief overview of those challenges.

Security for mobile devices such as PDAs and cellphones can be split into several main areas:

► Transmission security: Security within wireless WANs (for example, on CDMA or GSM networks) or wireless LANs (for example, 802.11a/b)

► Device security: Security provided to unlock access to device only, can be password or even biometrical based access

► Operating system security: Security provided to access the data on the device

► Application security: Security provided by the application itself

There are several weaknesses in all of these areas, some examples are:

► Weaknesses in cellular networks.

Cellular wireless wide area network protocols contain cryptographic weaknesses that could allow data to be disclosed by eavesdroppers.

► Weaknesses in wLAN (802.11)and wPAN (Bluetooth) networks.

Wireless Local Area Networks (wLAN) have already been deployed by a number of companies to support flexible provisioning of mobile services even in public areas like airports and hotels. However, by default, wLANs offer little security and unless additional security measures are deployed, WLAN networks are wide-open to outside intervention like "drive-by hacking/war-driving"[1], potentially exposing personal, corporate and business-critical data. Even the security feature within the WLAN standard, Wired Equivalent Privacy (WEP) is weak due to a flaw in the standard.

Bluetooth Wireless Personal Area Networks (wPAN) are also an efficient way of connecting mobile devices and intelligent appliances, but without adequate security measures in place, this too could provide an opportunity for unauthorized access to data.

---

[1] Hackers are cruising around metropolitan areas in cars and on bicycles, with their laptops listening for the beacons of wireless networks

- Limited security built into mobile devices.

  Most mobile devices have little or no built-in security functions. Even something simple like a password can have endless security implications —users who choose to deactivate their passwords could allow unauthorized access to data should the device be lost, stolen, or tampered with. Additionally, wireless devices often have Over The Air (OTA) remote configuration facilities that could be exposed and abused.

- *Always-on* connectivity increases the window of threat opportunities.

  While always-on connectivity is perhaps one of the more attractive features of wireless technology, it is also one of the most dangerous with regards to security. Not only does it increase the window of opportunity for hackers to access your system, always-on means that this can be done often without the user knowing it—if a device is in a purse, a pocket, or a briefcase, the user will not be able to detect that something has gone amiss.

- Rapidly developing technologies, increased complexity, and immature standards.

  Mobile technologies are evolving at a rapid rate, with new products, services, and gadgets. You have to stay ahead of the pack, but implementing a new service is not as simple as it sounds: New technologies often do not have full or suitable tested and verified security measures in place. Immature standards for user and device authentication, executable content security, and stores data security also create vulnerabilities. Additionally, your solution often depends on third-party providers to exchange your data through multiple networks, making it difficult for you to assure that all transactions and data transfers are secure. So who is responsible if a transaction fails, is eavesdropped, changed, or repudiated?

- Existing security controls will be pushed to their limits.

  While a wireless application needs certain hardware, software, and services to run properly, these services may also be reliant on existing security controls that may not have been initially designed to support wireless security services. It is not enough to simply attach wireless hardware and software to your existing infrastructure—while many of your current e-business investments can be leveraged for use in your mobile network, you need a strategy for how all of these components are going to link together.

The last topic will be described in more detail further on in this chapter.

The most common and relevant security design objectives for wireless data communications are basically the same as for wired communications:

- Authentication: The verification of the identity of the user attempting to send or receive the data or application. This is to make sure the clients or servers are really who they claim to be.

- Authorization: The granting or denying levels of access to data and applications. For example, a user (a person or an application) might have authorization to read a certain record, but not update it; or to update, but not to delete or create; or in Internet environments, to read (browse) but not run an executable or go deeper in a directory tree.

- Confidentiality: In data communications that data is being intercepted or shared without permission.

- Integrity: The assurance that data has not been altered in transit by a third party. This concern relates to forgery, fraud, tampering, and other unauthorized alteration.

- Non-repudiation: The preventing of the ability by the parties involved in a transaction to deny that they were involved. In other words, we want to prevent the buyer from being able to say "I did not authorize that purchase," and the seller from being able to say "I never said I would sell it at that price," and so on. This is to enforce the accountability for electronic transactions.

The above security design objectives for wireless data communications fit nicely as functional classes into the functional categories within the MASS architecture (audit, access control, flow control, identity/credentials, and solution integrity).

There are many techniques for achieving the most common security objectives. Such techniques include data encryption, message digest, digital certificates, packet filtering, address concealing, and more. The many implementations of these techniques have led to the popular security solutions or technologies such as the Internet Engineering Task Force (IEFT) and standard Transport Layer Security (TLS, formerly called Secure Socket Layer or SSL).

Transport Layer Security uses data encryption, message digest, digital certificate, and other techniques to achieve multiple security objectives, such as confidentiality, authentication, and data integrity. TLS is primarily used for TCP/IP networks. For a mobile/wireless architecture, TLS alone is not a solution, but is part of a solution. For data communications over wireless networks using the WAP protocol, there is a technique similar to TLS called Wireless Transport Layer Security (WTLS).

In the next section we will highlight the authentication issues within a mobile environment and will introduce a flexible architecture for wired and wireless access security.

We will focus on the Wireless Application Protocol (WAP) and the i-mode protocol because both are providing excellent security features that can be used together with Access Manager to grant access to resources within an enterprise.

The main goal is to achieve multi-channel access using different devices going (logically) through one *security portal* to get access to different back-end services.

8.2 Security mechanisms within WAP and i-mode

Today there are mainly two wireless services deployed as provided by the WAP Forum and by NTT DoCoMo of Japan.

We will have a closer look into the features of the Wireless Application Protocol and the i-mode service to show how the security features can be used in an Access Manager-based environment to enforce authentication and authorization.

Both approaches have the common focus on providing security specifications to enable secure e-commerce using mobile devices. Within the WAP standard you can implement client-side certificates and use them for client-side authentication and non-repudiation services. The current release of i-mode allows for E2E SSL with server-side authentication and is planning to support client-side certificates, too.

8.2.1 Wireless Application Protocol environment

WAP as an industry-initiated standard driven by the WAP Forum is designed for the presentation and delivery of information and services to wireless devices such as PDAs and cellphones.

The traditional WAP environment is quite analogous to a wired environment, where all connection services are provided by a (wireless) service provider.

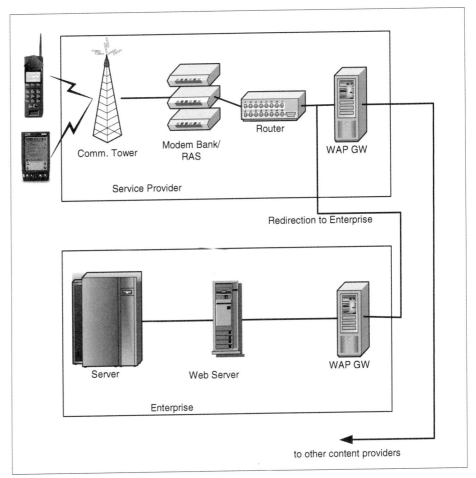

Figure 8-2   WAP environment for e-business purposes

The Wireless Service Provider handles all the communication processing like the translation of the wireless communication from the WAP devices through the transmission towers and Remote Access Server (RAS) to the WAP gateway.

The WAP gateway is used to translate the WAP protocols into the IP protocol stack. WAP protocols were optimized for mobile devices with limited capabilities such as memory, power, and display size. The WAP gateway is acting as a proxy and is providing the main functionalities such as:

▶ DNS services for resolving domain names in URLs
▶ Translating the WAP stack into the IP stack
▶ Management control point

Further services like transcoding of HTML (or even anyML) based content to the specific Wireless Markup Language (WML) can be done by the gateway, but mostly is part of an enterprise infrastructure. Transcoding tools like IBM WebSphere Transcoding Publisher can be used to achieve this transcoding. Transcoding is also responsible for providing WML deck-splitting to assure that the WML content will fit into the WAP device properly.

The back-end servers are usually placed in the enterprise space.

As showed in Figure 8-2 on page 187, there are circumstances where the WAP gateway should not be managed by the WSP, because there is a security gap in the WAP gateway due to the fact that the Wireless Transport Layer Security (WTLS) is ending in the WAP gateway and must be mapped into an SSL session. So the data is in clear until it is re-encrypted into SSL (Figure 8-3). There is a step towards an E2E security with WAP Version 2 that will be discussed later.

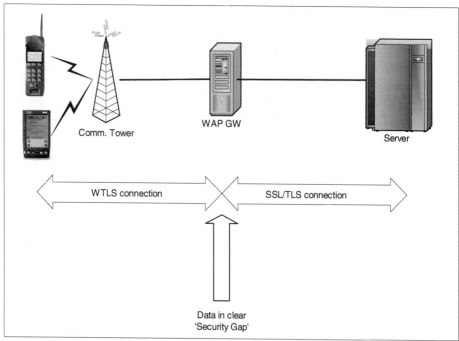

Figure 8-3   The WAP 1 security gap

The problem of managing your own gateway inside the enterprise is not the maintenance itself, but due to the fact that the mobile device does not have a DNS client, the enterprise still has to arrange a relationship with the WSP so that the WSP can reroute all the packets destined for the enterprise directly to the enterprise's WAP gateway instead of sending the packets to the WSP WAP gateway first.

8.2.2 i-mode environment

i-mode is a proprietary protocol of NTT DoCoMo of Japan. It was introduced in February 1999 in Japan, but due to global business connections i-mode is planned to be introduced in other countries of the world soon.

The i-mode Internet services use the Personal Digital Cellular-Packet (PDC-P) network and a subset of HTML for content description, the compact HTML (cHTML). i-mode is based on packet-switching on the wireless part and carried over TCP/IP for the wired part.

In this example the i-mode server is placed inside the provider's network; for administration reasons it is possible to place the i-mode server inside the enterprise production network. The i-mode server is responsible for service functions like relaying access to the Internet and handling i-mode and/or Internet mail.

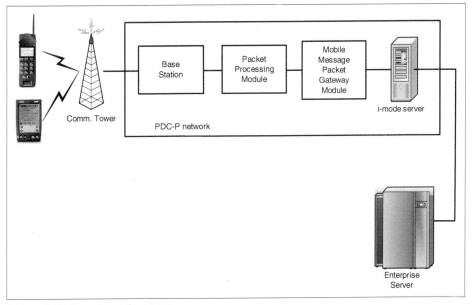

Figure 8-4   i-mode environment

The gateway that handles the conversion between the specific data transmission protocol and the i-mode server, the mobile message packet gateway, is included in the PDC-P network (Figure 8-4).

The i-mode server is a regular Web server that resides within an enterprise or at NTT DoCoMo.

8.2.3 WAP security architecture

The WAP architecture as of today comes in two flavours. The *real life* implemented WAP solutions are based on the WAP 1.2 specifications, but there are major changes in the new WAP 2.0 standard, which we will highlight. This new standard has some significant advantages so it is expected to see first implementations starting in 2002.

WAP 1.2 protocol specifications

The WAP specification defines open architecture and a set of protocols for the implementation of the wireless access to the Internet.

The WAP stack includes, among others:

► XML-type markup language and Wireless Markup Language, which is accessed by using standard HTTP requests

► A lightweight protocol stack to minimize bandwidth requirements enabling a lot of different wireless networks to run WAP applications

The mapping of the WAP 1.2 stack to the Internet stack is shown in Figure 8-5.

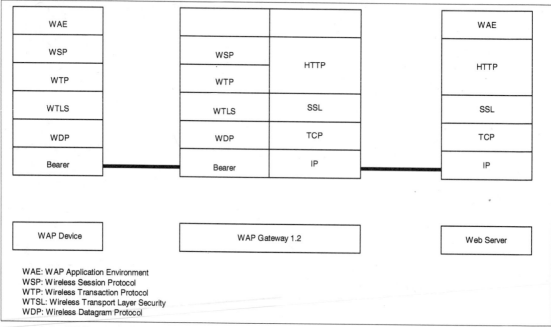

Figure 8-5   WAP 1.2 protocol mapping

Now let us have a closer look into the Wireless Transport Layer Security protocol. WTLS is based on the IETF SSL/TLS protocol. Within WTLS there are three different classes.

- ► Class 1: Unauthenticated key exchange to establish a session key (anonymous).

- ► Class 2: Enforcing of server-side authentication using PKI certificates similar to SSL/TLS protocol. The WAP gateway uses a WTLS certificate, which is a special X.509 certificate optimized for use in a small bandwidth environment.

- ► Class 3: If this is implemented on clients, they are able to authenticate using client-certificates (regular X.509 format).

While class 1 level is insufficient for secure wireless e-business, class 2 devices are currently available and even class 3 devices are already used in pilots and field tests.

Overview of achievable security levels using WAP devices

There are several levels of security that can be achieved by using WAP security. Provided within the WAP standard is the possibility of using a WMLScript Crypto Library to extend the possibilities of adding additional security, for example, digital security. We give a brief overview in Table 8-1.

Table 8-1 WAP security

Level	Meaning	WAP support
Authentication [part of MASS categories (access control and identity credentials)]	The other party who it claims to be	► WTLS classes 2 and 3 ► WIM module ► using application level security (Uid/Pw) ► PIN codes of mobile devices
Integrity [part of MASS category (solution integrity)]	The received information the same as the one originally sent	► WTLS class 1 ► Digital signature using WMLScript Crypto Library
Non-repudiation [part of MASS category (solution integrity)]	After receiving the message the other party cannot deny having sent it	► Digital signature using WMLScript Crypto Library
Secrecy/privacy [part of MASS category (flow control)]	Only the communication parties are able to understand what was meant	► WTLS class 1 ► Encryption within the wireless networks

The WAP Identity Module (WIM)

A WIM will support class 3 functionality and have embedded support for public key cryptography. An example of a WIM can be a smart card, which you can use in a mobile phone or PDA, or it can be part of a Subscriber Identity Module (SIM, in the case of GSM networks). A WIM should be tamper-resistant because it is holding the user's private key, which never should leave the WIM. Besides this, the WIM is capable of holding some number of user certificates; due to the fact that these are regular X.509 certificates, the memory of mobile devices can be used up quite fast. There are mechanisms like URL-based references for certificates; in this case a URL is used by the device to access back-end certificates. The details are beyond the scope of this book, but in 8.2.5, "Using digital signatures with WIM" on page 194, you can find a brief overview of how this can be implemented.

WAP client authentication

One option for client authentication is HTTP basic authentication. More commonly client authentication is done using the handshake protocol of Wireless Transport Layer Security. During the handshake process, in addition to negotiating security algorithms and exchanging cipher secrets, the WAP client sends a user ID and password. WTLS also supports authentication using mini-certificates (which are a kind of lightweight X.509 certificate).

WAP 2.0

The key feature of WAP 2.0 is the use of Internet protocols within a WAP environment. This support emerged from having high-speed wireless networks (for example, 2.5G and 3G[2]) that provide IP support directly to the mobile wireless device.

From a security point of view, this has a major advantage due to the introduction of Transport Layer Security (TLS). So, if the back-end servers are capable of TLS services, the above-mentioned WAP security gap will be eliminated because of having a secure E2E session from the mobile device to the back-end server, as shown in Figure 8-6 on page 193.

---

[2] 2.5 or 3 generation networks, such as wideband-CDMA

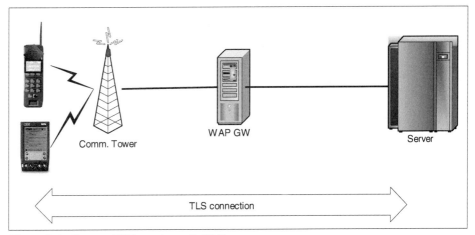

Figure 8-6   Secure E2E session with TLS

This can be done because the wireless profile for TLS defines a method for tunneling to support E2E security at the transport level (Figure 8-7).

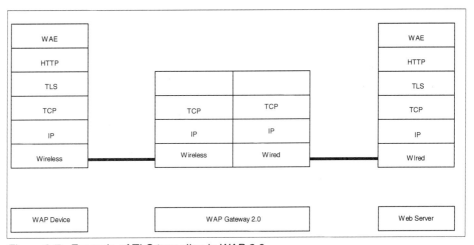

Figure 8-7   Example of TLS tunneling in WAP 2.0

8.2.4 Using WTLS certificates for server-side authentication

To provide at least a server-side authentication in a WAP environment you can use WTLS certificates of a WAP gateway. A WAP gateway WTLS certificate is a certificate that authenticates the identity of a WAP site to client devices such as WAP phones or PDAs using a WAP browser.

When a WAP user wants to send confidential information to a WAP gateway, the WAP browser will access the server's digital certificate. The certificate, which contains the WAP gateway's public key, will be used by the WAP browser to:

► Authenticate the identity of the WAP gateway.
► Encrypt information for the WAP gateway using the WTLS protocol.

The flow is basically the same as for regular browsers:

1. A WAP user (his browser) initiates a WTLS session by sending a Client Hello message requesting a secure session.

2. The WAP gateway responds with its server certificate.

3. The user's WAP browser verifies the validity of the gateway's certificate and proofs that it has been signed by a CA. The CA's certificate is stored in the WAP browser database.

4. If the certificate is valid, the WAP browser generates a session key and encrypts it with the WAP gateway's public key. The encrypted session key is sent to the WAP gateway.

5. The WAP gateway decrypts the message using its private key and recovers the session key. Now the session can be used to send encrypted information.

Note: This method does not authenticate the client, which is required, for example, to achieve non-repudiation (see 8.2.5, "Using digital signatures with WIM" on page 194).

8.2.5 Using digital signatures with WIM

Because of the importance (especially of non-repudiation) we will have a closer look on a possible infrastructure providing a certificates-based solution with WIM cards (or virtually any other smart card for wireless e-business).

The goal is to achieve an open solution with multiple partners, because you cannot assume that the complete infrastructure is implemented by only one company (Figure 8-8 on page 196).

The key players in this approach are:

► Wireless Service Provider (WSP)

The WSP is responsible for the wireless infrastructure (and eventually for the WAP gateway).

The WSP provides the wireless public key infrastructure (wPKI). The wPKI (WAP 1.2.1) incorporates WIM, which contains private RSA keys for authentication and non-repudiation, and certificate URLs pointing to standard X.509v3 certificates issued by the WSP Certification Authority (CA). The use of the keys on the WIM card is protected by personal PIN codes. Strong face-to-face registration of customers is recommended to form the reliable basis of digital identity guaranteed by the WSP CA. Wireless PKI provides means for strong user authentication and legally binding digital signature, including confidentiality and integrity of data and non-repudiation of transactions. The wPKI provides standard LDAP interface for service providers who trust the WSP's mobile certificates.

The WIM card is delivered by the WSP to the user. The WIM card together with the user PIN are used to generate digital signature.

To place the CA in the WSP organization is one way; there are others like governmental institutions. The key is trust in this organization.

► The point of transaction

This can be a digital point-of-sale (POS), a bank, a merchant, and so on. This organization provides the infrastructure to accept mobile payments and mobile transactions. It usually has a strong relationship with the CA. Main functions of this organization includes transaction processing, payment authorization, and account management. The *point of transaction* can also be subdivided into several organizations, for example, e-shops, virtual marketplaces, and financial departments.

► The mobile device

The mobile device is capable of holding the WIM card and of storing user information (for example, credit card information). Some mobile phones already support a digital wallet. The device must at least support WAP 1.2.1 standards. The signed content sent by the device is an encrypted message including the digital signature and the URL pointing to the WSP LDAP for the user certificate inquiry.

Note: If the device is capable of holding regular certificates instead or using the URL-reference approach, the device sends its certificate.

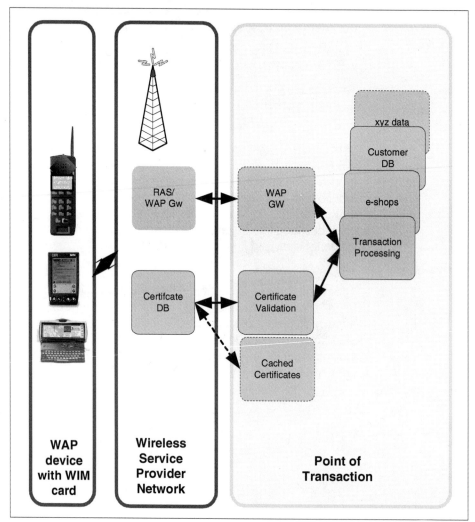

Figure 8-8   Architecture for digital signature use of WAP devices with WIM card

Message flow

The basic massage flow is as follows; we use a bank in this example:

1. The user is accessing the WAP site of the bank.

2. When a transaction is performed (for example, a wireless financial transaction), required fields in the WML form have to be filled out (this can be done automatically).

3. The transaction is received by the bank; the bank sends a kind of receipt back to the user.

4. The user signs this receipt and sends it back also including the certificate URL. The digital signature follows the PKCS#7 - Cryptographic Message Syntax Standard.

5. The bank validates the signed content, the digital signature, and the certificate using the connection to the wPKI LDAP of the WSP; here the certitude URL is used to access the issuer's certificate. (To speed this up, a cached version of the root CA certificate and the issuer's certificate can be used.)

6. The user receives a final response as to whether the transaction was authorized.

8.2.6 i-mode security architecture

There is not much published information of the security of i-mode available. In former times there were some open issues like the security of the wireless link between the mobile device and the cellular base station or things like password security.

But recently i-mode has adopted SSL supporting SSLv3 and SSLv2 connections, so i-mode now provides E2E security within a carrier's network and security between a carrier's network and its customers.

i-mode is able to handle server-side authenticated SSL sessions, so a SSL session is established between the i-mode device and the i-mode server. The i-mode server is typically installed within the enterprise.

At this time, i-mode devices are not capable of handling client-side certificates; this implies that non-repudiation is not possible with current implementations of i-mode (in contrast to the WAP/WIM architecture).

But there are plans to provide smart cards for security so the advantages will be similar to the WIM cards.

8.3 Access Manager support for mobile devices

Access Manager provides solutions for securing networks that use a Multiplexing Proxy Agent (MPA). This is a special variation of the authentication with customized HTTP headers.

Standard Proxy Agents (SPA) are gateways that support per-client sessions between clients and the origin server over SSL or HTTP. WebSEAL can apply normal SSL or HTTP authentication to these per-client sessions.

Multiplexing Proxy Agents are gateways that accommodate multiple client access. These gateways are sometimes known as WAP gateways when clients access via Wireless Access Protocol. Gateways establish a single authenticated channel to the origin server and "tunnel" all client requests and responses through this channel.

If you are not planning to use SSL between WebSEAL and the WAP gateway then MPA is not used. But be aware of the fact that if using HTTP only, the WAP gateway has to do the cookie handling for this sessions.

To WebSEAL, the information across this channel initially appears as multiple requests from one client. WebSEAL must distinguish between the authentication of the MPA server and the additional authentication of each individual client (Figure 8-9).

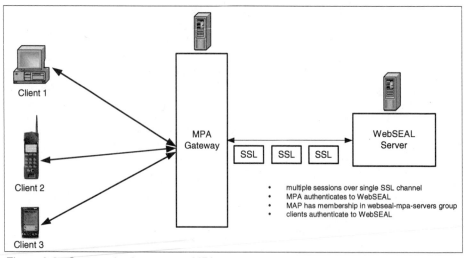

Figure 8-9   Communication over an MPA gateway

Since WebSEAL maintains an authenticated session for the MPA, it must simultaneously maintain separate sessions for each client. Therefore, the session data and authentication method used for the MPA must be distinct (different) from the session data and authentication method used by the client.

For valid session data types and authentication methods see *IBM Tivoli Access Manager for e-Business WebSEAL Administration Guide Version 3.9*, GC23-4682.

If Access Manager is used with IBM Everyplace Wireless Gateway and a user is authenticated at the gateway already, for example, to a RADIUS server, then WebSEAL can be configured to receive an authenticated ID from the gateway and not re-authenticate the user.

WebSEAL uses the WAP gateway for authentication through a WML form or, if a WIM is present, also a client-side, certificate-based authentication is possible.

The WAP gateway sends information to WebSEAL via an HTTP header or cookie. For a more detailed description on how to setup an MPA connection and its authentication flow, see Appendix F, "MPA authentication flow" on page 543.

8.4 Requirements for secure mobile access

The following parts will give a description of the specific requirements when integrating mobile users with different devices. We then will outline a flexible architecture ready to integrate into a given environment. The security design will be driven by the requirement of an integration with Access Manager.

8.4.1 Business requirements

Todays business requirements have clearly been extended by the ability to access information wherever you go. Current business models are expanded to meet the main new requirements to attract mobile users.

► Support of multiple devices used by a single user.
► Support of *legacy* dial-in devices such as laptops with full-blown browser.
► Support of open standards for security and presentation layers.
► Worldwide enablement with support of region-specific devices/services.
► Protect customers' personal data.
► Protect customers' transaction data.

8.4.2 Functional requirements

These business requirements lead to the following functional requirements. We focus on the mobile requirements; of course there are basic requirements that are also valid.

► Integration into existing enterprise infrastructure

The integration should be done via a migration with minor changes to the existing infrastructure.

► Independence from wireless service providers

The underlying wireless (bearer) services should be transparent to the enterprise; anywhere, anytime access should be possible.

► 365*24 availability

Small downtime, planned maintenance (of course this is not specific for mobile devices).

► Reasonable rate of mobile user authentication

Despite of unpredictable wireless network delays, the design of the authentication module must be sufficient to support a given rate of user authentications/second (for example, 25 authentications/second).

► Reasonable rate for throughput to mobile users

Despite unpredictable wireless network delays, the design of the content delivery module must be sufficient to support a given rate of delivered data (for example, 10 pages/second). Especially when supporting non-HTML data (for example, WML), the transcoding module must be sufficient.

It is most important to achieve the stickiness of a mobile user; user credentials should be propagated to target back-end servers.

► Standard security model, device independent

Security policies should be valid for mobile users too.

► Potential for growth

Scalability of the mobile module.

8.4.3 Security design objectives

The security design for mobile users is driven by the need to provide the same level as for wired users. There are also some additional objectives:

► Support for multiple mobile devices and their security features
► Authentication of mobile users (even new, un-authenticated)
► Authorization of subscribed users
► Protection of data in transit

- ► Accountability of transactions
- ► Pluggable into existing enterprise's security infrastructure

8.5 Wireless architecture

In this section we outline an architecture for mobile access to the enterprise system. We do not focus on additional security mechanisms like VPNs, which can be implemented additionally if enterprises have a special need. A more detailed look at transcoding issues can be found in Chapter 18, "Wireless integration" on page 477.

We follow a standardized approach based on SSL/TLS mechanisms to use with WebSEAL/Access Manager. Therefore we describe some basic scenarios that can be seen either as a start for a proof of concept or as a generic use case.

Note: While there are plans to provide i-mode based services in the US and Europe in the near future, there might be the requirement of supporting multiple different infrastructures (for example, WAP and i-mode) in one scenario. It might be applicable to use different WebSEAL instances to support this architecture. Access Manager Version 3.9 is able to support multiple instances of WebSEAL in one box, so hardware is not an issue anymore.

8.5.1 Basic architecture for WAP

A basic scenario for WAP-based access is shown in Figure 8-10 on page 202.

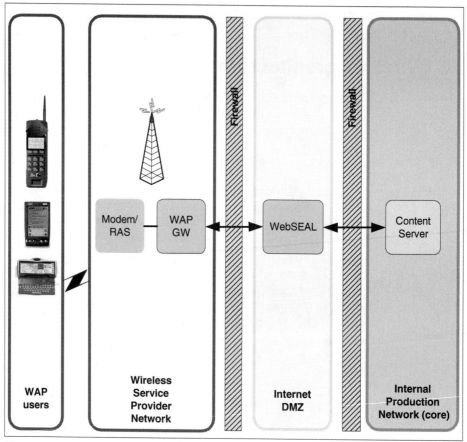

Figure 8-10   Basic integration.of WAP devices

As seen in 8.2.3, "WAP security architecture" on page 190, this is a case where we have to rely totally on the trust towards the service provider, which does not often meet enterprise requirements, especially in banking and insurance scenarios.

We have to adjust the architecture to meet the security design objectives of the enterprise:

▶ Elimination of the WAP security gap and use of our own WAP gateway
▶ Administration of WAP gateway within the enterprise

Architecture based on WAP 1.2

In the case of providing a secure access to the enterprise back-end system, we place the WAP gateway within the enterprise DMZ. A prerequisite of this design is that the WSP has to route all the incoming requests to the enterprise WAP gateway (Figure 8-11 on page 204). This way the potential security gap in the WAP gateway is within the trusted zone of the enterprise itself. In the case that the enterprise has established a distributed environment, you can enhance the security of the network link from the WAP gateway to the WebSEAL server implementing a virtual private network (VPN) link additional to the use of the MPA mode of WebSEAL (if you are using an SSL connection between WebSEAL and the WAP gateway).

As a further option the wireless gateway can use an external authentication server like Remote Authentication Dial In User Service (RADIUS).

The wireless gateway is capable of using a third-party RADIUS server for authentication as well. In this configuration, the wireless gateway is configured as a RADIUS client. WAP or dial-in clients may send user name and password information through a customizable prompt or through a framing protocol such as PPP, whose authentication packets carry this information. The wireless gateway can then forward this information to the RADIUS server.

The RADIUS server then authenticates the client based on a list of requirements that must be met. This list of requirements always includes verification of the password, but may optionally contain other criteria such as clients or ports that the user is allowed to access. Once the RADIUS server has authenticated the user, the wireless gateway adds an HTTP header containing client ID and user information to the request before forwarding it to back-end servers. Access Manager is intercepting all this traffic to apply its enterprise policies before granting access.

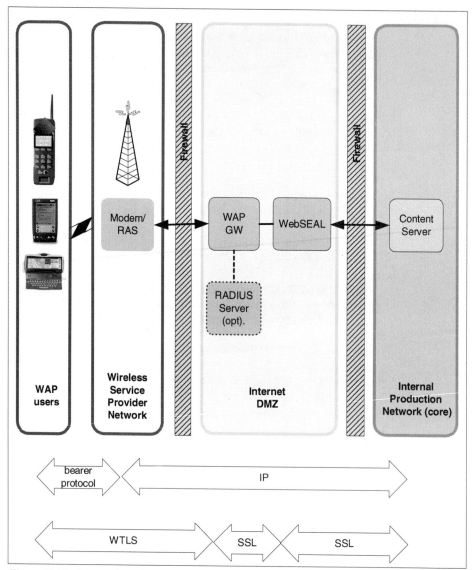

Figure 8-11   Integration of WAP 1.2 devices

In this scenario, WebSEAL is dedicated to be used in authorizing WAP flows. WebSEAL trusts the WAP gateway to have already authenticated the client.

Architecture based on WAP 2.0

Due to the major changes in WAP 2.0 regarding the introduction of TLS (see "WAP 2.0" on page 192), achieving E2E security might be easier.

To implement a secure access infrastructure for WAP 2.0 devices there now are the following options:

► The WAP gateway can be installed and maintained at the WSP site (because the WAP gateway now is capable of tunneling TLS from the client to the enterprise).

► The WAP gateway can be installed and maintained at the enterprise site.

But the world is not that easy; because there will be a migration overlap between WAP 1.x and WAP 2.0, you have to support both worlds. This is leading to the implementation of two different WAP gateways, one for each standard or a double WAP stack gateway. These double stack gateways are currently not available, but are likely to come soon.

For security and administration purposes we would recommend placing the WAP 2.0 gateway still in the trusted zone of an enterprise, but the final solution design depends on many requirements, such as maintenance, security needs, and TOC analysis to name a few.

The big difference in the WAP 2.0 scenario, shown in Figure 8-12 on page 206, is the E2E security provided by the tunneled TLS connection starting at the mobile device and ending in WebSEAL.

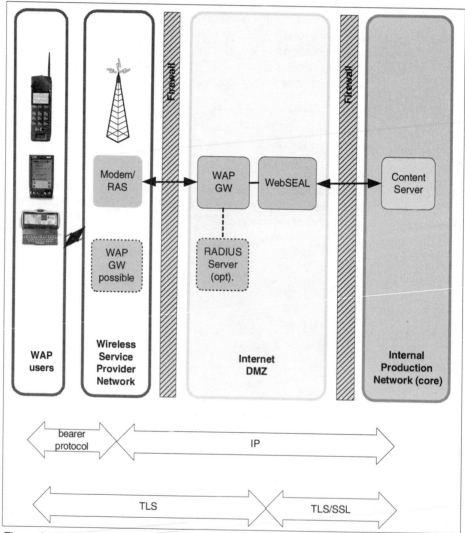

Figure 8-12   Integration of WAP 2.0 devices

Summary

In the proposed architecture (Figure 8-11 on page 204 and Figure 8-12 on page 206), we provide a modular setup for integration of WAP devices into an existing enterprise infrastructure.

► The wireless networking infrastructure is part of the WSP.

► Depending on the security requirements, the WAP gateway can be placed either in the DMZ or at the WSP site.

► The production network is enhanced by adding transcoding servers which handle the transcoding of the back-end content to the target WML for WAP devices.

► Important components (WAP gateway, transcoding server) are administered by the enterprise.

► Third-party authentication can be used (for example, RADIUS).

► Using TLS support in WAP 2.0 and Access Manager E2E security can be established.

► WebSEAL is the focal point for authentication and authorization to get access to the back-end systems.

Note: According to the service provider's environment, several identification mechanisms are possible:

► Identification by user-agent IP address

► Identification by user MS-ISDN number (Mobile Subscriber-Integrated Services Digital Network)

Both should be used in addition to the regular authentication methods (for example, basic authentication) because the above credentials are not necessarily associated with a human being, and can be impersonated.

8.5.2 Basic architecture for i-mode integration

A basic architecture for i-mode is shown in Figure 8-13 on page 208.

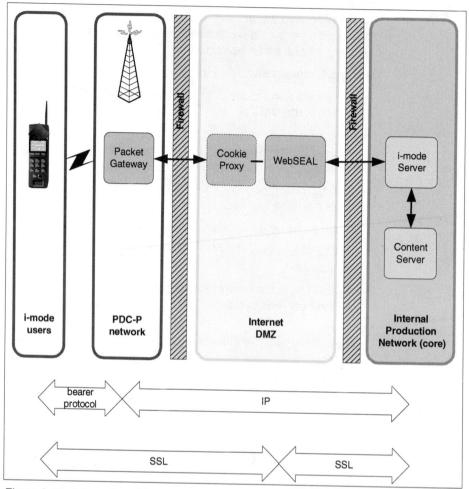

Figure 8-13   Integration of i-mode devices

In this approach the i-mode server is managed by the enterprise, which gives complete access control.

The session between the WebSEAL server in the DMZ and its back-end systems in the production network is secured by using an SSL session.

Because i-mode is SSL-enabled, there is also no potential security gap between the i-mode device and WebSEAL. The SSL CA root certificates are installed on the i-mode handsets during manufacturing.

While SSL renegotiation is used for the key-refresh (for example, every n message), which is important so that both the client and server basically agree on the mechanism for refreshing the session encryption, within i-mode SSL renegotiation is used for every *access*. This is surely not the best thing to do, so Access Manager uses basic authentication to establish a more session-based approach, rather than access-based.

i-mode supports neither client-side certificate logins nor cookies; forms-based authentication is also not supported.

To provide cookie support for i-mode devices, a Cookie Proxy is needed. You can use the IBM Everyplace Cookie Proxy, which is part of the IBM WebSphere Everyplace Server. This component is a plug-in for the Edge Server Caching Proxy and saves important information for Web browsers with limited functions. This can include cookie values and other values for session management and basic authentication. For a more detailed description of the i-mode cookie support, see Appendix D, "i-Mode cookie support" on page 529.

Note: Access Manager supports basic authentication for i-mode devices without the need of a Cookie Proxy; if forms-based authentication is needed, a cookie-proxy is required.

Summary
In the proposed architecture (Figure 8-13 on page 208) we provide a modular setup for integration of i-mode devices into an existing enterprise infrastructure.

► The wireless networking infrastructure is part of the WSP.

► The DMZ is enhanced with a Cookie Proxy.

► The production network is enhanced by adding transcoding servers that handle the transcoding of the back-end content to the target cHTML for i-mode devices.

► Important components (i-mode server, cooky proxy, transcoding server) are administered by the enterprise.

► WebSEAL is the focal point for authentication and authorization to get access to the back-end systems.

8.5.3 Legacy mobile devices
While we took a closer look especially at devices that are not capable of implementing a full-blown IP stack and all of its applications, mobile access is still dominated by using a laptop or a regular PC in order to get access to resources over the Internet or within a company.

Although these devices have virtually no lack of computing resources in terms of memory, screen size, computing power, and so on, there are still security exposures where you easily can imagine that sometimes it is more desirable to have a closed system (for example, in cars, white goods, and so on).

Dealing with legacy dial-in devices means dealing with legacy security issues like:

► Device security: User ID/password stored or not activated.

► Operating system security: Security leaks pop up quite often.

► Smart card issues: Even if you are using a smart card-based access system, tasks like encryption, decryption, and keystoring should be done by separate hardware or, even better, by embedded security hardware functions within the PC device.

Figure 8-14 shows a possible basic scenario where the wireless gateway is part of the enterprise DMZ. The intention of this is to gain control over incoming requests. If this and other requirements are not applicable, then the complete dial-in infrastructure can be placed within the service provider's premises.

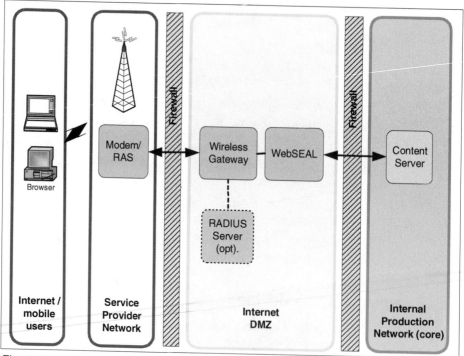

Figure 8-14   Basic architecture for legacy dial-in devices

8.6 Summary

In this chapter we have shown today's security requirements in a mobile environment.

Besides the already widely used dial-in devices like PCs, we especially focused on mobile-specific technologies like WAP and i-mode.

The access pattern is still valid even if more advanced authentication methods will be available (for example, mobile device certificates). This is crucial because otherwise every time the client's security methods are changing you have to change the complete flow of the authentication and authorization mechanisms.

Our approach is driven by the requirements to develop device-independent solutions and to enforce security policies to a wide range of client systems.

The main requirements in mobile security were mapped into the main categories of the MASS architecture so that we were able to define a flexible building block for mobile devices. These building blocks will be used in the following scenarios to show the possible integration of these devices into an existing infrastructure and make use of the focal security access point Access Manager to get access to various back-end systems.

## Part 2

Insurance environment

In this part we discuss a business portal solution for the Yellow Rose Insurance, Ltd. corporation, which is operating on a worldwide basis. They want to extend their current business model to use more e-business technology in order to grow and offer new services in a pervasive market.

Yellow Rose Insurance, Ltd.

This chapter provides an introduction to the overall structure of the Yellow Rose Insurance (YRI) corporation, including its business profile, current IT architecture and infrastructure, and medium-term business vision and objectives.

Note: All names and references for this company and other business institutions used in this chapter are purely fictional. Any match with a real company or institution is coincidental.

9.1 Company profile

Yellow Rose Insurance, Ltd. is a multinational insurance company that offers property-casualty, auto, and life insurances. Yellow Rose Insurance (YRI) serves a wide variety of customers, including individuals and businesses of all sizes.

YRI and its subsidiaries operate in over 60 countries, split into three administrative regions: Europe, the Americas, and Asia. Each region is responsible for maintaining a support structure for business partners and subsidiaries.

While much of its business comes in through business partners such as insurance brokers, there is still a sizeable YRI workforce dealing mostly with corporate customers.

YRI services include risk management, health care management, claims administration, and employee leasing/payroll processing. Yellow Rose Insurance conducts operations through several international operating divisions, all offering a wide range of products tailored for each region.

9.2 Current architecture

Each of the major regions (Europe, Asia, and the Americas) has its own network domain. These domains consist of several locations with their own network infrastructure.

Multiple HTTP servers running on Microsoft Windows NT are located in the DMZ behind the first firewall. Their purpose it to provide Web information services for the general pubic. These services consist of static HTML pages linked to the YRI home site. Each division in the company maintains their own various individual servers.

The information presented to the public is:

► News from YRI
► Insurance market information
► Details on different insurance policies and products
► Forms for request for offers

These Web servers are not using any form of transactions against the internal business systems today.

YRI is running an OS/390-based system for its business applications with many different applications covering the business requirements of YRI. The company employees access these applications using 3270 terminals.

There has been one application for the customer support center that YRI has developed to improve customer satisfaction. When initially dealing with customers over the telephone, an employee uses the customer number or name to search for details of an individual policy. The details of this policy can then be reviewed with the customer. However, the 3270-based application requires that the employee first ask the customer for the policy type and number, and then run the separate application as required. This process is slow and some customers complained about this cumbersome experience.

YRI has introduced a more effective customer care system using a Web-based application running on IBM WebSphere Application Server. After the employee has entered the customer number or name, a complete list of policy engagements for that customer is displayed. By selecting an individual policy, the details are displayed, and the individual application for that policy is activated.

To implement this new customer support application, YRI developed a new interface on the OS/390 called *Realtime Easily Accessible Customer Transactions (REACT)*. On the WebSphere server an application, based on servlets and EJBs, is passing the customer data to a CICS transaction using a CICS Transaction Gateway. The OS/390 application consists of a transaction manager that, for the appropriate CICS call, will collect this data and return the required list to the WebSphere application. The employees log on to WebSphere using their WebSphere user ID/password. The user credentials are then forwarded to the CICS transaction, which uses them for logging in the transaction system. The application has been very successful and customer feedback has been positive.

However, problems still exist in dealing with the insurance brokers. A hardcopy of price quotes still needs to be updated constantly, because an online version cannot be provided, due to the lack of an access control solution for the external Web servers. The process of issuing new insurance policies to customers is another painful process. After the broker sells the insurance to the customer, he has to physically send or fax it to YRI for verification. Only after verifying that the policy can be granted will the insurance come into effect. Unwanted delays in the distribution channel and the higher administrative costs result in lower profits when keeping insurance premiums at a competitive rate.

Access to the Lotus Domino-based e-mail system is enabled by using the Notes mail client from the intranet as well as through a Remote Access Server (RAS). While the RAS presents a possible security threat to the network, the business needs also dictate that mobile employees be able to access their e-mail and Web applications on the WebSphere Application Server utilizing the Internet channel.

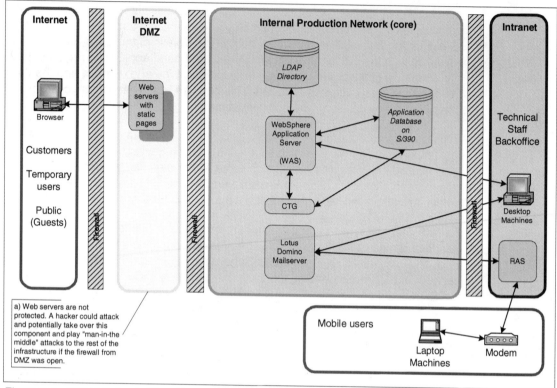

Figure 9-1   YRI Ltd's basic IT architecture

The IT architecture in a single region is visually represented in Figure 9-1. As you can see, the architecture relies on the following security measures:

► Access from DMZ to core network is completely disabled.
► Access between intranet and core network is controlled by a firewall.
► RAS is not directly in the core network, but in the intranet with an enabled mail connection to the Lotus Domino server.

As discussed earlier, this constitutes a relatively secure network, but it also limits the availability of key services such as e-mail and insurance applications residing on the WebSphere Application Server.

9.3 Corporate business vision and objectives

The global insurance market is becoming more and more competitive today. The company needs to offer new services to customers and agents quickly and cost-effectively in order to maintain profitability while increasing marketshare.

Therefore, Yellow Rose Insurance wishes to offer excellence of service to both its customers and its agents trough the use of the latest Web-based technology.

Customers should be able to gain global access to their insurance engagements around the clock, and to update information that will affect their premiums; for example, posting claims and adding additional items to their policies.

Third party agents and brokers should be able to conduct business transactions like commission statements, view account histories, view claim information, and complete insurance quotations online.

Since YRI is a global company with subsidiaries in Europe, the Americas, and Asia, they need to make transactions available across national borders for its agents and brokers.

In the long run, the intention is to enable remote transactions to take place on a real-time basis with digital signatures. This will not happen until the legislative side of digital signatures is clarified on an international basis; however, a Web-based solution with a centralized security infrastructure should allow for quick deployment of digital signature support without changes to the business application in the future.

Also, YRI wishes to make all corporate information available from the Internet. This includes everything from customer and contract management to e-mail and internal corporate data.

9.3.1 Initial design

After many internal meetings and discussions, the CIO and his group have decided that in order to cover the present and future security needs, the most suitable solution will be based on the IBM Tivoli Access Manager for e-business.

The decision was reached after successful proof-of-concept tests with Access Manager. Access Manager allows an organization to secure a broad range of Web servers and Java-based Web application servers *out of the box.*

Even when fine-grained access control decisions have to be obtained from within a Web application itself, they can implement this for their new Web applications with minimum development effort using Access Manager's standard Authorization API (aznAPI) or JAVA 2/JAAS classes, allowing these applications to be deployed faster and at a lower cost.

Furthermore, a future requirement for strong authentication will allow digital certificates or other authentication mechanisms and devices to be taken into production with minimal efforts.

After a decision has been made on what access control solution should be used, the group decided to implement the required solution in four separate projects. These four projects cover the following aspects:

- Laying the foundation for an enterprise-wide access control security infrastructure based on IBM Tivoli Access Manager for e-business and IBM WebSphere Application Server as described in Chapter 10, "Baseline security framework" on page 221.

- Integrating browser-based, secure access to the central e-mail system from intranet and Internet locations as lined out in Chapter 11, "Web mail integration" on page 287.

- Defining a new business model for a multiple-car insurance concept based on the integration of new pervasive devices as discussed in Chapter 12, "Pay-As-You-Drive" on page 301.

- Introducing internationalization with an easy-to-use and easy-to-administer single sign-on solution as shown in Chapter 13, "Cross-domain authentication" on page 309.

The requirements, design approach, architecture, and technical implementation for each project are described in their respective chapters.

## 10

Baseline security framework

This chapter provides a detailed description of the business and functional requirements as well as the design and implementation aspects for a security framework for an Enterprise Business Portal with Tivoli Access Manager for e-business.

The objective of this project is to provide Yellow Rose Insurance (YRI) with the baseline security framework needed for a centralized access control infrastructure for the current WebSphere application infrastructure as well as for future integration projects. We describe how this is achieved using Tivoli Access Manager components, which include extensions to provide JAVA 2 container-based authorization and centralized policy management for IBM WebSphere Application Server applications. New security functions will be added as plug-ins in later chapters.

10.1 Business requirements

Yellow Rose is in the early stages of implementing Web-based technology and an e-business infrastructure.

The CIO wishes to capitalize on the investments made for the current WebSphere Application Server application, used to review customer engagements by company employees. He would like to extend access to this application to individual customers and agents using the Internet.

In order to deploy this service, the CIO is looking for a secure solution that will enhance customer, employee, and agent confidence as well as protect the confidential data that is accessible via the current WebSphere Application Server application from unlawful and malicious access. The solution must also ensure that personal customer data is only revealed to an approved customer or agent. This new composition will provide a basic framework to which new services can be added securely in the future.

The CIO is concerned that the implementation of an advanced security solution will result in a complex system that will dramatically increase manpower cost. With this concern in mind, he requires a user friendly and an easily manageable system.

YRI wants to maintain their competitive edge in the insurance market. Their mission is to achieve excellence in bringing new services to the public by using Web-based technology. A requirement resulting from this is the need for a 24x7 availability of the system.

The CIO wants a Web portal that allows quick access to services for individual customers and agents. This portal also has to enable the general public to review the information available from the existing HTTP Web servers. Employees will continue to access business applications via the company intranet, with the exception of more and more mobile users, who will be using the Internet connection.

The CIO demands that central responsibility for the security system management has to be put in place. However this should not impede its expansion.

10.2 Functional requirements

The business requirements help us to describe the necessary functions in the well-planned security solution.

After a couple of workshops discussing these with YRI, the CIO and his team have determined the following key requirements:

► Support for integration to different cross-platform back-end servers

YRI needs to maintain operating system independence for Web-based application security. They are running their mail services on a Lotus Domino server based on Windows NT. The HTTP server for public information also runs on Windows NT, and multiple WebSphere Application Servers are based on AIX. There is an additional need to provide a single sign-on solution for Web-based applications. A user should only be required to log on once, independent of the resource he tries to access.

► Easy and user-friendly management of users and security policies

YRI is looking at ways to keep their IT-related costs down. They have learned that new technology, due to its complexity, naturally involves staff training for management and operations. However, it is important that the tools for management and operations are easy to use. This will help YRI justify investments and maintain a cost balance by using less experienced IT staff for the daily routine, and fully utilizing more experienced specialists for more complicated tasks.

► Centralized management for security policies

YRI uses WebSphere Application Servers that represent the strategic platform for existing and new enterprise business applications. They require the ability to centrally define and coordinate security policies for access to WebSphere Application Server resources and for resources that are unrelated to WebSphere Application Server. There is a need to enforce and delegate company security policies and standards through a central management system. This management system is required to manage the security policy across multiple servers. The solution will form the baseline for the company security policy and best practices.

► Standard security model that can be deployed for each region

YRI will initially enforce a security model in one region. If this is successful, the same components will be implemented in each location both nationally and globally. YRI has a strategy of using the same IT infrastructure for every location. This allows them to negotiate special prices from IT vendors. It also helps them to keep down the costs for IT staffing. They have the flexibility of moving their staff to locations that demand increased manpower without the need to retrain.

► Modular design so that new services can be added with minimal effort

Competitive situations constantly demand new services. YRI has to keep up with this demand, otherwise it will lose its customers. The security system will be implemented as a baseline security framework; however, as demand arises, it should be capable of adding new services without re-engineering.

- Ability to grow on demand

  The components of the security system should allow for increased demand for new services, application loads, and capacity. In one sense this is not really a direct function of the security software, but is more related to the overall IT design of the solution. However, the security system must be modular to allow for both a horizontal and vertical scaling. For example, when extra space is required for the user registry, extra disks can be added, or when Web traffic demands extra capacity, a new reverse proxy can be easily added.

- High availability and failover for security components

  YRI requires 24x7 availability of their Web services. The design will involve duplication and replication of multiple security components. Additional monitoring of services and generation of alerts for operational failure will be required.

10.3 Security design objectives

With the business and functional requirements clearly defined, we are now ready to document some of the most important design objectives for a security solution.

In our case, we are assuming that there has been an analysis carried out by IBM Global Services based on the MASS model. The IBM method for architecting secure solutions is described in the IBM Redbook *Enterprise Security Architecture using IBM Tivoli Security Solutions*, SG24-6014.

It is not our intention to repeat the MASS process in this section, but we remind the reader that in our effort to develop a system model for security for YRI, we have considered the *common criteria-based* method in MASS to describe the functions of the security system model. Using this model, we have broken down the security objectives and grouped them into five basic subsystems. The security objectives for YRI classified into the five subsystems, as follows:

- Access control subsystem

  - Access control will be enforced by using a user ID/password-based authentication mechanism for customers, employees, and agents. Since the applications invoked do not involve transactions such as transfer of money, the security level does not require enhanced security techniques such as PKI or token-based authentication.

- A single authentication process will be used across different back-end servers. Users are required to log on once in order to get authenticated. The authorization process can be delegated to the central authorization repository or to applications running on different or multiple back-end servers.

- Users requesting access to protected resources will be authorized according to access control information based on the company security policies.

- A central management capability for users and security policies will be put in place.

► Integrity subsystem

- Prevents unauthorized access attempts. The security implementation should be capable of preventing attempts to gain access to protected resources.

- Confidential information flowing between components exchanging sensitive information, that is, a user's browser and the Web servers in the production network are protected via SSL encryption.

- High availability. The security system should maintain a 24 hours/7 days a week access to services provided by YRI. This includes failover and duplication of hardware and software components.

► Information flow subsystem

- Enforces security policy for trusted or un-trusted credentials. There is a security requirement that sending or receiving requested information can be trusted by channel or path.

- For Internet access, YRI uses a firewall protecting the Internet DMZ. An additional firewall between this DMZ and the production network protects the back-end application systems and other IT management related resources. These firewalls are not discussed in this chapter. They protect the flow of information as part of the overall security policy and they are considered secure in our scenario.

- The Web servers in the production network consider requested access as trusted if the security system can signal this via path or certificate.

- Data flow within the production zone is classified as trusted.

- The intranet for employees is protected with a firewall configuration similar to the Internet. The same security policy defined for Internet users applies for the intranet, with one exception: Traffic from the intranet DMZ can be considered trusted.

► Credential subsystem

Central management of user credentials. Users requiring authorized access to services will be allocated credentials according to YRI's security policy. These credentials will be distributed to the access control subsystem for authentication and authorization decisions when requested.

► Audit subsystem

- Monitoring of user activity. For each request, a log needs to be created specifying the user ID of the requesting user (if authenticated) and the resource requested.

- Monitoring of access to resources. A log needs to be created to show the periodic use of components in this system.

10.4 Design approach

In designing this environment, we have to take several issues into account. The most important consideration is how to integrate the Access Manager solution with the existing approach causing as little trouble as possible. The solution also has to be expandable regarding performance, administration, and in terms of scalability when adding new components.

Another important factor is the high-availability of the solution. Therefore everything possible is *doubled-up*. For added availability, the solution has to be installed in two different locations. This will greatly increase availability in the event of a disaster that disables a whole site (blackout, flood, earthquake, and so on). These two sites can be anything from separate buildings in the same city to buildings on opposite sides of the globe. In our case they are two separate sites in different countries within the same region. For example, the primary location is in Finland and the secondary location in Norway.

While WebSEALs and Authorization Servers can be installed on as many boxes as needed, IBM Directory Server (LDAP) can only have one master server. Therefore, we use replicated LDAPs so that the downtime of an LDAP master server does not interfere with normal operations, as only write operations are disabled until a replica can be promoted to master. The promotion of a replica into the master server can be done in a matter of minutes by using a script or, alternatively, a manual operation.

While not supported out of the box, there is a way to configure a fail-over capability into the Access Manager Policy Server. See Appendix G, "Policy Server high-availability" on page 547 for more details.

Access Manager WebSEAL can handle all the Web authentication and authorization requests, but it was decided that the Access Manager for WebSphere Application Server plug-in was required to integrate the WebSphere Application Server authorization decisions into the Access Manager managed name space. The implementation of the plug-in also created the need for a trusted connection between Access Manager WebSEAL and WebSphere Application Server. These issues are discussed further in 10.5.5, "Tivoli Access Manager for WebSphere" on page 232.

To allow for flexible administration even if the solution grows more complicated, a delegated administration model will be used for administering users. See 10.5.3, "Delegated administration" on page 231, for more information on how delegated administration will be used in this project.

10.5 Implementation architecture

This section deals with the architectural decisions and designs for implementing an Access Manager environment to protect the WebSphere Application Servers containing transaction data and IBM HTTP Servers.

The Access Manager for WebSphere Application Server plug-in is discussed in 10.5.5, "Tivoli Access Manager for WebSphere" on page 232.

10.5.1 Before Access Manager installation

Since the aim of this project is to place all the back-end components into the internal production environment (core) and replace the front end with WebSEAL servers, the HTTP server that currently serves as the Yellow Rose Insurance general Web site located in the DMZ will have to be moved to the core network. The name and IP address of the server have to be changed to free them up for WebSEAL servers.

Even though this project describes the method of placing all components behind a WebSEAL server, it would still be possible to leave the server containing public information in the DMZ with the original www.company.com name. The WebSEALs would then have to use another DNS name, like secure.company.com. This is, of course, not as secure a solution as generally placing all Web resources behind Access Manager in the core network.

10.5.2 Components and communications

This section deals with the components needed for the new Access Manager architecture and the communications between them.

The components needed for the Access Manager implementation in this project are:

- IBM Directory Server (or other supported user registry)
- Access Manager Policy Server
- Access Manager Authorization Service installed on the WebSphere Application Server machine
- Access Manager WebSEAL server
- IBM Network Dispatcher
- Access Manager Web Portal Manager

Most of the components, with the exception of Network Dispatchers and WebSEAL servers, will be installed in the internal production network (core).

Communications to the components in the core network will be allowed from three directions: The WebSEALs in the Internet DMZ, the WebSEALs in the intranet DMZ, and from other components inside the core network itself. See 2.7, "Component configuration and placement" on page 45, for more discussion on network zones.

> **Note:** The ports listed here and in the examples are the default ports. The default ports are listed for clarity's sake; it is recommended that you change the default ports for back-end Web communications as discussed in Chapter 2, "Access Manager Web-based architecture" on page 33.

Communications from the Internet DMZ will be SSL-encrypted, with only one exception, which is the HTTP traffic to the IBM HTTP Server's public section. The required Internet DMZ to core network communications and the respective ports they use are listed here.

- WebSEAL communications with the Policy Server (ports 7135 and 7234)
- WebSEAL communications to the LDAP replica(s) (port 636)
- WebSEAL communications to the WebSphere Application Server(s) (port 443)
- WebSEAL communications to the IBM HTTP Server's public data (port 80); this is the only non-SSL connection
- WebSEAL communications to the IBM HTTP Server's confidential data (port 443)

> **Note:** You can further secure access to unsecured HTTP servers that listen on port 80 by configuring these servers to only allow incoming HTTP traffic from WebSEAL servers. This way *all* Web traffic, HTTP or HTTPS, has to be routed through WebSEAL. This will dramatically ease the administration and enforcement of the enterprise security policies.

Communications from the intranet DMZ will be mostly unencrypted (with the exception of Access Manager internal traffic and LDAP authentications). As before, these listed ports are the default ones.

► WebSEAL SSL communications with the Policy Server (ports 7135 and 7234)

> **Note:** Access Manager servers communicate with each other via SSL only.

► WebSEAL communications to the LDAP replica(s) (port 636)

Since access from WebSEAL to LDAP is SSL only, the same must apply for all other requests directed to LDAP, no matter the origin. While this is not optimal for performance, this solution provides more high-availability due to the fact that you do not have to configure a part of the LDAP replicas to answer SSL requests from the Internet DMZ, and a part of the LDAP replicas answer to TCP requests from the intranet DMZ. Also, security is increased because all LDAP traffic is encrypted.

► WebSEAL communications to the WebSphere Application Server(s) (port 80)

► WebSEAL communications to the IBM HTTP Server's public data (port 80)

► WebSEAL communications to the IBM HTTP Server's confidential data (port 443)

► WebSEAL communications to the Web Portal Manager (port 80)

Communications inside the core network will be mostly unencrypted. Here is a list of communication components and their ports.

► Web Portal Manager communication to Policy Server (port 7135)

► Web Portal Manager communication to the LDAP master server (port 389)

► Policy Server communication with authorization Service(s) (ports 7135 and 7136)

► Policy Server communication to the LDAP master database (port 389)

This component architecture and their communications are illustrated in Figure 10-1. Dashed lines represent unencrypted communications. While the CICS Transaction Gateway and its underlying OS/390 application database are not directly involved in the Access Manager and back-end Web architecture, they are shown in the figure in order to portray all the important components.

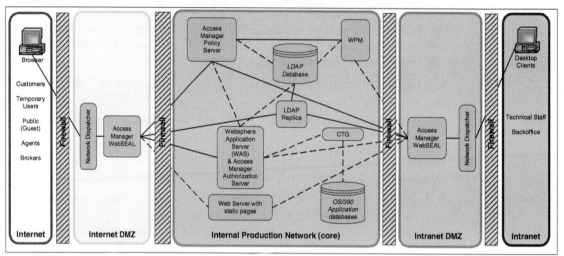

Figure 10-1   Component architecture overview

While the components in Figure 10-1 are shown as single boxes, this does not mean that there should be only one of each component installed.

High-availability

One of the most important requirements for Web-based environments today is high-availability. This section deals with that aspect of the solution.

The first step to high-availability is to install a replica of all the applicable components to a secondary location. While in YRI's case, the back-end components were already fault tolerant and operating in several locations, a fault tolerance scheme had to be designed for the new Access Manager components.

Of all the Access Manager solution components, the Access Manager Policy Server only supports replication functionality today; a hot standby implementation is not yet available. See more details in Appendix G, "Policy Server high-availability" on page 547.

The situation is much easier with the Authorization Service, Web Portal Manager and WebSEAL components. There can be any number of these installed in each Access Manager domain. The same goes for LDAP servers, but there can be only one master LDAP server; the other machines have to be configured as replicas.

The components required and their configurations are addressed in 10.6, "Technical implementation" on page 234.

10.5.3 Delegated administration

When creating large portals, the question of user administration becomes very important. In some cases it may still be prudent to create a pool of administrators who handle the administration of all the user accounts.

In our case, the better alternative is to use Web Portal Manager's delegated administration feature. This feature, which is discussed in more detail in 1.1.7, "Web Portal Manager" on page 10, allows you to create Enterprise domains, which in turn can contain several sub-domains. Each domain can support several different roles, such as senior administrators (responsible for the whole domain), support administrators (call center support personnel, for example), and of course users.

Each sub-domain can then be divided into further sub-domains in a treelike structure. Each domain's administrator only has control in his own domain and its sub-domains. This provides a secure method of operation in large corporate environments, with shared responsibilities.

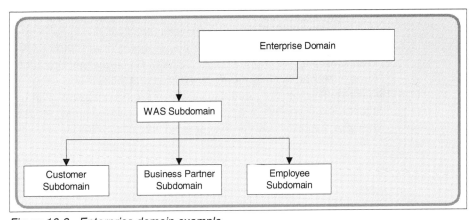

Figure 10-2 Enterprise domain example

As you can see in Figure 10-2 on page 231, the WebSphere Application Server sub-domain of the main enterprise domain has been split into three sections. Different people can be assigned the responsibility for managing the users in their respective domains. This can be achieved by adding them as administrators into their respective sub-domains.

10.5.4 Auditing

As WebSEAL supplies several logs by default (agent, referrer, and request logs), the most important is the *request.log*.

The request.log file contains the IP address, user ID (if authenticated), and the date and time of a request. In addition to the requested data, it provides information about the request type, result code, and number of bytes transferred. In short, as the request.log file contains all the basic data needed, there is no need to enable extra auditing.

In addition, the agent log shows which type of agent (browser) has been used, and the referrer log shows the referring URL (previous page).

Should the need arise, though, the webseald.conf file contains the settings for enabling detailed audits for authentication, authorization, and HTTP(S) requests. See the *IBM Tivoli Access Manager for e-Business WebSEAL Administration Guide Version 3.9,* GC23-4682, for further details on setting up logs.

10.5.5 Tivoli Access Manager for WebSphere

Tivoli Access Manager for WebSphere Application Server provides container-based authorization and centralized policy management for WebSphere Application Server Version 4.0.2. In our insurance scenario we use Access Manager for WebSphere Application Server to integrate existing WebSphere applications into the Access Manager authorization framework. Access Manager now manages WebSphere application security in a centralized manner. This not only means that there are no problems with user synchronization, but also that Access Manager tools can be used to centrally manage the users, rather than use native registry tools.

J2EE role-based security

In WebSphere Application Server Version 4.0.2, J2EE implements the concept of roles-based security. Roles are mapped to methods/resources, and users (principals) and groups are mapped to roles. The principal represents the identity of an entity that performs activities. A more detailed description of WebSphere Application Server security can be found in Chapter 6, "WebSphere application integration" on page 123, and the redbook *IBM WebSphere Version 4.0 Advanced Edition Security*, SG24-6520.

Table 10-1, taken from a sample insurance application, defines the roles and methods mapped to them. The entry *granted* means that the role can access the specified method.

Table 10-1   Mapping of roles to methods

Roles	Methods		
	getPolicy	changeDetail	closePolicy
Customer	granted		
Broker	granted	granted	
Superuser			granted

The roles shown in Table 10-1 can be mapped to principals and/or groups. The entry *invoke* in the table below indicates which principals or groups can invoke the methods that have been granted to that role.

Table 10-2   Mapping of groups/principles to roles

Principal group	Roles		
	Customer	Broker	Superuser
cust.group	invoke		
brokergroup		invoke	
chris		invoke	

From Table 10-2, the user chris can *invoke* the getPolicy and changeDetails methods, but can not invoke the closePolicy method.

Migration of roles to principals and groups

Tivoli Access Manager for WebSphere Application Server has a migration utility that maps the roles in WebSphere Application Server to Access Manager principals and groups. "Access Manager for WebSphere Application Server" on page 143 describes in detail the integration process.

10.5.6 Trust Association Interceptor (TAI)

The Trust Association Interceptor method is used to provide single sign-on to the WebSphere-based applications that are protected in Access Manager's secure domain.

Trust Association Interceptor mode is achieved by placing WebSEAL at the front end as a reverse proxy server. From WebSEAL's management perspective, a junction is created with WebSEAL on one end, and the WebSphere's Web server on the other end. A request for a Web resource, stored in WebSphere's protected domain, is submitted to WebSEAL, where it is authenticated against WebSEAL's security realm. If the requesting user has access to the junction, the HTTP request is transmitted to WebSphere via the junction. This HTTP request contains a header field that contains the user ID. This field is only information used between WebSEAL and WebSphere. WebSphere trusts the values in the header, and validates the request using the method validateEstablishedTrust. We refer to this as *validating the trust*. If the validation is successful, WebSphere authorizes the request. This is achieved by extracting the value of the iv_user HTTP header, and using the method getAuthenticatedUsername. If the client user has the required permissions to access the Web resource, the Web resource is delivered to WebSEAL through the Web server, which then gives it to the client.

TAI is described in more detail in "Web Trust Association Interceptor (TAI)" on page 135.

10.6 Technical implementation

We now describe the steps needed for creating the Access Manager security domain and Access Manager for WebSphere Application Server integration.

10.6.1 Access Manager components

This section lists the Access Manager components to be installed and the required configuration options, but it will not provide step-by-step instructions for such installation. Refer to the respective installation guides of Access Manager components for step-by-step instructions. The components that need to be installed are:

▶ IBM Directory Server LDAP master database in the primary location core network, unless this is already installed for WebSphere Application Server use, which we assume to be the case in this scenario.

▶ Access Manager Policy Server in the primary location core network.

- One or more LDAP replicas in the secondary location core network. These will be used for authentication as well as standby master servers, should the primary location become unavailable for some reason.
- One or more LDAP replicas in the primary location core network. These will be used for authentication as well as standby master servers.
- Access Manager Authorization Servers installed on the WebSphere Application Server machine located in the primary location core network.
- Access Manager Authorization Servers installed on the WebSphere Application Server machine located in the secondary location core network.
- One or more WebSEALs in primary location Internet DMZ.
- One or more WebSEALs in primary location intranet DMZ.
- Web Portal Manager in primary location core network.
- Web Portal Manager in secondary location core network.
- A Network Dispatcher in primary location Internet DMZ.
- A Network Dispatcher in primary location intranet DMZ.
- A Network Dispatcher in secondary location Internet DMZ. This is used as a hot-standby.
- A Network Dispatcher in secondary location intranet DMZ. This is used as a hot-standby.
- Optional: Access Manager Policy Server stand-by replica in secondary location core network.

The locations of the components are illustrated in Figure 10-3 on page 236. As mentioned earlier in this chapter, the locations can be physically remote from each other as long as they are connected by a network.

Tip: To save time later on, all LDAP traffic should be configured to be SSL-encrypted during Access Manager installation.

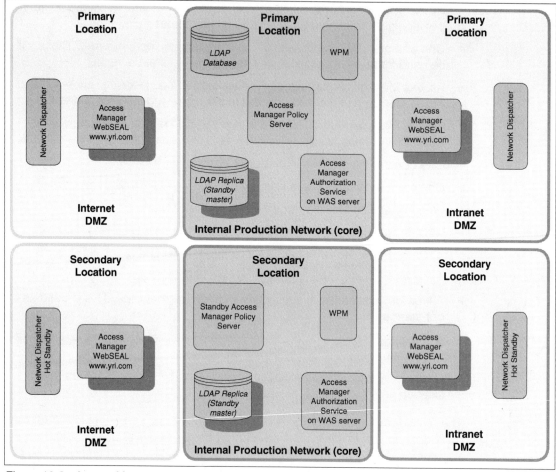

Figure 10-3   Access Manager components

Configuration

We assume that the components have been installed following their respective installation guidelines. We must now configure the security components, which include Access Manager, LDAP, Network Dispatcher, WebSphere Application Server, and the firewalls.

The firewalls have to be configured to only allow certain types of traffic to pass. For the Web application environment, only Web traffic should be coming into the DMZs on either port 80 or 443.

Additional security can be achieved by configuring all back-end Web servers to accept Web traffic only from the WebSEAL servers using their respective IP addresses. Other methods of operating system hardening should also be employed.

Access to the core network from the DMZs should be limited to the following:

▶ WebSEALs communicating to back-end Web servers on ports 80 and 443 (if possible, change these to something other than the default ports).

  You might want to impose even more refined restrictions here, with port 80 being open from the Internet DMZ WebSEALs to only the HTTP server, which contains the public information.

▶ Access Manager Policy Server access and authorization database notifications using ports 7135 and 7234, respectively, have to be configured between Access Manager Policy Server and the WebSEAL components.

▶ LDAP traffic over SSL from WebSEALs to the LDAP servers in the core network use port 636.

Once the firewall configurations have been completed, all the Access Manager components will need to be configured to access the applicable LDAP server(s).

Configure the WebSEALs in the DMZs to primarily contact the LDAP replica servers in their own location for read operations. Then you should prioritize LDAP connections in the ldap.conf configuration file and configure the WebSEALs to contact the LDAP replicas in the other locations for read operations if their primary connection to their LDAP replicas fail. For example:

```
replica = primarylocationldap1.yri.com,636,readonly,10
replica = secondarylocationldap1.yri.com,636,readonly,9
```

As you can see, in addition to different host names, the only difference is the priority setting, which is specified at the end of the configuration line. The valid ranges for the setting are between 1 and 10; the highest one will be contacted first, the lowest last. As the default for the LDAP master server is 5, it is recommended that you define your replicas in priority values higher than this.

Also, be sure to read Chapter 4, "Increasing availability and scalability" on page 79, for further information on making your environment more fault and stress tolerant.

10.6.2 Tivoli Access Manager for WebSphere Application Server

This section describes the process of integrating Access Manager with WebSphere Application Server Version 4.0.2 and assumes Policy Director for WebSphere Application Server Version 3.8. For detailed information on a step-by-step integration, refer to the *Tivoli Policy Director for WebSphere Application Server User Guide Version 3.8*, SC32-0832.

> **Note:** At the time we produced this material, Access Manager Version 3.9 was not released yet. Therefore, Access Manager for WebSphere Application Server Version 3.9 may or may not include changes to these instructions. Please refer to *IBM Tivoli Access Manager for e-Business WebSphere Application Server User's Guide Version 3.9*, GC32-0850.

Prerequisites

WebSphere Application Server requires the following prerequisites:

- IBM WebSphere Application Server, Advanced Edition Version 4.0, PTF 2 (4.0.2)

- The WebSphere Application Server Advanced Edition must be configured to use an IBM Directory Version 3.2.1 LDAP server or higher. This LDAP user registry is shared with Access Manager.

> **Note:** Access Manager for WebSphere Application Server does not require any additional components on the local computer. However, for optimized performance, we recommend installing the Access Manager Authorization Server on the same host as the WebSphere Application Server.

WebSphere Application Server must be able to access an Access Manager secure domain. The Access Manager secure domain consists of:

- An Access Manager Policy Server.

- An Access Manager Authorization Server.

- An IBM Directory Version 3.2.1 LDAP server (or higher). This LDAP registry is shared with WebSphere Application Server.

The Access Manager for WebSphere Application Server migration utility has to be installed onto the machines that contain EAR descriptor files.

> **Note:** The Access Manager for WebSphere Application Server migration utility can be installed on a remote machine in the network. However, there are software prerequisites required to enable this utility when executed remotely. For details refer to the *Tivoli Policy Director for WebSphere Application Server User Guide Version 3.8,* SC32-0832.
>
> The migration utility is available as a software download from the following URL:
>
> ```
> http://www.tivoli.com/secure/support/downloads/secureway/policy_dir/pd3.8/pd
> _was.html
> ```
>
> A valid login and password is required to access this Tivoli Customer Support software download site.

User registry prerequisites

Tivoli Policy Director for WebSphere Application Server User Guide Version 3.8, SC32-0832, provides the details of the prerequisites for the user registry, which must be satisfied before installing Access Manager for WebSphere. However, after importing the groups into Access Manager, we are required to integrate the groups with WebSphere.

By default, WebSphere determines group membership using the *member* and *uniqueMember* attributes of entries in LDAP of the type *groupOfNames* and *groupOfUniqueNames,* respectively. That is, when a user provides a user ID and password to the WebSphere Application Server authentication prompt, WebSphere Application Server does the following:

1. Searchs LDAP for entry with (uid=*input-User* & objectclass=eperson).
2. If found, performs an LDAP bind using the DN of this entry and the input password.
3. If the bind is successful, the password is correct and the user is authenticated.
4. Assuming that the DN found in step 1 was cn=User Name,o=yri, searchs LDAP for entries of the type groupOfNames or groupOfUniqueNames where attribute member or uniqueMember is cn=User Name,o=yri.
5. The cn of all returned entries names a group that contains the user.

> **Tip:** A useful tool for analyzing LDAP application use is the audit log.

In the WebSphere Application Server Admin Console click **Console -> Tasks -> Configure Global Security Settings -> User Registry -> Advanced**.

The LDAP Advanced Properties dialogue contains the search filters used by WebSphere Application Server to locate user entries, and determines user membership in groups.

The default LDAP search and mapping values for an IBM Directory Server are shown in Table 10-3.

Table 10-3 Default LDAP search and mapping values

Field	Value
User filter	(&(uid=%v)(objectclass=ePerson)
User ID	*:uid
Group filter	(&(cn=%v)(l(objectclass=groupOfNames)(objectclass=groupOfUniqueN ames)))
Group ID map	*:cn
Group member ID map	groupOfNames:member;groupOfUniqueNames:uniqueMember

Using these values, the LDAP audit log and the knowledge that Access Manager creates groups in LDAP using accessGroup entries, we can determine how to do the necessary modifications for the integration with Access Manager.

As we have seen, for users the default values work *as is*. Access Manager creates users entries of type *ePerson* and stores the Access Manager user ID in the attribute *uid* (remember, an LDAP entry can be composed of multiple types or *object classes*. The Access Manager user entries have the types inetOrgPerson and ePerson).

For groups, however, something different has to be done. The options are:

▶ Create groups outside of Access Manager (of type groupOfName or groupOfUniqueNames) and use the Access Manager group import command to provide Access Manager with the group definition accessGroup.

▶ Change the WebSphere Application Server search values to locate groups created by Access Manager.

In regard to the first option, once a group has been imported, Access Manager can manage its membership and inclusion in Access Manager ACLs, and so on. That is, all the functionality available to groups created to Access Manager is available to groups imported into Access Manager.

If Access Manager will be used for all group creation, then it is necessary to make these changes in the WebSphere Application Server LDAP Advanced Properties dialogue, based on the second option:

Directory type	Custom
Group filter	(&(cn=%v) (!(objectclass=groupOfNames) (objectclass=groupOfUnigueNames) (objectclass=accessGroup)))
Group member ID map	groupOfNames:member groupOfUniqueNames:uniqueMember accessGroup:member

After these changes are made, you should be able to control access for WebSphere Application Server applications by adding/removing Access Manager users to Access Manager groups.

> **Note:** Management of groups and users can be handled via Access Manager or WebSphere Application Server under the condition that the migration utility has not yet been executed.
>
> After the migration utility has been run, only Access Manager should be used for management of groups, roles, and users.

Authorization Server installation and configuration

We wish to optimize performance of Access Manager for WebSphere Application Server by running an Access Manager Authorization Server on the same machines as WebSphere Application Server. Before we continue with our integration installation, we must install and configure Access Manager Run Time and Authorization Server on each instance of WebSphere Application Server. Make sure that these components are correctly configured and running before continuing with the next step.

Install Access Manager For WebSphere

Follow the steps detailed in the *Tivoli Policy Director for WebSphere Application Server User Guide Version 3.8,* SC32-0832.

Note: Access Manager for WebSphere Application Server is available for download from URL:

```
http://www.tivoli.com/secure/support/downloads/secureway/policy_dir/pd3.8/pd
_was.html
```

A valid login and password is required to access the Tivoli Customer Support software download site.

After this download has been unpacked, the following three directories have been created: doc, migrate, and websphere. The doc directory contains the user guide in PDF format. The migrate directory contains the executable for the migration utility and should be copied to an Access Manager system that has access to the EAR file that needs to be migrated. In this case, it is the Access Manager Authorization Server located on the WebSphere Application Server machines. The websphere directory contains the jar files and configuration scripts for Access Manager for WebSphere Application Server and should be copied to each WebSphere instance that hosts secured applications.

Configure Access Manager for WebSphere

To configure the Access Manager for WebSphere Application Server authorization component for each WebSphere Application Server instance, complete the steps detailed in the *Tivoli Policy Director for WebSphere Application Server User Guide Version 3.8*, SC32-0832.

Access Manager for WebSphere Application Server is configured by running the supplied script and providing the relevant parameters.

The script for configuration of the authorization component requires the following values as input parameters:

`PDAdmin user Password PDMgrd Hostname PDACLd Hostname`

Where:

PDAdmin user Password   Is the UID and password of the pdadmin user.

PDMgrd Hostname   Is the host name of the Access Manager's secure domain Policy Server.

PDACLd Hostname   Is the host name of the Access Manager Authorization Server. This will be the local host name of the Access Manager Authorization Server when it is installed on the same machine as WebSphere Application Server.

Once the configuration has been completed and WebSphere Application Servers have been stopped and re-started, we can move on to the process for migration.

Migrating security roles to Access Manager

The final step in the integration of Access Manager for WebSphere Application server is to migrate the roles from the WebSphere application deployment descriptors to the Access Manager protected object space. This section will not describe how to use the migration utility. Migration of the security roles is detailed in the *Tivoli Policy Director for WebSphere Application Server User Guide Version 3.8*, SC32-0832.

> **Note:** Always make sure that the EAR file accurately reflects the application configuration before running the migration utility.

> **Tip:** The amount of migration data can be large and the execution time can be long. Therefore, the migration utility has a default time out after 60 minutes. This can be increased by using the -t <minutes> option when you run the migration utility. However, this value must not be greater than the SSL time out between the authorization API client and the Policy Server. The SSL time out value in seconds is set in the pd.conf file with the parameter ssl-v3-timeout and may be changed as required.

On completion of the migration, the Access Manager administrator can use the pdadmin command interface or the Web Portal Manager to manage the roles and modify or update the ACLs required for the protected objects.

10.6.3 WebSEAL forms-based authentication

In our scenario, forms-based authentication will be used between the client browser and WebSEAL. To enable forms-based authentication for SSL connections and disable basic authentication, modify the ba-auth and forms-auth entries in the webseald.conf file on all WebSEAL servers. The entries should read:

```
ba-auth = none
forms-auth = https
```

Then restart the server.

> **Note:** As you can see, authentication is only allowed through HTTPS connections. This is to prevent user IDs and passwords from being sent in the clear. Also, additional advantage of using the forms-based authentication is the fact that user ID and password are not stored on the client browser.
>
> However, some browsers (Microsoft Internet Explorer in particular) can cache the user ID and password submitted in a forms-based login page, should the user allow it. This may be a security risk and should be taken into consideration.

Authentication failover

Should one of the WebSEAL servers fail, fail-over cookies, which are discussed in "WebSEAL fail-over cookies" on page 87, should be configured on all WebSEAL servers.

10.6.4 Creating delegate domains

Implementing the delegated administration is a straightforward task once the structure has been decided on. All the actions can, and should, be performed with the Web Portal Manager. If you are not familiar with Web Portal Manager, see the step-by-step instructions in Appendix , "Creating delegate domains" on page 534, and for general information, see 1.1.7, "Web Portal Manager" on page 10.

▶ Create an Enterprise domain called yri_europe.

▶ Create sub-domain called was.

▶ Create three sub-domains under was.

  Call these sub-domains customers, partners, and employees.

▶ Assign an administrator to each of these domains.

  Using the superuser (sec_master) account, you can assign administrators to all the sub-domains. The administrators for employees, customers, and partners can be different persons, or one and the same. While you should assign a limited number of domain administrators, you should allow helpdesk operators support administrator privileges. This enables them to view Access Manager user account information and reset a user's password in problem situations.

Once these tasks have been performed, an Enterprise domain with a tree of sub-domains has been created, as shown in Figure 10-4 on page 245.

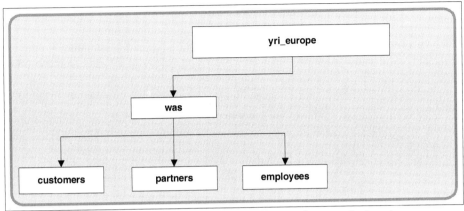

Figure 10-4   YRI enterprise and WebSphere Application Server sub-domains

Compare this figure with Figure 10-2 on page 231 to see the difference between abstract and real implementation.

10.6.5 Creating the junctions

To enable connection to the back-end servers, junctions need to be created. For more information about junctions, see "Platforms" on page 14.

WebSphere Application Server junctions

To enable Web connections to the WebSphere Application Server, the following steps must be completed.

Employees and business partners

Here is how to set up employee and business partner junctions:

For employee and business partner access, create the SSL junction /secure to point to the WebSphere Application Server on the Internet DMZ WebSEALs.

The easier, but less secure, way of configuring an SSL junction is using a one-way authentication, where only the back-end server sends a certificate to WebSEAL. But for testing purposes and non-production environments, these simple junctions will do fine. To create one, use the following syntax:

```
pdadmin server task webseald-servername create -t ssl -c iv_user -h WASserver1
-s /secure
```

The more secure method, the mutually authenticated junction, forces both WebSEAL and the back-end server to authenticate with a certificate. This provides additional protection against someone spoofing the back-end machine. While the back-end server requires its own certificate for all SSL connections, WebSEAL will require its own certificate to be sent to the back-end server for mutually authenticated SSL connections. If you already have a certificate that has been configured for use in WebSEAL, proceed with the following syntax:

```
pdadmin server task webseald-servername create -t ssl -c iv_user -s -h
WASserver1 -K certlabel -s /secure
```

> **Note:** If you do not yet have a certificate in a key database, go to "Key database" on page 538, for information on the steps required to create a database and configure it for WebSEAL.

Because employee access from the intranet DMZ does not require an SSL connection, create a TCP-based junction with the following syntax:

```
pdadmin server task webseald-servername create -t tcp -c iv_user -s -h
WASserver1 -s /secure
```

If you have several WebSphere Application Servers with the same content, and wish to employ these in a load-balancing formation, add these servers with the following command syntax:

```
pdadmin server task webseald-servername add -h WASserver2 /secure
```

Each time you run this command, it adds an additional server to the /secure junction.

> **Note:** When adding additional servers to the junction with the add command, the new server inherits the connection information from the existing junction. Therefore the syntax is the same for both TCP and SSL type junctions.

Customers

Here is the setup for customer junction: Junction /my to point to the WebSphere Application Server.

While employees and business partners can use the same channel to reach the WebSphere Application Server, the /my junction is created to allow for a more marketing-friendly URL for the users.

Switch explanations

In addition to the bare commands, let us briefly recall some of the important switches that have been used in the junction command:

- The switch -t ssl forces the junction to the back-end server to use the SSL protocol for all traffic.

- The -t tcp switch forces the junction to the back-end server to use TCP protocol for all traffic.

- The -c iv_user flag is in the command for the purposes of Trust Association Interceptor, which is discussed in more detail in "Web Trust Association Interceptor (TAI)" on page 135. The switch makes WebSEAL send the user ID in a field called iv-user inside the HTTP request to the back-end.

- The -h WASserver switch is for specifying the host name of the back-end server.

- The -K certlabel switch sets the certificate label to be used by WebSEAL when sending mutual authentication to the back-end server.

- The -s switch, for stateful, means that the so-called *sticky bit* is used. During a session, all the requests from a user are directed to the same server, if the server is available. This allows for consistent session control.

- The -f switch overwrites an existing junction. It is used when updating junctions; for example, when replacing the / junction with a new destination (used in the HTTP server junction).

- The /secure is the name of the junction. All junction names must always have the / in them.

HTTP server junctions

This section describes the steps needed to create junctions for the HTTP server.

- Replace (since it already exists) the root junction / as a TCP junction that points to the HTTP server. Do this on all WebSEAL machines.

```
pdadmin server task webseald-servername create -t tcp -h httpserver -f /
```

This means that any HTTP data being sent from the back-end Web server to WebSEAL will be unencrypted. But since there are no business transactions performed, nor are there any user IDs or passwords transmitted to the back-end Web server, this approach is perfectly sufficient. In this case the balance between risk and performance lets us chose a TCP instead of an SSL junction. Should the nature of the data stored on the HTTP server necessitate an encrypted connection from the Internet DMZ to the back-end HTTP server, use the following syntax on the Internet DMZ WebSEALs:

```
pdadmin server task webseald-servername create -t ssl -h httpserver -f /
```

This will create an SSL junction without mutual authentication. As there is no authentication data being passed, the use of mutual authentication to establish trust is not necessary.

► Local junction /cgi-bin %installdir%/PDWeb/www/docs/cgi-bin.

Local junctions to these paths may be needed since the / junction has been replaced to point to the HTTP server. If the /cgi-bin and /pics directories on the WebSEAL server have content that needs to be served, the junctions become necessary.

► Local junction /pics to point to %installdir%/PDWeb/www/docs/pics.

Note: If the cgi-bin and pics directories exist under the Web document root of your HTTP server, you can merely transfer the contents of the WebSEAL directories to corresponding directories on the HTTP server instead of creating two local junctions for them on the WebSEAL server. If you have placed something in WebSEAL cgi-bin, you should first check if the programs work on your HTTP server platform.

Web Portal Manager junctions

This section specifies the steps needed to create a junction that enables WebSEAL-controlled access to Web Portal Manager. On the intranet DMZ WebSEALs, use the following command for the first Web Portal Manager server:

```
pdadmin server task webseald-servername create -t tcp -b ignore -s -h
wpmserver1 /wpm
```

To add the second Web Portal Manager server to the junction, use:

```
pdadmin server task webseald-servername add -h wpmserver2 /wpm
```

Run these commands only on the intranet DMZ WebSEAL servers. Access to user management will not be available from the Internet.

Once all the junctions have been created, the resulting Web traffic flow should look like the one shown in Figure 10-5 on page 249.

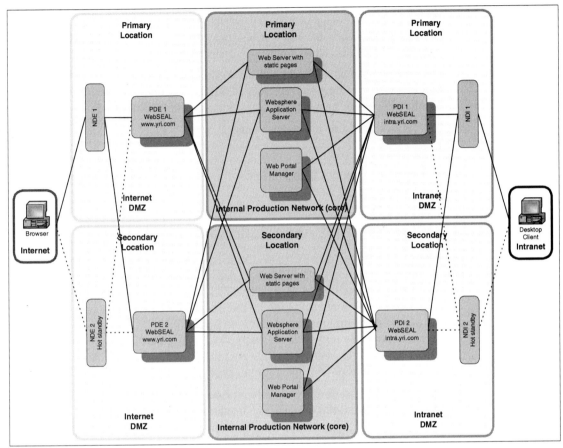

Figure 10-5   Web traffic overview

The dashed lines represent stand-by routes that are only activated by the failure of a primary Network Dispatcher.

10.6.6 External SSL configuration

Per default, WebSEAL creates an SSL certificate for external communications during installation; this certificate is self-signed. The users are forced to accept the certificate every time they connect to the WebSEAL server via SSL.

Instead of using the self-signed certificate, you should request an external certificate from your Certificate Authority. See "Key database" on page 538, for instructions on how to add a certificate into your production key database.

There are three exceptions to the instructions in "Key database" on page 538. These are:

- ► For your production certificate you should select a CA that is supported by most browsers (such as Thawte or VeriSign).

- ► The name of the server will be www.yri.com (alternatively, us.yri.com or asia.yri.com) for Internet DMZ WebSEALs, and intra.yri.com (alternatively, us.intra.yri.com or asia.intra.yri.com) for intranet DMZ WebSEALs.

- ► Set this certificate as the default one.

After restarting the WebSEAL service, you will be able to connect to the WebSEAL server without being prompted to accept the certificate because the browser can now trust it.

10.6.7 Configuration for Trust Association Interceptor

Enabling TAI between WebSEAL and WebSphere is a simple task. However, before this can be done we first have to decide what level of security should be applied to the junction. When you enable TAI, WebSphere completely trusts WebSEAL to authenticate and identify the user. For YRI we have chosen to use a mutually authenticated junction that forces both WebSEAL and the back-end WebSphere server to authenticate each other with a certificate. For more information about TAI, see "Web Trust Association Interceptor (TAI)" on page 135. To configure TAI, follow these procedures:

1. On WebSEAL, create the mutually authenticated junction if you have not already done so. Refer to 10.6.5, "Creating the junctions" on page 245.

2. On the WebSphere server change the values in the trustedservers.properties file located in the *WebSphere_base_install_directory*/Appserver/properties directory, as shown below.

```
trustedservers.properties
com.ibm.websphere.security.trustassociation.enabled=true
com.ibm.websphere.security.trustassociation.types=webseal
com.ibm.websphere.security.trustassociation.webseal.interceptor=com.ibm.ejs
.security.web.WebSealTrustAssociationInterceptor
com.ibm.websphere.security.trustassociation.webseal.config=webseal
```

3. On the WebSphere server, change the values in the webseal.properties file located in the *WebSphere_base_install_directory*/Appserver/properties directory as shown below.

```
webseal.properties
com.ibm.websphere.security.webseal.id=iv-user,iv-groups,iv-creds
com.ibm.websphere.security.webseal.hostnames=poolroom
com.ibm.websphere.security.webseal.ports=443
com.ibm.websphere.security.webseal.mutualSSL=true
com.ibm.websphere.security.webseal.username=pdirector
```

4. Download the WebSealTA.jar file from the WebSphere Advisor Web site onto your WebSphere Application Server machine, and make sure to put it first in your com.ibm.ejs.sm.adminserver.classpath in the admin.config file (and in the adminserver.bat file if you start your admin server from the command line).

5. Stop and re-start WebSphere.

> **Note:** The first thing you notice when you start WebSphere Application Server from the command line is that there are a few lines printed out after the DrAdmin line, which indicate that trust associations are in effect, and the signature string is displayed as `WebSEAL Interceptor Version 1.1`.

10.6.8 Securing access

In this section ACLs are created and attached to objects in order to allow members of each domain to access the appropriate resources assigned to their respective domains.

HTTP server ACLs

This section shows how to create the ACLs for opening most of the HTTP server's pages to the public through WebSEAL while still protecting a part of them.

1. First, make all pages on the HTTP server accessible to the general public.

   Create an ACL called open-acl that allows every user, even the unauthenticated ones, (T)raverse, (r)ead, and e(x)ecute rights. Allow normal administration rights to default administrators and admin groups, which are:

   ```
   iv_admin Tcmdbsvarxl
   sec_master Tcmdbsvarxl
   webseal_servers Tgmdbsrxl
   ```

Attach this ACL to the /WebSEAL/ object. This means you will be replacing default-webseal ACL with open-acl. Alternatively, you can attach the open-acl to /WebSEAL/servername object, but you would have to repeat the procedure on every WebSEAL server, and the effect would be the same.

2. Next, create the ACL to protect the pages on the HTTP server that should only be viewed by YRI employees and business partners.

   Create an ACL called yri_europe-info that allows (T)raverse, (r)ead, and e(x)ecute rights for the groups below to a Web resource, plus all the normal administration users and groups.

   ```
   yri_europe-was-employees-users
   yri_europe-was-employees-admins
   yri_europe-was-employees-domainadmins
   yri_europe-was-employees-sradmins
   yri_europe-was-employees-support
   yri_europe-was-partners-users
   yri_europe-was-partners-admins
   yri_europe-was-partners-domainadmins
   yri_europe-was-partners-sradmins
   yri_europe-was-partners-support
   ```

   Note: These groups were automatically created when you created the delegate domains described in 10.6.4, "Creating delegate domains" on page 244.

   Add the ACL to the /WebSEAL/servername/info/ object on all WebSEAL servers.

   With the exception of the /info/ subdirectory, all the information on your HTTP server is now available to the general public. This is shown in Figure 10-6 on page 253.

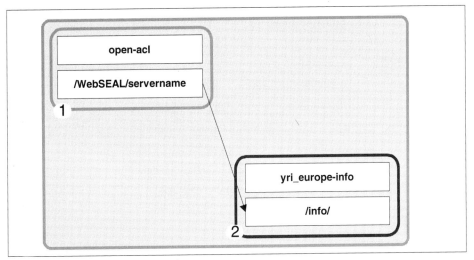

Figure 10-6 HTTP server security

The green box (1) shows the part of the object space open to everyone. The blue box (2) shows the serverspace protected by an ACL.

WebSphere Application Server ACLs

In this section ACLs are created to protect access to different parts of WebSphere Application Server. Employees, partners, and customers will each be allowed access to their respective subdirectories on the WebSphere Application Server.

► To protect access to the WebSphere Application Server's employee resources, complete the following steps:

Create an ACL called yri_europe-was-employees that allows (T)raverse, (r)ead, and e(x)ecute rights for the groups below to a Web resource.

```
yri_europe-was-employees-admins
yri_europe-was-employees-domainadmins
yri_europe-was-employees-sradmins
yri_europe-was-employees-support
yri_europe-was-employees-users
```

Also, add the rights for default admin users and groups.

Figure 10-7 on page 254 shows how the ACL should look at this point. Note the extra permissions that the sec_master user and iv_admin group have; these are the default rights for the maintenance of the object space.

Entry Name	Type	Permissions
☐ sec_master	User	Tcmdbsvarxl
☐ iv-admin	Group	Tcmdbsvarxl
☐ webseal-servers	Group	Tgmdbsrxl
☐ yri_europe-was-employees-Admins	Group	Trx
☐ yri_europe-was-employees-DomainAdmins	Group	Trx
☐ yri_europe-was-employees-SrAdmins	Group	Trx
☐ yri_europe-was-employees-Support	Group	Trx
☐ yri_europe-was-employees-Users	Group	Trx
☐	Any-other	T
☐	Unauthenticated	T

Figure 10-7   ACL example

> **Tip:** You can use a clone of the default-webseal ACL as a starting base again. Set Any-Other access to T(raverse), then add the yri-europe groups.

To allow this ACL to be used to protect WebSphere Application Server applications, add a special [WebAppServer](i)nvoke permission to the groups listed above. The [WebAppServer] action group has been created automatically by the WebSphere Application Server migration tool.

Attach the ACL to the /WebSEAL/servername/secure/employees/ object on all WebSEAL servers.

The WebSphere Application Server migration tool has created a new object space under /WebAppServer. Inside it you can find /WebAppServer/deployedResources/, which contains all the resources on your WebSphere Application Server.

Attach the ACL to all entries under /WebAppServer/deployedResources/ that you want the employees to be able to access. For example:

```
acl attach /WebAppServer/deployedResources/YRIListInsurance
yri_europe-was-employees
```

> **Note:** There may be an automatically created ACL already attached to the resource by the migration utility. In this case, detach the automatically created ACL and add the one you created.

▶ To protect access to the partners resources on the WebSphere Application Server, complete the following steps:

Create an ACL called yri_europe-was-partners that allows (T)raverse, (r)ead, and e(x)ecute rights for the groups below to a Web resource:

```
yri_europe-was-partners-admins
yri_europe-was-partners-domainadmins
yri_europe-was-partners-sradmins
yri_europe-was-partners-support
yri_europe-was-partners-users
```

Also, add the rights for default admin users and groups.

To allow this ACL to be used to protect WebSphere Application Server applications add a special [WebAppServer](i)nvoke right to the groups listed above.

Attach the ACL to the /WebSEAL/servername/secure/partners/ object on all Internet DMZ WebSEAL servers.

Attach the ACL to all entries under /WebAppServer/deployedResources/ that you want your business partners to be able to access.

▶ To protect access to the customer resources on the WebSphere Application Server, complete the following steps:

Create an ACL called yri_europe-was-customers that allows (T)raverse, (r)ead, and e(x)ecute rights for the groups below to a Web resource:

```
yri_europe-was-customers-admins
yri_europe-was-customers-domainadmins
yri_europe-was-customers-sradmins
yri_europe-was-customers-support
yri_europe-was-customers-users
```

Add default administration rights here too.

To allow this ACL to be used to protect WebSphere Application Server applications add a special [WebAppServer](i)nvoke right to the groups listed above.

Attach the ACL to the /WebSEAL/servername/my/profile/ object on all Internet DMZ WebSEAL servers.

Attach the ACL to all entries under /WebAppServer/deployedResources/ that you want the customers to be able to access.

► To create and implement the ACL that acts as a higher level protection to the WebSphere Application Server resources, complete the following steps:

Create an ACL that allows Unauthenticated and Any-Other (T)raverse access, because higher level admins and administration groups should be allowed traversing rights in order to administer their portions of the name space. Remove (r)ead and e(x)ecute permissions from this ACL.

Add this ACL to /WebSEAL/servername/secure and /WebSEAL/servername/my on all WebSEAL servers.

Now the access to the WebSphere Application Server Web resources is enabled for all users and administrators belonging to the appropriate groups. Customers can only access the /my/profile/ object, while employees can only access the /secure/employees/ object, and business partners will be able to access the /secure/partners/ object.

The structure of the object tree and the ACLs that protect them is illustrated in Figure 10-8 on page 257. The small green box (1) depicts an area where unauthenticated access is available; blue boxes (2) depict areas where access is allowed only to certain group(s). The red area (3) contains resources where no read and execute access is available; only traversing to a lower level of the tree to check for rights is allowed for non-administrators.

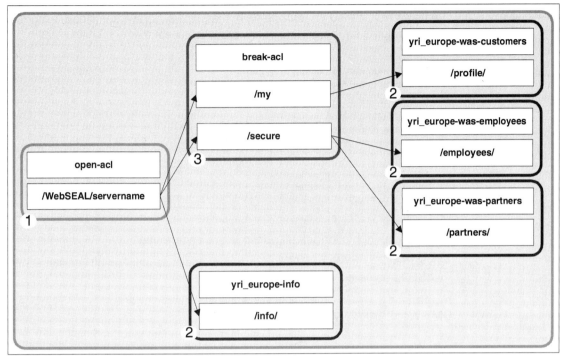

Figure 10-8   WebSphere Application Server and HTTP server security

For added security, there is an ACL on the WebSphere Application Server root level (/secure and /my junction point to the root of the WebSphere Application Server) to disallow all access unless specifically allowed further down the tree.

In some cases it might be important to limit access to Web pages for some administrators. For example, to disallow customer Support Administrators access to the Web resources assigned to their domain, the following changes must be made: The yri_europe-was-customers (or partners or employees) support group must be removed from the employee, partner, and customer ACLs.

This way you can lock out helpdesk operators from the Web resource, while still allowing them the rights to perform support tasks for users in their domain.

Web Portal Manager ACLs

This section shows how to create and attach the ACLs that protect the Web Portal Manager server while allowing administrators access to user information.

To enable security for the Web Portal Manager servers, do the following:

1. Create an ACL called yri_europe-wpm that allows (T)raverse, (r)ead, and e(x)ecute rights for the groups below to a Web resource.

```
yri_europe-was-employees-admins
yri_europe-was-employees-domainadmins
yri_europe-was-employees-sradmins
yri_europe-was-employees-support
yri_europe-was-customers-admins
yri_europe-was-customers-domainadmins
yri_europe-was-customers-sradmins
yri_europe-was-customers-support
yri_europe-was-partners-admins
yri_europe-was-partners-domainadmins
yri_europe-was-partners-sradmins
yri_europe-was-partners-support
```

Also, add the rights for default admin users and groups.

2. Attach this ACL to /WebSEAL/servername/wpm/pdadmin/ on all intranet DMZ WebSEAL servers.

3. Next attach the ACL break-acl to /WebSEAL/servername/wpm/ on all intranet DMZ WebSEAL servers.

Now all Web access to Web Portal Manager servers is blocked, except for the /pdadmin/ subdirectory, which contains the administration tool. Access to the /pdadmin/ directory is allowed for all the administrators of different sub-domains, as shown in Figure 10-9 on page 259.

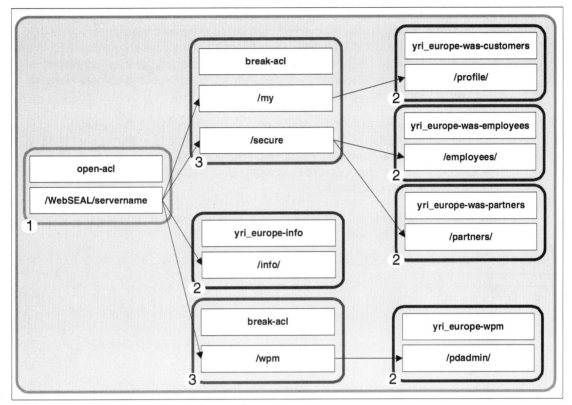

Figure 10-9   Complete server security overview

As you can see in Figure 10-9, all access to WebSphere Application Server and Web Portal Manager servers is restricted by default, with three subdirectories as exceptions. The HTTP server, on the other hand, allows all access to the /info/ subdirectory.

10.6.9 Network Dispatcher installation

The Network Dispatcher machines, located in the DMZ, are used to provide high availability and load balancing for the WebSEAL reverse proxy servers. The Internet and the intranet DMZ each have a Network Dispatcher machine allocated for this purpose. The balanced Web traffic is routed to two WebSEAL machines that are both located within the same secure domain. For example, PDE1 and PDE2 (see Figure 10-5 on page 249) host the Web domain www.yri.com. Network Dispatcher NDE1 will send a request for access to www.yri.com through PDE1 WebSEAL or PDE2 WebSEAL according to the configured load-balancing algorithms defined for NDE1.

Should the PDE1 Machine fail, Network Dispatcher NDE1 will simply route the traffic to www.yri.com through PDE2. In addition to the load-balancing mechanism, this provides the Web site with a fail-over capability. In Figure 10-5 on page 249 additional Network Dispatcher machines are shown as NDE2 in the Internet DMZ and NDI2 in the intranet DMZ. These are hot stand-by Network Dispatcher machines, which will take over the function of the primary Network Dispatcher machines should these fail.

This section describes the installation and configuration of the Network Dispatcher machines that are placed in the Internet and in the intranet DMZ. We will not describe Network Dispatcher in detail in this section. For more information, see the *Network Dispatcher User's Guide Version 3.0 for Multiplatforms,* GC31-8496.

We have added IP addresses to Figure 10-10 on page 261; these will be used in this section to illustrate the configuration examples.

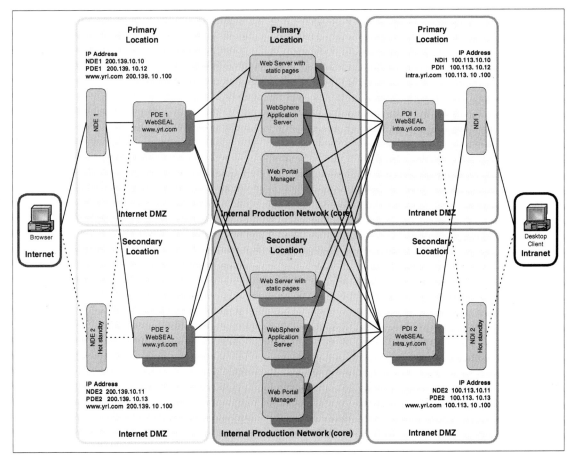

Figure 10-10 Network Dispatchers with IP addresses

Setup for the YRI installation

The following components and settings have been selected for Network Dispatcher:

► IBM RS/6000-based machine

► IBM AIX Version 4.3.3

► 50 MB of available disk space for installation

Note: Additional disk space will be needed for logs.

- ► 100 Mb Ethernet
- ► IBM Java Development Kit (JDK) Version 1.1.8 or higher (but not 1.2.x versions)
- ► Netscape Navigator 4.7 (or higher) or Netscape Communicator 4.76i (or higher) for viewing online Help

Note: The Network Dispatcher software is shipped on the WebSphere Edge Server CDs.

Network information and terms used

The following network information and terms are used:

Cluster address
    The IP address used by the clients to reach YRI's Web services

Non-Forwarding Address (NFA)
    The IP address of the Network Dispatcher host machine

The host machines running Network Dispatcher functions are:

```
NDE1.intra.yri.com (200.139.10.10)
NDE2.intra.yri.com (200.139.10.11)
NDI1.intra.yri.com (100.113.10.10)
NDI2.intra.yri.com (100.113.10.11)
```

The host machines running WebSEAL are:

```
PDE1.intra.yri.com (200.139.10.12)
PDE2.intra.yri.com (200.139.10.13)
PDI1.intra.yri.com (100.113.10.12)
PDI2.intra.yri.com (100.113.10.13)
```

The CLUSTER acronyms and addresses are:

```
www.yri.com        IP 200.139.10.100
intra.yri.com      IP 100.113.10.100
```

Note: For better readability we are using capitalized host names in the configuration files although the real world configuration will probably use lowercase names.

Preparations before installing Network Dispatcher

The following tasks need to be performed before actually installing and configuring Network Dispatcher.

1. Where possible, configure your Network Dispatcher and WebSEAL machines so that they are located on the same LAN segment. If this is not possible, ensure that network traffic between Network Dispatcher and WebSEAL does not have to pass through any routers or bridges that will change the IP packets.

2. Configure the network adapters on the Network Dispatcher machines. For this example we will assume you have the following network configuration:

Network Dispatcher Machines

```
NDE1.intra.yri.com (200.139.10.10)
NDE2.intra.yri.com (200.139.10.11)
NDI1.intra.yri.com (100.113.10.10)
NDI2.intra.yri.com (100.113.10.11)
```

> **Note:** In our example the machines contain only one standard Ethernet network interface card.

3. Ensure that Network Dispatcher machines can ping both WebSEAL machines.

4. Ensure that the WebSEAL machines are operational.

5. Use a valid IP address for the Web domains. This is the address we will provide for browser clients who wish to access our site—it is the cluster address. For this example we will use:

```
Web address    ip Address      netmask
www.yri.com    200.139.10.100  255.255.255.128 (0xffffff80)
intra.yri.com  100.113.10.100  255.255.255.224 (0xffffffe0)
```

6. Configure the Internet WebSEALs to accept traffic for www.yri.com. You must add an alias for www.yri.com to the loopback interface on PDE1 and PDE2.

> **Note:** In our configuration we are using the mac forwarding method, the Dispatcher component does not change the destination IP address in the TCP/IP packet before forwarding the packet to a WebSEAL server. By setting an alias for the loopback device to the cluster address on WebSEAL servers, the Dispatcher machines will load balance and accept packets for the cluster address.

Use this command on PDE1 and PDE2 machines:

```
/usr/sbin/ifconfig lo0 alias 200.139.10.100 netmask 255.255.255.128
```

Add the same command line into the file /etc/rc.net within part II of the file as shown below:

```
# (Remember that if you have more than one interface,
# you'll want to have a different IP address for each one.
# Below, xx.xx.xx.xx stands for the internet address for the
# given interface).
#
/usr/sbin/ifconfig lo0 alias 200.139.10.100 netmask 0xffffff80 >>$LOGFILE
2>&1
#/usr/sbin/ifconfig en0 inet `hostname`  up >>$LOGFILE 2>&1
#/usr/sbin/ifconfig et0 inet xx.xx.xx.xx  up >>$LOGFILE 2>&1
#/usr/sbin/ifconfig tr0 inet xx.xx.xx.xx  up >>$LOGFILE 2>&1
```

After adding the ifconfig line to rc.net, make sure that it has the proper bit mask applied to the file. Use the command **ls -l /etc/rc.net** to list and verify that the bit mask settings are similar to:

```
-rwxrwxr--  1 bin     bin        7857 jun 01 11:10 /etc/rc.net
```

Check the loopback settings by issuing the following command:

```
ifconfig -a
```

It should produce an output similar to the following for the lo0 interface. (Notice the two addresses on the ln0-interface! One is the loopback address 127.0.0.1, and the other one is the cluster address=200.139.10.100.)

```
lo0:
flags=e08084b<UP,BROADCAST,LOOPBACK,RUNNING,SIMPLEX,MULTICAST,GROUPRT,64BIT
>
        inet 127.0.0.1 netmask 0xff000000 broadcast 127.255.255.255
        inet6 ::1/0
        inet 200.139.10.100 netmask 0xffffff80 broadcast 200.139.10.255
en0:
flags=4e080863<UP,BROADCAST,NOTRAILERS,RUNNING,SIMPLEX,MULTICAST,GROUPRT,64
BIT,PSEG>
        inet 200.139.10.12 netmask 0xffffff00 broadcast 200.139.10.255
```

7. Repeat the configuration steps shown in step 6 for the intranet WebSEALs to accept traffic for intra.yri.com. Use the correct IP address for this network segment.

Installing Network Dispatcher software

Network Dispatcher software is available on the CDs supplied with the WebSphere Edge Server Version 2.0 Suite. Here are the AIX installation steps:

1. Log in as ROOT.

2. Put the CD in the CD-drive, and start smitty. Go to **Software Installation and Maintenance -> Install and Update Software -> Install and update from latest available software**. At the Input device field, supply the necessary information to select the CDROM-drive, and select **List** to see the CD's contents. Select the file sets for Network Dispatcher.

   After you have successfully installed and applied the software, exit smitty.

3. Verify that the file sets for the product are installed. Enter the following command:

   ```
   lslpp -l | grep intnd
   ```

   If you installed the full product, this command returns the following:

   ```
   intnd.admin.rte              COMMITTED  ND Base Administration
   intnd.cbr.license            COMMITTED  ND Content Based Routing
   intnd.cbr.rte                COMMITTED  ND Content Based Routing
   intnd.cbradmin.rte           COMMITTED  ND Content Based Routing
   intnd.doc.rte                COMMITTED  ND Documentation
   intnd.iss.license             COMMITTED  ND Interactive Session Support
   intnd.iss.rte                COMMITTED  ND Interactive Session Support
   intnd.issadmin.rte            OMMITTED  ND Interactive Session Support
   intnd.msg.en_US.admin.rte  COMMITTED  ND Base Admin Messages -U.S.
   intnd.msg.en_US.cbr.rte    COMMITTED  ND CBR Messages -U.S. English
   intnd.msg.en_US.cbradmin.rte
   intnd.msg.en_US.doc        COMMITTED  Network Dispatcher
   intnd.msg.en_US.iss.rte    COMMITTED  ND ISS Messages -U.S. English
   intnd.msg.en_US.issadmin.rte
   intnd.msg.en_US.nd.rte     COMMITTED  ND Dispatcher Messages -U.S.
   intnd.msg.en_US.ndadmin.rte
   intnd.nd.driver              COMMITTED  ND Dispatcher Device Driver
   intnd.nd.license             COMMITTED  ND Dispatcher License
   intnd.nd.rte                 COMMITTED  ND Dispatcher
   intnd.ndadmin.rte            COMMITTED  ND Dispatcher Administration
   ```

   The software is now installed and ready for configuration.

10.6.10 Configuring Network Dispatcher components

This section will provide a configuration example for YRI. Detailed configuration, operation, and maintenance of the Network Dispatcher is covered in the Network Dispatcher manual, *Network Dispatcher User's Guide Version 3.0 for Multiplatforms*, GC31-8496. This PDF file comes with the Network Dispatcher distribution and can be found in the directory /usr/lpp/nd/documentation. In addition, there is a separately available IBM Redbook called *IBM WebSphere Performance Pack Load Balancing with IBM SecureWay Network Dispatcher*, SG24-5858.

Planning considerations

Have ready the cluster address, and NFA and WebSEAL server addresses, so that these addresses may be edited into the appropriate scripts. We assume that for the machines placed in the Internet DMZ (see Figure 10-5 on page 249), NDE1 will be the primary Network Dispatcher, and NDE2 will be the hot stand-by machine.

Configuring the Network Dispatcher for high availability

Three high-availability scripts are supplied with Network Dispatcher. They are used when the high-availability fail-over mode is enabled. They activate or deactivate the interface(s) for the cluster address when a dispatcher changes its state from standby to active, or active to standby. These scripts are not for you to execute manually. Just move them to the correct location and configure them according to your requirements.

Sample scripts are shipped with the product; they are:

```
/usr/lpp/nd/dispatcher/samples/goActive.sample
/usr/lpp/nd/dispatcher/samples/goStandby.sample
/usr/lpp/nd/dispatcher/samples/goInOp.sample
```

The scripts must be renamed and placed in this directory:

```
/usr/lpp/nd/dispatcher/bin/goActive
/usr/lpp/nd/dispatcher/bin/goStandby
/usr/lpp/nd/dispatcher/bin/goInOp
```

For NDE1 and NDE2 the scripts must be modified similar to these examples. The lines that have to be changed are in bold.

The GoActive script

```
#!/bin/ksh
#ND_LOGDIR=/usr/lpp/nd/dispatcher/logs
NETWORK=200.139.10
INTERFACE=en0
NETMASK=0xffffff00
#
#    date >> $ND_LOGDIR/ha.log
#    print "This machine is Active.  Aliasing cluster address(es) to NIC \n" >>
$ND_LOGDIR
/ha.log
   for CLUSTER in 100; do
      ifconfig lo0 delete $NETWORK.$CLUSTER
      ifconfig $INTERFACE alias $NETWORK.$CLUSTER netmask $NETMASK
   done
```

> **Note:** The goActive script is executed when a dispatcher goes into active mode and begins routing packets.

The goStandby script

```ksh
#!/bin/ksh
#ND_LOGdIR=/usr/lpp/nd/dispatcher/logs
NETWORK=200.139.10
INTERFACE=en0
NETMASK=0xffffff00
#
#   date >> $ND_LOGDIR/ha.log
#   print "Going into Standby mode.\n" >> $ND_LOGDIR/ha.log
#   print "Deleting the device aliases and adding the loopback aliases" >>
$ND_LOGDIR/ha.log
  for CLUSTER in 100; do
     ifconfig $INTERFACE delete $NETWORK.$CLUSTER
     ifconfig lo0 alias $NETWORK.$CLUSTER netmask $NETMASK
  done
```

> **Note:** The goStandby script is executed when a dispatcher goes into standby mode, monitoring the health of the active machine, but does not route any packets.

The goInOp script

```ksh
#!/bin/ksh
#ND_LOGDIR=/usr/lpp/nd/dispatcher/logs
NETWORK=200.139.10
INTERFACE=en0
#
#   date >> $ND_LOGDIR/ha.log
#   print "Executor has stopped.  Removing loopback and device aliases. \n" >>
$ND_LOGDIR
/ha.log
  for CLUSTER in 100; do
    ifconfig lo0 delete $NETWORK.$CLUSTER
    ifconfig $INTERFACE delete $NETWORK.$CLUSTER
  done
```

> **Note:** The goInOp script is executed when a dispatcher executor is stopped and before it is started for the first time.

This should be repeated for NDI1 and NDI2 dispatchers using the correct IP address for the machines in the intra.yri.com domain.

Configuration script for Network Dispatcher

The configuration script is located at
/usr/lpp/nd/dispatcher/samples/configuration.sample.

Copy and rename it /usr/lpp/nd/dispatcher/configurations/configuration and make
sure that the script is owned by root and has permissions 0700.

The lines that have to be added or changed are in bold.

Remember to do the same for all Network Dispatcher machines.

```
#!/bin/ksh
#
# configuration.sample - Sample configuration file for the Dispatcher
component.
#
# This script must be placed in Network Dispatcher's configurations directory
# (nd/dispatcher/configurations/) to be used by Dispatcher, and it needs to
have
# root read and execute permissions.
#
# Ensure the root user is the one executing this script.
#
iam=`whoami`
if [ "$iam" != "root" ]
  then
    echo "You must login as root to run this script"
    exit 2
fi
#
# First start the server
#
ndserver start
sleep 5

#
# Then start the executor
#
ndcontrol executor start

#
#  The Dispatcher can be removed at any time using the "ndcontrol executor
# stop" and "ndserver stop" commands to stop the executor and server
# respectively prior to removing the Dispatcher software.
#
#  The next step in configuring the Dispatcher is to set the NFA
# (non-forwarding address) and the cluster address(es).
#
```

```
#  The NFA is used to remotely access the Dispatcher machine for administration
# or configuration purposes.  This address is required since the Dispatcher
# will forward packets to the cluster address(es).
#
# The CLUSTER address is the hostname (or IP address) to which remote clients
# will connect.
#
# Anywhere in this file, you may use hostnames and IP addresses
# interchangeably.
#
#DMZ addresses
#
# NDE1.intra.yri.com (200.139.10.10)
# NDE2.intra.yri.com (200.139.10.11)
#
#
# INTRA addresses
#
# NDI1.intra.yri.com (100.113.10.10)
# NDI2.intra.yri.com (100.113.10.11)

#

# the cluster addresses involved
# DMZ - www.yri.com (200.139.10.100)
# INTRA - intra.www.yri.com (100.113.10.100)


# NFApri is the IP address of the primary network dispatcher in a high
# availability env.
# NFAbackup is the IP address of the backup network dispatcher in a high
# availability env.
NFApri= 200.139.10.10
NFAbackup= 200.139.10.11
CLUSTER=200.139.10.100


# If on a PRIMARY ND, use the following 2 lines. Then comment out these
# two lines.
echo "Loading the non-forwarding address"
ndcontrol executor set nfa $NFApri

# If on a SECONDARY ND, use the following 2 lines. Remember to remove
# the comment signes.
#echo "Loading the non-forwarding address"
#ndcontrol executor set nfa $NFAbackup


#
#  The next step in configuring the Dispatcher is to create a cluster.  The
# Dispatcher will route requests sent to the cluster address to the
# corresponding server machines defined to that cluster.You may configure and
```

```
# server multiple cluster address using Dispatcher.
# Use a similar configuration for CLUSTER2, CLUSTER3, etc.
#
echo "Loading first CLUSTER address "
ndcontrol cluster add $CLUSTER


#
# Now we must define the ports this cluster will use.  Any requests received by
# the Dispatcher on a defined port will be forwarded to the corresponding port
# of one of the server machines.
#
echo "Creating ports for CLUSTER: $CLUSTER"
ndcontrol port add $CLUSTER:80+443


#
# The last step is to add each of the server machines to the ports in this
# cluster.Again, you can use either the hostname or the IP address of the
# server machines.
#
# PDE1.intra.yri.com (200.139.10.12)
# PDE2.intra.yri.com (200.139.10.13)
#
SERVER1= 200.139.10.12
SERVER2= 200.139.10.13


echo "Adding server machines"
ndcontrol server add $CLUSTER:80+443:$SERVER1+$SERVER2


#
#  We will now start the load balancing components of the Dispatcher.  The main
# load balancing component is called the manager and the second load balancing
# components are the advisors.  If the manager and advisors are not running the
# Dispatcher sends requests in a round-robin format. Once the manager is
# started, weighting decisions based on the number of new and active
# connections is employed and incoming requests are sent to the best server.
# The advisors give the manager further insight into a servers ability to
# service requests as well as detecting whether a server is up. If
# an advisor detects that a server is down it will be marked down (providing
# the manager proportions have been set to include advisor input) and no
# further requests will be routed to the server.
# The last step in setting up the load balancing components is to set the
# manager proportions. The manager updates the weight of each of the servers
# based on four policies:
#    1. The number of active connections on each server.
#    2. The number of new connections to each server.
#    3. Input from the advisors.
#    4. Input from the system level advisor (ISS).
# These proportions must add up to 100. As an example, setting the manager
# proportions to ndcontrol manager proportions 48 48 4 0
```

```
# will give active and new connections 48% input into the weighting decision,
# the advisors will contribute 4% and the system input will not be considered.
#
# NOTE: By default the manager proportions are set to 50 50 0 0
#


echo "Starting the manager..."
ndcontrol manager start

#echo "Starting the FTP advisor on port 21 ..."
#ndcontrol advisor start ftp 21
echo "Starting the HTTP advisor on port 80 ..."
ndcontrol advisor start http 80
# echo "Starting the Telnet advisor on port 23 ..."
#ndcontrol advisor start telnet 23
# echo "Starting the SMTP advisor on port 25 ..."
# ndcontrol advisor start smtp 25
# echo "Starting the POP3 advisor on port 110 ..."
# ndcontrol advisor start pop3 110
# echo "Starting the NNTP advisor on port 119 ..."
# ndcontrol advisor start nntp 119
echo "Starting the SSL advisor on port 443 ..."
ndcontrol advisor start ssl 443
#


echo "Setting the manager proportions..."
ndcontrol manager proportions 58 40 2 0


# The final step in setting up the Dispatcher machine is to alias the Network
#Interface Card (NIC).
#
# NOTE: Do NOT use this command in a high availability environment. The go*
# scripts will configure the NIC and loopback as necessary.
# ndcontrol cluster configure $CLUSTER


# Added for high availability services. This configures the machine as the
# primary ND server on reboot. If you are on a secondary ND, comment out the
#following 2 lines
ndcontrol highavailability heartbeat add $NFApri $NFAbackup
ndcontrol highavailability backup add primary auto 10089


# Added for high availability services.  This configures the machine as the
# backup
# ND server on reboot. If you are on a primary ND, leave the 2 following lines
#commented out.
#dcontrol highavailability heartbeat add $NFAbackup $NFApri
#dcontrol highavailability backup add backup auto 10089
```

```
# If your cluster address is on a different NIC or subnet from the NFA use the
# following format for the cluster configure command. ndcontrol cluster
# configure $CLUSTER tr0 0xfffff800 where tr0 is your NIC (tr1 for the second
# token ring card, en0 for the first ethernet card) and 0xfffff800 is a valid
# subnet mask for your site.
#
#Setting Sticky time interval in seconds
echo " Setting stickybit to 720..."
ndcontrol port set $CLUSTER:80 stickytime 720
ndcontrol port set $CLUSTER:443 stickytime 720
```

> **Note:** By default, the sticky bit is set to 0 and this means a non-persistent session. For a client session, the dispatcher routes each request according to the load on the WebSEAL servers. The result could be that the dispatcher sends the session cookie to the wrong WebSEAL server, and the session would be lost. When the sticky bit is given a value greater than 0, this value is used to define a time in seconds for a session persistence. With this sticky bit set, Network Dispatcher will ensure that the cookie is sent back to the originating WebSEAL server. The time required for a persistent session will depend on the Web application and can be set accordingly.

```
# The following commands are set to the default values.
# Use these commands as a guide to change from the defaults.
#  ndcontrol manager loglevel     1
#  ndcontrol manager logsize      unlimited
#  ndcontrol manager sensitivity 5.000000
#  ndcontrol manager interval     2
#  ndcontrol manager refresh      2
#
#  ndcontrol advisor interval ftp    21  5
#  ndcontrol advisor loglevel ftp    21  1
#  ndcontrol advisor logsize  ftp    21  unlimited
#  ndcontrol advisor timeout  ftp    21  unlimited
#  ndcontrol advisor interval telnet 23 5
#  ndcontrol advisor loglevel telnet 23 1
#  ndcontrol advisor logsize  telnet 23 unlimited
#  ndcontrol advisor timeout  telnet 23 unlimited
#  ndcontrol advisor interval smtp 25 5
#  ndcontrol advisor loglevel smtp 25 1
#  ndcontrol advisor logsize  smtp  25  unlimited
#  ndcontrol advisor timeout  smtp  25  unlimited
#  ndcontrol advisor interval http 80  5
#  ndcontrol advisor loglevel http 80  1
#  ndcontrol advisor logsize  http  80  unlimited
#  ndcontrol advisor timeout  http  80  unlimited
#  ndcontrol advisor interval pop3 110 5
#  ndcontrol advisor loglevel pop3 110 1
```

```
# ndcontrol advisor logsize   pop3 110 unlimited
# ndcontrol advisor timeout   pop3 110 unlimited
# ndcontrol advisor interval  nntp 119 5
# ndcontrol advisor loglevel  nntp 119 1
# ndcontrol advisor logsize   nntp 119 unlimited
# ndcontrol advisor timeout   nntp 119 unlimited
# ndcontrol advisor interval  ssl  443 5
# ndcontrol advisor loglevel  ssl  443 1
# ndcontrol advisor logsize   ssl  443 unlimited
# ndcontrol advisor timeout   ssl  443 unlimited
```

This script must be executed when the Network Dispatcher machine is rebooted, or if the Network Dispatcher must be restarted. Modify the file /etc/rc.tcpip and add the following line to the end of the file:

```
/usr/lpp/nd/dispatcher/configurations/configuration
```

To start the Network Dispatcher software, run this configuration script. Remember to do the same for NDE2, NDI1, and NDI2.

> **Note:** When two dispatcher machines are run in high-availability configuration and are synchronized, it is recommended that you enter all ndcontrol commands on the standby machine first, and then on the active machine.
>
> When running two dispatcher machines in a high-availability configuration, unexpected results may occur if you set any of the parameters for the executor, cluster, port, or server (for example, port stickytime) to different values on the two machines.

Network Dispatcher verification

Set up of the cluster, port, and server information can be verified with the following commands shown as examples executed on NDE1 or NDE2.

Server status command

```
ndcontrol server status 200.139.10.100:443+80:200.139.10.12+200.139.10.13
```

The output should look similar to this:

```
Server Status:------------
Server address ................ 200.139.10.12
Port number ....................443
Cluster address ............... 200.139.10.100
Server up ......................Y
Weight .........................10
Fixed weight ...................N
Sticky for rule ...............Y
Remote server ................. N
```

```
Router address ................. 0.0.0.0
Collocated .....................N

Server Status:------------
Server address ................. 200.139.10.12
Port number ....................443
Cluster address ............... 200.139.10.100
Server up ......................Y
Weight .........................10
Fixed weight ...................N
Sticky for rule ................Y
Remote server .................. N
Router address ................. 0.0.0.0
Collocated .....................N

Server Status:------------
Server address ................. 200.139.10.13
Port number .................... 80
Cluster address ............... 200.139.10.100
Server up ...................... Y
Weight ......................... 10
Fixed weight ................... N
Sticky for rule ............... Y
Remote server .................. N
Router address ................. 0.0.0.0
Collocated ..................... N

Server Status:------------
Server address ................. 200.139.10.13
Port number ........... ........ 80
Cluster address ........... .... 200.139.10.100
Server up ...................... Y
Weight ......................... 10
Fixed weight ................... N
Sticky for rule ............... Y
Remote server .................. N
Router address ................. 0.0.0.0
Collocated ..................... N
```

Cluster status command

```
ndcontrol cluster status 200.139.10.100
```

The output should look similar to this:

```
Cluster Status:
---------------
Address ............................... 200.139.10.100
Number of target ports ................ 2
Maximum number of ports................ 8
```

```
Default maximum number of servers ...... 32
Default sticky time ................... 0
Default port weight bound ......    20
Default port type .................... tcp/udp
Default stale timeout ................. 300
Primary Host Address ..........          200.139.10.10
```

Port status command

```
ndcontrol port status 200.139.10.100:80
```

The output should look similar to this:

```
Port Status:------------
Port number ................... 80
Cluster address ............... 200.139.10.100
Number of servers ............. 2
Stale timeout ............ .... 300
Weight bound .................. 20
Maximum number of servers ...... 32
Sticky time ................... 720
Port type .................... tcp/udp
Sticky mask bits .............. 32
Cross Port Affinity............ 80
```

Checking the weight and other related information please use the following command:

```
Ndcontrol manager report
```

Checking the Network Dispatcher operational status

To check whether the Network Dispatcher processes are running properly, use the **ps** and **netstat** commands to verify that the required ports are established.

First, a **ps -ef** command should reveal whether the Network Dispatcher overseer program is running on port 10099. **0>ps -ef** results in the following output:

```
UID      PID  PPID  C   STIME   TTY  TIME CMD
15102 pts/0 A      0:43 java com/ibm/internet/nd/server/SRV_ConfigServer 10099
```

Second, a **netstat -an** command should reveal whether the configuration file has been read and necessary ports are established. **0>netstat -an** results in the following output:

```
Active Internet connections (including servers)
Proto Recv-Q SND-Q Local Address      Foreign Address      (state)
tcp4     0     0  *.10004              *.*                  LISTEN
tcp4     0     0  *.10005              *.*                  LISTEN
tcp4     0     0  *.10099              *.*                  LISTEN
```

If these processes and sockets are not correct, then you will have to start the Network Dispatcher overseer and load the configuration file. Checking primary and backup synchronization can be done with the following command:

```
ndcontrol highavailability status
```

It should produce an output similar to this one on the primary (the active) dispatcher:

```
High Availability Status:-
Role ................ Primary
Recovery strategy .... Auto
State ............... Active
Sub-state ........... Synchronized
Primary host ........ 200.139.10.10
Port ................ 10089
Preferred target ..... 200.139.10.11

Heartbeat Status:-------
Count ............... 2
Source/destination ... 200.139.10.10/200.139.10.11
Source/destination ... 200.139.10.11/200.139.10.10

Reachability Status:--
Count ............... 0
```

The same output on the backup (secondary) dispatcher would be:

```
High Availability Status:--
Role ... ............ Backup
Recovery strategy .... Auto
State ............... Standby
Sub-state ........... Synchronized
Primary host ........ 200.139.10.10
Port .................10089
Preferred target ..... 200.139.10.10

Heartbeat Status:
-----------------
Count .......................... 1
Source/destination ... 200.139.10.10/200.139.10.11
```

Stop and start of Network Dispatcher

When the RS/6000 is rebooted, it may be necessary to restart the Network Dispatcher processes manually. To do this, run the configuration script located in /usr/lpp/nd/dispatcher/configurations/configuration.

To stop the Network Dispatcher completely, issue the command:

```
ndcontrol executor stop
```

You can also use the AIX **kill** command. Get hold of the process ID by issuing a **ps -ef | grep nd**. One of the lines will contain dispatcher. Use the **kill** command to kill the process listed by the **ps -ef | grep nd** command.

You can stop the individual Network Dispatcher processes with the following commands:

```
ndcontrol executor stop
ndcontrol advisor stop
ndcontrol manager stop ssl 443
ndcontrol manager stop http 80
```

More information on these commands can be found in *WebSphere Edge Server: Working with Web Traffic Express & Network Dispatcher*, SG24-6172.

10.6.11 Hosting multiple Web domains

In the scenario described in this section we have used a single Web domain for YRI, www.yri.com. We have assumed that Yellow Rose Insurance could offer to the public all its new and existing Internet services through a single Web domain with the URL www.yri.com. Therefore, the architectural design shown in this section has used a single primary WebSEAL instance, and a single secondary WebSEAL instance, running on an AIX server. In the Internet DMZ these WebSEALs are hosting www.yri.com, and in the intranet DMZ they host intra.yri.com.

Many companies today offer their Internet service to the public though different Web domains. The reasons for this vary; it may be historical, a takeover of a company with a Web site, for example, where the parent company wishes to maintain separate profiles. It may be due to company branding; that the easy-to-remember brand name is used in the Web domain name. Whatever the reason, from an Access Manager perspective there is a real need to host these Web domains using multiple WebSEAL instances on the same server. Access Manager Version 3.9 includes the ability to have multiple WebSEAL servers running on the same machine.

Suppose that YRI can justify the use of multiple WebSEAL instances; let us look at how this would affect the original architectural design. We will assume for the purpose of this exercise that YRI has a shipping subsidiary that will retain its own Web domain; the URL for this is www.ship-yri.com.

In this case, a different WebSEAL server instance is used for each hosted site, and it is running on the same machine. Each protocol of each server instance requires a different IP Address/port combination. Since Web Services are usually expected to be on port 80 and 443, this usually requires that either multiple IP addresses are allocated, or that there is a front-end device (load balancer, for example) that can map incoming requests to different ports of the same IP address.

> **Note:** The way in which multiple WebSEAL instances are used to host different sites running on the same machine is not virtual hosting the way you might understand it. In virtual hosting, only a single TCP/IP port is used by the server for each protocol (HTTP/HTTPS), but it will give the appearance of different Web sites based on the contents of the HTTP Host Header. This is usually considered true virtual hosting. The DNS names of the hosted sites each map to the same IP address. When a request is received at the server, the Host Header is examined to see which site the user is actually requesting.

Since WebSEAL does not support virtual hosting using the Host HTTP Header, this means that a different IP address/port combination must be used for each protocol (HTTP/HTTPS) of each instance.

By default, a WebSEAL server will bind to the ports on all IP addresses specified on the local machine. In this case, each instance must use a different port number. Clients can access the WebSEAL instances via any of the local IP addresses, but they must specify the correct port number to connect to the desired instance.

If the same ports are to be used by multiple instances (port 80 and 443, for example), then each of these instances must be configured to bind to a different IP address. When a WebSEAL instance is bound to a single IP address, clients must connect to that IP address in order to reach the server. Therefore, there are two ways we can use a multiple WebSEAL instance for our scenario.

WebSEAL with specified ports using the same IP address

Figure 10-11 on page 280 show how we would install two instances of WebSEAL on the same machine with the same IP address, using different port numbers. The advantage of this is that we do not require separate IP interfaces and are not subject to physical or network address limitations.

The WebSEAL instances are configured to bind to a specified port on the same interface. Refer to the *IBM Tivoli Access Manager for e-Business WebSEAL Administration Guide Version 3.9,* GC23-4682, for step-by-step configuration instructions. Each WebSEAL instance is a completely separate environment. Each has its own Web space, junctions, and authentication mechanisms. For YRI we have installed two instances, one for www.yri.com on ports 80 and 443, the other instance for www.ship-yri.com on ports 90 and 543. Normally the client requesting Internet access to these sites would need to specify the unique IP/port combination as part of the URL.

In this case we have an advantage, since Network Dispatcher was included in the original scenario. We can use the Network Dispatchers to map the domain names to their unique IP/port address. For clients requesting access, the Network Dispatchers will effectively translate a URL to its respective IP/port address. This will be transparent for the client, and the Web domain name (without the port number) can be used for or as part of the URL.

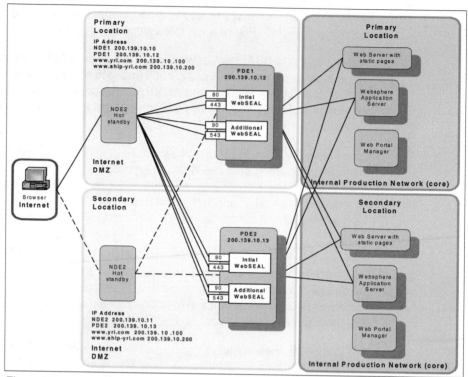

Figure 10-11   WebSEAL using different ports with same IP address

Before we show the configuration changes, refer to Figure 10-11 and consider the following:

▶ The Network Dispatchers will be configured for load balancing and failover in the same way as described earlier in 10.6.9, "Network Dispatcher installation" on page 259.

▶ The unique IP/port addresses for www.yri.com are:
  – HTTP = 200.139.10.12:80 and 200.139.10.13:80
  – HTTPS = 200.139.10.12:443 and 200.139.10.13:443

▶ The unique IP/port addresses for www.ship-yri.com are:
  – HTTP = 200.139.10.12:90 and 200.139.10.13:90
  – HTTPS = 200.139.10.12:543 and 200.139.10.13:543

The cluster address for www.yri.com is 200.139.10.100, and for www.ship-yri.com is 200.139.10.200. What we have to achieve using Network Dispatcher is to map the cluster address to the start or root URLs. They should point to the correct and unique IP/port address for the respective WebSEAL instance. Here is how we configure this mapping in the /usr/lpp/nd/dispatcher/configurations/configuration file.

In the configuration script file we add the cluster address as we did in our first dispatcher.

```
echo "Loading first CLUSTER address "
ndcontrol cluster add 200.139.10.100
ndcontrol cluster add 200.139.10.200
```

Next in the script, we define the ports that these clusters will use.

```
#
echo "Creating ports for CLUSTER: $CLUSTER"
ndcontrol port add 200.139.10.100:80+443 method nat
ndcontrol port add 200.139.10.200:80+443 method nat
```

Note: The option method nat on the command line indicates to the Network Dispatcher to use its Network Address Translation (NAT). This feature must be turned on to enable mapping of the cluster address to specified IP/Ports on the WebSEAL machines.

Finally in the script we add the WebSEAL server and map the IP/port address for each WebSEAL instance to the cluster address.

```
# NFApri is the IP address of the primary network dispatcher in a high
# availability env.
# NFAbackup is the IP address of the backup network dispatcher in a high
# availability env.
NFApri= 200.139.10.10
NFAbackup= 200.139.10.11
CLUSTERA=200.139.10.100 # www.yri.com
CLUSTERB=200.139.10.200 # www.ship-yri.com

SERVER1= 200.139.10.12
SERVER2= 200.139.10.13

echo "Adding server machines" For www.yri.com
ndcontrol server add $CLUSTERA:80:$SERVER1 mapport 80 returnaddress $NFApri
ndcontrol server add $CLUSTERA:80:$SERVER2 mapport 80 returnaddress $NFApri
ndcontrol server add $CLUSTERA:443:$SERVER1 mapport 443 returnaddress $NFApri
ndcontrol server add $CLUSTERA:443:$SERVER1 mapport 443 returnaddress $NFApri

echo "Adding server machines" For www.ship-yri.com
ndcontrol server add $CLUSTERB:80:$SERVER1 mapport 90 returnaddress $NFApri
```

```
ndcontrol server add $CLUSTERB:80:$SERVER2 mapport 90 returnaddress $NFApri
ndcontrol server add $CLUSTERB:443:$SERVER1 mapport 543 returnaddress $NFApri
ndcontrol server add $CLUSTERB:443:$SERVER1 mapport 543 returnaddress $NFApri
```

Note: The Network Dispatcher must act like a reverse proxy when IP/port translation is in effect. All traffic to and from the client will pass through Network Dispatcher. Therefore, the option returnaddress, which is the IP address of the Network Dispatcher instance, must be specified.

Be careful when specifying this address—it will be different for the primary or secondary Network Dispatcher and must be corrected in the relevant script.

Multiple WebSEALs using different interfaces

Figure 10-12 illustrates how we would install multiple WebSEAL instances on the same machine with separate IP interfaces.

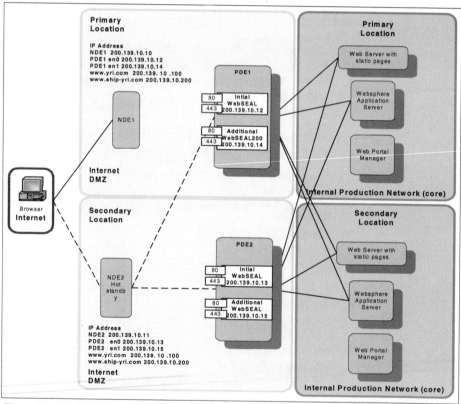

Figure 10-12   Multiple WebSEALs with different interfaces on the same machine

If physical or network limitations are not restrictive, this configuration has the advantage that it is very simple to secure with Network Dispatcher. The WebSEAL instances are configured to bind to a specified interface on the same machine. As seen in Figure 10-12 on page 282, the same ports can be reused. Refer to the *IBM Tivoli Access Manager for e-Business WebSEAL Administration Guide Version 3.9*, GC23-4682, for step-by-step configuration instructions.

Once each WebSEAL instance is set up and configured for a separate IP interface, the Network Dispatchers do not require any special setup. They can be configured as described in "Network Dispatcher installation" on page 259.

10.7 Conclusion

By comparing the objectives with the achievements, we can conclude that this phase of the project has been successful.

To break this down, see the functionality requirements as discussed in 10.2, "Functional requirements" on page 222:

► Support for integration to different cross-platform back-end servers

As Access Manager uses existing platform-independent standards (such as SSL, TLS, and HTTP) to communicate with back-end servers, the solution can be integrated with the current and future platforms.

► Easy and user-friendly management of users and security policies

The simple management tasks can be done with Web Portal Manager, and the Access Manager Administration API can be used to create a customized interface, should future projects require it. The pdadmin command and the API can be used for more advanced functions.

► Centralized management for security policies

All access control data is now stored on Access Manager, allowing for detailed security policy control data in a single storage.

► Standard security model that can be deployed for each region.

As the solution mechanics of Access Manager WebSEAL are transparent to the end user, and its only visible part, the error and login pages, can be customized to suit individual regions, the solution can be deployed in the same manner in any number of regions.

- Modular in design so that new services can be added with minimal effort

  Access Manager allows for any number of new services to be added by just adding them as junctions and configuring authentication, authorization, and single sign-on in the same manner as it was configured in this project.

  Also, more delegated administration domains can be added in the same manner as the ones in this project. These domains will provide for administration facilities for all new services.

- Ability to grow on demand (scalability)

  There are two important components for scalability in an Access Manager domain. These are the LDAP and WebSEAL servers. As the portal grows, any number of new WebSEALs and LDAP replicas can be easily added.

- High availability and failover for security components

  Like in scalability, the most important components here are the WebSEAL and LDAP servers. The procedures used in this project can be used to add any number of new servers.

  One of the most important components is Network Dispatcher. And while there cannot be multiple Network Dispatchers running at the same time, the hot-standby capabilities provide for automatic failover to a replica, and you can configure multiple hot-standby dispatchers.

  Of the other, less critical, components, the Access Manager Policy Server can currently only be replicated in a limited manner. But as only ACL database and user modifications are affected by Access Manager Policy Server's absence, this is not a critical component on a short time frame.

  The Authorization Servers, while not critical either, can also be installed in any number.

While some of the security requirements mentioned in 10.3, "Security design objectives" on page 224, have already been fulfilled by complying with the functionality requirements, there are a few of them that can be discussed here:

- Simple user password authentication for customers, employees, and agents

  Access Manager forms-based login is currently configured as the user ID/password authentication. In the future, however, new forms of authentication may be needed, such as PKI, SecurID active cards, or even biometrics. All of these and more are supported as authentication mechanisms with WebSEAL.

► Information flow subsystem

While most of the features protecting the back-end Web servers come from Access Manager, firewalls and operating system hardening still play a crucial role.

Because attackers constantly develop new methods and techniques for gaining unlawful access to protected resources, it is important that the security products and their components have the flexibility to add new security features to counter these attacks, and that these features do not involve re-engineering the of security solution.

But in the end, it does not matter how well WebSEAL can protect a Web resource if access to the Web resource is allowed from other, unprotected sources. Therefore this project took into account the placement of components and firewall port configuration needed to protect the back-end servers.

As always, security is not dependant on a single product, no matter how good.

11

Web mail integration

This chapter describes the business and functionality requirements for integrating a Lotus Domino Mail Server into the Access Manager environment described in Chapter 10, "Baseline security framework" on page 221. Also, the design and implementation steps needed to implement this functionality are described.

This project can be regarded as a component approach that could conceivably fit into any Access Manager environment with only minimal customization.

11.1 Business requirements

As a multinational company, YRI has many subsidiaries, business partners, and customers around the globe. Many of the company's employees spend most of their time traveling from one location to another.

In addition to being able to access customer account data, constant access to e-mail is required. Current dial-up solutions to the corporate Domino servers require that the user carry his/her own laptop with him/her at all times.

Other problems are the security implications of a direct dial-up to corporate network and the inherent unreliability and slow speed of phone networks in many regions of the world.

Employees must be enabled to access their mail in a fast, reliable, and, most of all, secure manner, even when they do not have access to their personal laptops. Also, time zone considerations dictate that e-mail be made available 24 hours a day.

11.2 Functional requirements

To accomplish the business requirements outlined by the CIO's statement, the project should consummate the following requirements:

► Enable secure Web-based access to e-mail.

While the primary concern is making e-mail available through the Internet, one of the objectives is to take a step towards the mobile office inside the company. Therefore, workstation and software independent intranet access to e-mail is a secondary requirement.

► The solution must fit into the existing Access Manager architecture.

The project must not require a reorganization of the existing component architecture or a restructuring of the security design.

► The administration cost of this solution must be minimized.

With Domino having its own security realm that still needs to be enforced for people using Lotus Notes clients, the security administration in the Access Manager environment should be minimized for this component.

► This solution must not interfere with existing Lotus Notes client-based e-mail connections.

- E-mail services should be integrated into a single sign-on environment; users should not have to memorize more than one user name and password.

  For obvious reasons, only one set of a user ID and password should be used. The ultimate aim of this approach is to have all the services available and personalized to the user with one authentication process.

- The solution must be highly available.

11.3 Security design objectives

In addition to the security requirements set for the basic Access Manager environment in 10.3, "Security design objectives" on page 224, the most important considerations are:

- Domino Web mail service must only be accessible through WebSEAL.

  While the Notes client access should still remain open on a one-to-many basis, WebSEAL must be used as a central point for security on the Web-based e-mail access.

- User access to mail should not enable access to other areas.

  While temporary users, like seasonal workers should have access to e-mail, it may not be prudent to allow them access to other secured back-end servers.

11.4 Design approach

Because this project is to be based on the existing Access Manager architecture, there are only a few considerations that prevent this solution from sitting on top of the existing framework without the need for any customization.

The first challenge is the single sign-on requirement. Since in this case, Access Manager and Domino do not share a common user database, we basically had two password-based solutions available. These are discussed further in 11.5, "Implementation architecture" on page 290.

The second challenge is the question of administration. This includes both the delegated administration of users in Access Manager, and the delegation of some of the more fine-grained access control decisions in Domino. Because of administrative conformity, we decided to implement the same model of delegated administration as was created for the WebSphere Application Server in the previous project.

Since there is not a comparable plug-in available for Domino as there is for WebSphere Application Server and Access Manager, the access control database in Domino is left in place. Access Manager handles the coarse-grained decisions on the Is this user allowed to contact the Domino server? level.

In other respects, this solution fully utilizes the existing security architecture. No additional components or services need to be installed.

11.5 Implementation architecture

As all employee mail is located on Domino servers, the Lotus Domino Mail Server is the logical way to allow Web-based access to e-mail for employees.

The Access Manager base architecture, created for the WebSphere Application Server integration, can handle the business needs and security implications of opening Lotus Domino for Web-based access without the need for further customization. For Lotus Domino integration, the following things need to be addressed:

► Providing single sign-on

   There are two different approaches to provide a single sign-on solution, which are discussed in 11.5.1, "Global sign-on (GSO) approach" on page 290, and 11.5.2, "Dummy password approach" on page 294. For this project, the dummy password method was selected, due to easier maintenance and better performance implications.

► Delegating access control

   As stated in the requirements, Lotus Domino has its own access control lists already in place and there remains the need to manage them for Notes client-based access. Therefore, Access Manager should be configured to only pass on requests from users allowed to access Domino, with more fine-grained control residing on the Domino server.

11.5.1 Global sign-on (GSO) approach

This approach uses the global sign-on feature of Access Manager to allow a mapping of user names and passwords between Access Manager WebSEAL and back-end servers.

In this section we discuss the implications of the GSO method particular to this scenario. To get a broader and more detailed understanding on the GSO method, see the *IBM Tivoli Access Manager for e-Business WebSEAL Administration Guide Version 3.9*, GC23-4682, and Chapter 5, "Authentication and delegation with Access Manager" on page 97.

Let us assume that your Access Manager user name/password combination is pduser1/pdpass1, and your Lotus Domino Internet user name/password combination is lnuser1/lnpass1.

Every time pduser1 requests a page from Lotus Domino, Access Manager realizes that the Domino junction is a GSO junction, and it retrieves pduser1's user name and password for the Domino GSO resource by consolidating its user directory (in this case, LDAP). It sends this credential (lnuser1/lnpass1) to the Domino server in the basic authentication header.

For a simple representation of GSO's operation, see Figure 11-1.

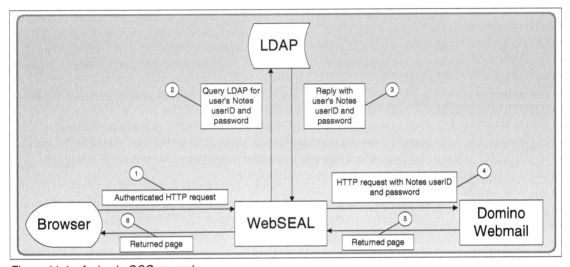

Figure 11-1   A simple GSO example

To implement this solution, follow these steps:

1. Configure a GSO junction and add it as a GSO resource to Access Manager.

2. Create a script that will copy the Domino user names as GSO mappings for respective Access Manager users.

3. Find out all the Domino passwords and add them as GSO mappings to the respective Access Manager users. Alternatively, create a script that rewrites the password in Domino and the Access Manager GSO mapping to be the same.

Administration and management issues

Typically, with the WebSEAL GSO capability, there are certain administration and management issues that have to be addressed before the actual deployment can take place. Following, we address some of the common issues. However, very often the way to tackle these issues may vary and be handled differently case-by-case, depending on the individual environment and architecture. Anyone who is responsible for the integration deployment should be aware of it. It is also the customer's responsibility to come up with a solution that best fits their environment and conforms to the corporate policy.

► Initial GSO credential population

To achieve single sign-on, the WebSEAL GSO junction requires creation of GSO resource credentials to individual users or groups, and these resource credentials have to be created and ready before WebSEAL can utilize the single sign-on capability to the back-end junctioned server. To populate the resource credentials for users, there are two common mechanisms we used to adopt:

a. Batch processing

A one-time application or utility can be created to retrieve the user name/password combination for each user in the junctioned application and populate it into the corresponding user GSO resource credential.

b. Self-serving

Whenever a user tries to access a back-end application through WebSEAL and there is no (or an incorrect) GSO resource credential defined for the user, an HTML form can be returned to the user in order to enter his/her user name/password for that particular back-end application. The CGI or servlet can be written to retrieve the information from the form and populate it into the resource credential.

The following shows the related pages from WebSEAL 3.9 that can be customized for this GSO self-serving:

```
PDWeb directory/www/lib/errors/C/38cf025a.html
PDWeb directory/www/lib/errors/C/38cf025b.html
PDWeb directory/www/lib/errors/C/38cf025c.html
PDWeb directory/www/lib/errors/C/38cf025e.html
```

Different customers may have different scenarios. There could be a situation where both of the above have to be adopted, or something completely different is required.

- Multiple point of access

  Ideally, with the Access Manager WebSEAL acting as a reverse-proxy and security agent, any direct accesses to the back-end junctioned servers and applications should be blocked, except those from WebSEAL. However, there are cases when an enterprise may want to still keep the direct access capability to servers and applications. For instance, one may want to secure access from the Internet while allowing direct access within the corporate intranet.

  Whether or not both of the access paths have to be secured, it depends on the individual corporate security policy and the nature of the back-end servers and applications. However, this is something that has to be considered when architecting the entire corporate security framework. More importantly, giving multiple point of access to servers and applications, could introduce password synchronization problems (which are addressed next).

- Password management and synchronization

  Ideally, with the WebSEAL GSO junction, after the user's GSO resource credentials are populated, the user name and password on the back-end junctioned server/application should become static. Any password polices dynamic in nature on the back-end should be deactivated, such as periodic password update. However, in many cases these credentials within the back-end system may remain active, particularly when the user is still allowed to access the server/application directly within the corporate intranet, as mentioned previously. In this case a user may change his password on the back-end server while he is directly accessing it, thereby causing the password in the WebSEAL GSO resource credential to get out-synced; hence, the SSO through WebSEAL to this server fails.

  To address this problem, a corporation must define a certain policy and mechanism to control or manage the password synchronization between the WebSEAL GSO resource credentials and the back-end servers or applications.

  A self-serving mechanism as discussed above could be one option, where a user will be prompted to update his GSO credential when it was out-synced.

GSO summary

In short, for any integration solutions that require the use of a WebSEAL GSO junction, it is important to understand the possible impacts on technical implementation and management issues caused by the GSO, as discussed above. Having a plan and solution to address those issues plays an important part and ensures the success of the entire integration and Access Manager deployment.

If you can ensure that the Notes Domino Web mail application can only be invoked by users after they have individually been authenticated by WebSEAL, the dummy password approach might be much more attractive, as you can see in the next section.

11.5.2 Dummy password approach

Access Manager WebSEAL has the ability to send user information coupled with what is known as a dummy password. This is a preconfigured password that is the same for every user. The dummy password gets sent to the back-end server in a basic authentication header along with the real Access Manager user name. See Figure 11-2 for an example flow of how the dummy password is used.

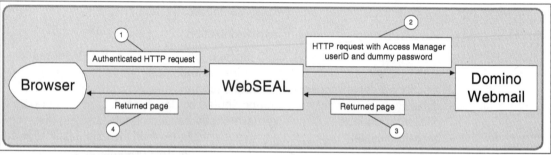

Figure 11-2   Dummy password example

Since WebSEAL stores the dummy password in a configuration file, the need for an extra LDAP query is removed, positively affecting performance.

> **Note:** While this section deals with some of the implications of the dummy password approach, it is not a comprehensive discussion. Please refer to *IBM Tivoli Access Manager for e-Business WebSEAL Administration Guide Version 3.9*, GC23-4682, for more detailed information on this feature.

Although all the users in Domino seem to share a single Internet password, this does not affect security because Web-based access to Domino will only be allowed from WebSEAL servers via SSL, and all users have to authenticate to WebSEAL first. Also, the password is not known to anyone but administrators. And unlike normal passwords that need to be remembered, this one is remembered by the configuration file, allowing for a longer and more complex password.

Note: Lotus Domino can have multiple passwords for different purposes. The password that is used when accessing your mail with a Notes client is not the same one as the Internet password discussed in this section.

11.5.3 Delegating access control

With no need to enforce fine-grained authorization twice, Access Manager is configured to perform coarse-grained access control only. There are two ways to implement this approach.

The first solution combines all users that are allowed to access Domino Web mail into a single group, and only this particular group is granted access to the Domino Mail server application.

Another method is to use the delegated administration feature of Access Manager, which allows you to create Enterprise domains, which in turn can contain several sub-domains. Each domain can support several different roles, such as senior administrators (responsible for the whole domain), support administrators (call center support personnel, for example), and users.

Each sub-domain can then be divided into further sub-domains in a tree-like structure. Each domain's administrator only has control in his own domain and its sub-domains. This provides a secure method of operation in large corporate environments, with shared responsibility.

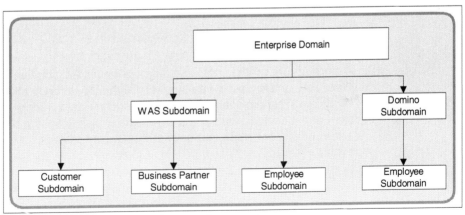

Figure 11-3   Enterprise domain example

As you can see in Figure 11-3, the WebSphere Application Server sub-domain of the main enterprise domain has been split into three sections with different administrators being responsible for managing the users in their respective domains. The Domino domain, however, has only one sub-domain.

As stated earlier, this is not quite as simple and straightforward as just adding all Domino users into a group and granting access based on group membership. But it does make for better expandability in the future, should the Domino server, for example, be used for delivering data to the customers and business partners as well.

For more information on delegated administration and the different administrative roles, see 1.1.7, "Web Portal Manager" on page 10, or *IBM Tivoli Access Manager for e-Business Base Administration Guide Version 3.9*, GC23-4684.

11.6 Technical implementation

This section describes the technical specifications for allowing secure access to Domino-based mail using the Web interface.

11.6.1 Creating the junction

This section shows how to create the junctions needed to access Domino Web mail through WebSEAL.

1. Create an SSL junction named /mail using the -b supply flag on the Internet WebSEALs.

   The easier, but less secure, way of creating an SSL junction is one-way authentication, where the back-end server sends a certificate to WebSEAL only. But for testing purposes and non-production environments, these junctions will do fine. Use the following syntax:

   ```
   pdadmin server task webseald-servername create -t ssl -b supply -h
   dominoserver -j /mail
   ```

   A more secure method, the mutually authenticated junction, forces both WebSEAL and the back-end server to authenticate each other using a certificate. This provides additional protection against someone spoofing the back-end machine. You need a certificate, which is sent to the back-end server when performing mutually authenticated junctions. Use the following syntax:

   ```
   pdadmin server task webseald-servername create -t ssl -b supply -h
   dominoserver -K certlabel -j /mail
   ```

   If you do not yet have a certificate in a key database, see Appendix E, "Step-by-step instructions" on page 533, for information on the steps required to create a database and configure it for WebSEAL.

2. Create a TCP junction named /mail using the -b supply flag on the intranet DMZ WebSEALs.

Since the intranet DMZ is considered secure, there is no need to create SSL junctions. Use the following syntax when creating the junction:

```
pdadmin server task webseald-servername create -t tcp -b supply -h
dominoserver -j /mail
```

Now access is enabled to the Domino Mail Server through WebSEAL.

11.6.2 Creating the delegated administration domain

This section lays out the steps needed to create a delegated administration domain for Domino.

1. Use WPM to create a sub-domain named domino.
2. Inside the domino sub-domain, create another sub-domain called employees.

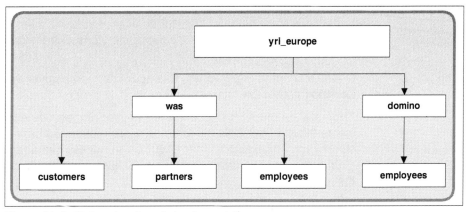

Figure 11-4   Enterprise domain implementation

The lowest sub-domain level will then be yri_europe/domino/employees, as portrayed in Figure 11-4.

Compare this figure with Figure 11-3 on page 295 to see the difference between abstract and real implementation.

11.6.3 Securing access

In order to secure access to the Domino Web-based mail resource for all users and administrators belonging to the yri_europe/domino/employees sub-domain, the following steps need to be completed:

1. Create an ACL called yri_europe-mail that allows (T)raverse, (r)ead, and e(x)ecute rights to a Web resource for the following groups:

    ```
    yri_europe-domino-employees-users
    yri_europe-domino-employees-admins
    yri_europe-domino-employees-domainadmins
    yri_europe-domino-employees-sradmins
    yri_europe-domino-employees-support
    ```

2. Add the ACL to the /mail junction.

11.6.4 Synchronizing users

While all the employees already exist as users in the WebSphere Application Server/Access Manager joint LDAP, their user names still differ from the Domino Internet user names. In order to use the dummy password feature, the user names need to be synchronized.

1. Create a script to copy Access Manager user names over their respective Domino Internet user names.

    To create the mapping between the two user names, use either manually created lists, LDAP DNs, or common parts in user names, whichever is most convenient. For example, if the LDAP DN in Access Manager is cn=John Doe, o=yri, c=eu and in Domino John Doe/EU, just use the common name part for the mapping.

2. Create a script to replace the Domino Internet passwords with the dummy password.

    The script to replace passwords is separate because it may be required in the future, while the Access Manager Domino Internet user names script is only needed once.

3. Set the dummy password in the webseald.conf file on each WebSEAL server, and restart each of the WebSEAL services.

    Modify the basicauth-dummy-passwd field. The following is an example of a dummy password configuration line:

    ```
    basicauth-dummy-passwd = dj42KtM5p2Srh7Qdnsd
    ```

    As stated in 11.5, "Implementation architecture" on page 290, the password does not have to be remembered by anyone; therefore it can be made very secure.

Tip: Every time the passwords are going to expire on the Domino server, all that needs to be done is running the script to change the Domino Internet passwords, reconfiguring the dummy password in the webseald.conf file on each WebSEAL machine, and restarting WebSEAL.

Pay-As-You-Drive

This chapter describes the business and functionality requirements for an exciting new business model. The *Pay-As-You-Drive insurance (PAYDI)* means that the vehicle's insurance premiums are based directly on how much or how often it is driven. There are many ways to implement this business model, some of them depending on built-in automotive solutions. YRI wants to pioneer this market with a specific customer section to open this model for other mobile customers later on.

This project shows how to integrate new requirements based on new business models into an existing environment. It can be easily expanded to meet similar requirements.

12.1 Business requirements

YRI wants to offer their customers who are owners of only occasionally driven vehicles (for example, old-timers or collectors), to use an optional usage-based pricing model to pay for their extra coverage. The following list will highlight some of the basic requirements:

► Convenient access using a mobile phone.

   As soon as the owner decides to take his car for a ride, he has to dial in with his cellphone in order to register for insurance coverage. No fancy dialogs other than security-related (for example, user ID/password) prompts should be provided.

► The YRI offer is based on a per-day (24 hour) charge default schema.

   Once registered, the driver is insured for 24 hours. If he wants to he can extend this period for another 24 hours by calling again, or he can call in earlier to cancel the insurance (should the trip be cancelled or be shorter than expected). At this point he will be charged at an hourly rate, which is rated twice as much as the per-day rate, so 12 hours will cost as much as one day. The customer will be charged the price that is more advantageous for the customer.

► The driver is able to check his usage data by accessing the YRI customer Web site (using a regular browser).

We are aware that this model is based on the trust between the driver/user and YRI, because this model is based on the assumption that the driver will dial-in.

Since the trend in the automotive sector is the integration of the car-system electronics (for example, GPS navigation, diagnosis, odometer) into the mobile communication-system, this manual process will eventually be replaced by an integrated communication system in the future. Today's cars carry much more equipment than just a cup holder, so in the near future, the car itself will be a mobile device that is able to communicate even without user interaction. This so-called pervasive computing model will lead to new possibilities in the automotive sector. Automatic emergency calls in case of an accident, tracking of stolen cars, and anonymous tracking of the car movement to analyze traffic conditions (floating car data), to name a few. This is not the focus of this book, but it is mandatory to understand these upcoming requirements.

YRI, as an innovative company, is aware of these new possibilities and wants to gain some experiences with this kind of insurance business model.

12.2 Functional requirements

To implement the business requirements, the project should realize the following functional requirements:

- Enable WAP-based access for mobile device.

  While there are possibilities of implementing this model even with non-WAP cellphones, YRI decided to go with WAP devices due to the fact that most of today's cellphones are WAP-enabled.

- The solution must fit into the existing Access Manager architecture.

  The project must not require a reorganization of the existing component architecture or a restructuring of the security design.

- The costs of this solution should be minimized.

  YRI will not implement its own remote access service (RAS) infrastructure, but in order to gain control over the WAP sessions, it will implement a WAP gateway within its own premises.

- The solution should be based on current standards and be open for further enhancements.

- The user must be able to control his data by accessing the YRI customer Web site.

- The solution must be highly available.

12.3 Security design objectives

In addition to the security requirements set for the basic Access Manager environment, the most important considerations for the mobile environment are:

- Use built-in security features in WAP.

  The WTLS layer of WAP must be used (8.2.3, "WAP security architecture" on page 190).

- No access to other Web resources should be possible through this access path.

12.4 Design approach

The above requirements lead to a straightforward design to implement these new services.

- Use the RAS infrastructure of a wireless service provider.

- Place a WAP gateway in the DMZ.
- Provide a convenient enrollment process for customers.

   Since customers are not willing to fumble with their cellphones, we want to minimize input requests to user ID and password.
- KISS: Keep It Super Simple.

   After passing the user's credentials, the back-end server application generates a time-stamped record as an entry in the user's PAYDI record. There will be only two pages that need to be accessed in this manner: The Start insurance and Stop insurance pages.
- Enable future enhancement.

   After the first 24-hour period is over, the user can be informed by using a mobile messaging gateway (for example, Short Messaging Service or WAP Push service). These services will become more common when the upcoming next generation networks are available (for example, 2.5 and 3 G like GPRS and UMTS).

12.5 Implementation architecture

Based on Figure 12-1 on page 305 we have a closer look onto the data flow especially from the security view.

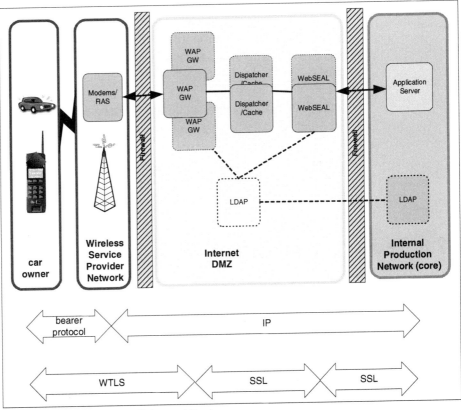

Figure 12-1 Pay-As-You-Drive architecture

The following assumptions are made:

► The user has stored his user ID and password in the profile on his cellphone.

In this case the user dials in and the user ID/password is automatically transmitted in the header so the user does not have to type in anything. This is convenient, but also a security leak in case the phone gets lost.

► The user has not stored his user ID and password in the profile in his cellphone

In this case, the user is prompted by a WML form and has to provide user ID and password.

► The default WAP gateway stored in the profile on the cellphone is located at the WSP site. Due to security requirements, an automatic redirection to the YRI WAP gateway will be forced by the WSP (8.2.1, "Wireless Application Protocol environment" on page 186).

- First the user is authenticated by the WAP gateway using user ID and password.

- The mobile user request is then routed to WebSEAL.

- WebSEAL is configured to receive an authenticated user from the WAP gateway and will not re-authenticate the user but perform further authorization if needed.

- WebSEAL uses the MPA support to connect to the WAP gateway (Appendix F, "MPA authentication flow" on page 543).

> **Note:** Non-repudiation is not addressed in this scenario, but as mentioned in 8.2.3, "WAP security architecture" on page 190, it can be achieved by using a digital signature.

12.6 Technical implementation

This section describes some specifics of this solution; common prerequisites were mentioned in the previous scenarios already.

Authentication method

The authentication method used for the mobile WAP devices is basic authentication. Due to the flexibility of our approach even upcoming technologies based on wireless PKI (wPKI) and certificates can be easily integrated at a later time.

Common LDAP directory

When using the IBM WebSphere Everyplace Wireless Gateway and its WAP capabilities, WebSEAL and EWG can be set up to use the same schema in the LDAP directory. They both can exploit a common inetOrgPerson entry for a given user. IBM WebSphere Everyplace Wireless Gateway will attach a wlUser auxiliary object to the inetOrgPerson, and WebSEAL will create a secUser object under the inetOrgPerson.

Distributed environment

If the wireless gateway is placed in a trusted zone, and WebSEAL is physically placed at a different trusted location, additional mechanisms like VPN should be used to establish secure links.

High availability

In order to handle high traffic networks, IBM WebSphere Everyplace Wireless Gateway can be implemented in a clustered environment. Clustering means that several machines are running one instance of the IBM WebSphere Everyplace Wireless Gateway software. Workload from one or more network connections are distributed across them.

Load balancer and caching proxies should be used to achieve high availability of WebSEAL and content servers.

12.6.1 Integration into existing infrastructure

The security infrastructure based on the Access Manager infrastructure and WebSEAL is expanded by integrating the WAP gateway into the authentication process.

Because of the lack of heavy transactional processing, transcoding of different back-end content will not be used in the first step, so YRI decided to develop the required WML coding (for example, WML forms) on its own. But YRI is already thinking of deploying new services to its clients and of course integrating pervasive computing models like intelligent cars. Therefore a transcoding model, as discussed in Chapter 18, "Wireless integration" on page 477, is also suitable for future services.

YRI already plans future enhancements like intelligent notification and location-based services for its clients using WebSphere Everyplace Server as a platform (see Appendix A, "IBM WebSphere Everyplace Suite - An overview" on page 489).

12.6.2 Conclusion

We have shown in this scenario that a given infrastructure can be extended to meet new business requirements. To assure secure access for mobile devices today's WAP environment and its WTLS support is already suitable to provide a certain level of wireless security.

The main requirement to use WebSEAL as the focal point for authentication and authorization issues is met using the features of WebSEAL to connect to WAP gateways in a secure way and to assure that no other back-end resources than the required ones can be accessed.

Cross-domain authentication

This chapter provides a detailed description about the business and functional requirements as well as the design and implementation aspects for authenticating users between different Access Manager domains.

13.1 Business requirements

While the customers and agents conduct most of their business in their home countries and regions, there is an increasing demand for cross-regional services.

While falling under a common corporate umbrella, our local subsidiaries in each region are best positioned to make tailored solutions to our customers. For example, to provide a US-based customer with a competitive premium quote for his villa on the French Riviera, a local consultant is an absolute requirement.

While the Yellow Rose Insurance corporation itself is composed of many smaller companies operating in different countries, they wish to present a unified look and feel to the customer, no matter which region he is dealing with.

When a customer comes in to view his insurance information, he should also be allowed to do the same thing with insurances he has in other regions.

13.2 Functional requirements

The following functional requirements can be derived from the business goals:

► The solution should allow single sign-on access between different regional domains.

Employees, customers, agents, and brokers must be allowed to access all information pertinent to them in all regions without separate user names and passwords for each.

► The addition and maintenance of users should be a simple process, not requiring extra work in each additional region.

All replication of users and their access data should be semi-automated and handled from their home region.

► The solution should fit on top of existing architectures.

13.3 Security design objectives

The following security items should be addressed by the solution:

► Users should only be able to log on into their home domain. The transparent logon to other domains should be implemented via CDSSO (see 7.2, "Distributed security domains" on page 166).

- ► Any replication of user data should be handled securely, preferably using the existing corporate backbone solution used for WebSphere Application Server data replication to minimize administration overhead.

13.4 Design approach

Prior to the installation of this solution into the existing architecture with the least amount of administrative hassle, we need to consider two things.

First, in order for CDSSO to work, the users must have an entry in the destination domain's user registry. Because the user IDs do not necessarily have to be the same, there will be a mapping requirement if the user IDs are different in different domains. A solution had to be designed to handle user ID and access control management. This is discussed in 13.5.1, "User management architecture" on page 312.

Second, CDSSO functionality has to be specifically initiated with a customized link. This creates the need to change links in the back-end servers, and while the back-end server structure might be the same now, this may not be the same always. Best approaches for different situations had to be designed. This topic is further discussed in 13.5.2, "CDSSO links" on page 312.

Otherwise, the CDSSO solution works seamlessly with the existing Access Manager architecture.

13.5 Implementation architecture

There are two ways to handle distributed authentication. One is the Cross-Domain Single Sign-On (CDSSO) and the other is e-community single sign-on. These approaches and their advantages are discussed in 7.2, "Distributed security domains" on page 166. Refer to that section for more detailed information.

For automatically logging on users from their home regional domain to other Access Manager domains, CDSSO is the simplest choice; therefore, it is used in this example.

13.5.1 User management architecture

Unless you want to go through the troublesome process of mapping user IDs during logon procedures, CDSSO requires the same user ID to exist in each domain. This means that all the people who need to have access to other regions, have to be provisioned for these domains. These people include business partners, employees handling international accounts, and customers with insurance policies in more than one region.

Just adding users from three different regions into one database can turn into an administrative nightmare; therefore, each region's root suffix will have organizational units containing users from the two other regions.

In order for users to retain the same access rights they have in their home region, group information should be sent over to other domains, as well as in user IDs.

13.5.2 CDSSO links

In order to pass the credentials of a user from one domain to another with CDSSO, special Web links that activate this feature have to be constructed.

There are two basic approaches to create the links:

► Mass replace. Replace all existing and future links to other domains with these links.

   In most cases, this is the most convenient method, as current software allows for automatic replacement of links, no matter how many there are.

► Creating a limited number of gateways. Only replace links in strategic places with CDSSO links.

   While replacing all links with current tools is a fairly easy task, there is still some administrative overhead. As a lighter solution you may choose to implement only a few links. As an example in our scenario, customers viewing their insurance data would be presented with links saying:

   ```
   View your insurances in Asia
   View your insurances in the US
   ```

   These links would take them to the pages that show a user's insurance in other regions.

   Also, if the directory structure is the same in each region, using things like JavaScript to create a dynamically changing link becomes relatively easy.

To keep the administrative load on changing the links as easy as possible, the latter solution is used in this scenario.

13.6 Technical implementation

In this section we describe the steps necessary to create a CDSSO trust between different domains of the YRI enterprise. However, this section does not contain detailed instructions for configuration. Refer to Chapter 6, "Cross Domain Sign-On Solutions," in the *IBM Tivoli Access Manager for e-Business WebSEAL Administration Guide Version 3.9*, GC23-4682, for step-by-step instructions for configuring CDSSO.

13.6.1 User management

As mentioned in 13.5, "Implementation architecture" on page 311, the users and their group information must be copied to all regions. User provisioning can be achieved with several methods.

► Generic commercial software that fits the purpose, such as IBM Tivoli Identity Manager

   The advantage of this solution is its expandability. Most of the features are already built in and require only configuration.

► Creating software inside the company

   This software can be created directly for the purpose of managing users. It can be a script utilizing the PDAdmin command line tool or a program created with the PD Administration API. For more information on the Administration API refer to the *IBM Tivoli Access Manager for e-Business Administration Java Classes Developer's Reference*, SC32-0842, or *IBM Tivoli Access Manager for e-Business Administration C API Developer Reference Version 3.9*, GC32-0843.

No matter which solution selected, you should create the organizational unit (OU) suffixes in each region's LDAPs before starting user provisioning. For example, in order to create containers in Europe for users who are being maintained from the Asia or US region, create the organizational units asia and us under the main suffix, which is o=yri. The resulting tree structure is illustrated in Figure 13-1 on page 314.

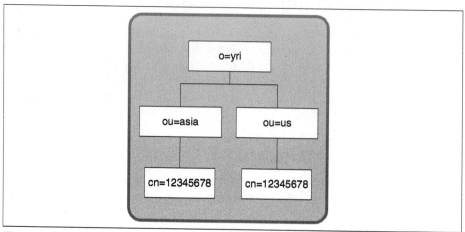

Figure 13-1   LDAP tree example

A customer whose home region is in Asia and customer number 12345678 would show up in the European LDAP database as the entry cn=12345678,ou=asia,o=yri.

The OUs can thus be used to distinguish which region "owns" a user. All updates to the user should come from the user's home region. This means that if the user's account is disabled or the user is deleted, the provisioning component must transmit the disable or delete command to the other to regions as well.

This sort of transaction should be performed via VPN inside the corporate network. The Figure 13-2 on page 315 shows the YRI user database structure and replication pattern.

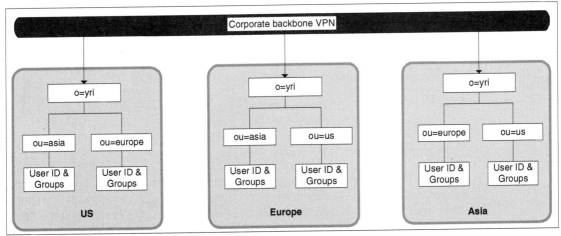

Figure 13-2   Provisioning in a corporate environment

Please keep the following guidelines in mind when implementing your provisioning component:

► Once a user ID has been created in another region, add the user to groups in that region.

Trying to add the user ID to a group called yri_europe-was-customers in the US domain will not work. The corresponding group there would be yri_us-was-customers.

► While a password is required when creating a user, the provisioning tool may be configured to enter a long random string to the remote domains because the user authentication is not based on a password when using CDSSO. The home domain should have a normal password though.

An even more secure solution is disabling the user's password. This will completely prevent the user (or anyone pretending to be the user) from logging on directly to any other than his home domain, where he can enter other domains by activating links.

13.6.2 CDSSO configuration

In order to enable CDSSO in the first place, you need to create the common key file, distribute the key, and configure the WebSEALs to accept CDSSO logins from the WebSEALs of the two other regions. As mentioned earlier, see Chapter 5, "Cross Domain Sign-On," in the *IBM Tivoli Access Manager for e-Business WebSEAL Administration Guide Version 3.9*, GC23-4682, for detailed instructions on implementing CDSSO.

After the basic configuration has been completed you must configure links that point to the other domains. These links are in the format:

`/pkmscdsso?destination-URL`

For example, to jump from the customer's homepage in the www.yri.com domain to the customer's homepage in YRI Asia:

`https://www.yri.com/pkmscdsso?https://asia.yri.com/my/profile`

or

`/pkmscdsso?https://asia.yri.com/my/profile`

While all these links are static, you can also create dynamic links. For example, to create a CDSSO link that takes the customer from a page in the www.yri.com domain to the corresponding page in the Asian domain, the following steps have to be completed with CGI scripting, JSP, JavaScript, or other means.

► Extract current pages location. For example:

`https://www.yri.com/my/profile/insurances.jsp`

► Replace the DNS name in the address with the Asian domain's DNS name.

`https://www.yri.com/my/profile/insurances.jsp` would become `https://asia.yri.com/my/profile/insurances.jsp`

► Add the CDSSO call in front of the address.

`/pkmscdsso?https://www.yri.com/my/profile/insurances.jsp`

► Write the link to a Web page.

For example:

`<a href="/pkmscdsso?https://www.yri.com/my/profile/insurances.jsp">Jump to Asia/a`

This example of dynamic links relies on the fact that the URL structure in both domains is the same. It is still possible to easily create dynamic links if there is just a difference in naming conventions of directories.

For example, if /my/profiles/ were named /your/insurances/ in Asia, you will just need to take this into account. So when changing the DNS name to Asia, the link generator would have to look up a directory name mapping and replace the directory names as well as the DNS name. This will work if a part of the directory names differs. If there is little or no consistency in directory structure, dynamic links become impractical.

Now that you have your configurations and links in place and have provisioned the users to other domains, the CDSSO implementation is done.

Part 3

Banking environment

ABBC is a banking institution that wishes to centralize its application security management, not only for its existing Internet banking application, but also for its message queueing and customer relationship environment, which means the tight distinction of different user groups and access mechanisms and locations.

Armando Brothers Banking Corporation

This chapter provides an introduction to the overall structure of Armando Brothers Banking Corporation, including its business profile, its current IT architecture and infrastructure, and its medium-term business vision and objectives.

Note: All names and references to company and other business institutions used in this chapter are purely fictional. Any match with a real company or institution is coincidental.

14.1 Company profile

Armando Brothers Banking Corp. (ABBC) is a financial institution that traces its history back to the early days of industrialization. It was a time of radical change and growing financing needs. The Armando brothers were open to new ideas and founded a bank situated in Austin, Texas to help pioneers of those days to finance their business ventures. ABBC, a bank very open to new technologies, expanded rapidly and became one of the most important banks with tradition in retail and private banking offering customized services for customers around the world. One reason for their success is their ability to explore different markets with specialized teams. ABBC is represented in all continents and all major cities with at least one office.

ABBC began soon to elaborate the new business opportunities offered by electronic banking. They were among the first banks offering their customers online access to their accounts. Additionally, other user groups like business partners and subsidiaries gained access to their computing environment. Over the years multiple IT systems offering a Web interface have been installed.

Recent reports about intrusion attacks and closely connected damage to business and reputation have forced ABBC to rethink their corporate security policy. Some of the major concerns are:

► ABBC faces significant challenges in keeping Internet information technology abreast of the demands of the banking business, much less a step ahead of those demands.

► Customers and business partners are not satisfied with ABBC's heterogeneous access to banking services.

On the other hand, increased competition forces ABBC to elaborate business opportunities offered by new technologies especially through the Internet. The new strategy for business now motivates the development of a uniform, pervasive security access method that offers ABBC's services through different channels like Internet and mobile access.

14.2 Current architecture

ABBC's current architecture has grown along with evolvement in IT technology. No wonder that multiple systems of different vendors using different technologies have been installed. Being inconsistent in the way they handle security, ABBC is faced with complex management tasks. ABBC's current IT architecture is depicted in Figure 14-1 on page 323.

There are four zones in our drawing to represent the common divisions for a Web infrastructure:

- ► External networks: All external users (customers, visitors, vendors) that require interaction with the business functions have networked access to this channel. This is an uncontrolled environment from the bank perspective.

- ► Internet DMZ: This is the first environment where the bank controls and defines the network and firewall controls to make sure that only authorized traffic passes. The controls here cover routing protocols, firewall rules, intrusion detection, system monitoring, link performance, and other technical measures.

- ► Production network(s): This are the inner system networks that are available for the business applications and machines. This is a secure, trusted environment that the bank has total control of.

- ► Intranet: This is the internal corporate network. It is allowed for internal users to have access to the banking systems available in the production network space, but this is also a controlled, as-needed access. Although the internal networks are considered trusted, firewalls enforce that only authorized traffic is allowed to access the Web-facing banking systems as well.

14.2.1 Existing environment architecture

Let us take a look at our working environment, which is made of many interdependent components such as:

- ► Network and firewalls: Although the network and firewall infrastructure discussion is out of the scope for this book, it is worth mentioning that we do recognize its existence and importance for proper secure implementation. Some firewall rule requirements are necessary for the environment to work and this is assumed to be true.

- ► Operating systems: We have a heterogeneous environment basically running Windows NT/2000 and Unix (AIX/Solaris). Server redundancy or high availability is part of all business machines in order to provide a 99.9 percent availability.

- ► Web servers: The Web server layer (or Web farm) is able to handle all external requests with the highest SSL security available. Load balancing and other techniques make sure that static content is readily available without physical I/O requests.

- Application servers: Applications are available for external users and internal users as well as for Web services and integration with other internal components with different purposes and access levels. There are two application severs, one for internal and one for external users. The internal application server is separated from the external application server for the following reasons:

  - For security reasons external users should not be able to get access to the internal application server because the total content provided is different. The internal server has system maintenance code and pages that should not be installed on the external server.

  - Internal and external machines can be scaled independently because there are many more external than internal users. It is worth mentioning that this may not be the case for others and thus, all application server code could reside in one consolidated entity, making it a unique point of service.

  - From an architecture perspective, the application servers may require different product support and thus, different operating system drivers, disks, and so on.

- Database servers: There is a high dependency on the database servers to perform transactional operations for users, which include external users, visitors, and internal users. Transactions may be simple query operations or complex update operations in many different points.

- Middleware server: This is an abstraction layer to integrate and isolate specialized systems that are not part of the core infrastructure, but are necessary to process specialized information (for example, accounting or brokerage). The middleware server is designed to keep front-end applications independent of the back-end system. ABBC operates world-wide and the applications of the back-end may vary from country to country. While each country has its own IT infrastructure, the middleware server is the only component that has to be adjusted to the local environment. The middleware is a transactional monitor that simply mediates the requests from one source system to one or more destination systems, as well as controls the flow of send/receive messages.

- Legacy systems: This is the most specialized system in the environment. Each system processes one particular service, but it has no direct integration with the other legacy systems. Integration is accomplished through middleware calls that can pass and receive requests from the internal legacy systems.

- Mobile infrastructure: Mobile devices have an independent gateway server that provides the integration between an external service provider and the bank system. While the business logic is the same, the presentation layer is customized to fit those devices.

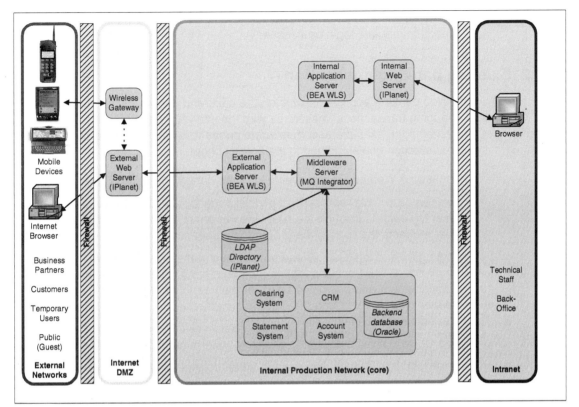

Figure 14-1 Current bank architecture

The dotted line in the drawing represents a communication link that is being used depending on the process (for example, authentication). The solid lines represent the main flow of the system and the intra-communication dependencies.

The troubles caused by the current architecture are:

▶ Different access paths with different authentication and authorization methods for internal and external users. This situation causes complexity, management overhead, and holds the imminent risk of unauthorized access.

▶ No integration of back-end applications due to lack of centralized security management.

▶ Current environment causes slow time-to-market due to complexity of user and security management. Developers need to implement security inside their applications.

▶ There is no central security policy for applications.

- Authentication is only a back-end feature. While this is good for back-end services, this also poses an additional complexity for the application that needs to mediate login processes.

14.2.2 Existing banking application

The Web banking application runs on the back-end application servers exchanging transactional messages with the internal systems. Our implementation example assumes some pages and functionality to describe the main protection goals outlined in the project chapters.

The following Web pages are available to the bank application:

- welcome.jsp: This represents the initial page for the site. This page allows the user to navigate through the site. One important feature is the login option that redirects the user to the proper login pages.

- login.html and login.jsp: These are existing authentication pages for the application. The front-end login page (login.html) is the presentation layer that provides user and password fields for the user. The login.jsp page is responsible for executing the credential authentication, as well as back-end session establishment.

- logout.jsp: This is the page to finalize and terminate the user session.

- undercon.jsp: This page is a place holder for the functionality we do not have in the example.

- exec_trn.jsp / query_trn.jsp: These pages represent the transactional code for customers. They have additional controls to enforce that only logged-in customers can access this functionality. This is part of the session controls that the application pre-populates during the login phase.

Figure 14-2 on page 325 shows the relation between the main pages and the system flow during normal login processing, which affects user identification, authentication, and authorization.

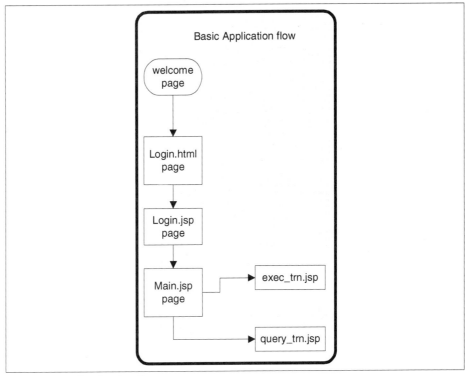

Figure 14-2   Application flow

14.3 Corporate business vision and objectives

To keep pace with the development and raising demands of the banking market, ABBC has to constantly improve their services in a profitable way. As to where the company wants to go, the ABBC company requested the Pforster Financial Group, one of the largest consulting companies, to elaborate their business vision and future goals to keep competitiveness and high standard services. Here is the outcome of their report:

► Innovation: As part of the Pforster recommendation, ABBC is planning to add important business processes under the common Web interface for insurance, brokerage, scheduled operations, and the stock market. This includes development of a uniform, pervasive security model that offers ABBC's services through different channels. These channels have to have authorization integration, using the same secure infrastructure already outlined as the basis. The security infrastructure components in place must follow the market trends without in-house coding and also provide enough integration capabilities to cope with future trends.

- Flexibility: ABBC plans to distribute its business model to other countries, as well as other local branches in all countries in which it operates. This requires great flexibility to easily and smoothly accommodate new changes and integration challenges. The strategy of the company is to have world-wide coverage to allow customers to interact and share services that are common in all countries.

- Open standards: This is a key element for the ABBC corporation and the product set in order to enable cross-platform integration with other components. It is important for ABBC to implement solutions based on open standards that are widely used and can be easily implemented with different technologies, allowing future changes to be design and implementation steps only, without re-engineering or throwing away components.

- Time to market: As for any company, the time to market factor is important for ABBC. The existing technology is well suited to support the number of customers today. The more users, transactions-per-user, and office communication that is part of this emerging business, the more pressure exists for new and improved services. ABBC's plan is to have a distributed development life cycle with collaboration from many countries in order to develop applications and services that are more cost-effective than in the past. A team of business analysts and system integrators will work in parallel, according to the market changes, to design and deploy new solutions that are well accepted for customers in general, as well as specific, tailor-made services for those that need them.

14.4 Project layout and implementation phases

As for any implementation, it is important to know the goals and measure expectations about the final product and how long it takes for the implementation to become effective. Let us describe the major steps that we cover in the following sections for the banking scenario.

Defining the main security goals for the implementation, we shall assume the following:

- Phased implementation: We will work in scenarios starting from a basic implementation and increasing complexity as we move towards the next steps so that Access Manager can be implemented and integrated accordingly.

- Business and security enhancements: As part of the implementation strategy, we present the additional business objectives and also the Access Manager benefits that each new step adds.

- Pervasive security: It is part of the design principle to make security part of the environment without disrupting services or user experience. Therefore, the security goal is also to provide high quality security, without even being noticed.

- Centralized management for some infrastructure components such as network administration, messaging systems, desktop computing, and so on.

- Decentralized management for local businesses and new markets, leveraging the same know-how and infrastructure standards.

The project has the three high level phases described in the following sections.

Project phase I - Protection of external Web resources

General management and the IT department are aware of the need for a solid basis to implement their future goals. The current environment with multiple systems and different security methodologies is too complex and costly to handle. The main goal of the first project phase is to provide a centralized, solid, and easy-to-manage security architecture to protect ABBC's assets from external attacks. Having analyzed the market, ABBC chose Access Manager as the strategic product to implement their security policy. We show how Access Manager protects external Web resources and provides for centralized security management. In this stage, all external Web traffic is controlled by the new Access Manager infrastructure, making it robust enough to leverage existing applications without too much integration effort. This is a security goal for better authorization, architecture, consolidation, and security management of services, reducing cost and time. Some access control capabilities for group membership are also already integrated within Access Manager at this stage.

Project phase II - Application integration

In the second phase we add enhanced functionality, for example, more sophisticated grouping for external users, as well as the addition of internal groups. We integrate existing applications into the security infrastructure and enhance them by a more fine-grained authorization model. The internal Web access is also integrated into this access model, making sure that all Web traffic is centrally administered through Access Manager. The systems take benefits of the Access Manager API capabilities, making it possible to extend the controls for third-party applications.

Project phase III - Wireless and CRM integration

The third project phase demonstrates Access Manager's capabilities to adapt to new requirements. ABBC selected Siebel as their CRM system. In this scenario we show how to integrate Siebel in the security environment. Additionally, tight integration of Wireless access is the final step towards an integrated, secure, and flexible IT infrastructure.

15

Protection of external Web resources

This chapter provides a detailed description of the business and functional requirements as well as the design and implementation aspects for the first scenario of the banking institution, the external Web resource protection.

15.1 Business requirements

Since this is the starting scenario for our discussions, it is worth mentioning that business requirements are the first step for a successful implementation because they describe the scope and vision that the business needs to achieve. The security model must consider those requirements also as risk conditions to be measured and carefully handled to avoid business risks not properly assessed.

Business requirements are high-level objectives that consider the revenue, marketing, sales, and market share objectives to make the whole business is successful. The business requirements defined here are for the Web-facing banking channel, detailing the kind of business model that ABBC wants to offer over the Web. Therefore, it is vital that the outlined business requirements neither conflict with internal rules nor provide misguidance about where the business wants to go.

> **Restriction:** The specific internal banking requirements and discussions are out of the scope of this book, such as internal manual processes, reconciliation procedures, security administration, system maintenance, and so on.

Phase I requirements scope

Here we detail the list of items that the business has presented as relevant to this new Web market and some direction about what kind of users, products, and core functionality must be available. They are summarized in the following list:

► Provide services to external customers for transactions (query, money-related) over a Web channel.

► Provide limited Web services for visitors (non-customers) for a limited time (trial period).

► Provide the same customer experience services through other channels such as call centers or ATM.

► Provide advisory information such as research documents and monthly advisory news.

► Customer data must be protected. This is also a legal requirement.

► The customer is the most important external user. She is the only one that provides revenue for the services. Visitors and registered users are non-customers.

► Visitors can become registered users. Visitors can become customers.

► Registered users can become customers.

- Services must have general public reliance (confidentiality). The law requires proper controls over private data.

- Provide services that are online on a 24x7 base (availability).

- Information must be consistently processed (integrity).

- Provide support for multiple customer transactions at the same time.

- Provide statistics about the system usage.

- Provide services based on customer properties such as channel being used, amount to transact, and user type.

- Support emerging business with dynamic rules that require quick time to market.

- Provide support for multiple languages for the Web channel.

- Provide a customer-centralized database in one geographical location.

- Customers and internal staff should be able to see the same information from the same consolidated access point, but with different access levels depending who is accessing from what location.

- The customer is the center of the business. Therefore, there should be a common way to enter (access) the systems.

- The business may want to expand and may need to plan for connecting its main (back-end) systems to external companies to provide services for customers.

- There may be some vendor access to the infrastructure to provide support and specialized services for customers such as marketing campaigns.

- The business will start with a small customer database and grow as it acquires new customers.

- The business will have all its vital data in one consolidated location.

- The customer base may grow up to one million users (active and inactive).

- The system must handle up to 200 concurrent users (customers, registered users, and visitors) for Web access.

- The system must handle up to 100 concurrent users for API authorization requests (other than Web).

15.2 Functional requirements

In this paragraph we detail the technical implications of the business model and what they mean for security from a high-level perspective. In our scenario, the bank has some main categories inside the application space. Although some of them interact with each other, they can be considered independent applications under the same framework:

► The customers need to perform one login (authentication) in order to have access to the system functions. Query transactions are all available for customers without requiring any additional password while the session is alive. For money transactions the customer needs to type a second (authentication) password as a confirmation for every money transfer. The business logic may control specific operations, values, or destination accounts.

► The customers can switch between the pages and the system will maintain proper session controls about what the user is doing. Pop-up menus are available as quick entry points for the whole site.

► All applications are visible to customers. There is no limitation on customer access for any given application. The access control subsystem needs only to validate whether there is a valid customer session in place. Account restrictions apply to only show data that belongs to that particular user or any other joint account where he/she also participates.

► An integration with the existing infrastructure such as Web servers, application servers, firewalls, authentication and authorization subsystems, and their security features is to be pursued wherever possible.

Figure 15-1 on page 333 summarizes the functions available for users (customers and the general public). Figure 15-1 on page 333 defines the name of the category, as well as the specific functions that are available for users. Those functions are either independent Web objects (pages, EJB, and so on) or complete Web pages. For simplicity's sake, we use the same functional names to define the site map layout.

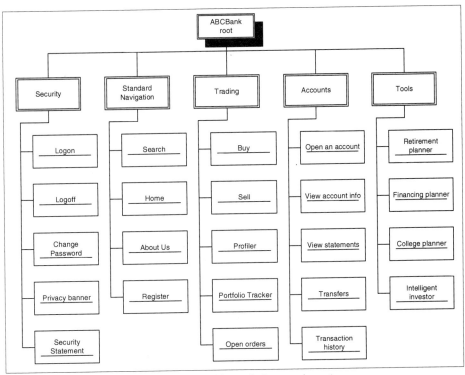

Figure 15-1   Functional requirements table and site map layout

Site map and functional details

Based on the high level site map we now define the functions available in each of the areas.

Security   Services related to access control, identification, and privacy information. These can be represented as a simple button, a full page, or a sequence of pages. The application logic that supports that functionality can be static HTML pages/content, dynamic pages, or EJB controls.

Standard navigation   General options available at any time for users. These are the navigation features implemented in all pages as a cross-reference for users to easily locate the services.

Trading	The applications and services are available for customers only. This section of the site implements all functionality for the trading business application. Any new application in our architecture becomes available as a main category. The options are then inserted underneath this category.
Accounts	The applications and services are available for customers only. This section of the site implements all functions related to account maintenance, account status, balances, notifications, and so on.
Tools	The applications and services are available for customers and registered users for viewing only. This section covers functionality that does not relate to a customer account itself, but uses input parameters to create trading and investment scenarios. Each option can be considered an independent application with its own logic and no relationship to the account or trading information for the customer applications.

15.3 Security design objectives

The security design objectives take into consideration the business requirements so that security can become a business enabler and implement a true pervasive security approach. Some of the security requirements have a direct one-on-one relationship to the business requirements previously stated. Some are implications to the business model proposed and thus can be considered add-ons to enable the business requirements. In general, the following topics need to be covered in order to understand what security is accomplishing to the business.

► Support multiple network entry access points.

The security model needs to provide good control for different existing source routes. Internet, intranet, Extranet are the most common groups that we have.

► Availability.

There has to be enough redundancy to fulfill existing service level agreements (SLA) with users in the system. From a security approach, there must also be controls to make sure that systems are properly secure and that only authorized users can access the servers.

- Integrity.

  The application must process the information precisely and be able to roll back pending transactions. The security goal in this arena is to make sure that the components can execute well-defined operations with reasonable access control checks, and that trust level definitions between the subsystems are in place. Anything wrong must be properly handled and orderly undone.

- Total security control.

  Security administration should try to control Web servers, application servers, integration components, and legacy systems in a uniform manner.

- Support secure communication and privacy.

  Critical information exchange, such as user ID and password data for authentication, must be stored and transmitted in an encrypted form. Applications and core system components should neither rely on weak nor clear text password processing or storage.

- Audit trails.

  The systems have to be configured to properly audit customer login, logout (when possible), and every transaction execution. Logging should include both successful and failed attempts.

- Identification.

  Since the external user scope consists of customers, vendors, and visitors, the system should be able to identify different types of users.

- Authentication.

  All external users have the same level of authentication enforcement using one login and one transactional password.

- Authorization.

  Different levels of authorization for users have to be enforced. They depend on what channel is used, date and time, and property values.

- Confidentiality.

  Application data must be processed, transmitted, and stored in a secure fashion.

Table 15-1 on page 336 describes the access control matrix. The system controls access based on identification and authentication information processed and stored during the session. Non-logged-in users are considered *public* or *visitors*, and thus are prevented from accessing privileged pages.

Table 15-1   Access control matrix

Security	Standard navigation	Trading	Accounts	Tools
public	*public*	*customers*	*customers*	*customers, registered users*

Three different groups are defined: *Customers, registered users*, and *public*. A user may only be a member in one of these groups. The application handles the session creation depending on the user type and whether there has been a successful authentication.

15.4 Design approach

Since we are focusing on external protection, it makes sense to add one layer to isolate the internal servers (including the Web server) from the users. One technique (which is also a security improvement) is the concept of a *reverse proxy*, which is implemented by Access Manager's WebSEAL blade. This way we can scale and divide the Web services without any disruption to user functionality, and use the existing Web infrastructure that could even be difficult to remove due to special filtering and integration with internal components. The WebSEAL layer provides two important security features.

► The authentication check is the first step in the user interaction, making it possible to control all user accesses before they reach any internal application server, thereby avoiding any malicious users' attempts to attack any server in the production DMZ.

► The authorization enforcement for all page requests, which is obviously a good security approach to allow only authorized requests to pass, makes it even possible to create audit trails about system access if required.

From an Access Manager perspective, WebSEAL is the external component that mediates the access requests from browsers to the internal Web space. Other internal components are also important (and required) to make this work. The location for those other components is best described in 15.5, "Implementation architecture" on page 337, with a detailed view of the components that Access Manager uses.

One of the major benefit is that Access Manager does not interfere with existing application architecture and processes. The implementation can leverage all the power of the application and still improve security without modifying the main business logic or environment connectivity.

15.5 Implementation architecture

Since it is part of the assumption that we start from a working environment, it seems logical that we need to accommodate some changes to make everything work properly. We define some basic categories to map the complexity of the scenario we are working and the changes that are necessary to make the new scope functional. Ideally, those changes have to be minimum, if none. As the scenarios become more complex, there may be a need for some special changes in one or two topics, but not all.

15.5.1 General implementation considerations

We define the following criteria to structure the changes in the solution that we are implementing in this as well as in the other banking scenarios.

Architecture changes

This is the high-level summary of the changes in the environment as a whole. Some categories are described in more detail since they have much more granular steps to be considered.

This section highlights changes with respect to:

► Application (general components, communication, hardware, redundancy)
► Network (routes, firewalls)
► Firewall (rules, logging, approvals)
► Security (availability, confidentiality, integrity concerns)

Security retrofit

This category describes the security changes that are required in the application and system level. For applications, this encompasses code changes and new code. For the system level, this includes agents, protocols, or software components that are new to the existing solution set. The items and questions covered are:

► Application (do we need to redo code?)

► Existing Web controls and logic (do we need to change/split pages?)

► In-house authorization engine (can it be used to coexist with legacy systems if required?)

Network changes

This includes the specific network changes required in the environment other than the security-specific ones.

The items addressed here are:

- DMZ re-engineering (do we need to re-model network zones and firewall machines?)
- System isolation (DMZ) and direct access to servers (is there any change necessary to support access to the environment?)
- Administrative networks (is there any change necessary to the management network?)
- VPN access (are there any changes necessary for external users coming through VPN channels?)

Production

This affects the machines, software, operating system, and personnel that maintain the environment. The items covered here include:

- Any new hardware for the Access Manager environment (physical requirements)
- Technical support access (is there any technical support restriction?)
- Production support access (can production support still operate the running systems? Is there any new component to be monitored on a regular basis?)

15.5.2 Implementation considerations

For our first project, *external Web resource protection,* we outline the major components and changes required to the running system. Figure 15-2 on page 339 shows the new Access Manager components required in our environment. The external WebSEAL server is the only entry point for external users. The Access Manager Policy Server is the main component for security policy administration. The Authorization Server is installed on the same machine. Although you can optionally install the Access Manager WPM features to manage most of the Access Manager resources using a graphical user interface implemented on one of the Web application servers, in our scenario we use the command line interface pdadmin to execute all the maintenance procedures as described in the next sections. The following bullets summarize the major changes in the environment:

- There are no significant architectural changes for the application in this phase. Since this is an add-on security implementation, there is little complexity in modifying application behavior. On the other hand, the overall system architecture now relies on a security reference monitor as part of the standard core features that require installation, customization, and maintenance to some extent.

- ► There are few security retrofit concerns to the existing applications. This approach is the simplest implementation considering an existing group of Web applications and thus does not pose severe or complex problems for configuration. In order to make the application receive the same session controls as it may be expecting for authentication, the login code should have some small changes.

- ► There are changes on the network level in order to fit the new hardware and software components. Some network and firewall reconfiguration is required to allow WebSEAL communication from the Internet DMZ to the Production Network. This is discussed in more detail in 15.6.3, "Network changes" on page 358.

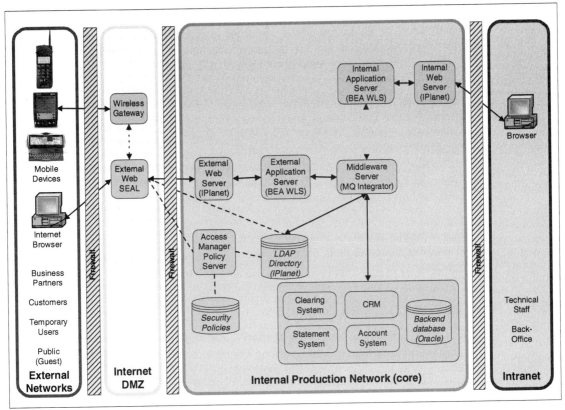

Figure 15-2   External protection example

15.6 Technical implementation

The main technical feature in this first scenario is the addition of the WebSEAL blade so that it creates an entry portal enforcing access control for all external Web requests. The benefit with this approach is that neither the end users access methods nor the applications need to be changed if you want to use standard authentication procedures for accessing the server. Depending on the application implementation, you may need to change the login pages to accommodate the new Access Manager components. Although we describe two different suggestions in this section, there may be other implementation strategies depending on your existing code.

The environment that we describe uses Policy Director 3.8, WebLogic Server 6.1 and iPlanet Directory Server 5.1 as the main components, all running on Windows 2000 Advanced Server. In order to use iPlanet Directory Server we used the manual configuration steps documented in the *Tivoli SecureWay Policy Director Error Message Reference Version 3.8*, GC32-0815.

> **Note:** Although this book generally covers the new Version 3.9 of the IBM Tivoli Access Manager, at the time we wrote this book that version was not yet generally available. The integration for the BEA WebLogic Server we are describing in this chapter was still based on the Tivoli Policy Director Version 3.8. Whenever we describe scenario details around Policy Director functions, we refer to Version 3.8 of the product—and whenever we talk about general information based on Access Manager, we refer to Version 3.9 of the product.

The implementation steps covered here change the authentication process only. The authorization logic is either non-existent or still part of the application and is not covered in this chapter.

15.6.1 Application changes overview

Assuming a situation where the current application uses a login page to execute a back-end login and creates session controls for the application, there is a modification required so that the login process can *trust* the authentication process performed by Policy Director and WebSEAL.

We describe two possible authentication implementation steps for this application. This is a minimum change approach for the application if it already implements some underlaying back-end authentication process. We start from a standard system with its own code and modify it so that it can utilize Policy Director. We define the two main flows as *login flow* and *transaction flow* to demonstrate the scope of the changes. Figure 15-3 shows the variations in all three cases, starting from the existing flow (present scenario), applying changes for basic authentication (approach I), and forms-based authentication (approach II).

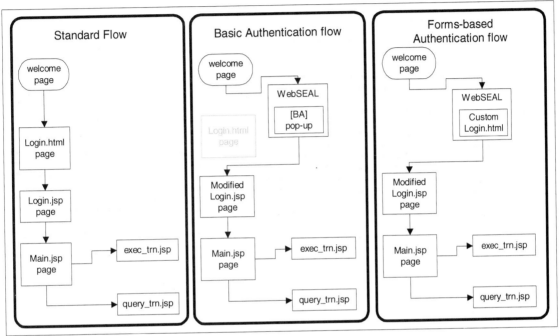

Figure 15-3   Application authentication flow scenarios

Present scenario: Standard flow

These are the current processes that the applications use, including the authentication process today. The authentication code may use a proprietary internal system, a flat password file, or a sophisticated database using LDAP or any other protocol. The bottom-line is that it is an application decision to evaluate whether the provided user authentication information is valid and whether the password is correct. The system flow is as follows.

Login flow (authentication)

The login flow is:

1. The user requests login page through browser (login.html) and waits for an answer.

2. The Web server sends an authentication request with user/password information to the application server (login.jsp).

3. The application server checks credential information using a proprietary authentication code to validate the user. This is still done by the login.jsp page together with the proprietary code communicating with some back-end systems.

4. If successful, the application server login.jsp code creates credential information for this user and makes it available by adding special session information, which can be further retrieved, for example, by exec_trn or query_trn, which are the business transactions that we have.

Transaction flow (authorization)

The transaction flow is:

1. The user requests a transaction page and selects the transaction that he wants to perform.

2. The application validates whether user has access for that given operation by checking session controls and group membership data available through the session and lets the request proceed or not.

3. The application executes the transaction and returns data for the user.

Basic authentication flow

In case the authentication is no longer being enforced by the application, the application needs to trust the security infrastructure components and that the credential information received is authentic. Authentication now becomes a core function of the infrastructure. The flows for that affect the login flow, as the following sections describe.

Login flow (identification and authentication)

The login flow is:

1. The user requests the login page through the browser (login.html) and waits for an answer.

2. WebSEAL executes the basic authentication process and requests user and password information from a pop-up dialog box.

3. WebSEAL performs the authentication.

4. If successful, WebSEAL creates credential information for the user and makes it available to the application by adding special header information, which can be further used by the modified application server (login.jsp) page.

5. The application login.jsp code uses the header information provided by WebSEAL and builds the specific session requirements for the application to work as usual.

Transaction flow (authorization)

This is the standard process that the application already uses without any code modification.

Forms-based authentication flow

This is the same fundamental principle as for basic authentication. The difference is a presentation improvement for the user who now can log in again using a custom HTML form and better session control (see 5.4.2, "Forms-based login with user ID/password" on page 109).

Login flow (identification and authentication)

The login flow is:

1. The user requests the login page through a browser (login.html) and waits for an answer.

2. WebSEAL sends the customized, user-friendly login.html page and waits for the user to submit the form using the fields username and password.

3. The user browser sends information to WebSEAL, which extracts data from the form and performs authentication.

4. If successful, WebSEAL creates credential information for the user and makes it available to the application by adding special header information, which can be further used by the modified application server (login.jsp) page.

5. The application login.jsp code uses the header information provided by WebSEAL and builds the specific session requirements for the application to work as usual.

Transaction flow (authorization)

This is the standard process that the application already uses without any code modification.

Next we look into the detailed specifications for the basic authentication and forms-based authentication approaches.

15.6.2 Changing the existing application

Looking closer at the application code, Figure 15-4 on page 344 shows an existing application with internal proprietary login code that validates the user and password information. This JSP page receives information about the user and password as part of the HTTPServletRequest interface. The authorization flow will be left untouched and is handled by the application as usual.

Without Policy Director, the application executes a myauth.checkuser() call to validate user and password information. If the return code (RC) is zero, then it is assumed to be a valid user and the application session data is properly added. If not, then the login page returns an error and does not create the session variables for the application. All the application components look for some or all session variables when performing operations and thus this data is vital for the application subsystem. A user can always select the logout option and end the application, invalidating the existing session.

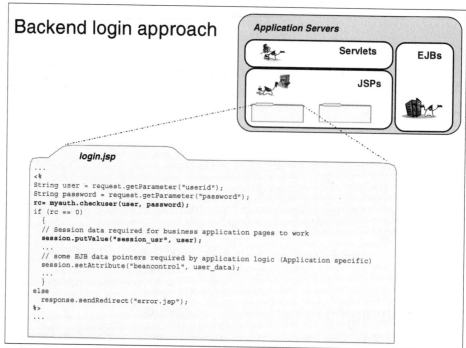

Figure 15-4   Backend login with application

Assuming an environment with Policy Director and WebSEAL already installed in production, it can leverage the initial authentication performed by WebSEAL and release the application from executing authentication calls. This also enhances the security processes that now are consolidated in a trusted condition. This process works well because Policy Director protects the resources in an existing application without any further modifications. The old login.html page is disabled since Policy Director now executes the same functionality. More information on trust concepts can be found in 5.3.2, "Trust" on page 104.

Figure 15-5 shows the modified "login.jsp page, which trusts the preceded WebSEAL authentication process. The key issue is to retrieve the "iv-user header information provided by WebSEAL, and use it to build the trust relationship for the session application data structures. Other data such as iv-groups and iv-creds are also important for future access control validations, which are covered in more detail in Chapter 16, "Application integration" on page 363.

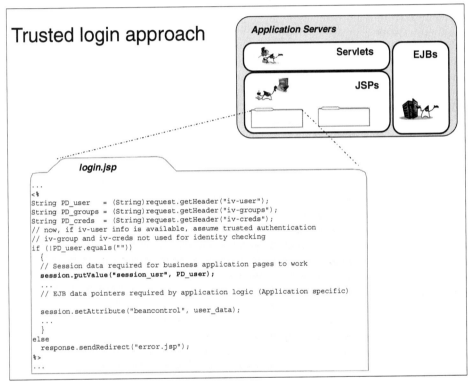

Figure 15-5   Application trust in WebSEAL

Approach I - Implementation with basic authentication

In this section we detail the technical Policy Director steps required to make the basic authentication idea work. The main items that we cover are:

- ▶ WebSEAL junction and webseald.conf configuration
- ▶ Policy Director ACL and object protection
- ▶ Business application and Policy Director object creation

► Using the modified application

WebSEAL junction and webseald.conf configuration

The junction is the key element that enables WebSEAL to handle a user request and route it to the corresponding Web server. By default, when WebSEAL is installed there is a root (/) junction available for the WebSEAL server as a local root junction. We use the root WebSEAL junction for simplicity in our example so that all resources in that WebSEAL blade are automatically handled by this junction. In other environments you may wish to define additional WebSEAL junctions and assign them to your target Web servers.

Since Policy Director needs a WebSEAL junction definition in order to validate incoming requests, we define a junction for the external WebSEAL blade as the root (/) so that all page requests will be validated by this junction definition. You need to define the junction by using the **pdadmin** command as described in Example 15-1.

Example 15-1   Defining a WebSEAL junction for the back-end WebLogic Server

```
pdadmin> server task webseald-w2ktst create -t tcp -p 7001 -h w2ktst -c all -f
/
Created junction at /

pdadmin> server task webseald-w2ktst show /
    Junction point: /
    Type: TCP
    Junction hard limit: 0 - using global value
    Junction soft limit: 0 - using global value
    Active worker threads: 0
    Basic authentication mode: filter
    Authentication HTTP header: insert - iv_user iv_groups iv_creds
    Remote Address HTTP header: do not insert
    Stateful junction: no
    Scripting support: no
    Delegation support: no
    Mutually authenticated: no
    Insert WebSphere LTPA cookies: no
    Insert WebSEAL session cookies: no
    Server 1:
        ID: 64a99738-1792-11d6-a0e1-006094572b0e
        Server State: running
        Hostname: w2ktst
        Port: 7001
        Virtual hostname: w2ktst
        Server DN:
        Query_contents URL: /cgi-bin/query_contents
        Query-contents: unknown
        Case insensitive URLs: no
        Allow Windows-style URLs: yes
```

```
Total requests : 1
```

The previous command shows a definition of a WebSEAL junction / defined for machine webseald-w2ktst that forwards requests via a TCP channel to port 7001 in the target server (-h w2ktst) where port 7001 is the standard BEA WebLogic HTTP port. Production environments should use SSL with a valid certificate installed for added security. The -c flag is required for WebSEAL to propagate the credential information so that the application can extract the credential information to use in the login code. For further junction information, please see the *IBM Tivoli SecureWay Policy Director WebSEAL Administration Guide*, GC32-0684.

> **Important:** For security reasons, you should only allow HTTPS as the protocol for basic authentication.

Next we configure the file *install root*/etc/webseald.conf to make sure we have selected basic authentication by checking the ba-auth entry in the [ba] stanza as HTTPS, which is the default setting. We also modify the standard pop-up banner to show ABBC Bank's name, as shown in Example 15-2.

Example 15-2   Webseald.conf configuration for basic authentication

```
...
ba-auth = https

basic-auth-real = ABBCBank - Basic Authentication Realm. [ba] stanza in
webseald.conf
...
```

Policy Director ACL and object protection

As this is our first Policy Director implementation, we define one access control list for customers (ALL-CUSTOMERS-EXT) and one for registered users (ALL-REGISTEREDUSERS-EXT). Public access is controlled by standard ACL definitions using the unauthenticated and any-other entries for now.

In Example 15-3 we create the required ACLs and execute a simple **show** command. Note that we also could have used the WPM graphical interface to administer ACLs.

Example 15-3   Defining ACL

```
pdadmin> acl create ALL-CUSTOMERS-EXT
pdadmin> acl create ALL-REGISTEREDUSERS-EXT
pdadmin> acl modify ALL-CUSTOMERS-EXT description "General customer ACL"
pdadmin> acl modify ALL-REGISTEREDUSERS-EXT description "General Registered
User ACL"
pdadmin> acl show ALL-REGISTEREDUSERS-EXT
```

```
ACL Name: ALL-REGISTEREDUSERS-EXT
Description: General Registered User ACL
Entries:
     User sec_master TcmdbsvaBl
```

Business application and Policy Director object creation

Figure 15-6 shows the application definition as it appears in the WebLogic
console. The application code (html, jsp, classes) is deployed in one location only
and the public Web application name is ABCBank.

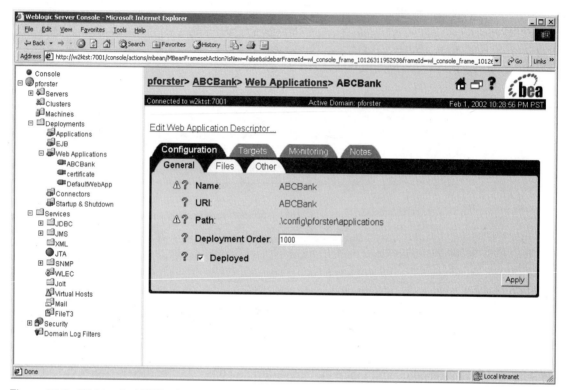

Figure 15-6   WebLogic ABCBank application

Assuming a single WebLogic Web application space, which is defined in the
server pforster as ABCBank, we now define the Policy Director objects and
groups and assign the proper ACLs to them. Figure 15-7 on page 349 shows a
sample of the CUSTOMER space in the iPlanet Directory server screen. Those
users are already part of the CUSTOMER group in our application.

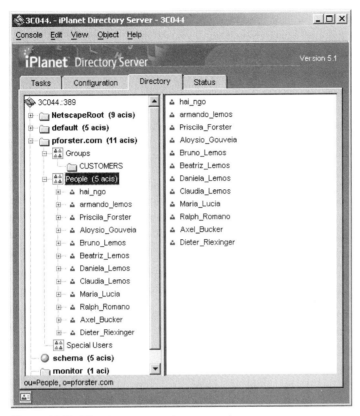

Figure 15-7   Directory server view

Shown in Example 15-4, we now modify the existing ACL information to include the Policy Director CUSTOMER group so that it can enforce access control for those users when that ACL is used. Finally we attach the ACL to the ABCBank application.

Example 15-4   Assigning Policy Director ACL to objects and defining groups

```
pdadmin> group show-members CUSTOMERS
Hai Ngo
Armando Lemos
Claudia Lemos
Daniela Lemos
Bruno Lemos
Beatriz Lemos
Priscila Forster
Ralph Romano
Aloysio Gouveia
Axel Bucker
```

Dieter Riexinger

```
pdadmin> acl modify ALL-CUSTOMERS-EXT set group CUSTOMERS rxT

pdadmin> acl show ALL-CUSTOMERS-EXT
    ACL Name: ALL-CUSTOMERS-EXT
    Description: General customer ACL
    Entries:
        User sec_master TcmdbsvaBl
        Group CUSTOMERS Trx

pdadmin> acl attach /WebSEAL/w2ktst/ABCBank ALL-CUSTOMERS-EXT

pdadmin> object show /WebSEAL/w2ktst/ABCBank
    Name : /WebSEAL/w2ktst/ABCBank
        Description : Object from host w2ktst.
        Type :  (Management Object)  : 16
        Is Policy Attachable : yes
        ACL : ALL-CUSTOMERS-EXT
```

Using the modified application

Now we can log in to the application and check whether WebSEAL is enforcing the authentication and passing the data to the back-end application.

1. After typing in the URL `https://w2ktst/ABCBank/welcome.jsp`, WebSEAL's basic authentication pop-up box appears, as depicted in Figure 15-8.

Figure 15-8   WebSEAL basic authentication pop-up box

2. Enter a customer user ID and password for authentication. The welcome screen appears, as shown in Figure 15-9.

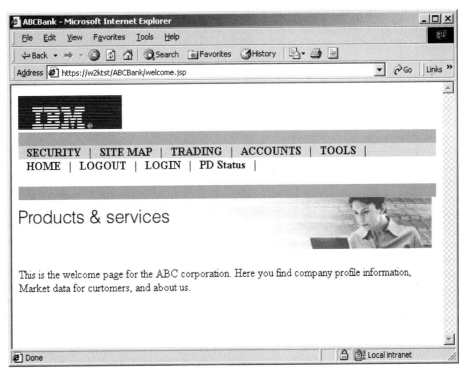

Figure 15-9   Successful login to the ABCBank Web environment

3. Select the **PD Status** option in the navigation bar. Figure 15-9 shows the Policy Director credential information that was made available to the application for user armando lemos. The internal application controls are not visible (that is, populated) yet, and we have enabled a simple test option to make Policy Director controls available to the application. In a real environment, the welcome.jsp screen should call the modified login.jsp page to make sure that the internal application controls are properly set beforehand.

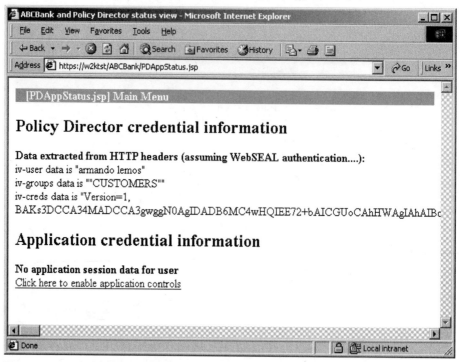

Figure 15-10   Policy Director credential information

In this example we added a link option for simplicity in order to understand the transition between the Policy Director parameters and the application controls (which should be handled together). By clicking the provided link you can see that the application has established its session control parameters as expected for normal usage (in our case sourceHost, sourceIP, usercode, and app_logged_in). This is shown in Figure 15-11 on page 353.

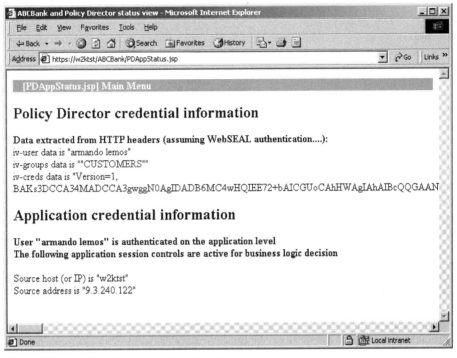

Figure 15-11   Policy Director and application trust

Note: The old login.html page should be deleted from the server. Since the sample code here still keeps the old login logic as well, you must make sure that the old authentication code is totally removed in the final version of the code.

Approach II - Forms-based authentication

Although Policy Director can be quickly implemented in any Web environment without modifications to the running application, there are cases where you may need to further customize the authentication process to make it more user friendly. Commonly, the application has a welcome screen with a nice looking login page with information about the system or how to perform the login procedure. This usually means National Language Support or other country-specific requirements that the business wants. The goal here is to enhance the customer experience to the Web site, using a nice looking HTML form instead of the WebSEAL pop-up dialog box.

Assuming the same application model that we described in the basic authentication scenario, the login.html page can now be used again as the presentation layer to prompt for user and password information using an identical look and feel as the other pages in the site. The application itself does not require any changes.

The main items we cover here are:

▶ WebSEAL junction and webseald.conf configuration
▶ Installing the new login page
▶ Policy Director ACL and object protection
▶ Using the modified application

WebSEAL junction and webseald.conf configuration

Assuming the previous configuration where we had basic authentication configured, we now must switch to forms-based authentication by changing ba-auth and enabling forms-auth in the webseald.conf file, as shown in Example 15-5.

Example 15-5   Enabling forms-based authentication in webseald.conf

```
...
ba-auth = none
...
forms-auth = https
...
```

This enables WebSEAL to use the predefined HTML template files that are located at *webseal install*/lib/html. The actual files are stored in a language-specific directory. The default United States English directory is:

```
lib/html/C
```

Installing the new login page

We need to store our existing login.html file to *webseal install*/lib/html/C so that WebSEAL can use it as the predefined login form. Since this is a template directory only accessible to WebSEAL, and assuming that there may be locale issues so that it makes sense to have the login page fully available for WebSEAL itself (including the images), then we also have to store it in the doc-root tree in the same WebSEAL machine. Let us assume an image directory *doc-root*/images for storing all images for the HTML forms including the login.html that we are changing. Since we are converting an existing HTML page, there are three things that must be in place so that WebSEAL can present the form properly:

▶ The user field in the form must be called username.
▶ The password field in the form must be called password.
▶ The FORM tag must have the ACTION statement set as /pkmslogin.form.

> **Note:** It is not mandatory to have the images on the WebSEAL server. You can also have a junction /images pointing to the Web server. The only requirement is that the objects be accessible to unauthenticated users.

Example 15-6 shows an extract of the code with those changes.

Example 15-6   Forms-based authentication and required changes

```
...
<script language='javascript'>
   function submitForm(formValue,form)
   {
    var username = document.index.username.value;
    var pass = document.index.password.value;
    if (formValue == 0)
      {
        if((username == "") || (pass == ""))
           { alert("please enter all fields.");
            formValue = 1;
           }
           else
           { document.index.action="/pkmslogin.form";
            document.index.submit();
           }
      } //end of if form value==0
    else
      { document.index.reset();
      }
   }

   function myInputType(frm)
   {
    var myVal=frm.username;
    document.index.username.value = "************";
   }
</script>
...
<IMG src="/images/lanim.gif" border="0" ></TD>
      <table BORDER=0 CELLSPACING=0 CELLPADDING=0 BGCOLOR="#FFFFFF" >
        <caption><form name='index' method='post'></caption>
...
```

Also, we changed the relative path for the images to an absolute path as <IMG src="/images/lanim.gif"> in the HTML code because WebSEAL needs to access them as external resources. We also need to define a junction (as described in the following section) so that the page shows the images correctly. All images required for the login.html page in our example are located at *doc-root*/images on the WebSEAL machine. This is shown in Figure 15-12.

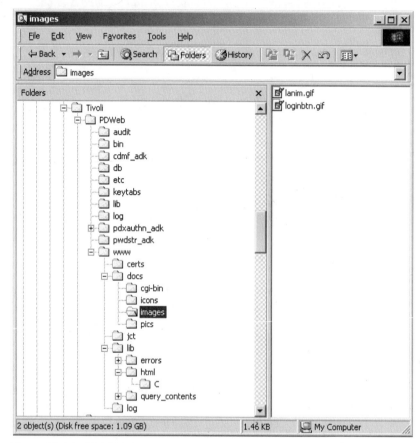

Figure 15-12   WebSEAL root-doc and HTML library locations

Policy Director ACL and object protection

As in the previous example, we need to define some access permissions so that the login page can be displayed correctly and the junction definition is important for proper WebSEAL object location. We define a new Policy Director ALL-PUBLIC group to allow external users to access the image directory. We need to define a junction for the external WebSEAL (webseald-w2ktst) as /images, so that image requests can be validated by this junction definition. Issue the `pdadmin` commands, as in Example 15-7 on page 357.

Example 15-7   Defining the /image junction and Policy Director ACL

```
pdadmin> acl create ALL-PUBLIC

pdadmin> acl modify ALL-PUBLIC set any-other Trx

pdadmin> acl modify ALL-PUBLIC set unauthenticated Trx

pdadmin> acl show ALL-PUBLIC
    ACL Name: ALL-PUBLIC
    Description:
    Entries:
        User sec_master TcmdbsvaBl
        Unauthenticated Trx
        Any-other Trx

pdadmin> server task webseald-w2ktst create -t local
-d "e:\program files\tivoli\pdweb\www\docs\images" /images
Created junction at /images

pdadmin> acl attach /WebSEAL/w2ktst/images ALL-PUBLIC
```

Using the modified application

The application execution is basically the same as described in the previous section. After typing in the URL `https://w2ktst/ABCBank/welcome.jsp`, the WebSEAL forms-based authentication now presents the login page, as shown in Figure 15-13 on page 358.

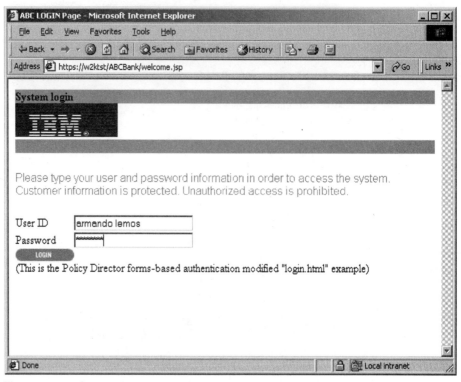

Figure 15-13   Custom forms-based login screen

The login page executes the same code as before and opens the welcome.jsp page for the user. This is exactly the same behavior as in the previous example with basic authentication. The biggest difference in this case is that users can experience the same look ad feel as before by accessing a user-friendly login page, with possibly different options and language settings. This is all done with Policy Director integrated to the identification and authentication.

15.6.3 Network changes

The addition of Policy Director requires some firewall changes. Due to the fact that WebSEAL may take over the old IP address from the Web sever(s), the Internet firewalls may not require changes at all, keeping the HTTP/HTTPS rules as the (only) required ports for the Web functionality.

Note: You may have other services such as mail, FTP, and so on, that may require other firewall rules to exist.

Assuming the Web server(s) are now located inside the production network, there must be a new firewall rule to allow communication from WebSEAL to the Web server(s) inside, obviously with the new IP addresses since the Web server(s) now belong to a different network. Figure 15-14 shows the network ports that should be configured.

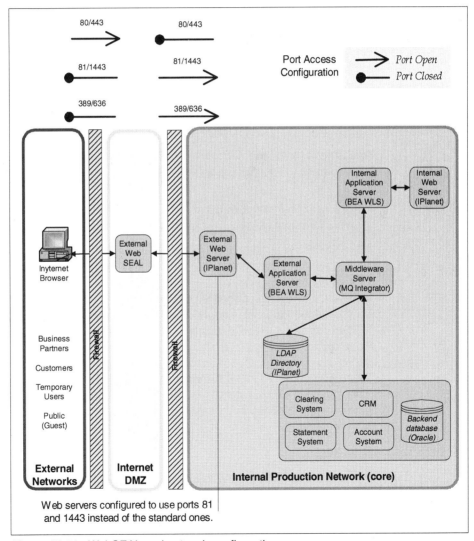

Figure 15-14   WebSEAL and network configuration

For security reasons, it is advisable to change the Web server ports to different ports. In our case, we defined HTTP port as 81 and HTTPS as port 1443 for the Web server. You must now create a firewall rule that allows TCP traffic from the WebSEAL IP addresses to port 81/1443 going to the Web server(s) new IP addresses. Also, WebSEAL requires LDAP ports to be opened. For added security you should open port 636 (LDAPS) only, but you may also consider opening port 389 (LDAP) if the firewall rules are consistent and the network segregation and isolation prevents external access to those services. This may even be required if you plan for high volume authentication, where an LDAP replica could be needed.

You should configure your external Web servers to only allow incoming HTTP/HTTPS traffic from the IP addresses of your WebSEAL server(s). This increases the trust relationship towards WebSEAL since no other session can be established except those coming from WebSEAL.

There is no routing or major network requirement other than assigning the new IP addresses to the servers in the subnetworks. There are no additional firewall rules.

For further information about Policy Director and network protection please see 2.7, "Component configuration and placement" on page 45.

> **Important:** Make sure that WebSEAL, and no other Web or Web application server, is the only externally visible server for HTTP/HTTPS access.

15.6.4 Production

There are no new components required for production other than the additional WebSEAL components. New hardware is required for the Access Manager Policy Server and WebSEAL. Although the sizing of the servers is out of the scope of this chapter, you may consider one set of machines for the WebSEAL blades as well as another set of machines for the Access Manager Policy Server. Depending on the load for authentication, you may need to consider additional LDAP replicas. Further details on this topic can be obtained in Chapter 4, "Increasing availability and scalability" on page 79.

15.6.5 Conclusion

We have demonstrated how to integrate a production application with little changes into a new login flow so that Access Manager call now remove the burden of the authentication complexity from the application. It is also true that this introduces new benefits such as user activity logging, central management and cost reduction as more applications take more benefit of the Access Manager infrastructure, as we describe in the following banking scenarios. The external Web access now implements a new, robust protection feature that improves flexibility and easy system architecture changes.

Application integration

This chapter provides a description of the business and functional requirements for the banking scenario, adding new design and implementation aspects for improving the banking application. The main goal of the second project phase is to fully protect all Web traffic for external and internal users, adding fine-grained access controls for user groups as well as integrating existing applications into the security infrastructure. Existing Web applications make use of the security functionality provided by Access Manager using J2EE security.

16.1 Business requirements

This project is based on an increased number of business requirements with direct implications to application behavior. The initial project I covered the addition of Access Manager components creating the secure infrastructure so that we can expand new security features based on that.

16.1.1 Phase II requirements scope

The following are complementary requirements from the business process owners:

- ► Support different types of customers: Classic, Gold, Premium.
- ► Provide differentiated content depending on which customers logged in.
- ► Support internal staff and operations employees that need to interact with customers, such as call centers or sales, through an internal (but similar to the external) Web interface.
- ► Support multiple internal staff users (support, back-end operations, technology, call center) and levels (operator, manager, and so on).
- ► Web tools should utilize coarse-grained controls on the page (can/cannot access specific pages) as well as customized presentation depending on the customer privileges.
- ► Reduce management overhead in the current IT environment.
- ► It is required to enhance the privacy and confidentiality for data sent through the internal network.

Some of these requirements are implemented with new functionality to the Web site, as we cover in the next section. Others are simply leveraged by the new secure infrastructure such as privacy, coarse-grained controls, and reducing management overhead.

16.2 Functional requirements

The new security features we are adding to the system are directly related to supporting new users and user types, and defining different groups to segment external users in order to better fit the new business model.

16.2.1 New user groups

The system must enable or disable different functions for the users depending on their group membership. This is valid for customers and internal users as well. In order to comply with the new business requirements, we must now define categories or roles to map different user entities. Our original Customer group may now span different subgroups such as:

► Classic: Standard customers or customers that have just opened an account. They can be promoted to higher category at any time.

► Gold customers: Customers with a certain account balance or partnership status with the bank. These users cannot be downgraded to Classic, but can be promoted to higher categories.

► Premium customers: This is the highest level of customer in the system. These customers can only be downgraded to the Gold category if they do not keep a minimum amount in the bank.

The different customer categories here are related to new tools that can be used by the different user groups. Therefore, there are now different tools for different types of external users. All other functions still remain the same.

16.2.2 More granular authorization

Customer restrictions still apply in terms of requiring one login password for query operations and one additional password for transactions. On the other hand, the system must handle internal user requests in such a way that it operates queries and transactions on behalf of customers, but using the internal user's authentication requirements instead. Sales and call center users have different access to customer information.

The standard pages for external users are also available for the internal sales and CRM users, depending on their group membership. We assume this kind of authorization is controlled by the application already.

Figure 16-1 on page 366 shows the access control modifications required in the functional table to cope with the new business requirements. Note the bold names defining the new access restrictions or additions with a plus sign (+) before the name. In our example, the Accounts subtree has additional groups including the ones defined in the high-level hierarchy (such as SALES, BO-STAFF, and CONTROLLING), while the Tools subtree redefines access to some of the groups (College Planner, for example, stays the same as Tools).

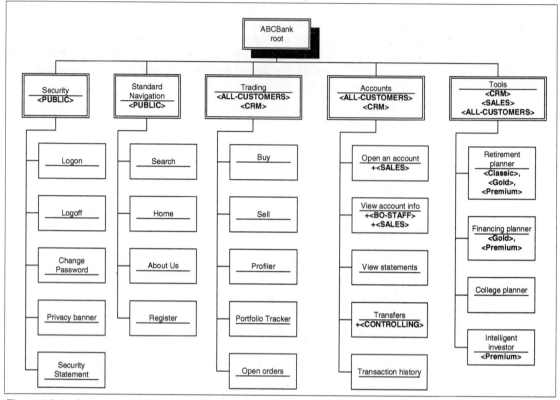

Figure 16-1   Access control and functional requirements

From an internal perspective, staff users may need to execute transactions on behalf of external users, such as query, monitoring, consolidation, reporting, and so on. Those functions are backoffice operations that must be carried out on a daily basis in order to execute the end-of-day (EOD) processing. Also, sales and call center employees must have different access rights to interact with customers.

The following internal groups have additional access to the system:

► Backoffice operations (BO-STAFF): Users that execute account checking, maintenance, trades, and other financial checks.

► Controlling operations (CONTROLLING): Users that validate banking information and customer trades.

► Sales (SALES): Users that interact with customers over the phone or personally. They are allowed to query their customer base and to open new accounts.

- Call center representative (CRM): Users that interact with customers over the phone. They are allowed to execute any transaction on behalf of customers.

Those users have access through an internal and independent application system, so that it is also more secure for them to execute those specialized functions. The concept is to have a Web infrastructure to serve hundreds of concurrent customers with load balancing and hot stand-by technologies and another small-scale infrastructure to serve a smaller number of peak requests for the internal team, allowing better scalability and phased code migration.

16.3 Security design objectives

This scenario creates some Access Manager challenges with respect to broadening the scope of protection and also controlling each of the components in a more detailed fashion.

16.3.1 Support for multiple network entry access points

We need to add new WebSEAL servers for the intranet users to make sure that only authorized staff has access to the internal Web and Web application servers. Already discussed for external protection only in Chapter 15, "Protection of external Web resources" on page 329, we now need to assure that all Web resources are properly controlled, independently of the entry point.

16.3.2 Identification

Since the application user scope is external (customers, vendors, visitors, staff) and internal (staff, vendors), the system needs to be able to identify and handle different types of users and use that identity as part of the authorization checking to grant or deny access based on user type or category. The external user types segregate customer categories and product offerings targeted to their needs (or in case they buy the service). Internal user types are controlled on a "need-to-have" or "need-to-know" principle to execute operations on behalf of external users.

Additional controls are introduced for customer groups by creating the new classic, gold, and premium groups and assigning users to them.

16.3.3 Total security control

Although applications may have different security requirements, users, and groups, the infrastructure that we deploy must handle all the different needs in a consolidated manner. Since the application server is the core component for storing business logic and presentation, we dedicate special attention to its security, for example, by integrating the WebLogic Custom Realm with Access Manager.

16.3.4 Authentication

Different levels of authentication are required, especially for internal users. All customers still use the dual password concept, one password for login and standard query operations and one additional password every time they execute a money transfer-related transaction. Both passwords are static for simplicity, but the transactional password could even be randomly generated by token devices or tables that could provide additional security. Internal users are also required to have dual authentication in order to execute the same set of money-related transactions by using their own private passwords.

16.4 Design approach

The new scope modifies the external functionality for customers, but it also enhances the internal capabilities quite a bit, allowing other types of users to share the same components to better serve the customers. The existing architecture allows the presentation layer (Web interface) to share the same system back-end operations. Some changes are necessary in the presentation layer and in passing the trust information on the authenticated principals to the application.

The following major security goals are now important:

► Enforce access control for both external and internal users.

It is extremely important to understand the different internal roles in the system and the different access levels. Since the application already exists for customers, it is also desirable that internal users share the same look and feel, especially for those internal groups with customer interaction. This makes it is easier for both to clarify issues and assist with system navigation, if requested. The internal application server will hold all internally modified code to enforce segregation and independence of services.

- Allow only authorized users to access any given Web application, regardless of the source (entry point).

  The idea of segregation for external and internal users creates a baseline infrastructure for enforcing different access control enforcement points for those entry channels, because there may be cases where you need to enforce users to only use one specific channel (that is, internal users should access the internal application server only).

- Control access to the application pages based on the user's group membership.

  This can be accomplished either by application coding (that is, programmatic) or by using WebSEAL (that is, independent). The ideal approach is to use WebSEAL, keeping the access control functions transparent and independent from the application.

- Allow transaction execution only for particular group members or individual users.

  This requirement is related to the way the application handles transactions and how many internal back-end systems it needs to check in order to execute a transaction. This is a more programmatic approach in the sense that the application needs to combine different business logic to decide whether a user is authorized for a particular operation, which can be different for other users. This situation can even go to the limit of only allowing operation for a user under a very special situation, such as allowing money transfers only to predefined accounts.

16.5 Implementation architecture

We start from a working environment with Access Manager already configured. The Access Manager Policy Server is installed in the production network, WebSEAL machines are part of the external infrastructure, and all incoming HTTP/HTTPS Web requests are directed to the WebSEAL servers in the DMZ.

The new system architecture also requires some additional component installation, in particular new WebSEAL servers for internal access control. The application may require some restructuring for some of the controls, especially to transfer some of the WebLogic controls (as for roles) to Access Manager. Although this is done without affecting the application code, it is worth mentioning that any further control should now rely on Access Manager. Figure 16-2 on page 370 shows the new system architecture that we use with additional WebSEAL servers in the internal network, making the intranet path controlled by

WebSEAL as well. The other system components stay exactly the same. The internal users are not impacted since the transition keeps the same system resources visible, but now with a secure and unique entry point provided by the WebSEAL layer.

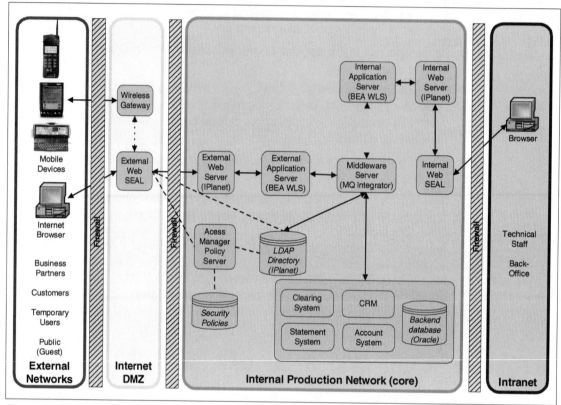

Figure 16-2   Internal access protection

16.5.1 Single sign-on for WebLogic with WebSEAL

One of the major security concerns has always been the multitude of passwords and different login mechanisms. Web single sign-on (SSO) is the technical response to the challenge of implementing some level of trust between Web application components.

The Web server's trust relationship towards WebSEAL is maintained through the junction defined between WebSEAL and the Web server. Figure 16-3 on page 371 shows an example how WebSEAL accomplishes the trust concept by using junctions.

These junctions can be configured for different levels of trust:

► They can use SSL encryption for data transfer between WebSEAL and the back-end Web servers.

► When using an SSL junction, WebSEAL automatically verifies the server-side certificate of the back-end Web server.

► Both WebSEAL and the back-end Web server can implement mutual authentication using the SSL junction.

To learn more about the details of configuring junctions, refer to the *IBM Tivoli Access Manager for e-Business WebSEAL Administration Guide Version 3.9*, GC23-4682.

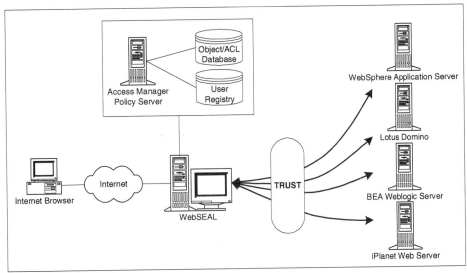

Figure 16-3   WebSEAL trust concept

The other essential aspect of trust is the WebLogic target application server's trust of the requester. This requires WebSEAL to act as a front-end authentication server while the WebLogic Server applies its own authorization policy onto the user credentials that WebSEAL passes on. To learn more about the different configuration options on how to pass on user credentials, refer to Chapter 5, "Authentication and delegation with Access Manager" on page 97.

In our particular approach, both of the previously mentioned aspects of trust are maintained. Additionally, all of the advantages of WebSEAL (high availability, load balancing, state management, scalability, support for multiple identity mechanisms, and so on) and of products that work with Access Manager apply.

The Access Manager Custom Realm is the foundation for this level of integration. The combination of WebSEAL and the Access Manager Custom Realm allows single sign-on, as well as user/group-based authorization decisions. This means that an Access Manager administrator can move users between groups that are mapped to the required roles in the J2EE application and thus affect which functions they are authorized for.

16.5.2 WebLogic and WebSEAL single sign-on

The single sign-on procedure is as follows:

1. When a user attempts access to a protected resource, WebSEAL requests proof of identity from the user. This proof of identity may be provided via a user name/password, certificate, user name and RSA SecureID, or a custom authentication mechanism supported by a WebSEAL Cross Domain Authentication Service (CDAS).

2. The identity material is presented to Access Manager WebSEAL or to a custom CDAS. WebSEAL first authenticates the user and then creates his credentials, the EPAC. When a CDAS is installed, it authenticates the user on behalf of WebSEAL and returns an Access Manager user identity to WebSEAL. WebSEAL can now perform checks such as account validity and time-of-day access restrictions.

3. The user's credentials are used to determine if the user is authorized to access the requested resource. The authorization is made by the Access Manager authorization engine using a locally cached copy of the authorization policy database and includes such considerations as account validity, time-of-day, authentication mechanism, and so on.

4. WebSEAL forwards the user's principal name and a password as basic authentication data to the WebLogic Server. The password, however, does not correspond to the client's Access Manager principal. Instead, it corresponds to another principal, known as the *configured user*, used solely for the purpose of authenticating the WebSEAL server to the back-end application server.

5. The WebLogic Server transparently passes this user name and configured user password through to the configured Access Manager Custom Realm, which verifies via Access Manager authentication services that the password provided by WebSEAL is correct for the special principal described above (that is, this password provides the basis of trust that the request's origin is WebSEAL).

6. If successful, the Access Manager Custom Realm returns the user's identity to the WebLogic Server.

7. If the client request requires the user to be in a role, then the WebLogic Server passes (one at a time) each group that is mapped to the role in the relevant deployment descriptor to the Access Manager Custom Realm.

8. The Access Manager Custom Realm uses the Access Manager Administration API to obtain the set of users that belong to that group, and returns the user list to the WebLogic Server.

9. The WebLogic Server makes an authorization decision using the user's group membership and either processes or rejects the user's request.

10. The output of the request is returned to the user via WebSEAL.

16.5.3 Application security variations

After introducing an overview of the possible application security variations we chose the one to use with our Access Manager security project. This discussion is important in order to define the relationship between Access Manager and the running environment for the application. An application can be classified as a collection of resources such as HTML forms, JSPs, servlets, back-end classes, and beans, each one of them having some or no security context or interface.

We can group the application security into three main categories:

► Programmatic approach

When applications control security by themselves using an internal proprietary process, code, and database to grant, deny, log, and manage security, they have implemented programmatic access control. Generally, the applications request principal information about users and resources, and they use security API calls to retrieve access control information for those principals. Finally, the application logic enforces security by granting or denying access to specific resources provided by the application.

Using this approach, applications become the decision factor for security and may even bypass important security checks. Usually this is done when there is no general infrastructure in place to handle security. This encompasses all resources for the application such as Web pages, back-end classes, and EJB, if available.

► Declarative approach

Applications use declarative access control by using an external source for the actual access control checking. There is no proprietary logic and the application communicates with the access control system using a specific and well-known set of rules defined by an API interface. The application does not implement or combine access rules, it just uses the ones provided, limiting the access control check to what the API can offer.

After querying the access control subsystem as to whether a given principal may access a requested resource, the application receives a simple yes or no answer, and based on that answer it either grants or denies the respective access. This can be considered the ideal situation, since it defines the scope and responsibility of the application in the autorization request and transaction execution steps. This also implies that the application does not control the actual flow of the logic, and that it is more difficult, if not impossible, to bypass the authorization layer in this case.

► Mixed

This is not really a category of its own, but covers the situation where applications take benefit of the infrastructure available when possible (using declarative techniques) and implementing only a few special controls using standard API calls (ideally compliant with JAAS, J2EE, or some other well-known standard). We recommend that you carefully use the programmatic approach to enhance the rule checking mechanism by providing fine-grained access controls when there is a lack of native APIs to offer that capability, but still utilizing one unique API set to handle the core requests.

Figure 16-4 shows each application component separated in secure/not secure sections. Since we want to discuss the security measures that we can accommodate in Access Manager, we concentrate on examining the secure components.

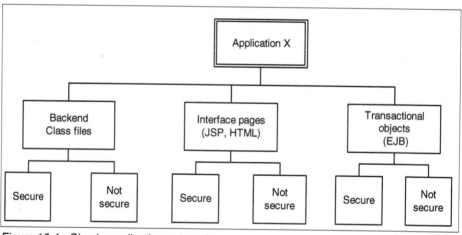

Figure 16-4   Simple application categories

Figure 16-5 on page 375 provides a view for each secure component showing which kind of controls we can add using Access Manager, and combining those possibilities with the application categories.

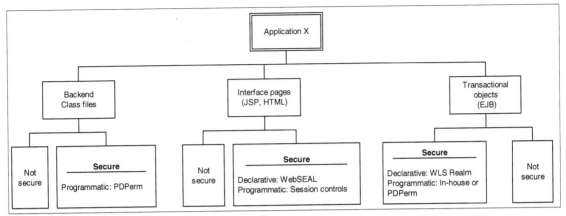

Figure 16-5   Security options for each component

16.6 Technical implementation

The major new technical components in this scenario are the addition of new WebSEAL machines for the internal users, new user types to control more detailed user groups for external users, the addition of new internal groups, WebLogic EJB controls, and Access Manager Custom Realm and Application controls using JAVA API calls to Access Manager security classes (PDPermission). We assume that the application has internal controls to manage very specific user conditions, and Access Manager can handle much of the authorization decisions including Web page requests and WebLogic Bean access, as described in the previous section.

The environment that we describe has Policy Director 3.8, WebLogic Server 6.1, and iPlanet Directory Server 5.1 as the main components, all running on Windows 2000 Advanced Server. Figure 16-6 on page 376 shows our sample configuration with two servers. WebSEAL is listening on port 80/443 for external HTTP/HTTPS requests. WebLogic Server 1 (WLS-1) is the primary machine for HTML and JSP code. WebLogic Server 2 (WLS-2) is the primary machine for EJB resources. In a real production configuration, the WebSEAL components should be deployed as machines independent from the application servers.

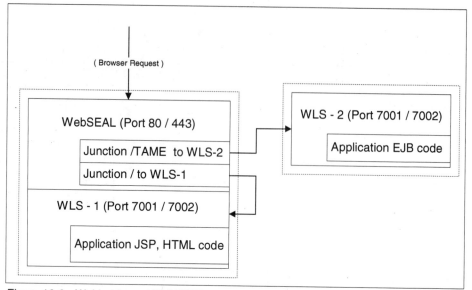

Figure 16-6   WebLogic and WebSEAL sample installation

Note: The implementation steps covered here change the authentication process and authorization as well, with respect to the Access Manager Custom Realm and Java-based PDPermission calls.

16.6.1 Architecture changes summary

This is the high-level summary of the changes in the environment and the application as a whole. The next sections cover in detail all topics listed either as a separate item or as part of the general discussion.

▶ Add new WebSEAL machines for internal users.

▶ Reconfigure internal firewalls.

▶ Make WebSEAL the only externally visible server for Web access.

▶ Create new Access Manager objects to control new customer groups and internal users.

▶ Use the Access Manager Custom Realm to enable access control for WebLogic objects such as EJBs supporting single sign-on via WebSEAL as well as a common, Access Manager-administered, user registry.

▶ Insert additional API calls in the application layer to check additional controls that are managed by Access Manager (PDPermission).

16.6.2 Access Manager Custom Realm

We describe how to install the Access Manager for WebLogic Server component in order to control the users and resources in one single location. We start our discussion with some of the possible EJB security issues related to WebLogic and how to leverage the same definitions in our migration scenario.

> **Important:** For detailed installation questions please see the *Tivoli Policy Director for WebLogic Server User Guide Version 3.8*, SC32-0831.
>
> The installation package for Policy Director 3.8 is available as a software download from the following URL:
>
> `http://www.tivoli.com/secure/support/downloads/secureway/policy_dir/downloads.html`
>
> A valid login and password is required to access the Tivoli Customer Support software download site.
>
> The BEA WebLogic Custom Realm is a base component in the Tivoli Access Manager 3.9 release.

Assuming that the existing banking applications use JavaBeans to execute transactional operations such as query customer account information, buy funds, sell stocks, check for wire transfers, and so forth, the beans may either be protected by WebLogic roles and group mappings (which now become an administration problem since users and groups need to be maintained), or left unprotected and leaving it up to the application code to instantiate and execute any bean they may need, which can also open other security concerns.

The ideal solution is to keep the existing security enforcement for the EJB objects (if any exist) and define an additional common layer that can be used to integrate EJB role controls and Access Manager, taking benefit of the unified user repository and enhanced authorization functionalities provided by Access Manager.

We demonstrate here the use of a stateless bean using a new integration feature called IBM Tivoli Access Manager Custom Realm for BEA WebLogic Server 6.1, which is a WebLogic Custom Realm that supports single sign-on via WebSEAL as well as a common, Access Manager-administered, user registry.

Also, by using the new Access Manager Custom Realm we can extend the group protection for customers to grant access only for those authorized to call the Bean objects, making the total Web space more secure for transactional operations.

Installation and configuration procedure

This procedure assumes that WLS 6.1 is currently installed without a custom realm and is launched using startWebLogic.cmd. Also, PDRTE, PDMgr, PDWeb, and PDAcld (only required if the Access Manager Custom Realm is to be configured as a *remote mode* application) are installed and configured as described in the relevant Access Manager manuals. Only PDRTE is required to be co-resident with the Access Manager Custom Realm. The aznAPI is only used for authentication of the *configured user*. Furthermore, this authentication only occurs once because the result is cached. Since no authorization decisions are made via the aznAPI, it is recommended to use the aznAPI in remote mode.

The key to variables for the installation are detailed in Table 16-1.

Table 16-1   Key variables for Access Manager WLS Realm installation

Variable	Description
BEA home	The BEA installation directory. In a standard installation, this value would be C:\bea or \bea.
BEA domain directory	The directory of the installed domain of the WLS server. In a standard install this value would be C:\bea\wlserver6.1\Config\mydomain or \bea\ wlserver6.1\Config\mydomain.
webseald server name	Name of the Access Manager server for WebSEAL, generally of the form webseald-hostname.
PDRealm	Name of the Access Manager Custom Realm that will be added to WLS. This name can be anything you choose.
AZN conf file path	The fully qualified path of the aznAPI.conf file that is generated from configuring an aznAPI application using svrsslcfg.
PD work directory	A directory that will be used to store the aznAPI.conf file, as well as the Access Manager certificates that will be used by the WLS server to communicate with the Access Manager servers. It will also be used as a temporary folder.
<configured user>	The special user that is configured in the Access Manager Custom Realm configuration data in order to form a trust relationship between WebSEAL and WLS. The name of this user can be any valid user name.

Variable	Description
<configured user password>	The password of the *configured user*.
WLS server	Host name of the WLS server.
WLS listen port	The port that the WLS server is listening on.
junction target	URL target of the junction.
pdadmin context user	Name of the user that will be used to create a pdadmin context. This user must be in the iv-admin user group or be delegated enough permission to be able to create/delete/modify/list users and groups. You can do this by giving the user the following permissions on an ACL attached to the /Management object TcmdbsvatNWA. The name of the default ACL attached to the /Management object is default-management.
pdadmin context user password	Password for the above user.

The installation and customization steps required to have the WLS custom realm properly set up are:

1. Register WLS as an aznAPI application.
2. Configure Custom Realm in WLS.
3. Configure the WLS junction.
4. Check that the configuration works.
5. Access Manager Custom Realm demo procedure.

Register WLS as an aznAPI application

Follow these steps on the WLS machine:

1. Install and configure PDRTE and AuthADK as per the *IBM Tivoli Access Manager for e-business Base Installation Guide Version 3.9,* GC32-0844. Example 16-1 on page 380 shows a configuration pointing to a Policy Server installed at server w2ktst and running LDAP services on port 3890. Figure 16-7 on page 381 shows the additional configuration summary for PDRTE, if you do not have the certificate file available during the initial setup. You can run the pdconfig utility to reconfigure any of the components at a later time.

Note: Make sure that you have the pdcacert.b64 file available if you are separately installing PDRTE using the ezinstall_pd scripts. Copy the file from your management machine and save it in your new target machine as, for example,
C:\Program Files\Tivoli\Policy Director\keytab\pdcacert.b64.

Example 16-1   Sample configuration options for PDRTE script

```
IBM Global Security Toolkit
------------------------------------------------------
Option                                      Value
1. Installation Directory ................. C:\Program Files\IBM\GSK

IBM SecureWay Directory Client
------------------------------------------------------
Option                                      Value
1. Installation Directory ................. C:\Program Files\IBM\LDAP

Tivoli SecureWay Policy Director Runtime Configuration Options
------------------------------------------------------
Option                                      Value
 1. Configure Using This Registry Type ....... ldap
 2. LDAP Server Hostname .................... w2ktst
 3. LDAP Server Port ........................ 3890
 4. Suffix ................................. secAuthority=Default
 5. Enable SSL with LDAP Server ............. n
 6. LDAP SSL Keyfile ........................
 7. LDAP SSL Keyfile DN .....................
 8. LDAP SSL Key File Password ..............
 9. LDAP Server SSL Port .................... 636
10. Installation Directory ................. C:\Program Files\Tivoli\Policy
Director
11. Policy Director Management Server Hostname w2ktst
12. SSL Server Port for Policy Director Management Server.. 7135
13. Policy Director CA Certificate Filename ..
```

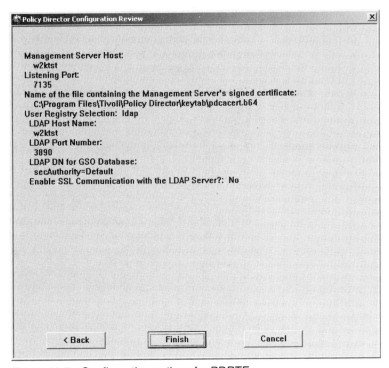

Figure 16-7   Configuration options for PDRTE

2. Configure aznAPI using svrsslcfg (shipped with PDRTE) as described in the
   *Tivoli SecureWay Policy Director Authorization ADK Developer Reference
   Version 3.8,* GC32-0810. The svrsslcfg command should be something like
   the following:

   ```
   svrsslcfg -config -f cfg_file -d kdb_dir -n server_name -s server_type -r
   port -P admin_pwd -S server_password
   ```

   Note: Paths should be specified as full paths, not relative paths.

   Where:

   cfg_file   Configuration file name.

   kdb_dir   The full directory that is to contain the key ring database
                         files for the server.

   server_name   The name of the server. The name may be specified as
                         either server_name/hostname or server_name, in which
                         case the local host name will be appended to form
                         name/host name. The names ivacld, secmgrd, ivnet, and
                         ivweb are reserved for Access Manager servers.

server_type   The type of server being configured. The value must be either local or remote.

port_num   Set the listening port number for the server. A value of 0 may be specified only if the [aznapi-admin-services] stanza in the configuration file is empty.

admin_pwd   The Access Manager administrator password. If this parameter is not specified, the password will be read from stdin.

server_pwd   The server's password. You can request that a password be created by the system by specifying a dash (-) for the password.

If the aznAPI is configured in remote mode, the [manager] stanza of the aznAPI configuration file must also be updated with a replica entry. This can be done by simply editing the configuration file or using the **svrsslcfg -add_replica** command. The aznAPI.conf file shipped with Policy Director 3.8 contains an example of a configured replica.

An example configuration would be to:

a. Create the *PD work directory*, such as C:\bea\CustomRealm\.

b. Copy the sample configuration file from *PD-install-dir*\example\authzn_demo\cpp configuration\ aznAPI.conf to this directory, rename it as pdrealm.conf and use it as a parameter input to the **svrsslcfg** command.

c. Edit pdrealm.conf and comment-out the line AZN_ADMIN_SVC_TRACE.

```
...
[aznapi-admin-services]
#
# Sample AZN Admin. Service Definitions
#AZN_ADMIN_SVC_TRACE = pdtraceadmin
...
```

d. Issue the svrsslcfg utility to create the aznAPI configuration file using the following syntax:

svrsslcfg -config -f pdrealm.conf -d *full path* -n *pdwlsrealm* -s remote -P *sec_master password* -S *PD-WLS-password* -r 0

For our example use this command:

```
C:\bea\CustomRealm>svrsslcfg -config -f pdrealm.conf -d
c:\bea\CustomRealm -n wlsmachine.anyname -s remote -P pdadmpw00 -S
wlsecretpw00 -r 0
```

```
Configuration of server wlsmachine.anyname is in progress.   This may
take several minutes...
```

The -n parameter specifies the name for your server and thus can be any
name you want. The configuration utility will create the proper server
identification based on the name you provide.

> **Note:** The -d path must be specified as a fully qualified path.

e. After executing this command, you can see the new Access Manager
   server via pdadmin:

```
pdadmin> server list
    webseald-w2ktst
    wlsmachine.anyname-3C044
    3C044-3C044
    authzn_local-w2ktst
    ivacld-w2ktst
pdadmin> server show wlsmachine.anyname-3C044
    wlsmachine.anyname-3C044
        Description: wlsmachine.anyname/3C044
        Hostname: 3C044
        Principal: wlsmachine.anyname/3C044
        Port: 0
        Listening for authorization database update notifications: no
```

Configure Custom Realm in WLS

Follow the next steps on the WLS machine:

1. Extract the contents of PDWLS_Realm.jar to *PD work directory*. This creates
   a subdirectory called image with the following files in it:

   - pdlib.dll
   - pdAuthzn.jar
   - libpdlib.a
   - libaznjni.a
   - pdadmin.jar
   - aznjni.dll
   - PDRealm.jar

> **Note:** We used C:\bea\CustomRealm\ as *PD work directory.*

2. Copy the appropriate shared libraries for your operating system (*.dll on Windows and *.a in AIX) from above into a directory that is in the system path (that is, Program Files/Tivoli/Policy Director/bin on Windows or /usr/lib on AIX):

```
C:\bea\CustomRealm\image>copy *.dll "C:\Program Files\Tivoli\Policy
Director\bin"
aznjni.dll
pdlib.dll
        2 file(s) copied.
```

3. Copy pdadmin.jar, pdAuthzn.jar, and PDRealm.jar to a directory on your file system. A recommended location would be the *BEA home*\lib directory.

```
C:\bea\CustomRealm\image>copy pdadmin.jar c:\bea\wlserver6.1\lib
        1 file(s) copied.
C:\bea\CustomRealm\image>copy pdAuthzn.jar c:\bea\wlserver6.1\lib
        1 file(s) copied.
C:\bea\CustomRealm\image>copy PDrealm.jar c:\bea\wlserver6.1\lib
        1 file(s) copied.
```

4. Stop the WLS Server if it is running. We will perform some additional configuration with the server down and then restart it a few steps further on.

5. Add the fully qualified path of pdadmin.jar, pdAuthzn.jar, and PDRealm.jar to the CLASSPATH variable that is defined in the startWebLogic.cmd batch file located in *BEA domain directory*.

```
...
set CLASSPATH=.;.\lib\j2ee12.jar;.\lib\weblogic_sp.jar;.\lib\weblogic.jar
set
CLASSPATH=%CLASSPATH%;c:\bea\wlserver6.1\lib\pdadmin.jar;c:\bea\wlserver6.1
\lib\pdAuthzn.jar;c:\bea\wlserver6.1\lib\PDRealm.jar
...
```

6. Create the WebSEAL *configured user* using the Web Portal Manager or pdadmin. In our example we simply added a user cnfusr3C044 in the existing DIT ou=people,o=pforster.com.

```
pdadmin> user create cnfusr3C044 cn=cnfusr3C044,ou=people,o=pforster.com
cnfusr3C044 cnfusr3C044 cnfusrpw00
pdadmin> user modify cnfusr3C044 account-valid yes
```

> **Attention:** If you are using the iPlanet Directory server, make sure that all user create commands (user create *user-name dn cn sn pwd password*) must have a valid and consistent DN, if using the cn attribute as part of the DN qualifier. For example, if you create a user with a DN as cn=userX,ou=people,o=abc.com, then the user create command should be `user create cn=userX,ou=people,o=abc.com userX sn_user pwuser`, where userX must match in both the *dn* and the *cn* fields.

7. Create the *pdadmin context user* that the custom realm uses to create a context with PDMgr using the Web Portal Manager or pdadmin. Remember, this user must either be added to the iv-admin group or be delegated sufficient permission such that he can add/delete/modify/list users and groups. You can do this by giving the user the following permissions on an ACL attached to the /Management object TcmdbsvatNWA. The name of the default ACL attached to the /Management object is default-management. For simplicity, we add the user admusr3C044 to the iv-admin group.

```
pdadmin> user create admusr3C044 cn=admusr3C044,ou=people,o=pforster.com
admusr3C044 admusr3C044 admusrpw00 iv-admin
pdadmin> user modify admusr3C044 account-valid yes
```

8. Restart the WebLogic Server.

9. Launch the WLS server console in a browser using the following URL:

```
http://WLS_host:WLS listening port/console
```

10. Under **Security -> Realms** configure a new custom realm.

   a. Name: TAME Realm.
   b. Realm Class Name: com.tivoli.wlsrealm.PDRealm.
   c. Add all required input configuration data as shown in Table 16-2.

Table 16-2 WebLogic Custom Realm startup parameters

Realm property	Valid values	Description
webseal.sso.configured	True or false; set as yes in our example	Defines whether WebSEAL will be configured and whether to attempt to perform SSO.
pdadmin.user.name	*pdadmin context user*; in our example, admusr3C044	Name of the user that will be used to create a pdadmin context. This user must be in the iv-admin user group or be delegated sufficient permission such that they can add/delete/modify/list users and groups.

Realm property	Valid values	Description
pdadmin.password	*pdadmin context user password*; in our example, admusrpw00	Password of the above user.
pdrealm.registry.listing	True or false; in our example, true	Defines whether the Access Manager Custom Realm should list users and groups (including group memberships) to the WLS console window. It is recommended that this be set to false in a production environment or in a test/development environment involving a user registry with greater than 3000 users.
connection.pool	1-n; in our example, 5	Where n is an integer defining the number of Realm objects to instantiate in the Realm pool.
pdrealm.tracing	True or false; in our example, true	Turn PDRealm tracing on or off. Trace will be sent to the console and the WebLogic log defined in the console.
wls.admin.user	*configured user*; in our example, cnfusr3C044	The special user that is configured in the Access Manager Custom Realm configuration data in order to form a trust relationship between WebSEAL and WLS.
group.dn	A valid DN; in our example, ou=groups,o=pforster.com	DN where groups are defined in LDAP.
user.dn	A valid DN; in our example, ou=people,o=pforster.com	DN where users are defined in LDAP.
aznapi.conf.file	*AZN conf file path*; in our example, C:\bea\CustomRealm\pdrealm.conf	The fully qualified path name of the aznAPI.conf file generated by the configuration of the aznAPI.

Figure 16-8 shows the WebLogic console and some of the parameters we provided.

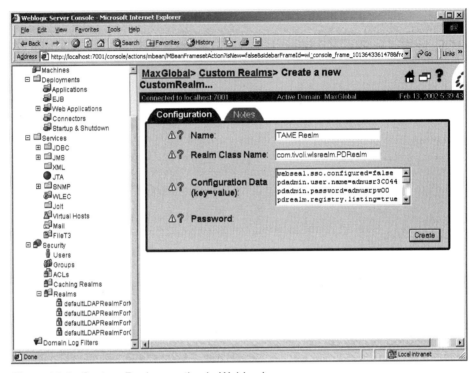

Figure 16-8   Custom Realm creation in WebLogic

11. Configure a new caching realm:

Name   TAME CachingRealm

Basic realm   TAME Realm

Case-sensitive   Yes

Figure 16-9 on page 388 shows the WebLogic configuration screen and the input fields. Use defaults for the caching settings.

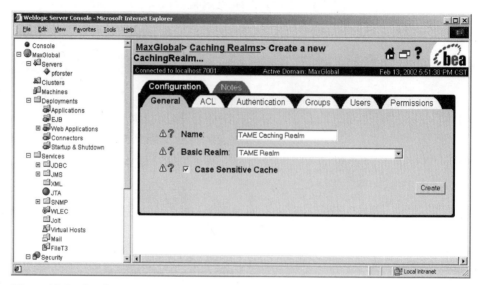

Figure 16-9   Configuring the Caching Realm in WebLogic

12..Go to **Security -> FileRealm** and set it to TAME CachingRealm. Leave all other fields unchanged, as shown in Figure 16-10.

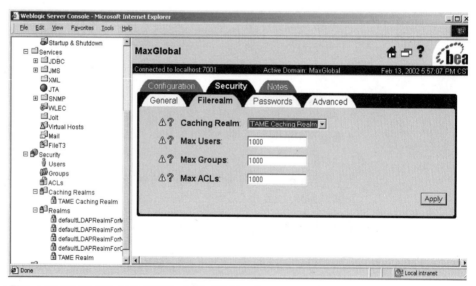

Figure 16-10   Setting the File Realm in WebLogic

13. Restart the WebLogic Server for the security settings to take effect.

Configure the WLS junction

In order to configure the WebLogic junction on the WebSEAL machine do the following:

1. Update the following configuration stanza in webseald.conf:

   ```
   basicauth-dummy_password = configured user password
   ```

   Assuming the user is cnfusr3C044 with password cnfusrpw00, apply the changes as follows:

   ```
   ...
   # Global password used when supplying basic authentication
   # data over junctions created with the "-b supply" argument.
   basicauth-dummy-passwd = cnfusrpw00
   ...
   ```

2. Stop and start the WebSEAL service for the changes to take effect.

3. Create a junction as described in *IBM Tivoli Access Manager for e-Business WebSEAL Administration Guide Version 3.9*, GC23-4682, using the syntax:

   ```
   pdadmin> server task <webseald_server_name> create -t tcp -p WLS listen
   port -h WLS server -b supply junction target
   ```

   The following example shows how to define and verify a junction called /TAME:

   ```
   pdadmin> server task webseald-w2ktst create -t tcp -p 7001 -h 3C044 -b
   supply /TAME
   Created junction at /TAME
   pdadmin> server task webseald-w2ktst show /TAME
        Junction point: /TAME
        Type: TCP
        Junction hard limit: 0 - using global value
        Junction soft limit: 0 - using global value
        Active worker threads: 0
        Basic authentication mode: supply
        Authentication HTTP header: do not insert
        Remote Address HTTP header: do not insert
        Stateful junction: no
        Scripting support: no
        Delegation support: no
        Mutually authenticated: no
        Insert WebSphere LTPA cookies: no
        Insert WebSEAL session cookies: no
        Server 1:
            ID: f1d440fe-21bf-11d6-9b0f-006094572b0e
            Server State: running
            Hostname: 3C044
            Port: 7001
            Virtual hostname: 3C044
   ```

```
Server DN:
Query_contents URL: /cgi-bin/query_contents
Query-contents: unknown
Case insensitive URLs: no
Allow Windows-style URLs: yes
Total requests : 1
```

Verifying the configuration

Check that the custom realm is working by first using the WLS console to create a new test user TAME_test, as shown in Figure 16-11.

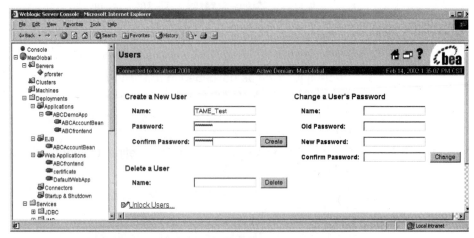

Figure 16-11   Defining a new test user in WebLogic

Next go to the pdadmin prompt and execute the **user show** command:

```
pdadmin> user show TAME_Test
Login ID: TAME_Test
LDAP DN: cn=TAME_Test,ou=people,o=pforster.com
LDAP CN: TAME_Test
LDAP SN: TAME_Test
Description:
Is SecUser: yes
Is GSO user: no
Account valid: yes
Password valid: yes
Authorization mechanism: Default:LDAP
```

The Access Manager Custom Realm SSO solution allows a single authentication step via WebSEAL that transparently authenticates the user to the WLS Server. This can be confirmed by running the demo application as described below. For download instructions for the demo application please see Appendix H, "Code examples for Armando Brothers Banking Corp." on page 553.

Access Manager WLS Realm demo procedure

This example demonstrates two types of authorization:

Declarative   The deployment descriptor ensures that only users in the BankMembers group can access the ABCDemo Servlet.

Programmatic   Using programmatic security, the EJB ensures that only the owner of each account has the permission to view his own account balance, that is, Armando cannot view Priscila's balance.

To run the demo application, perform the following steps:

1. Copy ABCDemoApp.ear into *BEA domain directory*applications. Note that this directory is not compulsory; you can place the EAR file into any directory on your file system.

2. Using the WLS console install the application shown in Figure 16-12.

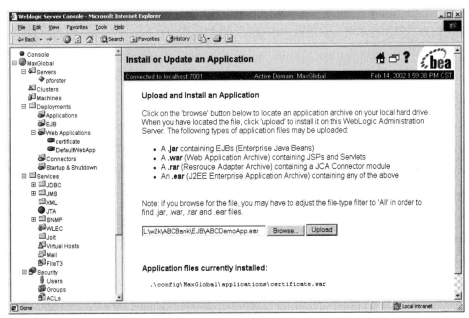

Figure 16-12   Uploading the ABCBank.ear archive file

3. Create the following users: Armando, Priscila, Bruno, Hai, and Aloysio using the WLS screen or the pdadmin **user create** command. Note that if you create the users by hand you still need to activate them manually. Those users are the only ones that you can use in this example.

```
pdadmin> user create Armando cn=TAME_Armando,ou=people,o=pforster.com
TAME_Armando Lemos passwd01
```

```
pdadmin> user create Priscila cn=TAME_Priscila,ou=people,o=pforster.com
TAME_Priscila Forster passwd01
pdadmin> user create Bruno cn=TAME_Bruno,ou=people,o=pforster.com
TAME_Bruno Lemos passwd01
pdadmin> user create Hai cn=TAME_Hai,ou=people,o=pforster.com TAME_Hai Ngo
passwd01
pdadmin> user create Aloysio cn=TAME_Aloysio,ou=people,o=pforster.com
TAME_Aloysio Gouveia passwd01
pdadmin> user modify Armando account-valid yes
pdadmin> user modify Priscila account-valid yes
pdadmin> user modify Bruno account-valid yes
pdadmin> user modify Hai account-valid yes
pdadmin> user modify Aloysio account-valid yes
```

4. Using the WLS console as shown in Figure 16-13, create a BankMembers group, assigning all of the users created above to be members of this group.

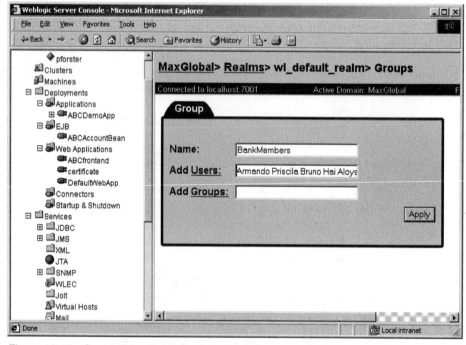

Figure 16-13   Creating the BankMembers group

5. To access the demo enter the following URL:

```
http://WLS server:WLS listening port/demo/snAccount
```

Authenticate with one of the users defined above. You will be prompted with a basic authentication form, as in Figure 16-14 on page 393.

Figure 16-14   Basic authentication with Access Manager and WebLogic

6. Only users defined in the BankMembers group can access the servlet. Furthermore, the authenticated user will only be allowed to view his own balance, and not the balance of any other user, as shown in Figure 16-15 on page 394. For example, select the user Priscila and **View Balance**, as shown in Figure 16-16 on page 395.

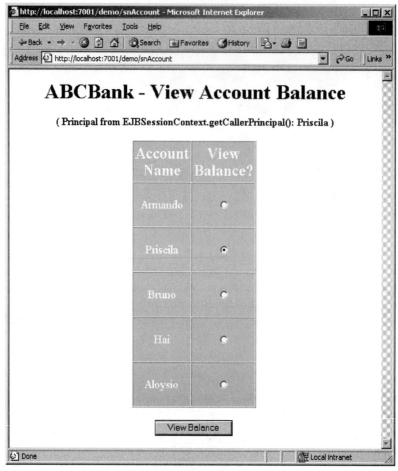

Figure 16-15   Accessing the servlet and EJB

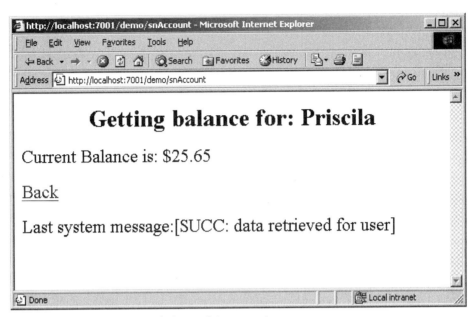

Figure 16-16 Valid account balance data request

Figure 16-17 on page 396 shows a simple deny example, when the test program tries to request account balance data for the user Armando, but still with the user Priscila as the current session user.

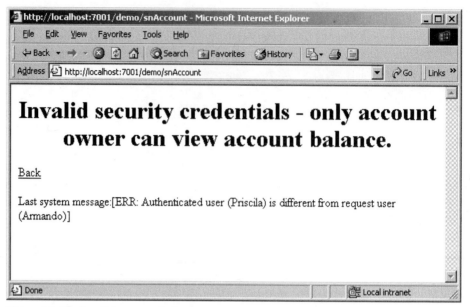

Figure 16-17   Invalid account balance request

To test the WebSEAL single sign-on, perform the following steps:

1. Open the browser and access the WebSEAL server using the syntax:

   ```
   https://webseald server name/junction target/demo/snAccount
   ```

2. In our case, we use https://w2ktst/TAME/demo/snAccount. WebSEAL will prompt you to authenticate.

3. Authenticate as one of the users defined above. We used Bruno, as shown in Figure 16-18 on page 397.

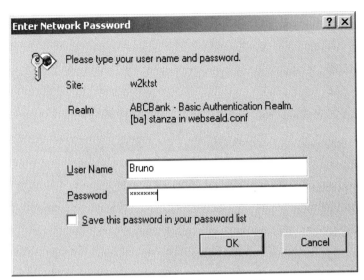

Figure 16-18   Basic authentication for Access Manager realm

4. This process will sign-on the user to the WLS server and the servlet can be invoked later without requiring a second authentication. When accessed via WebSEAL, the ABCDemoApp application will show identical behavior to that shown when accessing the WLS server directly, as in Figure 16-19 on page 398.

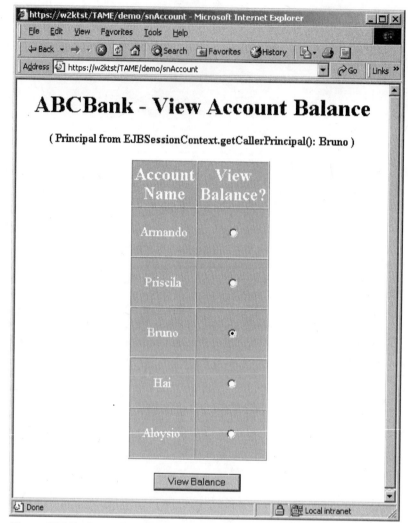

Figure 16-19 Accessing WebLogic using WebSEAL junction

Figure 16-20 on page 399 shows the output for the user request after selecting
View Balance.

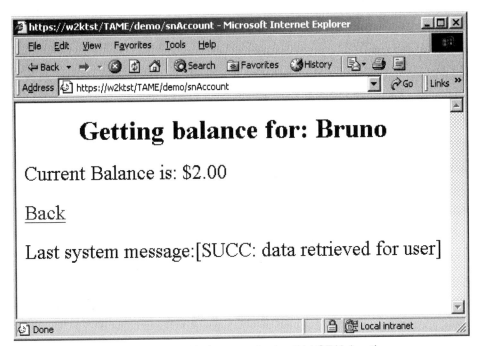

Figure 16-20 Output for the WebLogic request using WebSEAL junction

Example 16-2 and Example 16-3 show output information from the WebLogic logs demonstrating the execution of the requests as the authenticated principal.

Example 16-2 WebLogic access.log output

```
9.3.240.122 - Bruno [15/Feb/2002:10:26:00 -0600] "GET /demo/snAccount HTTP/1.0"
200 4696
9.3.240.122 - Bruno [15/Feb/2002:10:27:46 -0600] "POST /demo/snAccount
HTTP/1.0" 200 350
```

Example 16-3 Output log information stored in weblogic.log file

```
####<Feb 15, 2002 10:27:46 AM CST> <Debug> <PDRealm> <3C044> <pforster>
<ExecuteThread: '12' for queue: 'default'> <Bruno> <> <000000> <Entry Point:
getUser()>
####<Feb 15, 2002 10:27:46 AM CST> <Debug> <PDRealm> <3C044> <pforster>
<ExecuteThread: '12' for queue: 'default'> <Bruno> <> <000000> <Exit Point:
getUser()>
####<Feb 15, 2002 10:27:46 AM CST> <Debug> <PDRealm> <3C044> <pforster>
<ExecuteThread: '12' for queue: 'default'> <Bruno> <> <000000> <Entry Point:
getUser()>
####<Feb 15, 2002 10:27:46 AM CST> <Debug> <PDRealm> <3C044> <pforster>
<ExecuteThread: '12' for queue: 'default'> <Bruno> <> <000000> <Exit Point:
getUser()>
```

```
####<Feb 15, 2002 10:27:46 AM CST> <Debug> <PDRealm> <3C044> <pforster>
<ExecuteThread: '12' for queue: 'default'> <Bruno> <> <000000> <Entry Point:
getGroup() with parameter, name BankMembers>
####<Feb 15, 2002 10:27:46 AM CST> <Debug> <PDRealm> <3C044> <pforster>
<ExecuteThread: '12' for queue: 'default'> <Bruno> <> <000000> <Entry Point:
getGroupMembersInternal() with parameter group name: BankMembers>
####<Feb 15, 2002 10:27:46 AM CST> <Debug> <PDRealm> <3C044> <pforster>
<ExecuteThread: '12' for queue: 'default'> <Bruno> <> <000000> <Exit Point:
getGroupMembersInternal()>
####<Feb 15, 2002 10:27:46 AM CST> <Debug> <PDRealm> <3C044> <pforster>
<ExecuteThread: '12' for queue: 'default'> <Bruno> <> <000000> <Exit Point:
getGroup()>
```

We also changed our existing root junction to use the banking application from project I using forms-based authentication and, therefore, use all resources available in the banking site accessing JSP pages, HTML pages, and Bean controls together.

In order to test this scenario we changed the following:

1. Modify the / junction to use the -b supply parameter:

```
pdadmin> server task webseald-w2ktst create -f -p 7001 -t tcp -h w2ktst -b
supply -c all /
Created junction at /
```

2. Make sure that webseald.conf is configured for forms-based authentication. For more details you can check "Approach II - Forms-based authentication" on page 353.

3. Access the site by typing `https://w2ktst/ABCBank/welcome.jsp` and providing the credential information, as shown in Figure 16-21 on page 401.

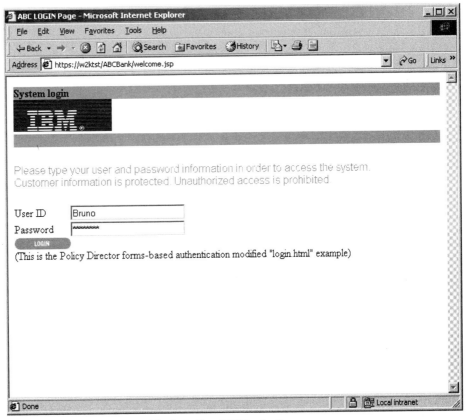

Figure 16-21   Forms-based login to the ABCBank site

4. Select the ***ACCOUNTS*** option from the navigation bar, as shown in
   Figure 16-22 on page 402. The next page displayed is the account page just
   like the previous examples for the user Bruno, as shown in Figure 16-23 on
   page 403.

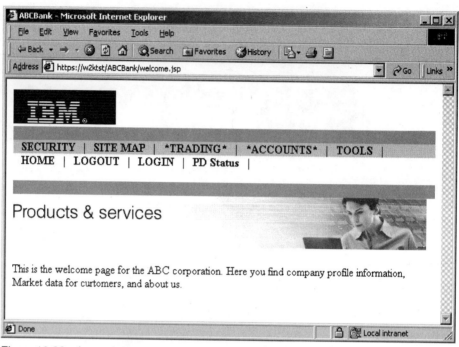

Figure 16-22   Accessing accounts resources for ABCBank

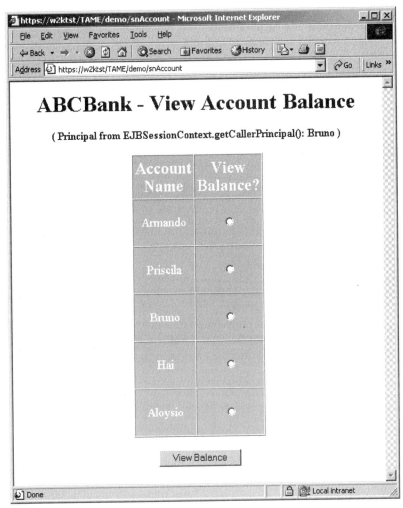

Figure 16-23   Account page for customer

This demonstrates that basic and forms-based authentication with Access
Manager are possible to control the existing ABBCBank resources through
WebSEAL junctions. Also, the Access Manager Custom Realm makes it possible
to use the existing role definitions in the deployment descriptors for the EJB
application in WebLogic. Another feature is that a customer can only see the
URL call as coming from the WebSEAL server (http://w2ktst/ or https://w2ktst),
but the actual resources can be in different servers (in our case the JSP
resources are in one machine and the account bean resources in another), which
shows that we have a true single sign-on process for as many different
application servers as we need.

16.6.3 Granular user groups in Access Manager

As stated in the requirements and functional design sections for this project, we need Access Manager to enforce different and more refined access controls to the existing groups (CUSTOMERS, REGISTEREDUSERS, and PUBLIC), and now make those more specific and even add new ones that did not exist in the first place. Depending on the case, you may have two distinct situations:

▶ Application does not control user groups.

This implementation does not require any changes to the application. The only thing required is to redefine the users and their visibility to the resources that you have.

▶ Application has internal user type definitions to handle proper group permissions.

This suggests that the application still has internal logic to perform access control (authorization), which should now be transferred to Access Manager as a core functionality.

Depending how the application directory structure is defined, the changes are mere configuration additions to Access Manager. We assume that the application directory structure already maps to a division between the high-level components, and thus we do not need to define discrete protection rules for each JSP object, but rather define one generic name for the whole directory subtree.

> **Note:** Should you have only one directory with all Web objects installed, then you may need to create individual ACLs using the `ACL ATTACH object acl` command.

Figure 16-24 on page 405 shows the new high-level access control rules for the system.

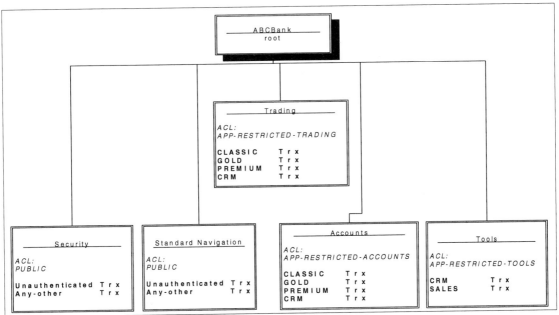

Figure 16-24   Application high-level ACL and group access layout

Figure 16-25 on page 406 shows the specific access levels for each subtree
segment. Note that some of them inherit the previous (ascendant) access level
and thus are not explicit in the drawing.

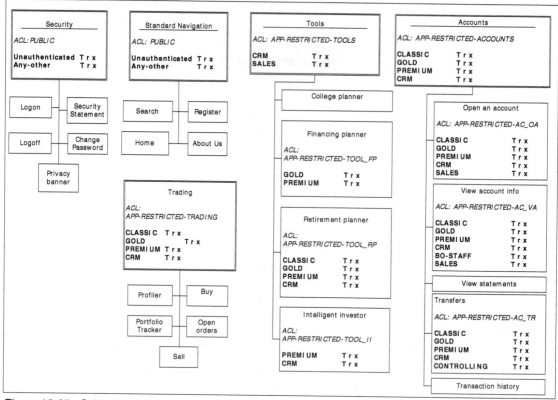

Figure 16-25   Subtree access levels

The main activities that we need to execute are:

1. Create the new customer groups in Access Manager.
2. Re-assign existing customer users to the new groups in Access Manager.
3. Create new staff users to Access Manager.
4. Assign the staff users to their respective group.
5. Define new ACLs and attach them to the WebSEAL objects.
6. Create the new customer groups in Access Manager.

Create the new Access Manager groups

Taking the list of users defined as in 16.2, "Functional requirements" on page 364, we must now create Access Manager groups for each new division (BO-STAFF, CONTROLLING, SALES, and CRM), as well as define the new customer groups (CLASSIC, GOLD, and PREMIUM) as shown in the following example:

```
pdadmin> group create BO-STAFF cn=BO-STAFF,ou=groups,o=pforster.com Backoffice
```

```
pdadmin> group create CONTROLLING cn=CONTROLLING,ou=groups,o=pforster.com
Controlling
pdadmin> group create SALES cn=SALES,ou=groups,o=pforster.com Sales
pdadmin> group create CRM cn=CRM,ou=groups,o=pforster.com CRM
pdadmin> group create CLASSIC cn=CLASSIC,ou=groups,o=pforster.com Classic
pdadmin> group create GOLD cn=GOLD,ou=groups,o=pforster.com Gold
pdadmin> group create PREMIUM cn=PREMIUM,ou=groups,o=pforster.com Premium
```

Re-assign users to new Access Manager groups

If you are considering a migration strategy this activity may require some manual tasks, pdadmin scripting, or API programming in order to transfer a potentially high volume of users to groups. We assume that existing users will be migrated during time according to some business revision (or automated process) not covered here. We define new customer users and assign existing ones to the different groups as shown in the following example:

```
pdadmin> group modify CLASSIC add "Armando Lemos"
pdadmin> group modify CLASSIC add "Hai Ngo"
pdadmin> group modify CLASSIC add "Aloysio Gouveia"
pdadmin> group modify GOLD add "Ralph Romano"
pdadmin> group modify GOLD add "Priscila Forster"
pdadmin> group modify PREMIUM add "Bruno Lemos"
pdadmin> group modify PREMIUM add "Beatriz Lemos"
pdadmin> group modify PREMIUM add "Maria Lucia"
pdadmin> group modify PREMIUM add AxelB
pdadmin> group modify PREMIUM add Dieter
```

Create new staff users to Access Manager

Assuming that we have not created the staff users so far, we must now define them to the system, so that they can use their user and password information to log in:

```
pdadmin> user create RuyForster cn=RuyForster,ou=people,o=pforster.com
RuyForster Forster secretpw01
pdadmin> user create RoseForster cn=RoseForster,ou=people,o=pforster.com
RoseForster Forster secretpw02
pdadmin> user create ClaudiaLemos cn=CLemos,ou=people,o=pforster.com CLemos
Lemos secretpw03
pdadmin> user create DanielaLemos cn=DLemos,ou=people,o=pforster.com DLemos
Lemos secretpw04
pdadmin> user create PauloNucci cn=PNucci,ou=people,o=pforster.com PNucci Nucci
secretpw05
pdadmin> user create JoaoAdamo cn=JAdamo,ou=people,o=pforster.com Joao Adamo
secretpw06
```

Assign staff users to groups

We must now define membership for the staff users so that when Access Manager performs authorization checks it can grant or deny access based on those accesses:

```
pdadmin> group modify SALES add RuyForster
pdadmin> group modify SALES add ClaudiaLemos
pdadmin> group modify CONTROLLING add DanielaLemos
pdadmin> group modify CRM add RoseForster
pdadmin> group modify BO-STAFF add PauloNucci
pdadmin> group modify BO-STAFF add JoaoAdamo
```

Define new ACLs for WebSEAL objects

Our fictitious example assumes some high-level segregation for the Web resources such as:

- ▶ /Security
- ▶ /StdNavigation
- ▶ /Trading
- ▶ /Accounts
- ▶ /Tools

Going back to Figure 16-1 on page 366; it shows the same group division with all the functions underneath the main categories. Since we have special access requirements for other components in the subtree, we need to define more specific fine-grained controls to totally control the resources as required. The resource protection must take into consideration the following access levels:

- ▶ /Security
- ▶ /StdNavigation
- ▶ /Trading
- ▶ /Accounts
- ▶ /Accounts/OpenAccount
- ▶ /Accounts/ViewAccountInfo
- ▶ /Accounts/Transfers
- ▶ /Tools
- ▶ /Tools/RetirementPlanner
- ▶ /Tools/FinancingPlanner
- ▶ /Tools/IntelligentInvestor

The next set of pdadmin commands shows how to define the objects and ACLs for those resources. Note that we only define the minimum set of profiles, making good use of generic capabilities and avoiding leaving objects not properly protected. We use the subtree definition as shown in Figure 16-25 on page 406 to define the commands required and create the resources.

```
pdadmin> acl create APP-RESTRICTED-TRADING
```

```
pdadmin> acl create APP-RESTRICTED-ACCOUNTS
pdadmin> acl create APP-RESTRICTED-AC_OA
pdadmin> acl create APP-RESTRICTED-AC_VA
pdadmin> acl create APP-RESTRICTED-AC_TR
pdadmin> acl modify APP-RESTRICTED-AC_OA description "Accounts / OpenAccount"
pdadmin> acl modify APP-RESTRICTED-AC_VA description "Accounts /
ViewAccountInfo"
pdadmin> acl modify APP-RESTRICTED-AC_TR description "Accounts / Transfers"
pdadmin> acl create APP-RESTRICTED-TOOLS
pdadmin> acl create APP-RESTRICTED-TOOL_RP
pdadmin> acl create APP-RESTRICTED-TOOL_FP
pdadmin> acl create APP-RESTRICTED-TOOL_II
pdadmin> acl modify APP-RESTRICTED-TOOL_RP description "Tools / Retirement
Planner"
pdadmin> acl modify APP-RESTRICTED-TOOL_FP description "Tools / Financing
Planner"
pdadmin> acl modify APP-RESTRICTED-TOOL_II description "Tools / Intelligent
Investor"

pdadmin> acl attach /WebSEAL/w2ktst/ABCBank/Security PUBLIC
pdadmin> acl attach /WebSEAL/w2ktst/ABCBank/StdNavigation PUBLIC
pdadmin> acl attach /WebSEAL/w2ktst/ABCBank/Trading APP-RESTRICTED-TRADING
pdadmin> acl attach /WebSEAL/w2ktst/ABCBank/Accounts APP-RESTRICTED-ACCOUNTS
pdadmin> acl attach /WebSEAL/w2ktst/ABCBank/Tools APP-RESTRICTED-TOOLS

pdadmin> acl attach /WebSEAL/w2ktst/ABCBank/Accounts/OpenAccount
APP-RESTRICTED-AC_OA
pdadmin> acl attach /WebSEAL/w2ktst/ABCBank/Accounts/ViewAccountInfo
APP-RESTRICTED-AC_VA
pdadmin> acl attach /WebSEAL/w2ktst/ABCBank/Accounts/Transfers
APP-RESTRICTED-AC_TR
pdadmin> acl attach /WebSEAL/w2ktst/ABCBank/Tools/RetirementPlanner
APP-RESTRICTED-TOOL_RP
pdadmin> acl attach /WebSEAL/w2ktst/ABCBank/Tools/FinancingPlanner
APP-RESTRICTED-TOOL_FP
pdadmin> acl attach /WebSEAL/w2ktst/ABCBank/Tools/IntelligentInvestor
APP-RESTRICTED-TOOL_II
```

We now define the groups that should belong to each ACL we created, as in Example 16-4.

Example 16-4   Adding groups to ACL definitions

```
pdadmin> acl modify APP-RESTRICTED-TRADING set group CRM rxT
pdadmin> acl modify APP-RESTRICTED-TRADING set group CLASSIC rxT
pdadmin> acl modify APP-RESTRICTED-TRADING set group GOLD rxT
pdadmin> acl modify APP-RESTRICTED-TRADING set group PREMIUM rxT

pdadmin> acl modify APP-RESTRICTED-ACCOUNTS set group CLASSIC rxT
pdadmin> acl modify APP-RESTRICTED-ACCOUNTS set group GOLD rxT
```

```
pdadmin> acl modify APP-RESTRICTED-ACCOUNTS set group PREMIUM rxT
pdadmin> acl modify APP-RESTRICTED-ACCOUNTS set group CRM rxT

pdadmin> acl modify APP-RESTRICTED-AC_OA set group CLASSIC rxT
pdadmin> acl modify APP-RESTRICTED-AC_OA set group GOLD rxT
pdadmin> acl modify APP-RESTRICTED-AC_OA set group PREMIUM rxT
pdadmin> acl modify APP-RESTRICTED-AC_OA set group CRM rxT
pdadmin> acl modify APP-RESTRICTED-AC_OA set group SALES rxT

pdadmin> acl modify APP-RESTRICTED-AC_VA set group CLASSIC rxT
pdadmin> acl modify APP-RESTRICTED-AC_VA set group GOLD rxT
pdadmin> acl modify APP-RESTRICTED-AC_VA set group PREMIUM rxT
pdadmin> acl modify APP-RESTRICTED-AC_VA set group CRM rxT
pdadmin> acl modify APP-RESTRICTED-AC_VA set group BO-STAFF rxT
pdadmin> acl modify APP-RESTRICTED-AC_VA set group SALES rxT

pdadmin> acl modify APP-RESTRICTED-AC_TR set group CLASSIC rxT
pdadmin> acl modify APP-RESTRICTED-AC_TR set group GOLD rxT
pdadmin> acl modify APP-RESTRICTED-AC_TR set group CRM rxT
pdadmin> acl modify APP-RESTRICTED-AC_TR set group CONTROLLING rxT
pdadmin> acl modify APP-RESTRICTED-AC_TR set group PREMIUM rxT

pdadmin> acl modify APP-RESTRICTED-TOOL_FP set group GOLD rxT
pdadmin> acl modify APP-RESTRICTED-TOOL_FP set group PREMIUM rxT

pdadmin> acl modify APP-RESTRICTED-TOOL_RP set group CLASSIC rxT
pdadmin> acl modify APP-RESTRICTED-TOOL_RP set group GOLD rxT
pdadmin> acl modify APP-RESTRICTED-TOOL_RP set group PREMIUM rxT
pdadmin> acl modify APP-RESTRICTED-TOOL_RP set group CRM rxT

pdadmin> acl modify APP-RESTRICTED-TOOL_II set group PREMIUM rxT
pdadmin> acl modify APP-RESTRICTED-TOOL_II set group CRM rxT
```

As a final step, we list all ACLs and check if the groups are exactly the ones we have defined in Figure 16-24 on page 405 and Figure 16-25 on page 406.

```
pdadmin> acl show APP-RESTRICTED-TRADING
    ACL Name: APP-RESTRICTED-TRADING
    Description:
    Entries:
        User sec_master TcmdbsvaBl
        Group CRM Trx
        Group CLASSIC Trx
        Group GOLD Trx
        Group PREMIUM Trx
pdadmin> acl show APP-RESTRICTED-ACCOUNTS
    ACL Name: APP-RESTRICTED-ACCOUNTS
    Description:
    Entries:
```

```
        User sec_master TcmdbsvaBl
        Group CLASSIC Trx
        Group GOLD Trx
        Group PREMIUM Trx
        Group CRM Trx
pdadmin> acl show APP-RESTRICTED-AC_OA
    ACL Name: APP-RESTRICTED-AC_OA
    Description: Accounts / OpenAccount
    Entries:
        User sec_master TcmdbsvaBl
        Group CLASSIC Trx
        Group GOLD Trx
        Group PREMIUM Trx
        Group CRM Trx
        Group SALES Trx
pdadmin> acl show APP-RESTRICTED-AC_VA
    ACL Name: APP-RESTRICTED-AC_VA
    Description: Accounts / ViewAccountInfo
    Entries:
        User sec_master TcmdbsvaBl
        Group CLASSIC Trx
        Group GOLD Trx
        Group PREMIUM Trx
        Group CRM Trx
        Group BO-STAFF Trx
        Group SALES Trx
pdadmin> acl show APP-RESTRICTED-AC_TR
    ACL Name: APP-RESTRICTED-AC_TR
    Description: Accounts / Transfers
    Entries:
        User sec_master TcmdbsvaBl
        Group CLASSIC Trx
        Group GOLD Trx
        Group CRM Trx
        Group CONTROLLING Trx
        Group PREMIUM Trx
pdadmin> acl show APP-RESTRICTED-TOOL_FP
    ACL Name: APP-RESTRICTED-TOOL_FP
    Description: Tools / Financing Planner
    Entries:
        User sec_master TcmdbsvaBl
        Group GOLD Trx
        Group PREMIUM Trx
pdadmin> acl show APP-RESTRICTED-TOOL_RP
    ACL Name: APP-RESTRICTED-TOOL_RP
    Description: Tools / Retirement Planner
    Entries:
        User sec_master TcmdbsvaBl
        Group CLASSIC Trx
```

```
              Group GOLD Trx
              Group PREMIUM Trx
              Group CRM Trx
pdadmin> acl show APP-RESTRICTED-TOOL_II
    ACL Name: APP-RESTRICTED-TOOL_II
    Description: Tools / Intelligent Investor
    Entries:
        User sec_master TcmdbsvaBl
        Group PREMIUM Trx
        Group CRM Trx
```

WebSEAL authentication and authorization will work for all users now sharing the same database rules and protecting both external and internal user access to the Web resources. Depending on the internal user requirements, it may also need some more access rules or special application integration for proper user restrictions, also known as fine-grained access control, covered in the 16.6.4, "Access Manager ADK and fine-grained access" on page 412.

16.6.4 Access Manager ADK and fine-grained access

There may be situations where you need to implement special access rule checking by programming some of the access validation within the application. The reason for this can be restrictions that your application imposes (for example, if it is a third-party application with predefined entry points or a customization layer) or if you have an in-house solution that is proprietary. If those applications offer enough flexibility for you to enhance the security model and remove some of the existing code, you can make them aware of the underlying Access Manager authorization infrastructure by using the standardized aznAPI calls.

In some cases you might have an abstraction layer already in place, and now you need to replace the actual application security by something more robust such as Access Manager. You would need to replace the existing application API wrapper code with Access Manager's aznAPI. Our examples are a case-by-case analysis where the bottom line is still the same: You want to have the flexibility to perform access control checking, and instead of using a proprietary logic that locks you into a specific application environment you want to rely on a robust security infrastructure providing these checks for a multitude of application environments in your enterprise.

Important: The Access Manager Authorization ADK is an application development kit that enables application developers to add Access Manager authorization and security services to applications. The *IBM Tivoli Access Manager for e-Business Authorization C API Developer's Reference Version 3.9*, GC32-0849, and the *IBM Tivoli Access Manager for e-Business Authorization Java Classes Developer's Reference Version 3.9*, GC23-4688, describe both a C implementation and a Java implementation of the Access Manager aznAPI.

Let us assume you have an application module that should only be available to some users under very specific situations. The logic to determine when to present that option is very specific, difficult, and time consuming. Let us also assume that access control checking is possible as a pre-execution code and thus there is an entry point to customize the specific API calls to make a decision in terms of proceeding with the transaction or not. Example 16-5 shows a very simplistic approach for an access control check call before executing the real transactional code myobject.execute(). The idea here is that there is at least one access check inside the code, but depending on the complexity of the transaction, you may need to execute multiple checks before actually allowing the business code to execute. Although this is very powerful, it also costs development and maintenance time, and thus you may use this for those situations that you cannot really leverage with existing Access Manager base features.

Example 16-5   Sample API check in code

```
...
if (myobject.check_access(user, resource) == OK)
    {
    rc = myobject.execute(trn, user, data);
    if (rc ==0)
       myobject.notify("transaction completed successfully");
    else
       myobject.notify("Error while executing transaction");
    }
else
    {
    myobject.notify("cannot execute transaction. User not authorized");
    }
...
```

We describe some examples using the JAVA API calls due to its simplicity. You may also want to evaluate the C version for performance reasons. The Access Manager Authorization Java Classes provide an implementation of Java security code that is fully compliant with the Java 2 security model and the Java Authentication and Authorization Services (JAAS) extensions, making it possible to consolidate different access control systems into Access Manager.

Let us consider that there is an in-house application that does not provide access control and we want to migrate some of the access control decisions to Access Manager and make it centrally managed. Let us also assume that it is a Java application that we can either modify or create a wrapper code for. The application checks some internal values, options, and dates in order to execute this hypothetical transaction, as shown in Example 16-6. The decision logic is based on different factors, such as the source address, the transaction code, the destination account number, the maximum limit for the user, and the day of trade, totalling five different business validation checks.

Example 16-6   Transaction and access control checks

```
...
String res1 = "SOURCE_IP_"+getSourceIP(); // IP is x.x.x.x
String res2 = "TRN/"+trnID; // trnID is "BUY_MF";
String res3 = "DESTINATION_ACCOUNT/"+Dest_Acc; // Dest_Acc is "261168-33"
rc1 = myobject.check_access(user, res1); // user is "ALEMOS"
rc2 = myobject.check_access(user, res2);
rc3 = myobject.check_access(user, res3);
...
// decision logic to execute transaction is:
// (valid source) AND (valid transaction) AND (valid account)
if ( (rc1==0) && (rc2==0) && (rc3==0) )
   {
   limit = my_oltp.retrieveCustomerLimit(user, Dest_Acc); // limit is "30000"
   dayTrade = my_oltp.isValidDate(curDate); // curdate: yyyy-mm-dd
   currency = my_oltp.getCurrency(); // currency is "USD"
   String res4 = "LIMITS/"+user;
   String res5 = "APP1/DAY_TRADE/"+dayTrade;
   rc4 = myobject.check_access(user, res4);
   rc5 = myobject.check_access(user, res5);
// decision logic to execute transaction is:
   // (valid limit) AND (valid daytrade)
   if ( (rc4==0) && (rc5==0) )
      {
      // data is "USD/1.000,00/265934-0"
      rc = myobject.execute(trnID, user, data);
      //
      // put other return code checking here and additional logic...
      //
      }
   else
```

```
        {
        myobject.notify("invalid transaction request");
        }
    }
else
    {
     myobject.notify("cannot execute transaction. User not authorized");
    }
```

The in-house Java class myobject performs many different tasks including access control checking, login, and application flow control. Assuming that the existing myobject.check_access() API performs some internal access control lookup to a database and returns a value based on some internal logic, we can replace this by Access Manager API calls, making it centrally managed, scalable and yet powerful enough to extend its access checking in the future. The current API declaration could be something like:

```
public int myobject.check_access(String user, String resource)
```

We can replace it by a new API call such as myobject.AM_check() or modify the existing check_access() code so that the integration becomes even easier. We assume the latter here so that the actual application code does not need any changes. The new check_access() class would look like Example 16-7.

Example 16-7 Access Manager and Java ADK API calls

```
....
public int check_access(String user, String resource)
    {
    int value          = 1 ; // assume not authorized by default (1)
    String accessLevel = "r";   // assume that all accesses are just for READ
    String rootTree    = "/UserDef/"; // user-defined placeholder for access
data
    try
        {
        System.err.println("testing "+rootTree+resource+" ...");
        PDPrincipal whoIsIt =new PDPrincipal(user);
        PDPermission whatTheyWant =new PDPermission(rootTree+resource,
accessLevel);
        if (whoIsIt.implies(whatTheyWant))
            value = 0;
        else
            value = 1;
        }
    catch (Exception e)
        {
        // Assume DENY as per the initialization previously done
        System.err.println(e.toString());
        }
```

```
    return(value);
    }
...
```

The new access control code relies on some fixed values for simplicity, such as r
for read operations and a user-defined name space /UserDef. Since we are
talking about access control to discrete objects on a boolean yes/no fashion,
checking for read is enough for the migration.

In order to use our test application, we need to populate Access Manager as in
Example 16-8, executing the **pdadmin** commands.

Example 16-8   Application authorization tree

```
pdadmin> objectspace create /UserDef "User-defined resource tree" 14
pdadmin> object show /UserDef
    Name : /UserDef
        Description : User-defined resource tree
        Type :  (Application Container Object)  : 14
        Is Policy Attachable : yes

pdadmin> object create /UserDef/SOURCE_IP "Source Address profiles" 14
pdadmin> object create /UserDef/TRN "Transactional Resources" 14
pdadmin> object create /UserDef/DESTINATION_ACCOUNT "Valid Account Space" 14
pdadmin> object create /UserDef/LIMITS "Trading Limits" 14
pdadmin> object create /UserDef/APP1/DAY_TRADE "Trading Days" 14
pdadmin> object create /UserDef/APP2/DAY_TRADE "Trading Days App2" 14
pdadmin> object create /UserDef/SOURCE_IP/10.XXX.XXX.XXX "IP range 10 network"
14

pdadmin> user create ALEMOS cn=armando.lemos,ou=people,o=pforster.com Armando
Lemos secretpw00
pdadmin> user modify ALEMOS account-valid yes

pdadmin> acl attach /UserDef ALL-CUSTOMERS-EXT

pdadmin> object SHOW /UserDef
    Name : /UserDef
        Description : User-defined resource tree
        Type :  (Application Container Object)  : 14
        Is Policy Attachable : yes
        ACL : ALL-CUSTOMERS-EXT
```

> **Note:** The object type 14 was selected because it best describes the type of name space we are extending. There is no hard requirement for this value other than the WPM GUI presenting a special icon based on this object type. There are no internal restrictions and you may choose other object types for other resource protection requirements in the future. For further details about object types please see *IBM Tivoli Access Manager for e-Business Base Administration Guide Version 3.9*, GC23-4684.

We use two users for testing. Example 16-9 shows a user that does not have any access to any of the resources we protect. This user is not assigned to any special group, and thus has no access.

Example 16-9 Sample execution - User with no access to any resource

```
E:\w2k\ABCBank\PDPerm>java -classpath
c:\jar\PDPerm.jar;c:\jar\ibmjcefw.jar;c:\j
ar\ibmjceprovider.jar;c:\jar\ibmjsse.jar;c:\jar\ibmpkcs.jar;c:\jar\jaas.jar;c:\
local_policy.jar;c:\US_export_policy.jar;. pforsterTH Dieter

IBM ITSO test program for PDPerm starting......
Testing user(Dieter)
testing /UserDef/SOURCE_IP/10.XXX.XXX.XXX ...
testing /UserDef/TRN/BUY_MF ...
testing /UserDef/DESTINATION_ACCOUNT/261168-33 ...
testing /UserDef/LIMITS/1500 ...
testing /UserDef/APP1/DAY_TRADE/2002-02-18 ...
Source IP is valid?        RC1(1)
Transaction is authorized? RC2(1)
Destination account valid? RC3(1)
Limit allowed?             RC4(1)
Day of Trade valid?        RC5(1)

Legend
RC = 0 : authorized
RC = 1 : denied
Transaction summary:DENIED
done.
```

Example 16-10 shows another user that belongs to the GOLD group. This group belongs to the ALL-CUSTOMERS-EXT ACL, and thus access is granted to the user.

Example 16-10 Sample execution - User with access to all resources

```
E:\w2k\ABCBank\PDPerm>java -classpath
c:\jar\PDPerm.jar;c:\jar\ibmjcefw.jar;c:\j
ar\ibmjceprovider.jar;c:\jar\ibmjsse.jar;c:\jar\ibmpkcs.jar;c:\jar\jaas.jar;c:\
local_policy.jar;c:\US_export_policy.jar;. pforsterTH ALEMOS
```

```
IBM ITSO test program for PDPerm starting......
Testing user(ALEMOS)
testing /UserDef/SOURCE_IP/10.XXX.XXX.XXX ...
testing /UserDef/TRN/BUY_MF ...
testing /UserDef/DESTINATION_ACCOUNT/261168-33 ...
testing /UserDef/LIMITS/1500 ...
testing /UserDef/APP1/DAY_TRADE/2002-02-18 ...
Source IP is valid?          RC1(0)
Transaction is authorized?   RC2(0)
Destination account valid?   RC3(0)
Limit allowed?               RC4(0)
Day of Trade valid?          RC5(0)

Legend
RC = 0 : authorized
RC = 1 : denied
Transaction summary:GRANTED
done.
```

This example shows the potential of the API and how one can migrate access control enforcement for existing application systems to a centrally managed system, making access decisions as uniform and reliable as possible. There are many other cases and variations that we are not covering here.

As a final integration idea, we have added the same check_access() API to the exec_trn.jsp page as a Web transaction that is validated for the same field information as in the previous examples. Figure 16-26 on page 419 shows the main input data as PDPermission.

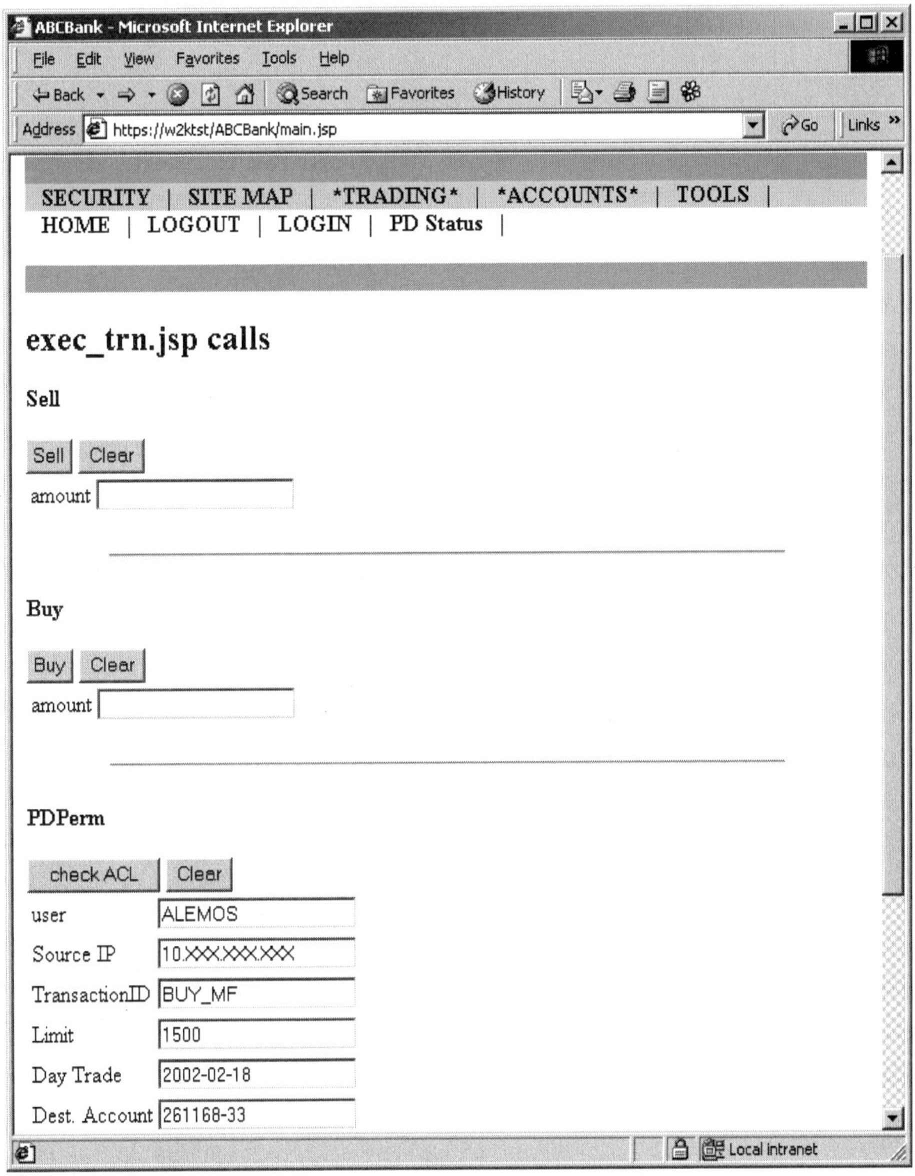

Figure 16-26   Fine-grained access checking - Input data

Figure 16-27 on page 420 shows the output for the test execution. Note that the results are exactly the same for the command line version previously executed. For simplicity, the access tree is not enforcing all possible fine-grained controls. This would be just a matter of adding the access control rules in Access Manager, leaving the application as it is.

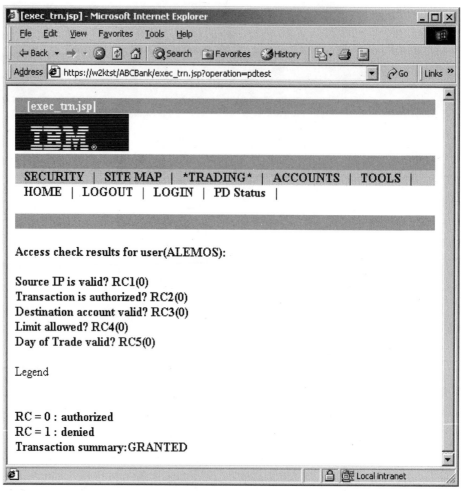

Figure 16-27   Fine-grained access checking - Validation results

16.6.5 Network changes

Since the internal users are accessing the internal Web server directly, we may
need to reassign new IP addresses for the Web servers and give the old ones to
WebSEAL so that users do not notice the changes. There are no firewall
changes necessary for the internal user setup, since all machines are already
installed in the production network.

Figure 16-28 on page 421 shows the network ports that should be configured.

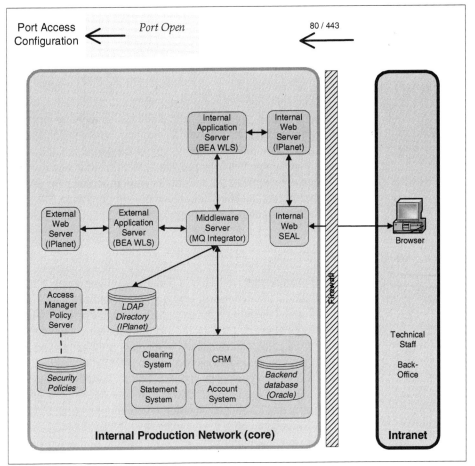

Figure 16-28   *WebSEAL and network configuration for internal users*

There is no routing or major network requirement other than assigning the new IP addresses to the servers in the sub-networks. There are no additional firewall rules.

For further information about Access Manager and network protection please see 2.7, "Component configuration and placement" on page 45.

> **Important:** Make sure that WebSEAL is the only visible server for HTTP/HTTPS access and no other Web server or Web application server can be accessed by any browser-based client.

16.6.6 Production

There are no new components for production to execute or monitor other than the internal WebSEAL components. The internal WebSEAL could be a replacement for the internal Web sever, should you not have any specific plug-in dependency between this internal Web server and the internal Web application server. If this is true, then there may be less machines for production to monitor, since you could disable the Web sever and make WebSEAL communicate directly with the application server.

16.6.7 Conclusion

We have demonstrated how to integrate a deployed application with few changes to the application environment, and taking benefit of all key security features already in place inside the application, and migrating those that could alleviate the application, such as performing authentication validation and expanding the access controls to all resources that now are only accessed if proper authentication is provided. Existing application authorization features were also migrated, now leaving security as an infrastructure responsibility and removing those tasks from the developers, who can now focus on application coding and let the environment do its part for validating access control. It is also true that this opens new benefits such as user activity logging, central management, and cost reduction, as more applications will take benefit of the Access Manager infrastructure over time (as we describe in the other banking scenarios). The external Web access now implements a new, robust protection feature that also improves flexibility and system architecture changes.

17

Backend integration

This chapter provides a description of the business and functional requirements for the back-end integration scenario. The main goal of the third project phase is to integrate existing applications into the security infrastructure. Integration of existing applications uses Siebel eFinance as an example for back-end systems and the middleware server based on MQSeries and MQ Integrator.

17.1 Business requirements and new challenges

ABBC realized that to sustain its growth in the competitive financial services arena, it needs a customer information management system that will enable it to provide superior service to its members. Up to now, most of the customers were assigned his or her own representative. The advantage is that customers are well known by their representative and experience a convenient service. But there are also disadvantages. A customer is more bound to the representative than to the bank itself. What if a representative is not available or even leaves ABBC? Customers would feel an immediate loss of service and ABBC is concerned about losing the customer. Therefore ABBC decided to create a single and global view of the customer across sales and services, which enables employees and representatives to serve any customer in any situation.

A second goal of the project is to secure internal traffic and implement detailed auditing to meet corporate auditing requirements. ABBC wants to elaborate its authorization framework developed in the previous projects. Existing applications will utilize this framework to ensure they are using trusted security mechanisms. Figure 17-1 shows an overview of the customer relationship channels towards ABBC.

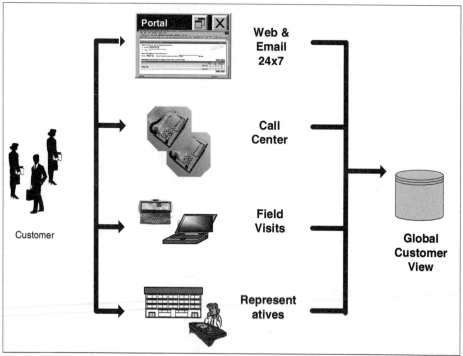

Figure 17-1   Global customer view using different channels

Important business requirements for this project are:

- Enhance customer service and satisfaction by:
  - Gaining faster response time for call center staff
  - Improving employee productivity
- Support more effective outbound marketing campaigns.
- Avoid too much dependency on representatives. Customers should only be "owned" by ABBC.
- Enhance cross-selling possibilities.
- Implement corporate auditing requirements.
- Non-repudiation for transaction processing for internal and external transactions.

17.2 Functional requirements

To fulfill the business requirements, ABBC decided to roll-out the existing Siebel customer relationship management system to all branch offices worldwide. All representatives have to have access to a global customer view and have to be able to provide updates to gather valuable customer data. Thus, more than 1000 internal and external users in call centers and all branch offices worldwide will have access to the existing CRM system.

Additionally, ABBC wants to extend their service operations to the Internet by a customer self-service system. Customers should be able to quickly resolve their own problems and questions, and escalate unsolved problems to product experts within ABBC or in any branch office.

The functional requirements are:

- Secure access of users in branch offices through intranet to sensitive data in the global CRM system.

  The access to the user's data must be controlled by a central security instance to guarantee the fulfillment of the bank's security policies.

- Non-repudiation for transaction-processing is important within ABBC's internal network. Thousands of internal users have access, and representatives perform transactions on behalf of their customers. The customer representative and the bank both need to have proof that the transaction has been executed and confirmed.

- Reduce service call response time to enhance customer satisfaction by processing inbound e-mails and providing a new Web site to enable full 24x7 customer self- and assisted service.

- The solution must fit into the existing security architecture. The project must not require a reorganization of the existing component architecture or a restructuring of the security design. Thus, Access Manager and back-end applications like Siebel and applications based on MQSeries have to be integrated.

- The cost of this solution should be minimized. Existing components in the infrastructure have to be reused as far as possible.

- The solution must be highly available.

- Reduce management overhead in current IT environment.

- Convenient access to the CRM system for internal and external users. Customers should experience an easy-to-use interface to provide valuable information.

17.3 Security design objectives

The typical security design requirements described in 15.3, "Security design objectives" on page 334, and 16.3, "Security design objectives" on page 367, were driven by an overall Web security approach. For integration of back-end systems like Siebel- or MQSeries-based applications we want to add the following concerns:

- Access control
  - Protect access to the now externally and internal available CRM system, applications, and data. Enforce and control their usage.
  - Enforce strict access control to MQSeries applications in the production network and intranet.
  - Quick deletion/locking of users on all systems.

- Authentication
  - Allow different authentication mechanisms for different type of users.
  - Support stronger authentication mechanisms. Representatives performing transactions on behalf of their customers and accessing protected data have to use PKI certificates.
  - Maintain simple user authentication with passwords for customers.
  - Single sign-on for all involved systems.

► Integrity

- Provide consistent management of users on all systems, Web application servers, MQSeries-based back-end applications, and CRM.

- Maintain a central repository of user identities among all systems.

- Provide system-independent security capabilities.

► Auditing

Allow monitoring of user activity and resource usage on all involved systems.

17.4 Design approach

Figure 17-2 depicts the current situation of ABBC's back-end system. Only a very limited number of internal users have access to the Siebel CRM system. MQSeries application queues are protected using user IDs of the local operating system. Messages sent between the different systems are not encrypted.

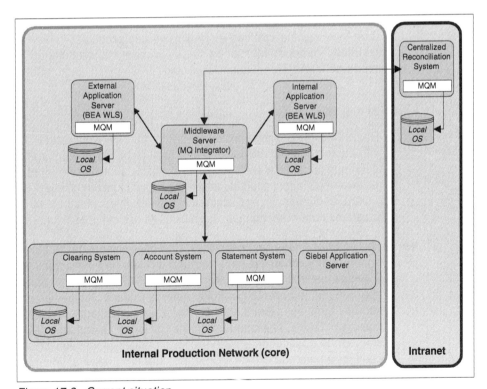

Figure 17-2   Current situation

The new scope modifies the external functionality for customers, offering new services and a customer self- and assisted service. It also enhances the internal capabilities, allowing other types of users (like representatives) to access and share customer data on the global CRM system. Access protection and data integrity become even more important and drive the design of our third project. The design goals of this project are:

▶ Protect queues using the new security framework based on Access Manager.

▶ Remove MQSeries access protection based on operating system IDs.

▶ Encrypt messages sent between the production network and intranet.

▶ Monitor activity of application queues.

▶ Offer Siebel applications to representatives in the intranet and Internet.

▶ Provide customer self-service capabilities by providing customers access to the applications running on the Siebel Application Server.

▶ Configure different authentication mechanisms in Access Manager WebSEAL.

Before we can design an architecture of our enhanced system, we have to take a short look into the involved technologies and products. In the following sections we briefly introduce MQSeries security model, Access Manager for Business Integration, and Siebel security policy.

17.4.1 MQSeries security

IBM MQSeries provides a simple means to allow applications to communicate with each other, regardless of platform or application language. The underlying technique is called message queuing. Applications using MQSeries write and retrieve application-specific data (messages) to/from queues, without having a private, dedicated, logical connection to link them. It is not even necessary that programs communicating through queues are executed concurrently.

The heart of MQSeries is the message queue manager (MQM), the MQSeries' runtime program. Its job is to manage queues and messages for applications. It provides the Message Queuing Interface (MQI) for communication with applications. In order to control access to queues, MQSeries provides its own security functions. The authorization engine is called the object authority manager (OAM). The queue manager calls the OAM to make a decision as to whether an application is authorized to perform a function on a queue. On each platform where you create MQSeries queue managers, you need to decide:

▶ How security is to be used and implemented
▶ Who is going to use the MQSeries system and resources (for example, queues)

Additionally, MQSeries has several exit points that can be used to provide additional functionality, especially related to security. For example, code exits can be used to encrypt messages being sent between queue managers. However, in sites where there is more than one system running MQSeries, there is no central security management from which control of who can access messages on queues can be achieved. Figure 17-3 shows MQSeries' security model.

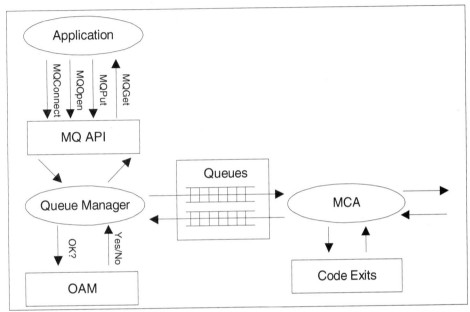

Figure 17-3   MQSeries security model

Within ABBC there are a number of systems running MQSeries. This leads to the issue of security being spread across a number of systems, with a number of different types of security systems in use. Today access to queues is controlled locally on the system where the MQSeries queue manager is running. For each platform that MQSeries operates on, the native security system for that platform is used to ensure that the resources MQSeries owns and manages are protected. This situation is depicted in Figure 17-3.

In our scenarios we want to show an example of a J2EE application running on the external BEA WebLogic Server of how Access Manager for Business Integration secures the communication to the middleware server. The application uses the MQSeries classes for Java Messaging Service (MQJMS) to exchange messages with the middleware server. MQJMS is a set of Java classes that implements Sun's Java Message Service (JMS) interfaces to enable JMS programs to access MQSeries systems. The use of MQJMS as the API to write MQSeries applications has a number of benefits. Some advantages derived from JMS being an open standard with multiple implementations are:

- The protection of investment, both in skills and application code

- The availability of people skilled in JMS application programming

- The ability to plug in different JMS implementations to fit different requirements

Other advantages result from additional features that are present in MQJMS, but not in MQ base Java, like asynchronous message delivery. You can find more information about the benefits of the JMS API on Sun's Web site at:

`http://java.sun.com`

17.4.2 Access Manager for Business Integration

Access Manager for Business Integration is a new part of the Access Manager product family. The first release of this product provides a way of integrating MQSeries with Access Manager. Access to queues can now be controlled by security policies defined using Access Manager, meaning that MQseries access can now be centrally managed.

In our scenario we do not only control access to queues, we also elaborate the digital signing and encryption functions of Access Manager for Business Integration to encrypt messages. This means that message contents are only viewable at the time when the application passes the message to MQSeries and when the message is retrieved by the application. At all other times while the message is passed between machines in the production environment and ABBC's central reconciliation system in Europe it is encrypted and thus cannot be viewed or tampered with. To sum up, using Access Manager for Business Integration provides the following benefits:

- Access Manager is used to control access in terms of who can *get* and *put* from a queue. You can find implementation details in "Access control" on page 431.

- Messages sent over the internal network can be signed and encrypted. Stored messages in MQSeries queues are also protected, as they are stored in encrypted format. You can find implementation details in "Encryption of messages" on page 433.

- Auditing of queue access is performed. You can find implementation details in "Auditing of queue access" on page 463.

Access control

Up to now, the access to applications and data operated by ABBC is tightly controlled. The number of users generally authorized to use these applications or have access to the data is essentially limited to a small number of employees or applications of the organization. Only the staff working for ABBC has been granted access to the applications and data provided.

Banking applications developed in the past have strong audit requirements in order to track every transaction that was initiated by an employee at any time. Audit trails are used to show what transactions a particular person uses, when the action occurs, and what specific task is accomplished. There is a strong urge that these types of applications would be able to positively identify the person running the application. Customers generally have to visit a branch office in person to interact with the business. However, the application system is always executed under the authority of an employee, who is in effect acting on behalf of the customer.

A main goal of ABBC is to open their existing applications to their employees and business partners, but the number of users increases dramatically, as it is no longer limited to employees of ABBC. The definition and access control for these users is currently done in the IT environment. The user ID is propagated to the back-end application systems. Employees and business partners use thin and thick clients to connect to ABBC's back-end systems.

At the example of a banking application we demonstrate how security is currently managed in ABBC. The application consists of Java servlets and EJBs being executed in the external BEA WebLogic Server. The application uses IBM MQSeries to communicate between the front end that handles interaction with end users on the Internet, and the back-end application that implements the business function. In between is the middleware server running MQ Integrator.

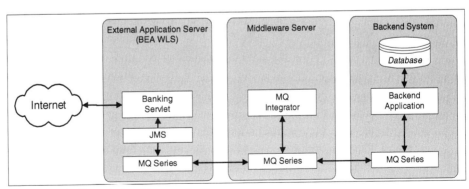

Figure 17-4   Sample banking application

In this sample banking application scenario depicted in Figure 17-4 on page 431, security has to be managed in several places:

► In BEA, controlling which users access Web resources and applications
► In MQSeries in the Internet environment
► In MQSeries in the middleware server
► In MQSeries in the back-end application environment
► In the security system used to control access for the back-end application

In this simple example only three queue managers are used. However, in a more complex scenario there could be many more queue managers involved. Each separate MQSeries system typically has its own security definitions. It can be a complex task to manage queue access on all involved machines. In the following sections we describe briefly with the example of an application using JMS, how security policy definition and enforcement can be managed centrally.

Using MQSeries classes for Java Message Service

Programmable options allow MQ Java to connect to MQSeries in either of the following ways:

► As an MQSeries client using Transmission Control Protocol/Internet Protocol (TCP/IP)

► In bindings mode, connecting directly to MQSeries

In our example we use MQ Java as an MQSeries client. Generally we can run MQ Java in three different modes:

► From within any Java-enabled Web browser
► Using an appletviewer
► As a stand-alone Java program or in a Web application server

In our scenario MQ Java is installed on the same machine as the BEA WebLogic Web server. MQSeries server runs on the same machine. The advantage is that we can exploit all reliability options offered by MQSeries. Please refer to the MQSeries documentation UsingJava.pdf for installation and verification procedures on supported platforms.

Using Access Manager for Business Integration

Figure 17-5 on page 433 depicts our sample banking application, but now using Access Manager for Business Integration to secure access to MQSeries' queues. Instead of defining the user IDs in the local operating systems, all internal and external user IDs and access control information are managed centrally by Access Manager.

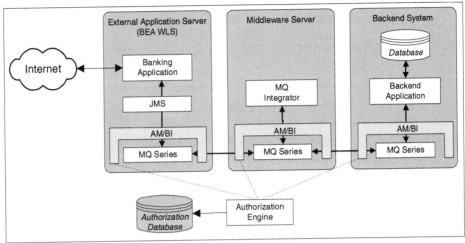

Figure 17-5   MQSeries communication secured by Access Manager

Encryption of messages

As mentioned earlier, it is possible to use MQSeries channel exits to encrypt messages written to a queue. Basically, channel exits provide MQ node to MQ node security. This is totally independent of any application design. There are different types of channel exits in MQSeries. The following list describes those types that can be used for security purposes:

▶ Security exit: This exit is used for authentication of the partner MCA when two MCAs connect to one another. The exit is invoked at MCA initiation and termination, and at channel startup after initial data negotiation, but before any user data is exchanged. A security exit does not have access to message data and, therefore, cannot be used for functions such as encryption. Each channel security exit uses a pair of public and private keys to verify itself during an initial handshaking phase with its partner.

▶ Message exit: A message exit is invoked once per message on either side of the channel. Among other purposes it can be used for encryption on the link.

▶ Send and receive exit: These exits are called once per message segment. This can be used for data compression and decompression or data encryption and decryption.

The necessary steps to encrypt messages in MQSeries are:

1. Select a cryptographic software package.

2. Store the queue manager's private and public keys in a private key file.

3. Define and implement a key distribution method. One method is to use MQSeries Channel Server Security Database (CSSD).

4. Design and implement a security exit program.

5. Design and implement a message exit or send and receive exit programs.

ABBC would need the following skills in order to implement encryption on MQSeries channels:

► Programming skills to implement the channel exit programs in the following ares:

 - C programming
 - Programming skills for the chosen cryptographic software package
 - Programming skills for all involved platforms
 - MQSeries programming skills

► In-depth knowledge of security concepts and PKI infrastructure.

For a more detailed description of how to use MQSeries channel exits to encrypt messages please refer to *MQSeries Security: Using a Channel Security Exit, Encryption, and Decryption*, SG24-5306.

Encrypting and signing messages

Using Access Manager for Business Integration for encryption and signing is totally transparent for MQSeries applications. There is no need to implement a single line of code. The only thing to do is to define a *protected object policy* (POP) and specify the protection level. Figure 17-6 shows the architecture of Access Manager for Business Integration. The Access Manager for Business Integration interceptor receives a message from the application.

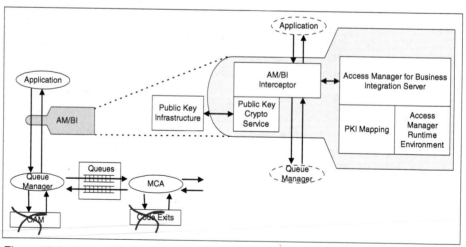

Figure 17-6 Access Manager communication between application and MQM

When Access Manager for Business Integration is performing the *put* process, it will check to see how many recipients are specified for this particular message. It is expected that there will be at least one recipient, but it could well be that there are a number of recipients. If the complete message was encrypted using the first recipient's public key so that only he could decrypt it, then this would mean that the second and subsequent recipients could not decrypt the message. This would imply that the complete message would have to be encrypted using the public key of each individual recipient. This would significantly increase the CPU processing required for the encryption phase and also dramatically increase the size of the message being sent.

To negate this extra CPU processing and increased message size, Access Manager for Business Integration does not encrypt the message using any of the recipients' public keys. Access Manager for Business Integration uses the GSKit to:

► Generate a random key.

► Use a standard algorithm to encrypt the message data using the generated random key.

► Use each recipient's public key to encrypt the generated random key.

► Build the complete message consisting of:

– One entry for each recipient containing the generated random key encrypted with the recipient's public key

– The original message data encrypted using the generated random key

This approach has the following advantages:

► CPU overhead is kept to a minimum.

► Only one copy of the encrypted message is required regardless of the number of the recipients.

► Impact on MQSeries response time is kept to a minimum.

Having encrypted the message, Access Manager for Business Integration puts the message to the corresponding queue. Thus, messages are stored encrypted and are only decrypted if an application gets a message from a queue. Thus transactions in a queue are protected. If channel exit applications perform message encryption, the messages are decrypted before being stored in a queue. Thus transactions in a queue are not protected at all.

Managing certificates

An important issue is deciding where to obtain your digital certificates. You obtain your digital certificates from Certificate Authorities (CA). Before you enable SSL communications for any application, you must decide whether you use a public CA or a private CA to issue certificates.

Public CAs include, among others, VeriSign, RSA, and Thawte. These commonly used Certificate Authorities are examples of public CAs. Advantages of using a public CA are:

► Your company does not need to operate a Certificate Authority, which mean less administrative overhead as you do not need to issue certificates to users.

► Your SSL configuration is simplified because many public CA certificates come pre-installed in the key databases of client applications. An example for this is the IBM GSKit. It already comes with public certificates of VeriSign, RSA, and Thawte.

Disadvantages of using a public CA are:

► You must ensure that the Certificate Authority's requirements to verify identification meet your security needs.

► You must trust the Certificate Authority not to lose or compromise its keys.

► The cost of obtaining certificates.

Certificates from public CAs are best for:

► Deployment on the Internet, such as with an e-commerce or other secure public Web site.

► Users that are loosely affiliated with your organization, such as business partners or vendors.

► Users that may already be using certificates from a well-known CA for other purposes. Therefore choosing certificates from a well-known CA creates less of an administrative burden on both the affiliated organization and your system administrator.

Advantages of using private CAs are:

► You can control which users or applications can be issued certificates. You can issue certificates that are based on your own certificate guidelines, rather than relying on a public CA's policies.

► Users specify whether to trust certificates that are issued by a particular private CA. The certificate's content may also be used to determine trust.

Disadvantages of using private CAs are:

► Using a private CA requires more administrative overhead.

► When you use a private CA, each client application that uses SSL to communicate with a server must obtain and store a local copy of the private CA's public certificate. Depending on the number of clients in your network, this may result in a higher management cost than purchasing certificates from a public CA whose CA certificate is often built into the client's certificate database.

Digital certificates from private CAs are best for:

► Deployment on a corporate intranet.

► Using locally issued certificates allows you to more tightly control who has certificates and what they can access with those certificates.

► Users that you want to have access to resources are under a user profile.

► Testing secure applications and environments without spending money on certificates.

Due to these reasons ABBC decided to use self-signed certificates in our scenario.

17.4.3 Siebel security system

In order to understand the integration work described in "Technical implementation" on page 446, we first provide a brief introduction of the Siebel 7 architecture, and then we introduce some concepts of the Siebel security system.

Siebel 7 overview

Siebel Systems, Inc. was founded in 1993 to address the growing need of organizations of all sizes to acquire, retain, and better serve their customers. Siebel eBusiness Applications provide an integrated family of e-business applications for managing, synchronizing, and coordinating all customer touchpoints and customer segments. By implementing Siebel eFinance, ABBC tries to capitalize on information captured during each customer interaction to more effectively cross-sell and up-sell additional financial products and services.

A general architecture of a Siebel implementation is depicted in Figure 17-7 on page 438. The shaded box represents ABBC's current Siebel implementation as it is used in our architecture diagrams.

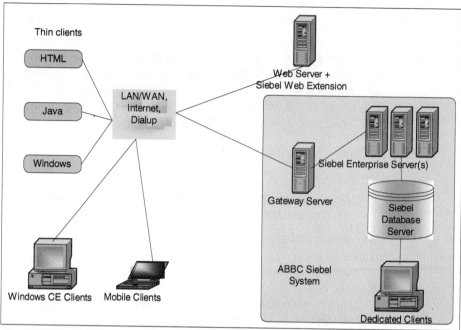

Figure 17-7   Siebel system high-level architecture

Siebel Database Server

The Siebel Database Server services database requests generated by the clients and the Siebel Application Server processes. It stores all the data used by the Siebel Enterprise Applications and is, in fact, nothing more than a relational database management system (RDBMS) such as an IBM DB2 server, managing the access to the data.

Siebel Application Server

The Siebel Application Server is a server within the Siebel Enterprise that executes many different Siebel processes as required by the individual implementation. While running these processes it also serves as the middle tier between the Siebel Database Server and the Siebel Remote and Thin Clients.

Siebel Gateway Server

The Siebel Gateway Server manages access to the Enterprise Server providing enhanced security, load balancing, and high availability.

The two services that operate within the gateway Server are the Name Server and Connection Brokering:

► The Siebel Name Server stores information about all the parameters that determines the configuration and operation of the Enterprise Server. It also keeps track of the availability of the components throughout the Siebel enterprise.

► As an optional component, Connection Brokering provides load balancing and fault tolerance. It works with Siebel Name Server to distribute client requests across multiple Siebel servers.

Siebel Web Extension (SWE)
SWE provides access to the Siebel Application Server via HTML clients.

Thin Client
Besides mobile, wireless, and dedicated clients, Siebel supports different types of Thin Client:

► HTML Thin Clients

   Siebel HTML Thin Clients is a set of components used for customizing and implementing the .com Web applications. They are part of a large system that also has a Siebel server, a Siebel database, and a Web server.

► Siebel Thin Clients for Windows and Java Thin Clients

   With these types of clients you can deploy the Siebel Enterprise Application over the intranet. They access the application dynamically over the network from any connected machine. These clients access the gateway Server to determine the Siebel Server, and access the Siebel database through the Siebel Server.

ABBC decided to use pure HTML clients to ease access to the system through the Internet for customers and representatives. Therefore a Web Server and the Siebel Web engine have to be added to the scenario.

Siebel security model
The Siebel security model, insofar as it can be externalized, is composed of the following entities:

► Roles
► Credentials
► Users

Roles
A role in the Siebel system is a user attribute from which access control or entitlements information is derived. A user can have one or more roles in the system. A role is defined by the single attribute that is the role name.

Credentials

Credentials are data that Siebel uses to authenticate a user to a data repository. The key, or index, of a credential is the type. A user may have one or more credentials. Siebel also has the concept of a default credential that could be shared by multiple users, should they not have a credential specific to them. A credential is defined by the following attributes:

► Credential type
► User name
► Password

Users

The user entity is the fundamental representation of a user in the system. Attributes of a user are:

► User name
► Password
► Account status
► Set of roles
► Set of credentials

All discussion in this section on attributes and behavior of these entities are statements on the externalized interface, not necessarily how Siebel uses these internally.

Siebel authentication

Siebel supports three approaches for authenticating users:

► Database authentication
► Security adapter authentication
► Web single sign-on

ABBC has to choose one of three fundamental authentication architectures for their Siebel application users:

► Database authentication

   This approach relies on the underlying application database for user authentication.

► Security adapter authentication

   This architecture provides for authentication to external services. Siebel provides security adapters to support Microsoft Active Directory Server and LDAP-compliant directories.

► Web single sign-on (Web SSO)

This approach uses an external authentication service to authenticate users. Siebel applications provide adapters for standards-based directories, such as LDAP directories, and also allows customers to create custom adapters.

ABBC may choose an approach for user authentication individually for each application. However, in order to reduce the administrative overhead, ABBC decides to use a consistent approach across all their Siebel applications. In fact, they decide to use Web single sign-on and a customized adapter for integration with Access Manager, the Access Manager security adapter for Siebel. The reason for this decision is outlined in Table 17-1.

Table 17-1   Comparison: Siebel authentication methods for ABBC environment

Functionality	Database	Security adapter	Web SSO (Access Manager)	Comments
Does not require additional infrastructure components.	X			Adapter for Web SSO is provided by Access Manager.
Centralized storage of user credentials and roles.		X	X	
Dynamic user registration in conjunction with Tivoli Identity Manager. Users are created in real-time through self-registration or administrative views.		X	X	For Web SSO users are managed using Access Manager administration.
Supports account policy. You can set policies such as password expiration, password syntax, and account lockout.		X	X	
Supports Web single sign-on, the capability to log in once and access all the applications within a Web site or portal.			X	

17.4.4 Access Manager security adapter for Siebel

The Siebel architecture allows development of security adapters to integrate with external authentication authorization and access protection systems. Siebel published the Siebel 7 security adapter interface that a security adapter must supply to integrate with Siebel. A security adapter is implemented as a DLL that supports these interfaces. It is a plug-in to the authentication manager. The security adapter uses the user credentials entered by a user or supplied by an authentication service to retrieve the Siebel user ID, a database account, and, optionally, a set of roles from the directory.

In the Siebel environment, a security adapter can be configured via a stanza in the service configuration file. Usually they are located in the bin directory of either the full Siebel client or the Web-based thin client.

The integration between IBM Tivoli Access Manager and Siebel 7 can also allow centralized management of Siebel roles/responsibilities and credentials in Access Manager. This provides the additional benefit of simplifying security policy management, and is achieved by installing the Access Manager security adapter for Siebel 7.

Figure 17-8 shows the network architecture for integrating Access Manager and Siebel Version 7.

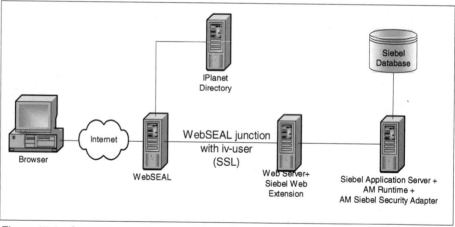

Figure 17-8   Siebel-Access Manager integration architecture for ABBC

17.4.5 High-level architecture

Based on the given business reasons, security requirements, and integration options we discussed, we can now start to design a solution for this project. Integration of MQSeries applications and customer/representative access to Siebel applications leads to the high-level architecture depicted in Figure 17-9.

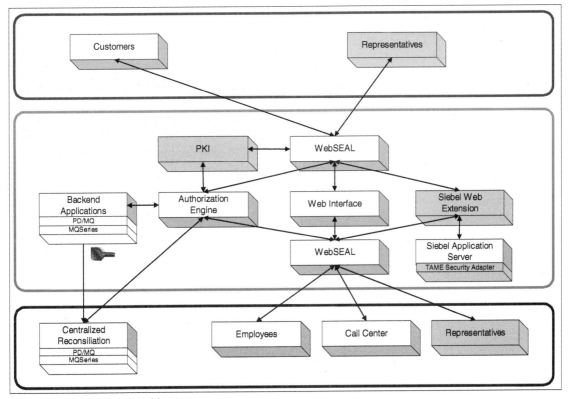

Figure 17-9   High-level architecture

At this point the components described are only on a logical level. The detailed architecture is described in 17.5, "Implementation architecture" on page 444. The dark shaded boxes are the only components new to the system.

► Siebel Web Extensions: The Siebel Web Extensions (SWE) provide access to Siebel applications via HTML-based clients.

► Access Manager security adapter for Siebel: The security adapter is used to provide centralized management of user credentials and roles.

► Representatives: New access groups of users with different levels of authentication. Depending on what kind of applications they access and transactions they perform, different authentication levels are required.

- PKI: The PKI infrastructure is necessary to support encryption of MQSeries messages, strong authentication for representatives, and signing of transactions.

- Access Manager for Business Integration: Access Manager for Business Integration is used to provide encryption functionality transparent for the MQSeries applications.

17.5 Implementation architecture

The implementation architecture is depicted in Figure 17-10 on page 445. The dotted lines indicate the authentication and authorization verification of Access Manager for Business Integration towards the Access Manager authorization engine. The local operating system is no longer used to authorize access to MQSeries queues. All messages in ABBC's environment can now be encrypted totally transparently for the application and without any need to implement additional software modules.

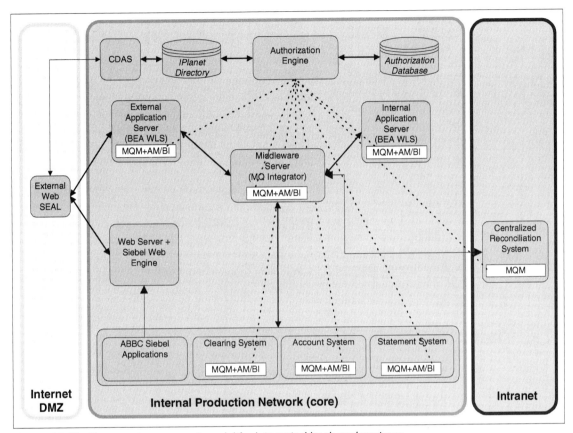

Figure 17-10 Proposed component model for integrated back-end systems

The main design decisions are:

► Access to MQSeries queues is protected by Access Manager for Business Integration using the Access Manager authorization engine. Certificates of internal users are also stored in the IPlanet directory.

► Messages between the intranet and internal production network are encrypted by Access Manager for Business Integration.

► Access to Siebel applications is protected by WebSEAL. Additionally WebSEAL is configured to provide single sign-on. Internet users and internal users need only a single user ID and password to access applications in ABBC's production environment.

► Different authentication methods are supported by WebSEAL. Among others, digital certificates can be used to authenticate users. Certificates are stored in the IPlanet Directory. An external certificate authority (CA) is not involved. Up to now, only representatives of ABBC are required to have a certificate.

- Centralized security management of Siebel roles/responsibilities and credentials in Access Manager. This provides the additional benefit of simplifying security policy management, and is achieved by installing the Access Manager security adapter for Siebel.

We implement the architecture in two steps. In the first step we install the Siebel Web engine and define junctions in WebSEAL to protect access. Next we change configuration of WebSEAL to support different levels of authentication. Furthermore, Siebel has to be configured to accept user names provided by WebSEAL in order to allow single sign-on as required. Details of how this is done are provided in 17.6.2, "Integration of Siebel applications" on page 466.

In the second step we install Access Manager for Business Integration on all MQSeries server systems. For all users we create certificates and store them in the IPlanet directory. Users of MQSeries queues are no longer to be defined in the local operating systems. Then we configure Access Manager for Business Integration to encrypt messages sent between the internal production network and the intranet. Details of how this is done are provided in 17.6.1, "Integration of MQSeries applications" on page 446.

17.6 Technical implementation

This section describes the implementation steps for our third project.

We assume that a complete MQSeries installation is already in place. First we describe installation and configuration steps of Access Manager for Business Integration.

In the second part we describe the installation and configuration of the Access Manager security adapter for Siebel. Again we assume that the Siebel Application Server software is already installed. A detailed installation description of all Siebel software would go far beyond the scope of this book. We only mention configuration steps that are necessary to integrate Siebel software in ABBC's security environment.

In the last step we configure WebSEAL for strong authentication. Representatives should use their certificates to log on if they perform transactions on behalf of their customers.

17.6.1 Integration of MQSeries applications

In the following sections we describe how to implement MQSeries queue access protection, encryption of messages, and how transactions can be audited.

The installation and configuration comprises the following steps:

1. Installing Access Manager for Business Integration
2. Configuring Access Manager for Business Integration
3. Protecting queues
4. Creating user certificates
5. Modifying user entries in LDAP
6. Encrypting messages
7. Testing the installation

Installation

The installation of Access Manager for Business Integration is straightforward. Please refer to Chapter 2, "Installation," in the *Tivoli Policy Director for MQSeries Administration Reference Guide 3.8* (which is provided with the product).

Configuration

The next step is to configure Access Manager to protect the queues. This task includes defining MQSeries objects such as queue managers, channels, and queues. In ABBC this task is already completed, as the current MQSeries environment is up and running.

Access Manager for Business Integration offers two configuration methods:

► Use of the command line utility for all configuration
► A graphical configuration wizard for Windows only

We used the graphical configuration wizard for the Windows 2000 platform to configure Access Manager for Business Integration. In order to configure Access Manager for Business Integration perform the following steps:

1. Write down the names of the MQM manager and error queues you want to configure.

2. Make sure that the dynamic link library MQM.DLL is not used by another process. Go to the Services window and check if the service IBM MQSeries or any other MQ process is running. Stop any process using MQM.DLL.

3. Before configuring Access Manager for Business Integration, the administrator must verify that the Access Manager for Business Integration daemon service has full control of the *install-path*\audit and *install-path*\db directories. Also, users that belong to the mqm group must have full control of the *install-path*\log directory. Complete the following steps to set the permissions for the audit, db, and log directories:

   a. Start the Windows NT or Windows 2000 Explorer.

   b. Right-click the name of the *install-path*\audit directory to display the pop-up menu.

c. Click **Properties** to display the audit Properties dialog box.

d. Click the **Security** tab.

e. Click **Permissions** to display the Directory Permissions window.

f. Review the Name box. If Everyone is not assigned Full Control, continue to the next step. If Everyone is assigned Full Control, you do not need to make any changes in the permissions for this directory and you can go to step l.

g. Click **Add** to display the Add Users and Groups window.

h. Select **MUSR_PDMQD**.

i. Click **Add** to display the selected user in the Add Names field.

j. Click **OK**.

k. Ensure that Full Control is displayed in the Type of Access field.

l. Click **OK** until you return to the Windows Explorer.

m. If you have not set the permissions for the *install-path*\db directory, repeat step 1 through step 12, but select the *install-path*\db directory in step 2.

n. If you have not set the permissions for the *install-path*\log directory, repeat step b through step l, but select the *install-path*\log directory in step 2 and select the group mqm in step h.

4. Then follow the configuration instructions in the *Tivoli Policy Director for MQSeries Administration Reference Guide 3.8* (provided with the product).

After successful configuration the Access Manager for Business Integration process starts automatically. During the configuration process Access Manager for Business Integration creates the corresponding objects in the Access Manager object space. Figure 17-11 on page 449 presents an example.

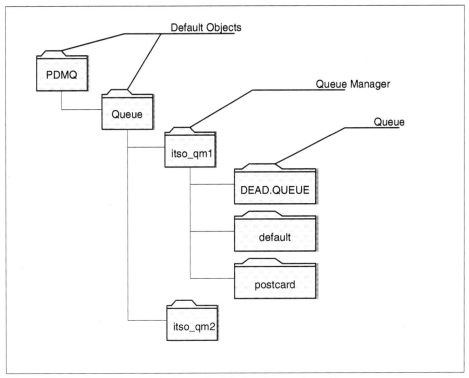

Figure 17-11   Example of objects created during the configuration process

The highest Access Manager for Business Integration object is always called PDMQ. The next object is always called queue. Under the queue object are objects at the queue manager level, itso_qm1 and itso_qm2. These queue manager objects are the names of the MQSeries queue managers you wish to manage. Beneath the queue manager objects are the queue objects, DEAD.QUEUE, default, and postcard. These are the names of queues defined to the MQSeries queue manager.

Protecting queues and messages

Protecting access to queues in MQSeries using Access Manager for MQSeries involves configuring Access Manager accordingly. The components that require configuration to achieve MQSeries queue protection are:

► Access control list (ACL)
► Protected Object Policy (POP)

We use the Access Manager Web Portal Manager for configuration. Usually the URL is `http://hostname/pdadmin`.

Access control list

In order to access a protected queue you have to attach an ACL to it. ACLs can be attached at the /PDMQ/Queue level and its properties cascade down to all objects beneath it. ACLs can also be attached at the queue manager and queue name object levels. An example screen shot of an ACL configuration screen in Access Manager Web Portal Manager is shown in Figure 17-12. New permissions are defined for Access Manager for Business Integration:

► E for enqueue

  Allows put access.

► D for dequeue

  Allows get access.

These permission bits are checked by Access Manager for Business Integration to determine whether a user can put or get to and from a given queue.

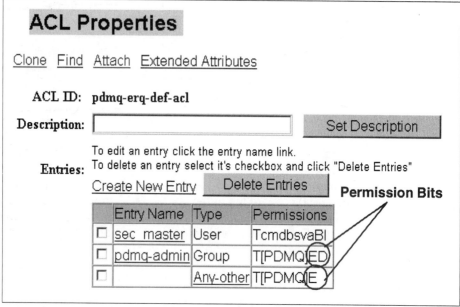

Figure 17-12   ACL configuration using Access Manager Web Portal Manager

Protected Object Policy

To create a new protected object policy select **POP Create** in the Portfolio frame of Access Manager Web Portal Manager. In the Create Protected Object Policy form give the POP a name and select the properties you want. When done, click **OK** to create the POP template.

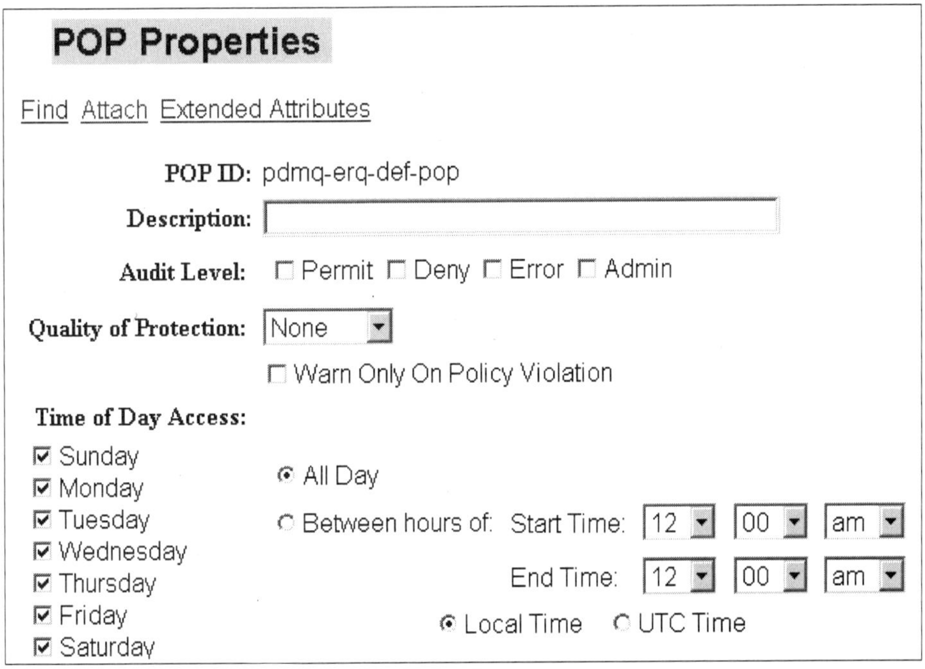

POP Properties

Find Attach Extended Attributes

POP ID: pdmq-erq-def-pop

Description: [   ]

Audit Level: ☐ Permit ☐ Deny ☐ Error ☐ Admin

Quality of Protection: [None ▾]

☐ Warn Only On Policy Violation

Time of Day Access:

☑ Sunday
☑ Monday   ⦿ All Day
☑ Tuesday   ○ Between hours of: Start Time: [12 ▾] [00 ▾] [am ▾]
☑ Wednesday
☑ Thursday   End Time: [12 ▾] [00 ▾] [am ▾]
☑ Friday   ⦿ Local Time   ○ UTC Time
☑ Saturday

Figure 17-13   POP configuration using Access Manager Web Portal Manager

The Quality of Protection attribute is used by Access Manager for Business Integration to determine what level of message protection is required. Valid values are:

▶ None: Messages are not to be signed or encrypted
▶ Integrity: Messages are to be digitally signed
▶ Privacy: Messages are to be encrypted

Where the quality of protection indicator for a queue is set to none, Access Manager for Business Integration will put the messages as native MQSeries messages, without any encryption. Each queue object defined to Access Manager requires a POP associated with it. The POP can be attached at the /PDMQ/Queue level and its properties allowed to cascade down to all objects beneath it. As with ACL templates, POPs can also be attached at the queue manager and queue name object levels.

Create user certificates

If an application or user needs to send an encrypted message, Access Manager for Business Integration requires that the recipients' certificates are stored in the key database. The steps to do this are:

1. Create a user certificate database for each user.

2. Create a user certificate.
3. Export the certificate.
4. Import the certificate in another key database file.

Create a user certificate database

Type gsk5ikm to start the Java utility. Click **Key Database File**; click **New**. The input mask is shown in Figure 17-14. Specify the key database type (to store certificates you should select the CMS key database file), the key database file name and location, and click **OK**.

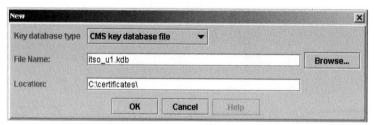

Figure 17-14   Create a key database file

The Password Prompt window is displayed, as shown in Figure 17-15 on page 453. Specify and confirm your password used to secure access to the key database file. If you specify an expiration date, you need to keep track of when you need to change the password. If the password expires before you change it, the key database is not usable until the password is changed.

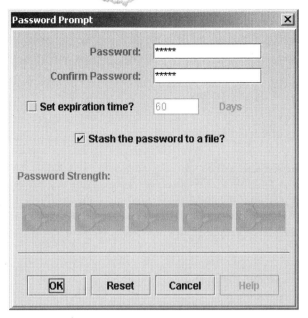

Figure 17-15   Password Prompt window

If you are creating a key database file for a non-interactive application, you must store the password into a stash file. Access Manager for Business Integration uses the stash file to open the key database file (instead of prompting the user for a password). To enable stash file support for this key database, check the box labeled Stash the password to a file. Click **OK** and the database will be created for you.

> **Attention:** Possession of a stash file and the associated key database are sufficient to impersonate the application associated with the public-private key pair and certificate stored in the key database. Ensure that these files are accessible only to the owner.

Create a user certificate

The next step is to create a user certificate. We want to use self-signed certificates for our scenario due to the reasons mentioned in "Managing certificates" on page 436.

To create a self-signed digital certificate in a key database, follow these steps:

1. Start gsk5ikm. The IBM Key Management window is displayed.

2. Click **Key Database File -> Open**. The Open window is displayed.

3. Select the key database file to which you want to add a self-signed digital certificate and click **Open**. The Password Prompt window is displayed.

4. Type the password and click **OK**. The IBM Key Management window is displayed. The title bar shows the name of the key database file you selected, indicating that the file is open and ready.

5. Select **Personal Certificates** from the pull-down list.

6. Click **New Self-Signed**. The Create New Self-Signed Certificate window is displayed, as shown in Figure 17-16.

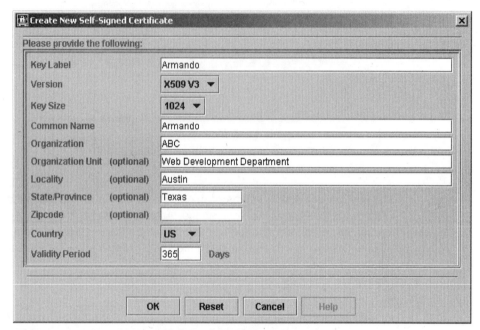

Figure 17-16   Create New Self-Signed Certificate window

7. Type in a key label for the self-signed digital certificate.

8. Type in a common name and organization, and select a country. For the remaining fields, either accept the default values, or type in or select new values.

9. Click **OK**. The IBM Key Management window is displayed. The Personal Certificates field shows the name of the self-signed digital certificate you created.

Repeat this task for all recipients of messages in your environment.

Copy certificates

We want to export a personal certificate from a source key database to be imported as a personal certificate in a target key database. Please follow these steps to export a certificate:

1. Open the source key database containing the certificate that you would like to add to another target key database as a personal certificate.

2. Select **Personal Certificates** from the pull-down list.

3. Select the personal certificate you want to export.

4. Select **Export/Import** to transfer keys between the current database and a PKCS#12 file or another database. The Export/Import Key window displays.

5. Select **Export** from Choose Action Type.

6. Select the key file type (for example, the PKCS12 file) from the pull-down to export list.

7. Type the name of the file to which you would like to export the certificate, or click **Browse** to select the name and location, and click **OK**. The Password Prompt window displays.

8. Enter a password for the certificate file, confirm the password, and click **OK**.

9. Select the encryption strength of the key file and click **OK**.

The certificate is now exported from the source database.

> **Attention:** The PKCS#12 file is a temporary file and should be deleted after use.

Please follow these steps to import the certificate into the target database:

1. Open the target key database to which you would like to import the certificate that has been exported above.

2. Select the personal certificates from the pull-down list.

3. If the target key database has no personal certificate, click **Import** to import keys from a PKCS#12 file or another database. The Import Key window displays. If the target key database has one or more personal certificates, do the following:

   a. Click the **Export/Import** key pushbutton; the Export/Import key window displays.

   b. Select **Import** from Choose Action Type.

4. Select the same key file type that you specified from the export.

5. Type the name of the file containing the certificate you exported, or click **Browse** to select the name and location. Click **OK**. The Password Prompt window displays.

6. Specify the password from when you exported the certificate. Click **OK**.

The certificate is now imported to the target database.

Modify user entries in LDAP

Before we can create users that will be active in Access Manager for Business Integration we need to add a new class called secPKIMap to the LDAP directory.

1. Start the IPlanet directory console.

2. Double-click **Directory Server** (*instance name*). The screen shown in Figure 17-17 is displayed.

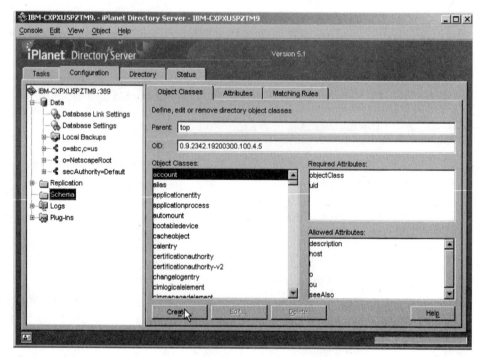

Figure 17-17   IPlanet Directory Server console

3. Select the **Configuration** tab.

4. Select **Schema**.

5. Click **Create**. The Create Object Class window is shown in Appendix 17-18, "Create Object Class window" on page 457.

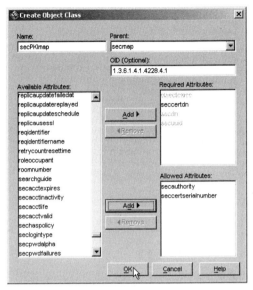

Figure 17-18   Create Object Class window

6. Type in the class name `secPKIMap`, select the parent **secMap**, and add the attribute secCertDN as the required attribute and secAuthority and "secCertSerialNumber" as allowed attributes.

7. Click **OK**. The new class is created for you.

> **Attention:** The IPlanet Directory Server currently does not distinguish between structural and auxiliary object classes.

The next step is to add the new attributes defined in secPKIMap to an existing user object. Perform the following steps:

1. Select the **Directory** tab.

2. Select **Users** under the Default entry.

3. In the list of users select the user you have just created and double-click it. The Property editor is opened, as shown in Figure 17-19 on page 458.

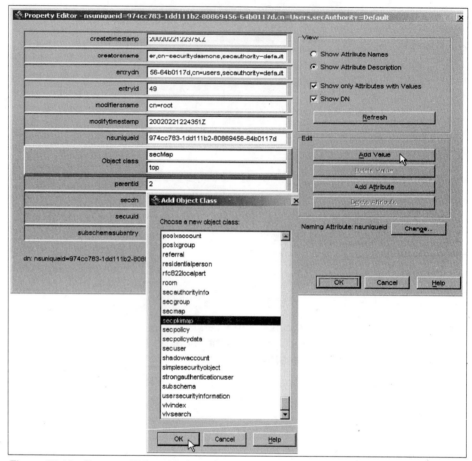

Figure 17-19   Property Editor window

4. Select the entry **secMap** in the Object class section and click **Add Value**.

5. In the next screen select **secPKIMap** and click **OK**.

6. You will find new attributes in the Property Editor window, as shown in Figure 17-20 on page 459.

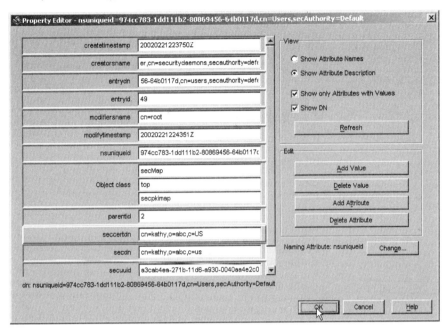

Figure 17-20   New attributes in Property Editor for secPKIMap

7. Type in the DN of the user's certificate. Make sure that you specify it exactly as used in the certificate. This is the place where Access Manager maps users to user certificates.

8. Click **OK** and repeat this for our second user, John.

Encryption of messages

Access Manager for Business Integration supports the following protection levels:

▶ None

Only access to the queue is controlled.

▶ Integrity

Integrity for a message means ensuring that it cannot be modified in any way after it has been created by the application program. This is achieved by digitally signing the message data using the originator's Private key before it is placed in the MQSeries queue.

▶ Privacy

Privacy for a message means that only authorized users are able to view the message content. It is achieved by digitally encrypting the message data using the recipient's Public key before it is placed in the MQSeries queue.

In order to encrypt messages you have to create an extended attribute at the queue level in Access Manager's object space. In Access Manager Web Portal Manager browse the object space and find the queue you want to encrypt. In our scenario it is the queue /PDMQ/Queue/itsomanager/itso_2. Click the queue name and the input form is displayed, as shown in Figure 17-21.

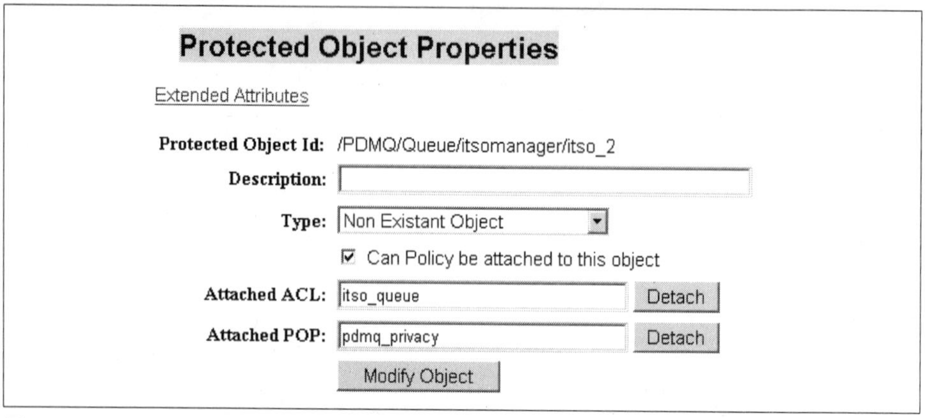

Protected Object Properties

Extended Attributes

Protected Object Id: /PDMQ/Queue/itsomanager/itso_2

Description: [   ]

Type: [Non Existant Object   ▾]

☑ Can Policy be attached to this object

Attached ACL: [itso_queue   ] [Detach]

Attached POP: [pdmq_privacy   ] [Detach]

[Modify Object]

Figure 17-21   Properties of the queue /PDMQ/Queue/itsomanager/itso_2

Click **Extended attributes**. In the following screen, shown in Figure 17-22, define a new attribute named Q-recipients and set the value to the DN of the recipient's certificate. Make sure that you type it in correctly, as these values are not checked by Access Manager. In our scenario we select the user John as the recipient.

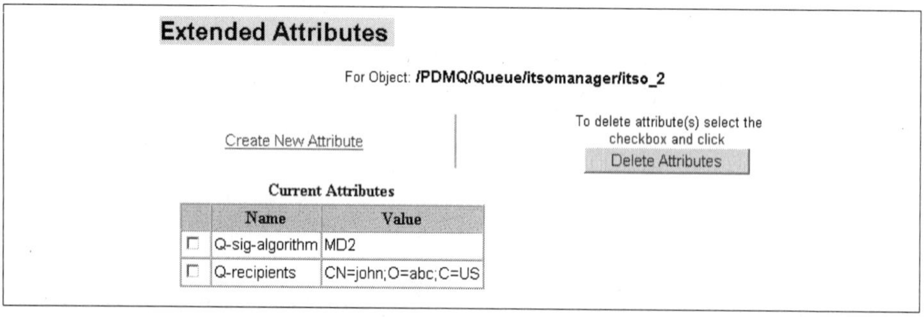

Extended Attributes

For Object: **/PDMQ/Queue/itsomanager/itso_2**

Create New Attribute

To delete attribute(s) select the checkbox and click
[Delete Attributes]

Current Attributes

	Name	Value
☐	Q-sig-algorithm	MD2
☐	Q-recipients	CN=john;O=abc;C=US

Figure 17-22   Extended Attributes screen

The last step is to modify the POP displayed in Figure 17-13 on page 451. Select the protection level you want to enforce and Access Manager for Business Integration will start to sign or encrypt messages.

Testing the installation

We test our scenario with the following test environment:

- ► Windows2000
- ► Access Manager 3.9
- ► MQSeries Server 5.2.1
- ► Two Access Manager users: Kathy and John with self-signed certificates
- ► One queue named /PDMQ/Queue/itsomanager/itso_2
- ► Operating system user ausres18

We define two test cases for our scenario:

- ► Test case *access*

  We test access to the queue.

- ► Test case *privacy*

  We test if a message is signed and readable only by the recipients.

For our tests we use the application amqsput to add messages to a queue and amqsget to read from a queue. These applications are provided for test purposes by MQSeries.

In order to see debugging output displayed in a command prompt we need to enable this feature. It will help us verify if our settings work correctly. Open the file routing on the Access Manager Policy Server and add the following line:

```
NOTICE:STDOUT:
```

On Windows2000 you find this file in c:\Program Files\Tivoli\Policy Director\var\svc.

The last step is to switch on interactive login in order to switch login contexts as needed. Enter the following command:

```
C:\> setlogin on
```

Test case access

We attach an ACL to the queue itso_2 denying access to everybody. We start the test application to write a message to the queue:

```
C:\>amqsput itso_2 itsomanager
```

A screen is displayed to enter key database file name and password, as shown in Figure 17-23 on page 462. Provide the entries and click **Login**. In the next screen we select the certificate for the user Kathy who is not granted access to the queue. Click **OK** and Kathy is logged in. On the login screen click **Exit** and amqsput continues.

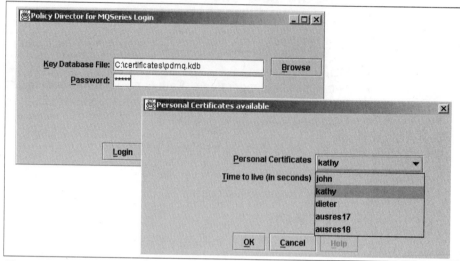

Figure 17-23   Selection of the login context

The result shown in Example 17-1 is displayed.

Example 17-1   Access denied by Access Manager for Business Integration

```
C:\>amqsput itso_2 itsomanager
Sample AMQSPUTO start
target queue is itso_2
MQOPEN ended with reason code 2217
unable to open queue for output
Sample AMQSPUTO end
C:\>
```

Obviously user Kathy was not allowed to open the queue. Now we grant Kathy access to the queue by changing the ACL. We grant her the permission bit E for enqueue. We start amqsput again and get the result shown in Example 17-2.

Example 17-2   Access granted by Access Manager for Business Integration

```
C:\>amqsput itso_2 itsomanager
Sample AMQSPUTO start
target queue is itso_2
test message

Sample AMQSPUTO end

C:\>
```

Test case privacy

We perform the same test but now change the POP to enforce encryption. At the queue level in the Access Manager protected object space we add the extended attribute named Q-recipients with the value CN=john;O=abbc;C=US to the queue itso_2. Again the user Kathy sends a mail to the queue.

Then we try to read the mail, also as the user Kathy. We see the output shown in Example 17-3.

Example 17-3 Kathy tries to read a message encrypted for John

```
C:\>amqsget itso_2 itsomanager
Sample AMQSGETO start
MQGET ended with reason code 2109
message <>
```

Access Manager for Business Integration could not decrypt the messages. The private key of the user John is required for that. We perform the test again. This time we change the user using the login utility and try to read the queue as the user John. We see the output shown in Example 17-4.

Example 17-4 Using John's login

```
C:\>amqsget itso_2 itsomanager
Sample AMQSGETO start
message <Another message for John (encrypted)>
no more messages
Sample AMQSGETO end
```

This time Access Manager for Business Integration was able to decrypt the messages using the private key of user John.

This successful proof of concept concludes the setup and configuration of Access Manager for MQSeries in a heterogeneous environment using different platforms: Windows NT and AIX, iPlanet directory, and J2EE applications using JMS running on BEA WLS 6.1.

Auditing of queue access

ABBC does have a business requirement for auditing. It is important for them to know who added or removed messages to a queue. With Access Manager for Business Integration this is an easy task. One thing we have to do is change the pdmqazn.conf file in the directory *pdmq-install-path*/etc, switch on auditing, and specify the audit log. The entries are shown in Example 17-5.

Example 17-5 pdmqazn.conf example

```
[aznapi-configuration]
logaudit=yes
```

```
auditlog =
...
auditlog = <pdmq-install-path>\audit\audit.log
```

The audit level is specified in the POP.

In Example 17-6 we list the audit.log entries for our test case privacy, which we
performed in the previous section.

Example 17-6   Test case privacy, adding a message to queue itso_2 for recipient John

```
<date>2002-02-22-20:12:10.257+00:00I-----</date>
<outcome status="0">0</outcome>
<originator blade="PDMQD"><component rev="0.1">pdmq</component>
<action>0</action>
<location>3C041</location>
</originator>
<accessor name="mq_pki_ldap">
<principal auth="IV_LDAP_V3.0">kathy</principal>
</accessor>
<target resource="0"><object>/PDMQ/Queue/itsomanager/itso_2</object></target>
<data>
</data>
<data tag="action">MQOPEN</data>
<data tag="operation">E</data>
<data tag="result">access allowed</data>
<data tag="qop">privacy</data>
<data tag="ProcessId">3320</data>
<data>
</data>
</event>
<event rev="1.1">
<date>2002-02-22-20:12:10.272+00:00I-----</date>
<outcome status="0">0</outcome>
<originator blade="PDMQD"><component rev="0.1">pdmq</component>
<action>0</action>
<location>3C041</location>
</originator>
<accessor name="mq_pki_ldap">
<principal auth="IV_LDAP_V3.0">kathy</principal>
</accessor>
<target resource="5"><object>/PDMQ/Queue/itsomanager/itso_2</object></target>
<data>
</data>
<data tag="action">MQOPEN</data>
<data tag="operation">N</data>
<data tag="result">MQOPEN call successful</data>
<data tag="ProcessId">3320</data>
<data>
```

```
</data>
</event>
<event rev="1.1">
<date>2002-02-22-20:12:13.132+00:00I-----</date>
<outcome status="0">0</outcome>
<originator blade="PDMQD"><component rev="0.1">pdmq</component>
<action>0</action>
<location>3C041</location>
</originator>
<accessor name="mq_pki_ldap">
<principal auth="IV_LDAP_V3.0">kathy</principal>
</accessor>
<target resource="5"><object>/PDMQ/Queue/itsomanager/itso_2</object></target>
<data>
</data>
<data tag="action">MQPUT</data>
<data tag="operation">E</data>
<data tag="result">MQPUT call successful</data>
<data tag="prot-operation">sign and encrypt</data>
<data tag="sign-algorithm">MD2</data>
<data tag="encode-algorithm">DEFAULT</data>
<data tag="recipients">CN=john;O=abbc;C=US
</data>
<data tag="MsgId">414d51206974736f6d616e6167657220972f743c12300300</data>
<data tag="MsgFormat">MQSTR   </data>
<data tag="ProcessId">3320</data>
<data>
</data>
</event>
<event rev="1.1">
<date>2002-02-22-20:12:13.132+00:00I-----</date>
<outcome status="0">0</outcome>
<originator blade="PDMQD"><component rev="0.1">pdmq</component>
<action>0</action>
<location>3C041</location>
</originator>
<accessor name="mq_pki_ldap">
<principal auth="IV_LDAP_V3.0">kathy</principal>
</accessor>
<target resource="5"><object>/PDMQ/Queue/itsomanager/itso_2</object></target>
<data>
</data>
<data tag="action">MQCLOSE</data>
<data tag="operation">N</data>
<data tag="result">MQCLOSE call successful</data>
<data tag="ProcessId">3320</data>
<data>
</data>
```

```
</event>
```

Auditing can be configured for each queue separately. With this tool ABBC can audit any access to queues and control if and when messages have been signed, encrypted, sent, and removed.

17.6.2 Integration of Siebel applications

In our scenario we do not focus only on Web single sign-on as a level of integration. Access Manager's integration with the Siebel model provides ABBC with the flexibility of leveraging a single security model that scales across their e-business applications. IBM Tivoli Access Manager security adapter for Siebel Version 7 enables ABBC to truly leverage a common security model for managing their Siebel resources. This means that means we can leverage a common user identity and common policy definition using Access Manager to manage Siebel applications.

The user is authenticated by WebSEAL. WebSEAL passes the user identity to Siebel Web Extensions (SWE). SWE explicitly trusts the information passed by WebSEAL.The Siebel authentication manager concludes that Web single sign-on is implemented and that the user credentials identify a user who is pre-authenticated by Access Manager. The Siebel authentication manager invokes the security adapter to verify that the credentials come from a trusted source and return a database account, a Siebel user ID, and possibly roles from the directory. The object manager opens a database connection using the database account and identifies the user by the Siebel user ID. Therefore you still need to have the Siebel users stored in the Siebel database. The authentication process is depicted in Figure 17-24.

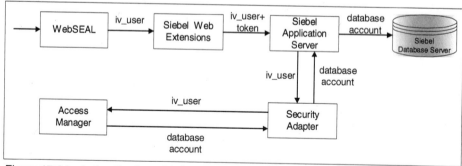

Figure 17-24 Authentication with Access Manager security adapter for Siebel

Access Manager configuration for single sign-on

Having already installed WebSEAL, the only thing to do is to define a junction between Access Manager WebSEAL and the Web servers running the Siebel Web Extension. This configuration option is called trust association. Trust association is described in detail in "Web Trust Association Interceptor (TAI)" on page 135.

When defining the junction to the Web server running the Siebel Web Extension, the -c iv_user flag must be used to pass the Access Manager user name in the IV-USER HTTP header, and the -j flag to enable processing of JavaScript. Communication should be secured using a mutually authenticated SSL junction. Additionally, the script-filter parameter in webseald.conf should be enabled. WebSEAL must be restarted for this change to take effect.

Other than that, there are no special requirements for the installation or configuration of the Access Manager environment.

Siebel configuration for single sign-on

Siebel Version 7 can be configured to extract the user's name from a variety of HTTP mechanisms. The simplest one for use with WebSEAL is the IV-USER HTTP header. The SWE configuration file, eapps.cfg, is located in the *Siebel-7*/Sweep/bin directory. The configuration file is modified to read the header and pass it to Siebel applications. Each application must be explicitly enabled. Example 17-7 shows how to enable SSO for the echannel and esales applications.

Example 17-7   Enabling SSO for the echannel and esales applications

```
[defaults]
...
SingleSignOn = TRUE
UserSpec = IV-USER
UserSpecSource = Header

[/echannel]
ProtectedVirtualDirectory = /echannel
...

[/esales]
ProtectedVirtualDirectory = /esales
...
```

By configuration, the Siebel Web Extension explicitly trusts the information it receives in the HTTP request, so it should be ensured that the only network path to the Siebel Web server's endpoint is via WebSEAL. A more secure way is to use a mutually authenticated SSL junction is described in "Web Trust Association Interceptor (TAI)" on page 135.

So that the Siebel applications can trust the information received from the SWE, a shared secret is distributed between the SWE and the security adapter. The secret is configured in eapps.cfg, as in Example 17-8.

Example 17-8   eapps.cfg configuration

```
[defaults]
...
TrustToken = sso_shared_secret
```

The TrustToken is nothing but a string you can select in order to protect against Web engine spoofing attacks. This setting must be the same on both the SWE and the security adapter. The adapter compares the TrustToken value provided in the request with the value stored in the application configuration file. If they match, the request comes from a trusted SWE.

The eapps.cfg file also contains the user name and password for a user identity that represents the privileges for an anonymous user. This user name and password should match a user in Access Manager, and the corresponding user ID should be found in the Siebel database.

Example 17-9   User name and password should match

```
[LDAP]
AnonUserName = anonymous
AnonPassword = <password>
...
```

This anonymous user allows a Siebel application home page to display to a user who has not logged in.

After changes are made to this file, the Web server must be restarted.

Attention: In our scenario we install the Access Manager security adapter for Siebel. If only single sign-on is to be used, you have to install another security adapter like the vanilla LDAP security adapter that ships with the Siebel software.

Plain spaces should be used as separators in configuration files. Use of tabs in the configuration file will cause problems.

Configuration of Access Manager

In order to install and configure the Access Manager environment for Siebel you have to perform the following steps:

1. Install the Access Manager infrastructure on the Siebel server machine.
2. Configure the infrastructure.
3. Install the Access Manager security adapter for Siebel.
4. Configure users, groups, and credentials in Access Manager.

Install Access Manager infrastructure

The minimum requirement for a machine running the Access Manager security adapter for Siebel 7 is:

► IBM GSKit (appropriate for the Access Manager RTE version).

► LDAP client (appropriate for the Access Manager RTE version). In our scenario we use the IPlanet LDAP directory client.

► Access Manager Runtime Environment.

Configure Access Manager infrastructure

The Access Manager RTE has to be configured for the existing Access Manager domain. Please refer to the *IBM Tivoli Access Manager for e-Business Base Administration Guide Version 3.9*, GC23-4684, for how to configure the RTE.

Install Access Manager security adapter for Siebel

The Access Manager security adapter for Siebel consists of a single shared library. The adapter for Windows is called PDSiebel.dll, and the adapter for AIX is named libPDSiebel.a. For both environments the shared library should be copied to the Siebel Server's bin directory. Usually the path is *Siebel-7*/siebsvrv/bin.

With the adapter come test programs that should be installed in the bin directory for the Access Manager runtime. Ensure this directory is in the path environment variable.

Configure users, groups, and credentials in Access Manager

An important issue during integration of different security systems is always the mapping between the particular entities. In this case it is the question of how to map the Siebel entities into the Access Manager security model. The Access Manager security adapter for Siebel implements the mapping described in Table 17-2.

Table 17-2   Mapping of Siebel entities to Access Manager security model

Siebel entity	Access Manager representation	Default prefix
Role	Group	SiebelRole-
Credential	Resource credential	SiebelCred-
User	User	N/A

Resource credentials in Access Manager can be seen as personalized ACL databases. Because Access Manager groups and resource credentials are also used for other purposes, there are configurable prefixes for the group names and resource credentials that map to Siebel roles and credentials. The default prefixes are shown in column 3 of Table 17-2.

> **Attention:** User credentials and roles are no longer stored in Siebel. You have to create users in Access Manager as GSO users. The GSO storage mechanism is used to hold Siebel credentials.

Configuration of Siebel 7 for centralized security management

In order to configure Siebel to use Access Manager security adapter for Siebel you have to perform the following steps:

1. Configure the Access Manager security adapter for Siebel.
2. Test the installation.

Configure Access Manager security adapter for Siebel

The Access Manager security adapter for Siebel has to be configured for all Siebel applications separately. It is configured via the Siebel client as follows:

1. Launch the Siebel client and log in as SADMIN.

2. From the View menu, choose **Site Map**.

3. Click **Server Administration**.

4. Click **Servers**.

5. Click **Show Components**.

6. Find the object manager for the application you wish to enable for use with the security adapter.

7. In the bottom frame, click **Component Parameters**.

8. Click **Query**, and search for Security*.

9. Change the value for Security Adapter Name to PD.

After these changes are made, the component group must be restarted from the same interface:

1. Show Servers.
2. Select **Server Component Groups**.
3. Highlight the component group to be restarted, for example, Siebel ISS.
4. Click **Shutdown**.
5. Wait until the component group has been stopped.
6. Click **Restart**.

The service configuration file is also modified to enable single sign-on and to specify the shared secret. This is a file like esales.cfg, scw.cfg, etc., usually located in the *Siebel-7*/siebsvrv/bin/enu directory. These parameters are specified in the stanza of the configured security adapter. Entries permitted in the service configuration file are described in Table 17-3.

Table 17-3   Entries in the Siebel service configuration file

Configuration item	Description	Mandatory	Default value
AdminName	Access Manager user name with administrative privileges.	Y	-
AdminPassword	Password for the Access Manager user.	Y	-
ContextPoolSize	Number of PD admin contexts created in the context pool. The context pool allows concurrent requests from the adapter without creating contexts (and SSL sessions) for short use.	N	5
RoleGroupPrefix	Prefix on PD group names that represent Siebel roles.	N	SiebelRole-
CredentialTypePrefix	Prefix on PD resource credentials that represent Siebel credentials.	N	SiebelCred-

Configuration item	Description	Mandatory	Default value
DisableChangePassword	Flag to disable the change password propagation to Access Manager.	N	0
DisableSetUserInfo	Flag to disable the propagation of account status or password changes to Access Manager.	N	0
DefaultCredentialUserid	This parameter specifies a user name in the Access Manager system to which default credentials are attached. If credentials cannot be found for a given user, this user name will be checked next in an attempt to find a valid credential.	N	-
TraceFile		N	-

Other mandatory parameters for the Access Manager security adapter are shown with sample values in Example 17-10.

Example 17-10   Sample entries in the service configuration files

```
[SecurityAdapters]
PD = PD
…


[PD]
DllName = PDSiebel.dll
AdminName = sec_master
AdminPassword = <admin_pw>
ContextPoolSize = 3
RoleGroupPrefix = SiebelRole-
CredentialTypePrefix = SiebelCred-
…
SingleSignOn = TRUE
TrustToken = sso_shared_secret
…
```

Test the installation

In the Access Manager security adapter for Siebel package the following applications are included:

▶ pdadmin_pool_test

This program tests the Access Manager administration context pool. It creates multiple threads to grab and use contexts. Trace output allows you to verify that a context is not used on any two threads at the same time. The program will also verify connectivity to the Access Manager Policy Server.

▶ PDSiebelTest

Tests all the interfaces in the security adapter. Configuration parameters normally found in the service configuration file are embedded in the program, so if they are to be changed, recompilation is required. Administrator user name and password are specified on the command line. The program operates (destructively) on a user called pdsiebel_testuser. This user should be pre-created as a GSO user before running the test program. Access Manager groups prefixed with PDSiebelTestRole- are looked for in the test. GSO resource names prefixed by PDSiebelTestCred- are also used. Resources named PDSiebelTestCred-Server and PDSiebelTestCred-Database must exist.

To simplify configuration of a PD environment to run this test program, two scripts, pd_siebel_test_setup.pdadmin and pd_siebel_test_cleanup.pdadmin, are provided to simplify the task. Use these scripts as follows:

```
pdadmin -a sec_master -p pwd < pd_siebel_test_setup.pdadmin
```

Example 17-11   Content of the pd_siebel_test_setup.pdadmin script

```
user create -gsouser pdsiebel_testuser cn=pdsiebel_testuser,o=tivoli,c=us
pdsiebel_testuser pdsiebel_testuser passw0rd
user modify pdsiebel_testuser account-valid yes
group create SiebelTestRole-Employee cn=SiebelTestRole-Employee,o=tivoli,c=us
SiebelTestRole-Employee
group modify SiebelTestRole-Employee add pdsiebel_testuser
group create SiebelTestRole-Manager cn=SiebelTestRole-Manager,o=tivoli,c=us
SiebelTestRole-Manager
group modify SiebelTestRole-Manager add pdsiebel_testuser
rsrc create SiebelTestCred-Server
rsrc create SiebelTestCred-Database
rsrccred create SiebelTestCred-Server rsrcuser testuser rsrcpwd password1
rsrctype web user pdsiebel_testuser
rsrccred create SiebelTestCred-Database rsrcuser TESTUSER rsrcpwd SECRET
rsrctype web user pdsiebel_testuser
```

After you have finished the test, the pd_siebel_test_cleanup.pdadmin script will clean up your environment. Use the script as follows:

```
pdadmin -a sec_master -p pwd < pd_siebel_test_cleanup.pdadmin
```

Example 17-12   Content of the pd_siebel_test_cleanup.pdadmin script

```
user delete -registry pdsiebel_testuser
group delete -registry SiebelTestRole-Employee
group delete -registry SiebelTestRole-Manager
rsrc delete SiebelTestCred-Server
rsrc delete SiebelTestCred-Database
```

If you are faced with any problems while testing the installation you may want to use the various log files provided by the components. Here are some hints where you will find them:

▶ The SWE log file is located in *Siebel-7*/SWEApp/log/ssYYMMDD.log.

▶ Turning on the LDAP server's trace capabilities may help to diagnose problems.

- For the IPlanet directory server, this is done using the iPlanet administration server console.

- For the IBM SecureWay LDAP server, this is done through the Web-based management tool.

▶ Setting the TraceFile parameter in the PD stanza of the application's configuration file will provide additional information.

> **Attention:** When single sign-on is enabled, direct access to the Siebel Web server endpoint will result in an error because the IV-USER header variable will not be present in the incoming request. All access must be via WebSEAL.

17.6.3 Strong authentication

Step-up authentication means that a user is not immediately shown a `denied` message when they try to access a resource that requires a higher authentication level that the one they logged in with. Instead, they are presented with a new authentication prompt that requests information to support the higher authentication level. If they are able to supply this level of authentication then their original request will be permitted. By default, Access Manager recognizes three authentication methods:

▶ Unauthenticated
▶ Password
▶ Token-card

In our scenario we use an e-banking application that offers customer functions to be used by customers and representatives and a special set of representatives functions that should be used by representatives only. In order to use them a representative needs to have a digital certificate. This situation is depicted in Figure 17-25. Step-up authentication would be the method to use.

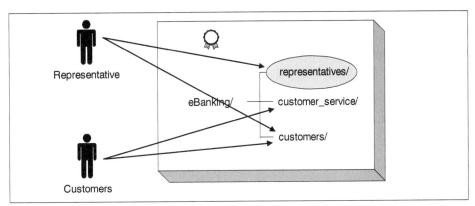

Figure 17-25   Protected object space for ABBC e-banking

In the current version of Access Manager, certificate authentication is not a supported method for step-up authentication. In order to protect part of the object space using certificates, we have to configure WebSEAL to require an additional certificate from the user. We elaborate a new feature of Access Manager WebSEAL, which is available since PD3.8 Fixpack 1, called virtual hosting. This allows us to run another instance of WebSEAL on the same machine. For details please have a look at 10.6.11.

We install a second version of WebSEAL on our WebSEAL server. For each WebSEAL instance we use a separate configuration file.

To start configuration of a second WebSEAL instance called usecert we use the following command:

```
ivweb_setup -u no -U yes -m chuy5 -i usecert -n 9.3.240.19 -M 7238 -R 443 -r 80
```

The next step is to modify the configuration file of this WebSEAL instance called webseald-usecert.conf. Example 17-13 the entries we have to modify.

Example 17-13   Configuration of WebSEAL instance

```
[certificate]
accept-client-certs = required

[authentication-mechanisms]
cert-ssl = C:\Program Files\Tivoli\Policy Director\\bin\sslauthn.dll
```

The last step is to define junctions for our scenario using pdadmin. We create for WebSEAL instances junctions to protect the root.

Example 17-14   Create junctions

```
pdadmin> server task webseald-nocerts create -t ssl -b filter -h coupland -p
8080 -f /
pdadmin> server task webseald-usecert create -t ssl -b filter -h coupland -p
8080 -f /
```

Access to the representative object space is protected and not available through the WebSEAL instance nocerts. An ACL grants access to the user group representatives only.

18

Wireless integration

This chapter adds additional business and functional requirements as well as the design and implementation aspects for a mobile banking scenario. It shows how to integrate mobile devices to an existing infrastructure without the need of redesign.

18.1 Wireless Banking business requirements

Today's banking and trading institutions realize they must move and move quickly to capitalize on new business opportunities in wireless banking and trading. Resistance to the implementation of wireless banking can lead to major losses at the business and market share levels.

Wireless services will soon be a necessity for the end-user. Although many technological barriers like small bandwidth and security needs need to be overcome, it is imperative to face the change in mobile banking.

Wireless banking and trading is only an extension of the product offerings for the financial institutions. It is not an extension of Web technology, because the back-end services are the same. It is a new business model with new requirements regarding the mobile environment.

Online banking and online trading works from standard Internet connections using a PC, while wireless applications present a much greater challenge.

Today, wireless banking lacks leadership in enforcing one standard. There are several network standards, PDA standards, browsing standards, and protocol standards. The challenge is to provide a generic architecture that can be used by most common wireless devices. The application itself must be device and network independent.

Important business requirements for wireless banking are:

► Convenient access to the system

   The user should be able to use more than one mobile device (that is, PDA and cellphone). The user can personalize the content via a portal by using a full-browser interface (personalization and profile changes are usually not done via mobile devices).

► Secure access to sensitive data

   The access to the user's data must be controlled by a central security instance to guarantee the fulfillment of the bank's security policies.

► Non-repudiation for transaction processing

   Non-repudiation is one of the most contesting issues in wireless banking and trading. Both the user and the bank need to have proof that the transaction has been executed and confirmed.

► Multi-channel security architecture

   The security architecture must be expandable without changing the environment. This allows starting with basic security requirements and moving to more sophisticated security models using, for example, certificates.

► B2A model support

The *business to anyone* model support will get more important. A user can make a wireless payment and have it automatically deducted form his account and transferred into the recipient's account.

18.1.1 Functional requirements

In addition to the requirements for the wired environment there are additional requirements for mobile devices:

► Enable WAP-based access for mobile devices.

Today the term *WAP banking* is quite common and is often used synonymously to mobile banking. WAP devices are not necessarily cellphones; the WAP stack and browsers are also found in a wide range of PDAs. Providing a WAP service is a must for today's financial institutions.

► The solution must fit into the existing Access Manager architecture.

The project does not require a reorganization of the existing component architecture or a restructuring of the security design.

► The cost of this solution should be minimized.

Due to the security requirements, the bank will not necessarily have to implement its own Remote Access Service (RAS) infrastructure, but to gain control over the WAP sessions, it will implement a WAP gateway within its own premises.

► The solution should be based on current standards and be open for further enhancements.

In the case of WAP in conjunctions with *real* transactions (rather than browsing stock quotes, account balance, and so on) the WTLS capabilities must be used (see 8.2.3, "WAP security architecture" on page 190).

► The solution must generate generic WML in order to be compliant to all WAP devices. A device-specific rendering of contents can be done using more sophisticated transcoding.

► The solution must be highly available.

Outline of the WAP application

The introduction of the new WAP services will be done in two major steps:

1. Access to *view only* information such as account balance or stock quotes
2. Access to financial transaction application

This is because of the different security models used in the first step usually one additional credential check is needed (for example, login password), in the second scenario a transaction may be accomplished by more than one additional user inputs (login password and transaction password, which can be a one-time pad).

In both cases the security relies on a *no-WIM* approach, so it is lacking non-repudiation.

The bank has identified two major areas that they want to support:

► Banking

This includes tasks like choosing an account, browsing a balance, and accounting transactions.

► Brokerage

This includes tasks like choosing a deposit, portfolios, order book, order details, stock quotes, near time quotes, and order transactions (buy/sell).

► Service

This includes tasks like changing/locking user password, activating/locking transaction password, and activating/locking one-time transaction password blocks.

Besides these areas, a setup and service WAP part has to be provided.

In a future step the bank plans to provide Intelligent Notification Services (INS) for their customers. This can be done using the IBM WebSphere Everyplace Suite as a platform (see Appendix A, "IBM WebSphere Everyplace Suite - An overview" on page 489).

18.1.2 Security design objectives

To build trust between the customer and the bank, the proposed solution has to use the security mechanisms provided by the WAP standard. Today the current WAP 1.2.1 standard is quite common, so the solution can use WTLS to ensure a certain level of data security.

This leads to the following main design objectives:

► Use your own WAP gateway within the bank's IT infrastructure.

► The WAP connection has to use WTLS; this implies that the offer for mobile customers depends on their WAP phones.

► Provide WAP settings on the bank's service Web site or even through *Over-the-Air (OTA)* provisioning.

- ▶ Use WTLS server side authentication (see 8.2.4, "Using WTLS certificates for server-side authentication" on page 193).

- ▶ Use additional security levels for WAP services like PIN changes or financial transactions.

  This can be achieved by a step-up authentication. Access Manager ensures this different authentication level to provide greater security to a junctioned region by applying a step-up POP policy. This requires a stronger level of authentication than the client used when he initially entered the WebSEAL domain.

18.1.3 Implementation architecture

The main goal of integrating mobile devices is to leave the business logic as it is. As shown in the banking scenarios before, we will rely on Access Manager as the focal security point. But there are two major components we have to introduce when implementing a wireless banking scenario. These are the WAP gateway and the way content from the back-end servers is delivered to the mobile devices; therefore, transcoding is a crucial element of this solution.

Integrating the WAP gateway

We will use our own WAP gateway within the banking IT environment to ensure security for a WAP scenario. The wireless service provider has to route all requests from their premises to the bank's WAP gateway.

In order to provide a high-availability environment, we decide to use the WAP gateway in a clustered way so that in the case of failure at least one WAP gateway is still available.

We will use the WAP gateway to serve WAP devices with WTLS support in the case a transaction is initiated. For unauthenticated users and simple browser tasks we will present a public page for mobile devices. WebSEAL will be used with basic authentication and SSL.

Integrating transcoding services

In order to provide a suited output for WAP-enabled devices we have to transform the existing content from the back-end servers to a WML-compliant output stream. We will focus on the capabilities of the WebSphere Transcoding Publisher, which supports a wide range of transcoding services for different in- and output streams.

WebSphere Transcoding Publisher can be used in different ways to achieve transcoding services. We will give a short introduction to see the pros and cons of these models.

The following modes of operations are available:

► Proxy
► Servlet
► JavaBeans

Proxy mode

In this mode of operation, WebSphere Transcoding Publisher transcodes output content, such as HTML and XML, generated by your applications. Images such as JPG and GIF can also be transcoded. One of the most important issues when running WebSphere Transcoding Publisher in this mode of operation is that your application content can be generated by any source or application server. The proxy can be implemented in two different ways:

► Stand-alone proxy

When running WebSphere Transcoding Publisher as a normal proxy, the data that flows from the original source will be transcoded in the proxy according to the device and network profile needed. This method would be suitable for users who have the ability to configure a proxy device in their browsers.

> **Note:** Some wireless devices do not have the capability to let you configure a proxy.

► Reverse proxy

When WebSphere Transcoding Publisher runs in reverse proxy mode, no special configuration is required on the part of the user. In this case, WebSphere Transcoding Publisher behaves like a Web server. It forwards requests for content received from client devices to the servers it has access to, and transcodes the content before returning it to the clients, based on the device and network profiles.

Using a Caching Proxy to cache transcoded pages: If you use an external cache server in your network, IBM WebSphere Transcoding Publisher can use it to store and retrieve transcoded Web pages and intermediate results. This may enable IBM WebSphere Transcoding Publisher to avoid repeating the transcoding of frequently accessed pages, thus giving better performance. Expiration of cached data follows HTTP specifications. The WebSphere Edge Server uses an API to invoke the WebSphere Transcoding Publisher for transcoding and tags it for possible caching and reuse.

Servlet mode

The bank in our scenario does not make use of the WebSphere Application Server, but we would like to mention another mode in which WebSphere Transcoding Publisher can be deployed. The servlet mode of WebSphere Transcoding Publisher allows a more secure implementation.

In this mode of operation, IBM WebSphere Transcoding Publisher Version runs as a WebSphere Application Server filter.

WebSphere Transcoding Publisher can be configured to operate as a servlet so that it can be administratively incorporated into WebSphere Application Server to transcode the content produced by other servlets. The advantage of this configuration is that the transcoding servlet can operate within the security context of the Web application server so that it can transcode information that will later be encrypted before it is sent to the client.

JavaBeans mode

It is also possible to separate the transcoders from the framework and run them independently as JavaBeans. This provides a means for other server programs, such as servlets, independent content-providing programs, or Java Server Pages, to invoke single transcoders directly.

There are several transcoders by WebSphere Transcoding Publisher as JavaBeans like image-converter bean, WMLBean, imodeBean.

18.1.4 Security implications with WAP and WTP

As we have seen already in 8.2.3, "WAP security architecture" on page 190, we can secure the connection between the WAP device and the WAP gateway using WTLS.

However, when running WebSphere Transcoding Publisher, as a proxy as shown in Figure 18-1 on page 484, the HTTP connection from a WAP gateway to WebSphere Transcoding Publisher must be in the clear (insecure) since WTP will not be able to transcode any HTML or XML content generated by the Web applications.

A Caching Proxy can be used to optimize the traffic. A WAP gateway will typically provide the capability to cache binary WML pages for WAP devices. In addition, WebSphere Transcoding Publisher, when running as a proxy, can be configured to connect to a Caching Proxy, such as the IBM WebSphere Traffic Express, a component of the WebSphere Edge Server (see Appendix C, "Access Manager and WebSphere Edge Server" on page 515).

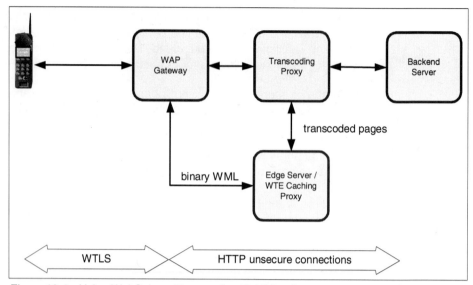

Figure 18-1   Using WebSphere Transcoding Publisher in reverse proxy mode

When using WebSphere Transcoding Publisher in a servlet mode, you will not only be able to secure the WAP connection from the WAP device to the WAP gateway, but, as illustrated in Figure 18-2, you can also secure the HTTP connection from the WAP gateway to the Web server using SSL (or TLS).

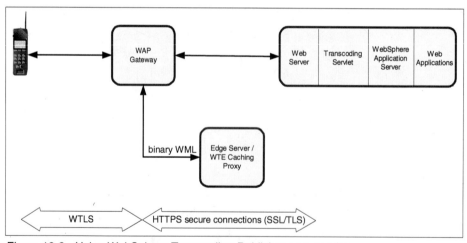

Figure 18-2   Using WebSphere Transcoding Publisher as a servlet

Conclusion

In our bank scenario we decide to use the proxy model of WebSphere Transcoding Publisher in conjunction with the caching capabilities of the WebSphere Edge Server (Figure 18-3 on page 486). The servlet model cannot be used due to the fact that we are relying on a BEA infrastructure.

Nevertheless, we have to ensure that the connection between the WAP gateway and the back-end server is secure, so we decide to rely on a virtual private network (VPN) connection based on IPSec.

The main requirements are met by this solution:

► Integration of mobile WAP devices into the existing application infrastructure

► Secure access to back-end services and financial information

► Integration into the WebSEAL infrastructure

► Control of the WAP gateway by the bank

► Flexible infrastructure to support various mobile end devices, starting with WAP

► Modular design of middleware components (transcoding, caching)

► High availability

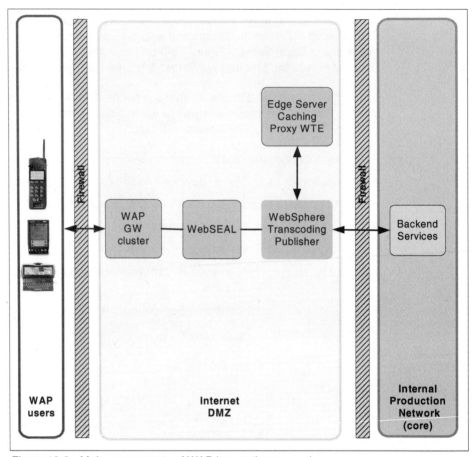

Figure 18-3   Main components of WAP integration scenario

Note: For a detailed description and more implementation issues of WebSphere Everyplace Server and WebSphere Transcoding Publisher we recommend reading the following Redbooks:

► *New Capabilities in IBM WebSphere Transcoding Publisher Version 3.5 Extending Web Applications to the Pervasive*, SG24-6233

► *IBM WebSphere Everyplace Server Service Provider Enable Offering: Enterprise Wireless Applications*, SG24-6519

► *IBM WebSphere Everyplace Server: A Guide for Architects and System Integrators*, SG24-6189

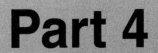

Part 4

Appendixes

IBM WebSphere Everyplace Suite - An overview

Today's solutions in a mobile environment often were developed step-by-step without taking care of the dependencies among each other. This has led to a situation in which companies have to manage and maintain several different systems independently due to the fact that applications were not separated from the infrastructure. Every task (like subscription management, security, device management, networking changes, etc.) has to be performed for different systems many times instead of doing it once (Figure A-1 on page 490).

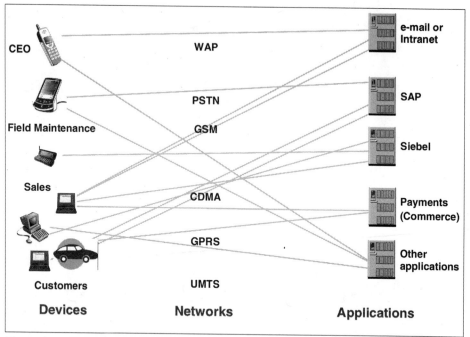

Figure A-1   Today's heterogeneous world

In the case of problem analysis, migration issues, or deployment of new applications, one is facing several *closed* subsystems. This ends up by realizing that former investments in these kinds of solutions were often lost (Figure A-2 on page 491).

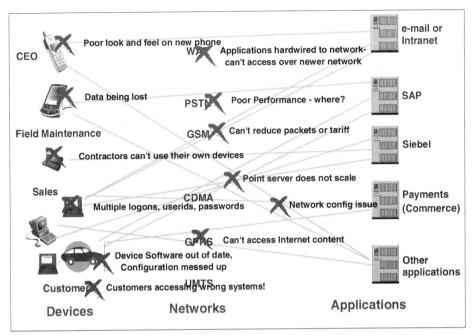

CEO

Poor look and feel on new phone

W?? Applications hardwired to network-
can't access over newer network

e-mail or
Intranet

Data being lost

PSTN Poor Performance - where?

SAP

Field Maintenance

GSM Can't reduce packets or tariff

Siebel

Contractors can't use their own devices

Point server does not scale

Sales

CDMA
Multiple logons, userids, passwords

Network config issue

Payments
(Commerce)

GPRS Can't access Internet content

Device Software out of date,
Configuration messed up

Customer Customers accessing wrong systems!
UMTS

Other
applications

Devices   **Networks**   **Applications**

Figure A-2 Problems causing a nightmare

To get out of this dilemma, IBM's approach is to provide a set of components
packed into the WebSphere Everyplace Server (Figure A-3 on page 492) to
streamline complexity and enable customers to make new services easier to
implement and to achieve: "Any device using any network having access to any
application."

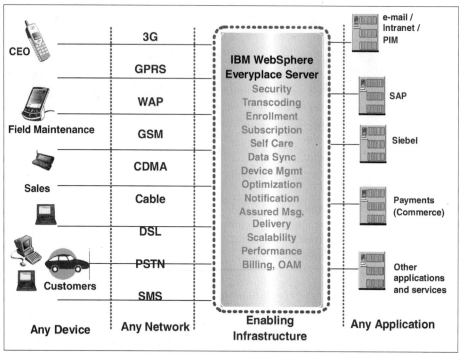

Figure A-3   The WebSphere Everyplace Server approach

This appendix gives a technical insight as to what you can expect from the possibilities of this flexible middleware solution.

WebSphere Everyplace Server is a components-based solution approach. It is not fixed in terms of providing a closed implementation. The strength of WES is providing the functions really needed in a mobile environment to enable customers to implement access, especially from mobile devices to back-end-services, quickly and reliably.

WebSphere Everyplace Server (WES)

The WebSphere Everyplace Server integrates multiple components and programs that are based on proven technologies. It is functionally rich and supports multiple open standards. Customers can begin mobile Internet and value-added services quickly by installing only some of the features provided by WES, and then add new features as necessary.

IBM WebSphere Everyplace Server combines (into one integrated, performance-tuned package) all the middleware infrastructure needed to connect, adapt, manage, transform, and scale today's Web applications and legacy data to a mobile environment (Figure A-4 on page 494).

► The IBM WebSphere Everyplace Server provides the components that enable communication protocol adaptation, AAA services, subscription services and notification services.

► WES establishes and authenticates communications connections to and from pervasive devices, bridges (connections to IP and other standard protocols), and load balances requests, and it keeps track of active sessions.

► WES delivers intranet and Internet Web content and data to pervasive devices matching the requirements of the user, device, and network.

► WES controls user enrollment, maintains repositories of user preferences and device capabilities, provisions devices, delivers applications and upgrades to devices, and supports trouble reporting.

► The IBM WebSphere Portal Server implements aggregation and rendering for content and applications. It is a separate, complementary product offering.

WebSphere Everyplace Server - A more detailed view

Some key features in Everyplace Server:

► Allows users or applications to more easily manage information with intelligent notifications that are triggered when events occur and/or content is available based on preferences.

► Supports location-based information to dynamically determine the user's device position information, pass that information to an application, and manage the privacy of that location information.

► Extends applications with hands-free access by integrating with the IBM WebSphere Voice Server, giving users voice recognition and voice application access and integration to application content.

► Incorporates encryption and authentication capabilities that enable you to deploy security-rich applications, and integrates with Access Manager for enhanced authorization and access control for fine-grained access control.

► Provides high availability and scalability to support enterprise-wide and service provider-sized deployments.

► Due to the flexible structure of WES, single components can be used in the beginning and later on be extended by adding new functions via additional components.

► For application developers, Everyplace Server provides access to pervasive services through IBM's industry leading WebSphere Studio and Visual Age Java tools.

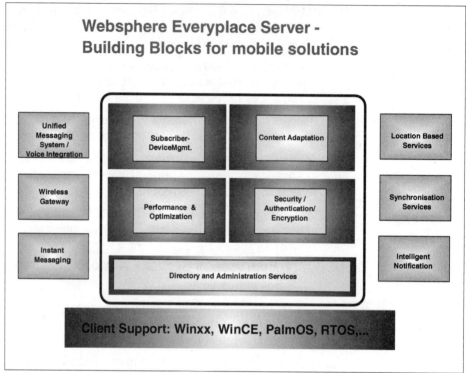

Figure A-4   WES main components

WebSphere Everyplace architecture: Building blocks

Everyplace Server provides capabilities in these main functional areas:

► Communication Protocol adaptation services/gateways/Intelligent Notification Services

► Authentication, authorization, accounting (AAA), and security services

► Content adaptation services

► Content delivery services (including notification services, location based services, etc.)

► Subscription and provisioning services

► Performance and Optimization for high-availability and scalable systems (see also Appendix C, "Access Manager and WebSphere Edge Server" on page 515)

► A sophisticated client support including several hand-held OS and Real Time OS (RTOS) for embedded systems as used in automotive areas or in pervasive devices such as residential gateways and set-top boxes

Communication Protocol adaptation services/gateways

Within WES, the communication protocol adaptation service is ensured by the Everyplace Wireless Gateway product.

The IBM Everyplace Wireless Gateway Server is a distributed, scalable, multipurpose UNIX communications platform that supports optimized, secure data access by both Wireless Application Protocol clients and non-WAP clients over a wide range of international wireless network technologies, as well as LAN and WAN wire line networks.

Everyplace Server securely extends e-business not only to Wireless Application Protocol phones and wirelessly connected PCs, but also to *sometimes connected* devices such as Workpads, Palm Pilots, and PocketPCs, and *always connected* devices such as residential gateways, internet access devices, and digital set top boxes.

This can be used with a client piece of code to achieve maximum reliability and security. If you intend to use the client pack, support for popular hand-held devices is given that enables secure, optimized wireless connections.

This includes support for WinCE 3.0 Handheld Professional and PC 2000, PocketPC, Palm OS, Windows ME, and embedded QNX/Neutrino, as well as Win95/98/NT/2000 wireless clients.

The IBM Everyplace Wireless Gateway also includes a new messaging gateway, enabling the Everyplace Wireless Gateway to act as an SMS Push Proxy to deliver SMS messages generated from an application over WAP and non-WAP networks. A toolkit is provided to exploit the push API and this messaging capability and support the latest WAP forum protocol spec and next generation networks like GPRS.

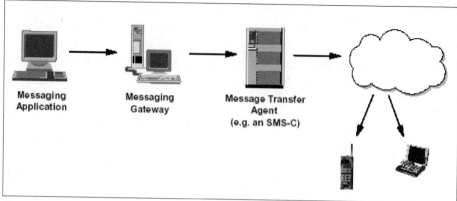

Figure A-5   Advanced messaging with WES

Messaging gateway overview

One of the advantages of using the messaging gateway is the set of APIs provided for application programmers. The messaging API provides a unified interface to many different types of networks and target client devices. An application programmer can push a message to an e-mail client or to a GSM-SMS phone by simply specifying different address types. The API hides the complicated details of how that message is to be encoded and the specific protocols for each network, maintaining connections to the network providers and other device- and network-specific activity. The application programmer can concentrate on creating and directing messages.

For example, an application might use the messaging gateway API to send stock quote alerts to a user's e-mail client during regular working hours and to the user's phone after hours. Other examples of typical push messages are airline flight status updates, news, traffic, and weather reports, and e-mail arrival notifications (Figure A-5).

The wireless gateway supports a broad range of target client devices, including:

► Wireless Application Protocol end-user devices

► Global System for Mobile Communications Short Messaging System (GSM-SMS) mobile phones

► Simple Mail Transfer Protocol (SMTP) e-mail clients

► Simple Network Pager Protocol (SNPP)-supported pagers and phones

► Mobitex end-user devices

The messaging gateway is an installable component of the wireless gateway. The wireless gateway can be installed without the messaging gateway, but the messaging gateway cannot be installed without the wireless gateway. The messaging gateway takes advantage of the accounting, logging, and tracing, and security subsystems of the wireless gateway. Additionally, the messaging gateway is configured using the wireless gateway's configuration utility (gatekeeper).

Authentication, authorization, accounting (AAA) and security

A secure connection equals user trust, especially when transmitting confidential information. The WebSphere Everyplace Server provides Virtual Private Network (VPN) technology, firewall protection, single-user logon, subscriber authentication, and device authentication where PKI capabilities exist on the client. This can be implemented in many ways.

Basic security software enables secure connections between mobile devices and applications across mobile and land line networks.

- ▶ Provides authentication and single sign-on for users of all functions within the WebSphere Everyplace domain.

- ▶ Integration with Tivoli Access Manager provides authorization and fine-grained access control, and limits application access by defined user privilege.

- ▶ Supports multiple authentication methods, including basic Web authentication, forms-based, certificates, and calling a phone number.

- ▶ Encrypts data transmission across wireless and land line networks.

- ▶ Supports of authentication by other vendor gateways.

In addition, WebSphere Everyplace Suite provides a RADIUS Server (included in the TPSM software component).

RADIUS is an open standard Internet protocol for security (authentication and authorization) and accounting. Key features of RADIUS are:

- ▶ Client/server architecture

    A network access server operates as a client of RADIUS. The client is responsible for passing user information to designated RADIUS servers, and then acting on the returned response.

- ▶ Network security

    Transactions between the client and RADIUS server are authenticated through the use of a shared secret that enables encryption. The secret is never sent over the network. In addition, any user passwords are sent encrypted between the client and RADIUS server.

► Flexible authentication mechanisms

The RADIUS server can support a variety of methods to authenticate a user. When the user provides a user name and original password, RADIUS can support point-to-point protocol (PPP), password authentication protocol (PAP), or challenge handshake authentication protocol (CHAP), and other authentication mechanisms.

A RADIUS server is used in our solution to authenticate users for dial-in remote access. Authentication information is stored in a local database, which is owned by the subscriber Management Database (TPSM). Authentication consists of two steps:

► Identification: A determination of who the user is
► Verification: Validation that the user identity is accurate

RADIUS accounting enables system administrators to track dial-in usage. This information is often used for billing purposes.

An accounting record is inserted into the Tivoli Personalized Service Manager database and may be used by an external mediation or billing engine for rating and billing purposes.

Content adaptation services
Content adaptation extends applications to new classes of mobile computing devices that have different characteristics (storage, screen size), and supports the intermittent nature of mobile device connectivity.

► Content transformation

WebSphere Transcoding Publisher (WTP) provides a standard set of transcoders for transforming and reformatting information to meet device, data, or user needs. It includes a developer toolkit for customizing existing transcoders, creating new transcoders, and creating new device profiles.

The following transcoders are already provided: HTML to WML; HTML to VoiceXML, which enables Web content access from voice; and HTML to ClipperML for Palm and Machine Translations.

► Voice integration

WebSphere Voice Server (WVS) integration provides the ability to voice-enable applications with support of the VXML 1.0 standard. VXML provides mechanisms for text-to-speech and speech recognition capabilities to create hands-free access to Web applications and content (for example, news, weather, sports, stocks).

► Synchronization

Everyplace Synchronization Manager includes conduits that provide direct synchronization between Palm OS or Windows CE and EPOC devices and Lotus Notes or Microsoft Exchange servers for e-mail, calendars, contacts, and tasks, and synchronization to any ODBC-compliant database.

► Reliable messaging

MQSeries Everyplace Server provides a reliable messaging infrastructure for connecting mobile clients with servers and enables applications to queue up data even when network connections are not present.

Content delivery services

Content delivery expands the sources and methods for delivering content across a variety of devices.

► Intelligent notification enables end users to be notified when certain events of interest occur. Notifications are delivered via the following SMS messages: WAP push messages, e-mail, and/or instant messaging. An intelligent notification server is part of the WebSphere Everyplace Suite.

► Location services provide privacy-based access to location information. It locates mobile end users (their longitude/latitude or city/state/country). It supplies information to applications, which can then deliver personalized content based on the location (for example, a restaurant application can identify the nearest restaurant to your current location).

► Users can control which applications are allowed to receive information about their location. A more detailed description of location-based services based on WES is given in a following appendix.

► Instant messaging provides awareness of individuals that are online and real-time communication for users on a variety of devices. The instant messaging function can be delivered by the Lotus Sametime product.

Subscription and provisioning services

Tivoli Personalized Services Manager is a WES component for supporting Internet subscriber services. Subscription Services have the ability to capture, retain, and handle information about users and about the end user-oriented services provided to them (Figure A-6 on page 500).

The Subscription Services within WES include:

► Enrolment: The application used by new subscribers to register with the service provider.

► Self-care: A suite of applications that allows subscribers to view and change personal information collected during enrollment. Allows subscribers to access and modify some of their profile data.

- Customer care: Customer care allows customer service representatives (CSRs) to view, add, or change subscriber data during customer service phone calls. All data viewed by CSRs is completely up-to-date and any changes are immediately activated and made accessible to the billing system and to any other integrated systems.

- Device management: Allows CSRs to centrally customize and configure user devices. The function gives access to control software downloads and welcome pages on devices. This is important in terms of maintenance.

- Provisioning: Gives the ability to trigger the automatic configuration of heterogeneous applications, servers, and devices to deliver services to end-users.

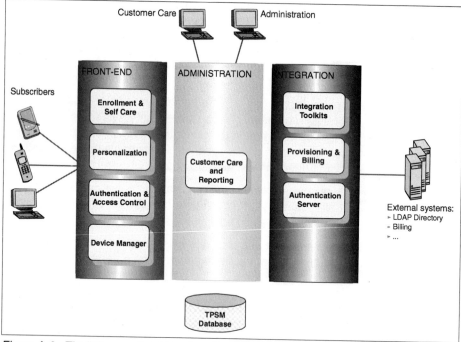

Figure A-6   Tivoli Personalized Services Manager TPSM overview

Administration services

On top of the list of above services, Everyplace Server provides integrated installation, configuration, and operation, which simplifies administration and enables customers to install only the services that meet their business objectives. The Everyplace Server Manager gives system administrators a central access point for administrative operations.

Everyplace Server also uses a lightweight directory access (LDAPV3) server that supports a variety of schema, referrals, authentication mechanisms, and related specifications.

WES components at a glance

Table A-1 lists the main software components of WES (and some optional components) and which requirements they meet.

Table A-1   WES components at a glance

Software component	Role within WES
WebSphere Edge Server	Provides performance and scalability including: ▶ Load balancing (Network Dispatcher) ▶ Caching Proxy (Web Traffic Express) ▶ Security functions (authentication)
Additional core components	Device data base: Directory of device characteristics for supported devices
Everyplace Wireless Gateway	Receives, manages, and authenticates wireless and wireline connections; supports WAP and non-WAP standards
Authentication Server	Performs multiple forms of authentication, SSO, reverse and forward proxy, and maintains table of active session; based on WebSEAL plug-in
Tivoli Access Manager	Performs fine-grained access control (optional component)
Speech Application VoiceServer and DirectTalk	Provides speech recognition and text2speech facilities (conversion from/to voiceXML; optional component)
WebSphere Transcoding Publisher	Provides content adaptation and customization facilities based on user, device, and network
MQSeries Everyplace Server	Provides asynchronous messaging and gateway to MQSeries platform
Everyplace Sync Server	Provides synchronization to various data repositories
TPSM and DMS	▶ Provides user enrollment services and self-care applications ▶ Provides software distribution, inventory services, and management services
Location Based Services (LBS)	Determines physical location of end user and supplies location-based information (LBS is not provided by WES, but can be plugged into WES)

Software component	Role within WES
Intelligent Notification Server (INS)	Provides notification of end user via SMS, WAP, e-mail, collaboration of application events and content

Scalability and performance

IBM has detailed experience in designing scalable systems for more than 20 years. High availability IT environments like the Olympic Games showed IBM's technical leadership in providing a scalable, high-availability software and hardware solution.

Optimization software provides functions such as load balancing and high availability. The underlying technologies, for example, network dispatching services and caching proxies like WebSphere Edge Server, part of the WES suite), were used in high traffic environments to achieve maximum reliability and robustness.

The following 20 million subscriber testbed scenario gives a glimpse of the robustness of an IBM-based wireless architecture.

IBM announced at SuperComm in June 4th, 2001, the WebSphere Everyplace Suite scalability benchmark 20 M users with WebSphere Everyplace Gateway in front of the whole architecture.

The high-end performances were displayed: More than 300 k concurrent users with a very good response time. WAP simulators have been designed for the 10 M benchmark and reuse for this year's 20 M benchmark. The simulation was made using the following hypothesis:

- ▶ One session consists of 11 WML page requests
- ▶ Users wait 10 seconds between requests
- ▶ Between 64 - 2K bytes of data per downloaded page
- ▶ The format of the pages were including WML/WBMP formats

Scalability benchmark results:

- ▶ 20 M subscribers loaded into LDAP
- ▶ Exercised WES scalability configuration options such as wireless gateway clustering
- ▶ Successfully ran WAP workload for 20 M subscribers

Integration of existing systems

To provide a specific architecture for a customer, IBM will support its customers in a detailed analysis of the existing systems and possible implementation and migration issues.

This generic picture (Figure A-7) shows a possible integration scenario.

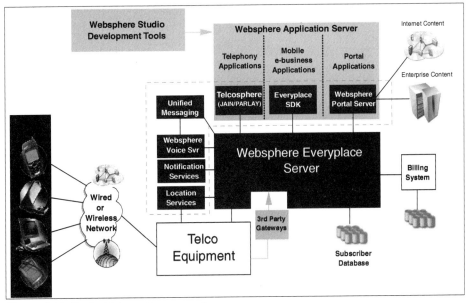

Figure A-7   Typical integration scenario

Security services

IBM security solutions provide comprehensive, scalable, and standards-based Authentication and Authorization Services for Web pages and Web applications, ensuring that only authorized users access data, services, and transactions. It allows Web application programmers to focus on business logic and to tie into its robust security infrastructure using Java-standardized security calls, thus avoiding the need for complex, proprietary security code in their applications. It also establishes clear definitions of user roles and security policy, which allow for easy accommodation of new personnel and new managed resources.

For user authentication and authorization all common standards are supported, like basic authentication, forms-based authentication, and certificate-based authentication. IBM's security architecture provides a strong integration into existing PKI infrastructure.

In case of encryption for data protection, all major standards are supported and, by providing an open interface based on Common Data Security Architecture (CDSA), the security needs can be adjusted in a flexible way. On the networking level, IBM supports all standards, like IPSEC and L2TP, to name a few.

In general, all described services within the WebSphere family make extensive use of security features to provide a secure access to all kinds of data.

These and many more security-related functions are provided by the IBM/Tivoli Security Suite, like Access Manager, for performing authentication and authorization tasks, and Risk Manager to correlate and analyze security risks (to name a few).

Hardware architecture

In terms of physical architecture, a detailed architecture study needs to be performed with the customer to adapt the configuration to the required number of subscribers, the number of concurrent requests, and network topology.

A typical architecture, fully scalable and high-availability, would look like Figure A-8.

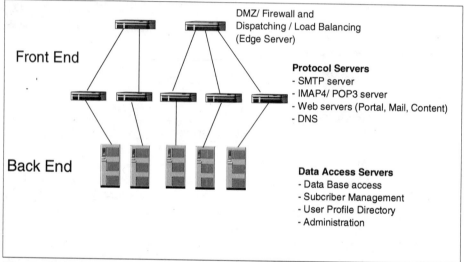

Figure A-8   Physical architecture

The architecture is divided in two parts:

► The front end, which is responsible for receiving and managing the requests of the users. The advantage of this solution is the ability to build a scalable solution when the traffic of the platform increases. The configuration of node is very simple, so the front end is based on clone machines that have the advantage of easily replacing it or adding it for maintenance reasons or when the traffic increases.

The key element to build this type of architecture is the WebSphere Edge Server, which is able to provide the functions of Load Balancing, high availability, and scalability for all the protocol servers. The Edge Server, combined with the DMZ, is the unique entry point for all the flow of the platform.

The edge server can also perform authentication functions through an Access Manager-based mechanism. This has the advantage of performing early additional security functions instead of passing these tasks to the back-end services. This approach is reducing security lacks as well as networking traffic and server load.

► The back end, which contains all the applications working on user information. These applications need to have access to user data stored on disks and databases.

Load balancing within the WES Edge Server

The dispatcher engine checks incoming client requests and re-routes them to the appropriate machines, which are configured to serve those requests. The principle is that the least loaded server gets the next incoming request. In addition, the dispatching engine should be able to recognize subsequent requests of the same client and direct it to the same server. This method is known as server-affinity dispatching, and is extremely important for e-business and e-commerce applications, where clients are directed through a meaningful work flow.

Since Internet communication scenarios follow a stochastic process, it is never predictable which load has to be handled at certain time intervals and how long a user session will take. According to that, the dispatcher engine fulfills a dynamic load-balancing approach.

Another part of the Edge Server is the Caching Proxy. Beside the regular tasks a Caching Proxy is performing, a WebSEAL plug-in is available. WebSEAL is a major component of Tivoli's Access Manager. It allows authentication tasks to be performed at the *entry* of a network instead of going first through the complete network just to perform an authentication request. Have a closer look at the Access Manager Plug-In for WebSphere Edge Server in Appendix C, "Access Manager and WebSphere Edge Server" on page 515.

High availability

WebSphere Edge Server embeds the functionality to set up high-availability configurations. Installing a pair of servers offers the possibility that both can observe each other, acting as primary and secondary (backup) dispatcher. In case of a failure, the back-up machine takes over, changes its IP interface configuration, and acts as the active dispatcher until the failed one rejoins the cluster.

In terms of high-availability of a cluster, IBM provides mechanisms as the High Availability Cluster Multi-Processing (HACMP) to run clustered uniprocessors or nodes of a SP complex. It detects system failures and handles failover to a recovery processor.

Conclusion

Introducing a flexible, standards-based middleware enables a company to provide an open framework for integration of its existing and future applications in a mobile environment.

WES can help customers streamline their infrastructure to get ready for the fast-paced mobile world. Together with IBM's complementary software based on open standards, customers can integrate their existing systems to protect their investments and implement a secure, scalable, and high-availability platform to reach the goal: Any device, any network, any application.

Putting it all together - WES and Access Manager

In the previous section we have shown the capabilities of WES. To have a closer view, especially at the edge server component and its Access Manager plug-in, see Appendix C, "Access Manager and WebSphere Edge Server" on page 515.

In this section we provide an architectural overview of how Access Manager is linked up to WES and back-end services. Access Manager plays a central role in the authentication and authorization process for the complete environment and can actually improve the security infrastructure of a company because it builds up the focal point for security services. This simplifies roll-out, administration, and maintenance in the area of security.

Figure A-9 on page 507 shows an overview of the architecture framework including even mobile devices.

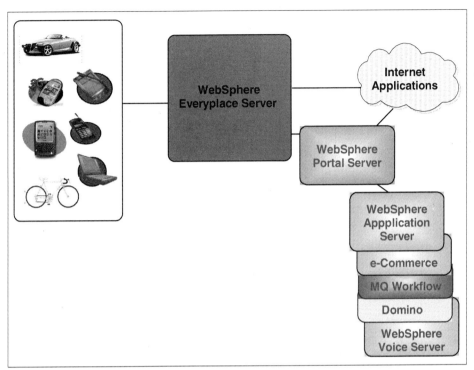

Figure A-9   E-business architecture framework

After unfolding the components we see a close interaction of the parts in WES together with the WebSEAL Plug-In for Edge Server and Access Manager.

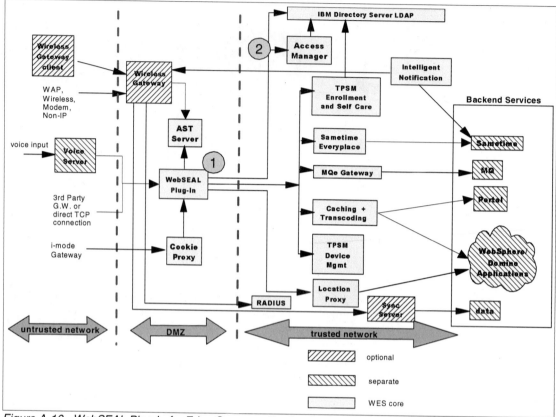

Figure A-10   WebSEAL Plug-In for Edge Server as the focal point of security

Figure A-10 [1]shows the main role of the WebSEAL Plug-In in the Edge Server (see Appendix C, "Access Manager and WebSphere Edge Server" on page 515) as the first instance in the process of authentication.

As you can see, even voice input can be authenticated by WebSEAL. This is because the voice server, which does voice recognition, generates an alias user ID to accommodate the Dual-Tone Multi-Frequency (DTMF) user ID. It is handled as a trusted device by the WebSEAL Plug-In for Edge Server (same as for the wireless gateway).

The second security instance is Access Manager itself, which is used for fine-grained authorization. It also can be used for checking if information provided by an application may be delivered even to an authenticated user.

---

[1] The figure shows a possible configuration with WES Service Provider Offering (SPO); WES also comes as an Enable Offering (EO), which is better suited to the needs of enterprises that are not a service providers.

As an example, imagine a mobile user wants to get information from a location-based service application, like an ATM or a restaurant finder, then Access Manager first checks if the user is authorized to use this service. If he is, the second check is done by Access Manager to determine if the location-based service itself is allowed to know the location of the user. Access Manager is used also to guarantee privacy, which is important for a mobile user because of the ability of a wireless provider to track their users while moving in the wireless network.

Note: For a more detailed view of WES there are currently two Redbooks available:

- ▶ *IBM WebSphere Everyplace Server Service Provider and Enable Offerings: Enterprise Wireless Applications, SG24-6519*
- ▶ *IBM WebSphere Everyplace Server: Guide for Architects and Systems Integrators, SG24-6189*

Basic setup for WAP client devices

This appendix gives a short overview of the basic parameters and networking configuration for WAP phones and WAP-enabled PDAs.

Common parameters for WAP devices

If you configure your WAP device you will find more or less the fields shown in Table B-1, which have to be filled in. These parameters are device-independent.

Table B-1   Basic parameters for WAP client devices

Parameter	Value	Comment
Profile name	Alphanumeric name	Chosen name for the WAP profile in the device
Homepage	http://....	URL of the WAP page
Connection type	Connectionless or connection-oriented/continuous	Type of connection; today most often connection-oriented
Connection security **or** gateway port	On/off or 920x [a]	WTLS on/off or specific port (for example, in case of GSM 9203)
Bearer	Data	Bearer service type
Dial-up number	Numeric Phone Number	Dial-up phone number of RAS
IP address (gateway, proxy)	Numeric IP address	IP address of the WAP gateway
Authentication type	Normal	PPP authentication; PAP or CHAP
Data call type or access type	ISDN or UDI	Type of data connection: Digital/ISDN (UDI) or analog (V.32)[b]
Data call speed	numeric value (for example, 9600)	Connection speed
User ID	Alphanumeric, case-sensitive	User ID[c]
Password	Alphanumeric, case-sensitive	Password
Timeout	Numeric in seconds	Automatic shutdown after x seconds
Image load	Yes/no	Wireless BMP loading
Response timer	Numeric in seconds	Maximum time to load a WML deck

a. This value defines the security used with WTLS:

9200: Insecure (no WTLS) connectionless session
9201: Insecure (no WTLS) connection-oriented session
9202: Secure (WTLS) connectionless session
9203: Secure (WTLS) connection-oriented session

b. ITU.T V.110 UDI ISDN

c. User ID and password often are generic and can be stored on the device; a second authentication will take place before accessing the application itself (for example, using WML forms)

Setup of WAP cellphones

Due to the vast amount of different cellphones we cannot provide a detailed description for all cellphones, but in Table B-1 on page 512 you will find all necessary values to use with your WAP phone.

There is another convenient way to set up the phone, using over-the-air configuration. In this case, you dial a special number and the parameter values are sent to your phone by the WSP (or the enterprise). From a security point of view there is a chance of misuse because the user has to trust the number he is dialing.

Setup of PDA

When using a PDA, there are two ways to use wireless services:

▶ PDA with integrated wireless device (cellphone capabilities or cardphone)
▶ PDA using a cellphone as modem

We will describe the second case in which the PDA uses the infrared link (or a cable) to the cellphone's modem.

The equirement for the PDA is a WAP browser, which can be found as freeware on the Internet; take care that the browser is WTLS-capable.

The main difference within the PDA families is the operating system, which is mainly WinCE (or PocketPC) or PALM OS. But the penguin is moving into this space too. In any case, the setup is basically the same.

PDA OS settings

For the PDA OS settings:

1. Define the connection to the cellphone (IrDA or IrComm).

2. Define connection speed.

3. Define dial-up number.

4. Define user ID and password (you can store it or be prompted every time the connection is setup).

5. If details can be setup like domain name services (DNS) and IP address, use the automatic value; for connection type, PPP is appropriate.

PDA WAP browser settings

Look for a programs folder and select your installed WAP browser, then:

1. Define WAP startpage (home page).
2. Define gateway IP address.
3. Define WTLS service and/or ports.

In this PDA scenario the phone is only used as a modem (connected to the PDA via infrared or cable), so no settings have to be done on the phone (except activating the infrared port).

Access Manager and WebSphere Edge Server

The IBM WebSphere Edge Server includes two products, formerly known as IBM WebSphere Network Dispatcher and IBM WebSphere Traffic Express.

The WebSphere Network Dispatcher provides functions for load-balancing between servers and clusters and can redirect incoming traffic to under-used servers or clusters based on defined criteria.

The WebSphere Traffic Express is a Caching Proxy engine with additional functionality like content-based routing and authentication support.

In this appendix we will have a closer look onto the WebSphere Traffic Express (WTE, a Caching Proxy).

The Edge Server can be used as a standalone product. It is also included in the IBM WebSphere Everyplace Server (WES). Especially within the WES (Appendix A, "IBM WebSphere Everyplace Suite - An overview" on page 489), it builds up a robust infrastructure for implementing wired and wireless business models.

Starting with Edge Server Version 2 and WES Version 2.1 (Appendix A, "IBM WebSphere Everyplace Suite - An overview" on page 489), a WebSEAL Plug-In for Edge Server is provided as a part of WTE within the Edge Server.

The WebSEAL Plug-In for Edge Server is a combination of powerful authentication mechanisms together with caching and proxy techniques. It is useful to put an authentication tool in front of a network at the edge to perform authentication tasks already at the start of a data flow rather than routing all authentication traffic to your security server first (Figure C-1).

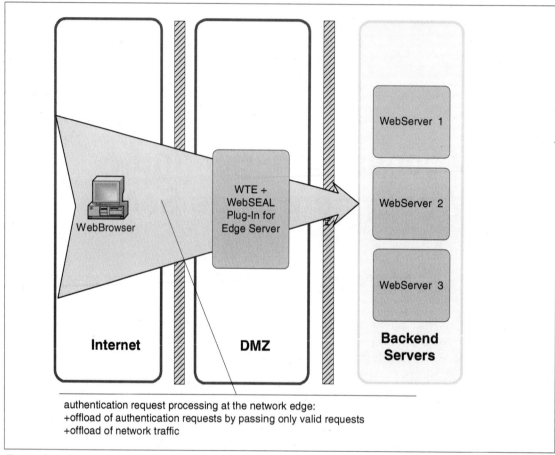

Figure C-1   Reduction of authentication and network traffic

WebSEAL Plug-In for Edge Server concepts

Typically, when a user issues a request to a Web site using a browser, the object represented in the URL corresponds to an object on a Web server. WebSEAL Plug-In for Edge Server provides access control by verifying that the user is allowed to access the requested object on the Web server before allowing the request to complete.

The Caching Proxy provides the functionality of a proxy server for the following protocols: HTTP, File Transfer Protocol (FTP), Gopher, and Real-Time Streaming Protocol (RTSP). The proxy server accepts the client request, regenerates the client request, and sends the request to the content server on behalf of the client. It then retrieves the data from the destination content server and forwards the request back to the client.

The WebSEAL Plug-In for Edge Server supports authentication via user ID/password challenge (basic authentication), forms-based login, and SLL client certificate.

A proxy server can be used for several different deployment scenarios:

▶ Forward proxy

   Clients can configure their browsers to direct all their Web traffic through a Caching Proxy. In this scenario, the Caching Proxy is configured as a forward proxy.

▶ Transparent proxy

   The client re-direction to access the Internet can take place at the network level by configuring routers to direct client requests transparently through the Caching Proxy. In this scenario, the Caching Proxy is configured as a transparent proxy. A transparent proxy is based on the same principle as a forward proxy. The difference is that in forward mode the user has to define the proxy settings in her browser.

▶ Reverse proxy

   Clients can connect directly to the Caching Proxy, which they believe to be the destination content server. For this scenario, the Caching Proxy is configured as a reverse proxy.

Together with the WebSEAL Plug-In for Edge Server there are two main authentication proxy modes. WebSEAL Plug-In for Edge Server provides access control in the following modes of operation of WTE:

▶ Reverse authentication proxy
▶ Forward/transparent authentication proxy

Setting up WTE with the WebSEAL Plug-In for Edge Server

The following sections describe setting up WTE with the WebSEAL Plug-In for Edge Server.

Reverse authentication proxy

Since a Web site's content may span multiple Web servers for performance and content distribution, Web Traffic Express may be used as a reverse proxy to the back-end Web servers so that the user believes the Caching Proxy is the content server.

The reverse proxy performs user authentication based on HTTP authenticate headers. In a domain where the authentication proxy is installed, no other origin server (content or application server) in this domain may do its own user authentication.

The reverse proxy concept is accomplished by configuring the Web site's public domain name on the WTE and specifying a route to the corresponding back-end Web server, as illustrated in Figure C-2 on page 519.

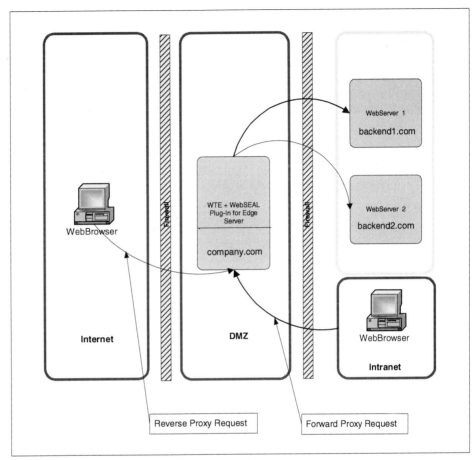

Figure C-2   WTE and WebSEAL Plug-In for Edge Server

In this example, the WebSEAL Plug-In for Edge Server would be configured to provide access control to the objects on company.com. After a user had been successfully authorized, the request would be routed to the corresponding back-end server by the WebSEAL Plug-In for Edge Server performing URL mapping.

WebSEAL Plug-In for Edge Server's access control is configured through its object space configuration file, osdef.conf. In this file, you would add the following entry to configure this Web site:

```
[Remote: /WebSEAL-Lite/reverse/company.com]
domains = company.com www.company.com
login_method = forms
form_login_file = http://company.com/pub/login.html
form_login_errorfile = http://company.com/pub/loginerr.html
```

```
form_logout_file = /account/logout.html
route = https://back-end1.com
```

This entry tells the WebSEAL Plug-In to authorize all requests for company.com and www.company.com using /WebSEAL-Lite/reverse/company.com in the Access Manager's object space, using forms as the login method and mapping every URL to the same Web server. By default, the WebSEAL Plug-In checks /WebSEAL-Lite/reverse/*domain name* for reverse proxy requests.

Forward/transparent proxy authentication

WebSEAL Plug-In for Edge Server may also be used to provide access control to outbound requests, as illustrated in Figure C-2 on page 519.

> **Note:** WebSEAL Plug-In for Edge Server with WTE can be used as a forward and reverse proxy. WebSEAL only supports reverse proxy mode.

Users on the intranet configure their browsers to use the same instance of WTE as proxy to get to the Internet. By default, the WebSEAL Plug-In for Edge Server checks /WebSEAL-Lite/forward/*domain name* for forward proxy requests. But you can explicitly override this by creating a server definition in the object space configuration file as shown below:

```
[Remote: /WebSEAL-Lite/forward/blockedsites]
domains = fun.com *.fun.com *.games.com
route = http://back-end2.com/pub/browsepolicy.html
```

In this example, all browser requests matching the above domain names would be redirected to the company's browsing policy Web page. Alternatively, you could place an ACL at this location in the object space that would prevent anyone from going to the listed Web sites.

Creating the object space

In order for you to specify what objects users are allowed to access on a Web server, ACLs must be associated with the objects provided by the Web server. This means that the Web server's object hierarchy needs to be represented in Access Manager's object space. The simplest way to do this is to import the Web server's file system into Access Manager's object space. After this has been done, ACLs may be placed on the desired objects. The WebSEAL Plug-In for Edge Server's object space manager, wesosm, generates the object space for the following Web servers:

▶ Web Traffic Express
▶ Other Web servers

Web Traffic Express

Although Web Traffic Express is a proxy, it can function like a Web server when requests are made directly to the primary domain name of the Web Traffic Express machine. Typically, informational and error messages are stored in the proxy's Web space. The WebSEAL Plug-In for Edge Server will enforce access control to these objects managed by Web Traffic Express. The following server definition in the configuration file is used to represent Web Traffic Express:

```
[Local: /WebSEAL-Lite/companypoxy.com]
domains = companyproxy.com
query_command = http://companyproxy.com/cgi-bin/query_contents?dirlist=/
```

The configuration tool executes wesosm to generate the object space for Web Traffic Express as its final step in configuring the WebSEAL Plug-In for Edge Server. After running the configuration tool, you should be able to place ACLs at the appropriate locations in the object space for Web Traffic Express. For example, informational and error pages should not require authorization for users to access.

Other Web servers

The object space manager, wesosm, may also be used to query a remote Web server's file system in order to create corresponding entries in Access Manager's object space. To do this, it reads the object space configuration file and creates object entries for each server definition in the file. In order to import a Web server's file system using this utility, another supplied utility, query_contents, must be placed in the cgi-bin directory on the Web server that is to be queried. Afterward, an entry must be added to the object space configuration file, telling wesosm how to query the remote Web server's file system. Using the example, you would place the following entry in the configuration file:

```
[Remote: /WebSEAL-Lite/reverse/company.com]
domains = company.com www.company.com
query_command = http://back-end1.com/cgi-bin/query_contents?dirlist=/
```

After the entry has been added to the configuration file, run the Object Space Manager from the WebSEAL Plug-In for Edge Server machine as shown below:

```
wesosm —run —infile location of osdef.conf -verbose
```

The utility will now proceed to connect to the Web server to query its file system. It will subsequently connect to the Access Manager server to create entries in the object space underneath /WebSEAL-Lite/reverse/company.com. If a server definition does not have a query_command associated with it, only the root branch will be created. After the object space has been created, you may place ACLs at the appropriate locations in it.

Over a period of time, the object space may become cluttered with obsolete entries that are no longer in use. To remove these obsolete entries from the object space, run the utility with the following parameters to remove the obsolete entries from the object space:

```
wesosm -run -infile location of osdef.conf -clean -verbose
```

The above example is based on the assumption that full Access Manager installation is available. To perform fine-grained access, this is the recommended way, but it is also possible to use the WebSEAL Plug-In for Edge Server within WTE as a stand-alone authentication tool. We will highlight both approaches in the next section.

Using the WebSEAL Plug-In without Access Manager

The WebSEAL Plug-In for Edge Server is made the central point of authentication.

The WebSEAL Plug-In is designed to be the first point of entry for all HTTP traffic from the Internet and third-party gateways. If you are using the IBM Everyplace Wireless Gateway (EWG), it routes all HTTP requests to the WebSEAL Plug-In, which is the next hop after the Everyplace Wireless Gateway. WebSEAL Plug-In for Edge Server intercepts all HTTP requests destined for back-end services and ensures that all the requests have been authenticated.

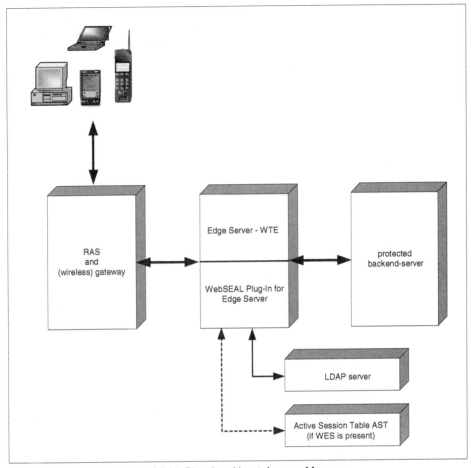

Figure C-3   Using the WebSEAL Plug-In without Access Manager

If the requests intercepted by WebSEAL Plug-In for Edge Server are from a trusted IP address that is owned by the Everyplace Wireless Gateway, then the WebSEAL Plug-In skips the authentication process (8.3, "Access Manager support for mobile devices" on page 198).

If the request does not arrive from a trusted IP address, that is, it arrives from the Internet or a third-party gateway, then it must have authentication credentials included within its header. If these credentials are not present, WebSEAL Plug-In for Edge Server will challenge the user for a user name and password. If the credentials are present, for example, in the user's response to the challenge, then the WebSEAL Plug-In queries the LDAP to verify the user credentials. If the credentials are accepted, it directs the user request to the back-end servers (Figure C-3).

Note: If IBM WebSphere Everyplace Server is present, WebSEAL Plug-In for Edge Server also maintains an Active Session Table (AST) to keep track of active and authenticated sessions. This improves performance in that for a second request from the same user (using the same credentials) only the AST is checked.

The proxy technology only allows a very basic access control (all or nothing). To address the need for a fine-grained access, WebSEAL Plug-In for Edge Server uses Access Manager as we will show next.

Using the WebSEAL Plug-In with Access Manager

When using Access Manager for access control, WebSEAL Plug-In for Edge Server checks with Access Manager to see if the user requesting an object has the appropriate permissions before sending the request to the back-end servers. These permissions are defined in ACLs associated with each object. If the user does not have the appropriate credentials, the WebSEAL Plug-In issues a challenge to the user. If the user cannot provide the appropriate credentials, then an access-denied message or error page may be returned.

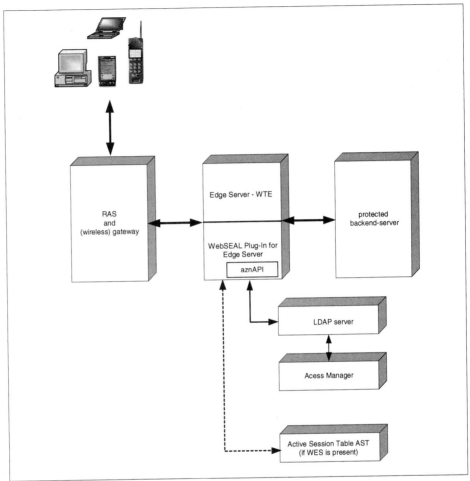

Figure C-4   Using the WebSEAL Plug-In with Access Manager

Access Manager extends the basic LDAP schema for the LDAP that it manages. It then stores the user credential information in its copy of the LDAP using these schema extensions. Because the information is stored using this schema extension, any access to this credential data must occur through the authorization API (aznAPI).

WebSEAL Plug-In for Edge Server authenticates against Access Manager's LDAP directory when Access Manager is installed. This means that the WebSEAL Plug-In authenticates against the LDAP directory through the authorization API, rather than through its LDAP client (Secureway Directory client).

When a user request is issued, WebSEAL Plug-In for Edge Server intercepts the traffic and checks if any credentials are provided in the HTTP header. If not, a challenge is issued (for example, basic authentication) and the provided credentials are checked against its cache (or the AST if WES is present).

> **Note:** The Access Manager Policy Server manages the master ACL database and publishes replicas to the Authorization Servers, of which the WebSEAL Plug-In is one. WebSEAL Plug-In for Edge Server checks against its copy of the ACL through the aznAPI. When there are changes to the ACL, the Access Manager Policy Server dynamically updates WebSEAL Plug-In for Edge Server's copy of the ACL and any entries in its cache. But the WebSEAL Plug-In does not bring user entries in its memory until the session is established.

If none exist, WebSEAL Plug-In for Edge Server sends the authentication request via the aznAPI to Access Manager's Authorization Server replica. If the authentication is successful, WebSEAL Plug-In for Edge Server will store this information combined with the appropriate permissions to access the requested back-end data in its local cache to improve the performance of subsequent requests (and create an entry in the AST, if WES is present).

Once authorization for the requested object has been granted, the WebSEAL Plug-In forwards the user request to the back-end servers.

For subsequent requests WebSEAL Plug-In for Edge Server uses the cached credentials to determine the access rights.

> **Note:** In both cases you can use WebSphere Everyplace Server (WES) and its components. This ensures a smooth integration of all middleware building blocks like transcoding, availability, and networking, and might ease the setup of a multi-channel scenario serving different client-devices from different back-end services. This approach is outlined in this appendix very briefly, because this is beyond the scope of this redbook.

WebSEAL Plug-In and WebSEAL - Comparison

This tables gives a quick overview of the different (and complementary) features of both.

Table C-1 WebSEAL Plug-In and WebSEAL comparison

Functions	WebSEAL	Edge Server and WebSEAL Plug-In
Reverse proxy	Yes	Yes

Functions	WebSEAL	Edge Server and WebSEAL Plug-In
Forward proxy	No	Yes
eCommunity	Yes	No
Edge Server 2.0 features	No	Yes
Step-up authentication	Yes	No
Virtual hosting (see Note below)	Yes	Yes

Note: Virtual hosting in WebSEAL terminology means that WebSEAL can handle multiple server processes (multiple instances). It is not able to use the HTTP host header to distinguish the servers (like Edge Server does). Find more information on multiple WebSEAL instances in 10.6.11, "Hosting multiple Web domains" on page 278.

i-Mode cookie support

The Cookie Proxy provides support for NTT DoCoMo i-mode phones. This component is a plug-in for Edge Server Caching Proxy and saves important information for Web browsers with limited functions. This can include cookie values, and other values for session management and basic authentication. When an HTTP response is downloaded, the IBM Everyplace Cookie Proxy reads its header and saves any cookie values (that is, name=value pair, path, and expires data) into its own table. Then, when the Web browser issues an HTTP request to the Web server, the Everyplace Cookie Proxy retrieves the saved cookie values, adds them to the request header, and passes the request to the back-end server.

> **Note:** Currently, the IBM WebSphere Everyplace Cookie Proxy is only available when installing on machines in Japan.

i-Mode cookie support

The Everyplace Cookie Proxy checks the expiration value of a cookie only when it is saved in its own table, and it does not check the expiration value of any cookies when they are retrieved. All saved cookie values remain in the Everyplace Cookie Proxy's table until the session is cleaned up by the cleanup daemon. This means that a cookie is passed to the back-end server as long as the cookie entry remains in the table, and monitoring for expiration is the responsibility of the back-end server.

When a user tries to access a Web application for the first time in a session (or after the expiration of a time-out delay since this user last had access to this application), the Everyplace Cookie Proxy generates a session ID. If the host name of the URL is that of the back-end server or the Everyplace Cookie Proxy, this session ID is added to the URLs of the hyperlinks in the HTTP response.

Every time an HTTP request is submitted, the Everyplace Cookie Proxy checks whether the incoming session ID is valid. This session information is stored in the table of the Everyplace Cookie Proxy until the session cleanup daemon removes it. The session expiration period and the cleanup interval can be defined during the configuration of the Everyplace Cookie Proxy.

If the Web browser submits an HTTP request and the back-end server requires basic authentication, but the Everyplace Cookie Proxy has not yet stored a valid user ID and password, the Everyplace Cookie Proxy sends a login form to the Web browser. (This form can be customized by the back-end Web application developer or the administrator who sets up the Everyplace Cookie Proxy.) When the user logs in, the Everyplace Cookie Proxy reads the body of the HTTP request and saves the user ID and password. Then, throughout the rest of the session whenever the browser submits an HTTP request, the Everyplace Cookie Proxy:

- ► Retrieves the user ID and password
- ► Adds the default realm after the user ID if the realm is specified in its configuration file
- ► Encodes the resulting string, using BASE64
- ► Adds the string to the request header
- ► Passes the header to the back-end server

Performance and scalability issues must be addressed when the Everyplace Cookie Proxy is implemented. The physical architecture will have an important effect on both performance and scalability, so for better throughput and security, the IBM WebSphere Edge Server Caching Proxy, including the Everyplace Cookie Proxy, should be installed on a machine separate from the other components of WebSphere Everyplace Server.

The use of HTTPS is one factor that affects the number of HTTP requests processed per unit of time and the turnaround time per request. In general, the overhead for processing HTTPS is much larger than the overhead for cookie processing by the Everyplace Cookie Proxy.

Step-by-step instructions

This appendix contains step-by-step instructions on how to create a multiple domain structure in Access Manager and how to generate a key database for use with certificates.

Creating delegate domains

This section shows how to use the Web Portal Manager in order to create an enterprise domain and any number of sub-domains.

While this example is written for the WebSphere Application Server scenario discussed in Chapter 10, "Baseline security framework" on page 221, the same steps can be applied to the creation of any enterprise domain.

Enterprise domain

From the left-hand pane of the WPM, select **Create Enterprise Domain**. You will then be prompted for the domain name, description, and ldap suffix, as shown in Figure E-1.

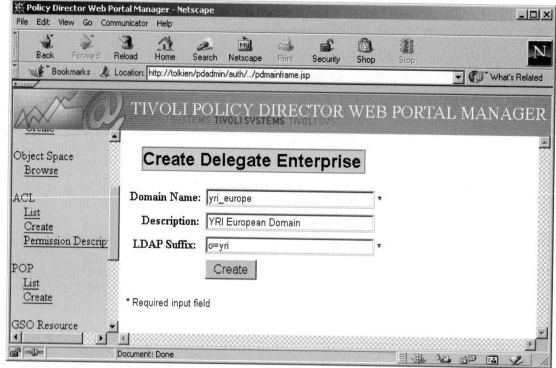

Figure E-1   Creating an enterprise domain

In this case the name of the domain is yri_europe and the LDAP suffix is o=yri. Enter the data and click **Create** to create the enterprise domain.

> **Tip:** The LDAP suffix is needed to store group information for the domain. It is possible to create different suffixes or organizational units (OUs) under current suffixes. Using a different suffix for each enterprise domain can help keep the LDAP tree more organized. Please note, however, that those modifications must be done manually and not via the WPM.

Sub-domains

Now that the enterprise level domain has been created, it is possible to add sub-domains.

From the left-hand pane, select **List Enterprise Domains**. This will bring up yri_europe on the right-hand side of the window. Selecting the domain will get you to the Delegate Domain Properties menu, as shown in Figure E-2 on page 536.

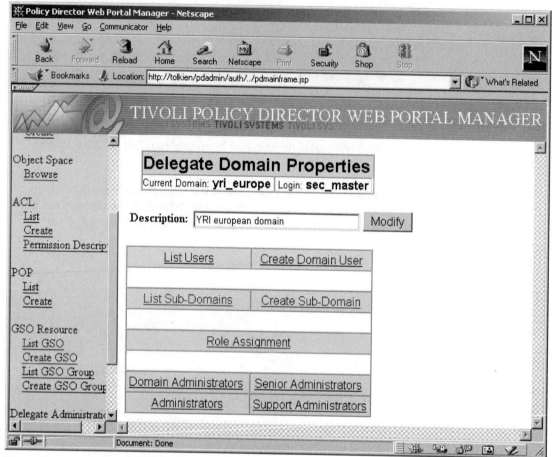

Figure E-2   Delegate Domain Properties menu

Select **Create Sub-Domain** to bring up the Create Delegate Domain dialog, as shown in Figure E-3 on page 537.

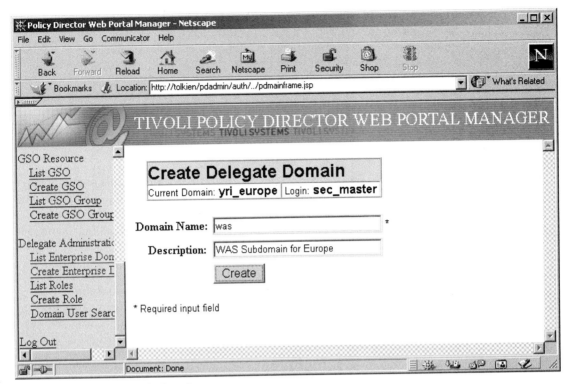

Figure E-3 Creating a sub-domain

Just enter a domain name into the appropriate box and a short description (not mandatory) and click **Create**. You have now created the first sub-domain.

Reuse this section to create any number of sub-domains, either under the enterprise domain or under other sub-domains.

Important: When you wish to create sub-domains under other sub-domains, make sure that you are in the right domain before you start. Removing domains created in a wrong place is a lengthy task. Use the List Sub-Domains link to navigate inside the domain tree and check the Current Domain box to make sure you are adding a new domain in the right place before clicking the **Create** button.

Key database

This section describes the steps needed to create a key database and populate it with certificates. WebSEAL needs this to communicate securely with clients and back-end servers. While this example describes how to acquire the certificate used for communication with a back-end server, you can also use this example to acquire the certificate used for external communications.

1. Create a key database.

   Start your GSKIT Graphical User Interface and select **Key Database File -> New**. You will be presented with a box like that shown in Figure E-4.

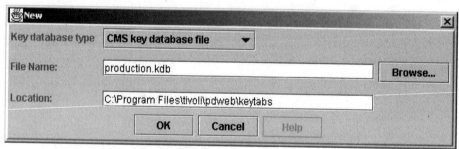

Figure E-4   Creating a new key database

Fill in the appropriate fields with the name and path of the key database file. Leave the type as CMS key database file.

You will then be prompted for a password, as shown in Figure E-5 on page 539.

Figure E-5   Creating a key database, password prompt

Important: As this is the password protecting your certificates, it should be extremely secure. Leaving this password open to guessing or brute force attacks may present a serious security hazard.

For additional security, stash the password to a file. This way you do not have to enter the password into any configuration files.

2. Create a certificate request for your Certificate Authority.

Once you have created your key database, you will be presented with a view of all the Signer Certificates recognized by WebSEAL. If your CA is not among these, you must get their root certificate and add it to the key database. Once this is done, select **Personal Certificate Request** from the menu, as shown in Figure E-6 on page 540.

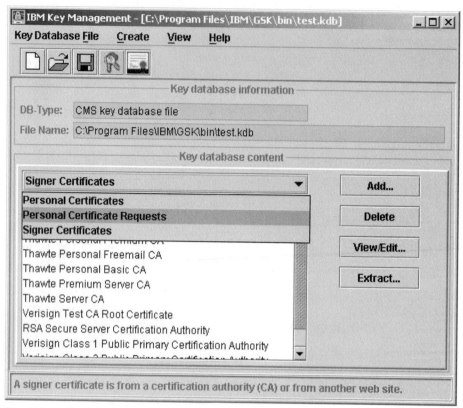

Figure E-6   Key Management, main view

Click **New** to open the window for certificate requests. As shown in Figure E-7 on page 541, fill in the required fields. While the name of the WebSEAL server and the Common Name field must match, the key label can be whatever is easy to remember. Often the best choice is the name of the machine without the DNS suffix.

Note: While the organizational unit and locality are listed as optional information in the screen shot, this might may not be the case for some CAs. In order to complete the certificate request process as quickly as possible, fill in all applicable fields.

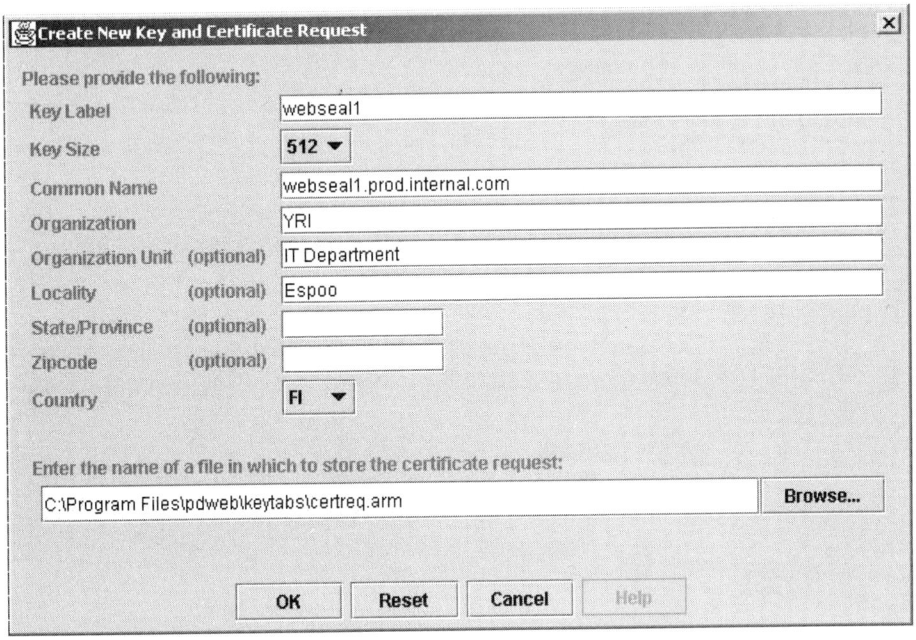

Figure E-7 Certificate request window

Repeat the certificate request step for all of your WebSEAL machines. Just change the Key Label and Common Name field. This will place all certificates in one file that you can copy across to all WebSEAL servers.

While it is possible to create self-signed certificates, it is better to obtain them from a widely known CA, to avoid the extra work of configuring the all back-end servers to trust your Access Manager WebSEAL machines.

3. Import the certificate you receive from your CA.

In the GSKIT main view, select the Personal Certificates menu from the drop box and click the **Receive** button. You will get a Receive Certificate dialog window, shown in Figure E-8 on page 542. Enter the path and name to the certificate you received from your CA.

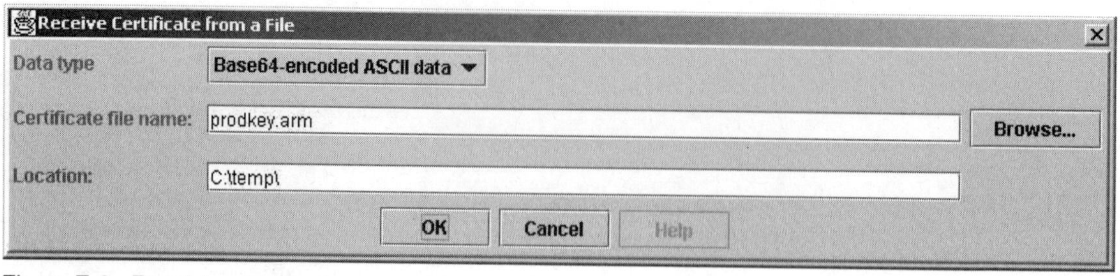

Figure E-8   Receiving certificate

The data type of the certificate may vary, depending on the choices you made when downloading, but Base64-encoded is the most common one.

> **Note:** Sometimes you may experience problems with the certificate being invalid. This is most likely caused by formatting introduced in some phase of the certificate transfer. Try to use only the most basic text editors and only save the certificate in ASCII format to avoid problems.

4. Configure Access Manager WebSEAL to use the certificate.

   To use the newly created key database, which we have placed under %installpath%\pdweb\keytabs\production.kdb, the WebSEAL's configuration file %installpath%\pdweb\etc\webseald.conf needs to be modified. To configure the key database file for WebSEAL use, modify the webseal-cert-keyfile entry to correspond to the name and path of the key database.

   ```
   webseal-cert-keyfile = C:/Program Files/Tivoli/PDWeb/keytabs/production.kdb
   ```

   Next, the stash file containing the key database password must be configured with the webseal-cert-keyfile-stash entry.

   ```
   webseal-cert-keyfile-stash = C:/Program
   Files/Tivoli/PDWeb/keytabs/production.sth
   ```

   Next, restart the WebSEAL server. If you have problems with starting the WebSEAL server or in initiating SSL communications, the most likely cause is that WebSEAL does not have the required rights to access the files.

MPA authentication flow

In this appendix we give a more detailed view of the authentication process when using the Multiplexing Proxy Agent (MPA) support in WebSEAL.

Authentication process

The following is the authentication process when using the Multiplexing Proxy Agent (MPA) support in WebSEAL.

1. The WebSEAL administrator performs the following preliminary configuration:
   - Enables support for Multiplexing Proxy Agents (MPA)
   - Creates an Access Manager account for the specific MPA gateway
   - Adds this MPA account to the **webseal-mpa-servers** group

2. Clients connect to the MPA gateway (for example, WAP gateway).

3. The gateway translates the request to an HTTP request.

4. The gateway authenticates the client.

5. The gateway establishes a connection with WebSEAL, forwarding the client request.

6. The MPA authenticates to WebSEAL (using a method distinct from the client) and an identity is derived for the MPA (which already has a WebSEAL account).

7. WebSEAL verifies the MPA's membership in the webseal-mpa-servers group.

8. A credential is built for the MPA and flagged as a special MPA type in the cache. Although this MPA credential accompanies each future client request, it is not used for authorization checks on these requests.

9. Now WebSEAL needs to further identify the owner of the request. The MPA is able to distinguish the multiple clients for proper routing of login prompts.

10. The client logs in and authenticates using a method distinct from the authentication type used for the MPA. So if the method used for the client is basic authentication, the method used for the MPA may be IP address-based.

11. WebSEAL builds a credential from the client authentication data.

12. The session data type used by each client must be distinct from the session data type used by the MPA.

13. The Authorization Service permits or denies access to protected objects based on the user credential and the object's ACL permissions.

Enabling and disabling MPA authentication

The mpa parameter, located in the [mpa] stanza of the webseald.conf configuration file, enables and disables MPA authentication.

To enable the MPA authentication method, enter yes.

To disable the MPA authentication method, enter no.

For example:

```
[mpa]
mpa=yes
```

Note: The use of the MPA support of Access Manager depends on the installed WAP gateway. Be sure to check how your gateway is set up. There are gateways in the market that use multi-SSL instead of single SSL (MPA).

Policy Server high-availability

While each Access Manager domain can have only one Policy Server, there are still many ways to increase the availability of Access Manager Policy Servers (PDMGR). The most frequently used methods are different types of clusters. And while these are very useful in many cases, clusters usually are very limited in geographic separation of participating machines.

This appendix deals with creating a lightweight, location and operating system-independent solution to increasing Access Manager Policy Server availability.

Access Manager Policy Server replication

Since Policy Director Version 3.8, which was the first version without DCE, the whole Policy Server configuration was just based on a few files and some LDAP entries. This has made it possible to create a lightweight replication solution.

> **Note:** There is some limited Policy Server replication support in Access Manager Version 3.9. The replication method presented here is a different approach that can be used regardless of version.

As mentioned earlier, the benefits of this solution compared to cluster solutions are its independence of geographic proximity and the fact that the same solution works on different operating systems. While this was not tested in the lab for this redbook, the solution should also work as a migration product, enabling the migration of Access Manager Policy Server from one platform to another.

The basic idea behind the solution is to copy the configuration, certificate, and authorization database files from one machine to another. The installation procedure for the second Policy Server depends on whether you have the master LDAP database on the same machine as the Policy Server.

Both cases are covered in the installation and recovery instructions.

> **Note:** While the instructions are detailed enough for people with some experience in Access Manager and LDAP, the lack of step-by-step instructions means that inexperienced personnel should not attempt to implement this solution without familiarizing themselves with LDAP and Access Manager Policy Server installation, as well as the basic principles of the operating systems they are using for the implementation.

Components

The servers involved in this scenario are:

► management1

This is the primary Access Manager Policy Server, and also the LDAP master server (unless LDAP master server is located on a machine separate from the PDMGR server).

► management2

This is the machine hosting the Access Manager Policy Server stand-by replica and LDAP replica server (unless the LDAP master server is located on a machine separate from the PDMGR server).

Installation

These installation instructions assume that the Access Manager Policy Server has already been installed on management1. Also, the paths mentioned here are the default paths for a Windows-based installation. Paths, for example, Solaris, differ slightly as Access Manager files are split between /opt and /var directories.

Complete the following steps:

1. On management2, install LDAP.

   This means a complete installation of the LDAP server, but without any of the Access Manager users and groups.

2. On management2, make a DB2 backup of the LDAP database.

   This will create an image of a clean database that will be needed later.

   > **Note:** Do this step only if the LDAP master server is located on management1, not if it is located on a separate machine.

3. On management2, the install and configure Access Manager Policy Server.

   When prompted for the LDAP database host name, enter management2. Other settings are not important, so do not waste time configuring SSL connections to the LDAP server.

4. On management2, shut down the Access Manager Policy Server service and disable the automatic startup on machine reboot.

   This is to make sure that when files are being copied from the active server to the stand-by, the files will not be locked (thus preventing copying).

5. On management2, do a DB2 restore of the LDAP database using the backup created earlier.

   This will remove the server name-specific entries made to the LDAP when installing and configuring Access Manager Policy Server on management2.

   You will then have a clean database, ready for data coming in from the LDAP master on management1.

   > **Note:** Do this step only if LDAP master server is located on management1, not if it is located on a separate machine.

6. On management1, make an LDIF backup of the LDAP database and copy the backup file over to management2.

This step and the following step are to be performed pre-replication in order to quickly transfer the existing user base and suffixes from the LDAP master to the LDAP replica.

While this transfer could not be called "fast" in an environment with users numbering in tens or hundreds of thousands, it is still a good method for smaller environments. In those large environments the LDAP master server should be on a separate machine anyway.

> **Note:** Do this step only if the LDAP master server is located on management1, not if it is located on a separate machine.

7. On management2, do an LDIF restore from the backup file you copied over from management1.

   Once this step is completed, management2 is ready to be configured as an LDAP replica.

> **Note:** Do this step only if the LDAP master server is located on management1, not if it is located on a separate machine.

8. On management1 and management2, configure replication with management1 as master and management2 as replica.

   This will transfer all the LDAP data to management2 when it is updated.

> **Note:** Do this step only if the LDAP master server is located on management1, not if it is located on a separate machine.

9. Complete the following step only if the LDAP master server is located on a machine separate from the Access Manager Policy Server(s):

   Uninstall the LDAP server from management2.

   If an LDAP server is already installed on a separate machine, the LDAP server on management2 has already served its purpose, which was to enable the installation of an Access Manager Policy Server, and can be removed.

10. Copy Access Manager configuration, certificate, and authorization database files from management1 to management2.

    The files are as follows:

```
%PDPATH%\db\master_authzn.db
%PDPATH%\keytab\ (you can copy this whole directory)
%PDPATH%\etc\ivmgrd.conf
%PDPATH%\etc\ldap.conf
%PDPATH%\etc\pd.conf
```

The %PDPATH% variable stands for the path where Access Manager is installed. For example, the default installation path on Windows 2000 would be c:\Program Files\Tivoli\Policy Director.

> **Important:** This procedure only copies a snapshot of the necessary files. A solution (a script or management software) should be used to copy files every time they are changed. The master_authzn.db file changes in rapid succession especially.

Now all the files that configure an Access Manager master server are replicated to the stand-by machine and the installation part is complete.

Recovery

This section explains how to get Access Manager Policy Server stand-by running after the primary server has suffered a breakdown.

1. On management2, configure the LDAP server as master instead of replica.

   This will enable the LDAP server for write operations coming from Access Manager Policy Server.

   > **Note:** Do this step only if the LDAP master server is located on management1, not if it is located on a separate machine.

2. Rename management2 to management1 and, if possible, change the IP address of management2 to that of management1.

   The changing of the name is imperative, because all the certificates are configured with the name management1; so are all the configuration files on the other Access Manager components (such as WebSEAL).

   If you implement this solution with two different physical locations, the IP address space may differ between these two locations. Therefore it might not be possible to configure management2 with management1's IP address.

   If it is not possible to change the IP address of management2 to that of management1, you need to change the IP address of management1 in DNS in order for Access Manager components to successfully connect to the new Access Manager Policy Server.

3. On management1 (formerly management2) configure Access Manager Policy Server service to start automatically on reboot and start up the service.

   Now that this is the active server, there is no need to keep the service shut down.

Note: In order to re-establish an MTS session (you will not be able to receive any ACL database changes without one) with the Policy Server, the WebSEALs and Authorization Servers have to be restarted. You can restart the servers one at a time, thus always preserving availability.

Code examples for Armando Brothers Banking Corp.

This appendix describes the Java code that we used in our examples in the banking scenarios, how to install and deploy it in WebLogic, and where the code is available for download. Details about how to use the application and the Access Manager changes that must also be done for the projects are documented in the project chapters Chapter 15, "Protection of external Web resources" on page 329, and Chapter 16, "Application integration" on page 363.

Restriction: The code snippets provided with this Redbook serve as example code to demonstrate possible implementation solutions to integrate different kinds of applications in an Access Manager authorization framework. Therefore we did not provide one single application in an EAR file. However, you may download and install the code to reconstruct the scenarios we describe in this book. The following pages will guide you through the installation procedures.

Code organization structure

The simple Java banking application that we used in our project discussions for the ABBC Bank. All sample banking source codes are available for download at the IBM site:

```
ftp://www.redbooks.ibm.com/redbooks/SG246556
```

We define the directory layout and files for the banking application in terms of the development structure (in case you want to modify it and enable additional functionality), as well as the production installation steps required in order to have the base code properly installed. Additional instructions are also available in each project section when necessary.

Directory structure

The banking application in this book is a JAVA application using HTML, JSP, EJB, servlet, and class files that we refer to as ABCBank application.

> **Note:** Do not get confused—although our bank is named ABBC, the code snippets are all showing ABC for Armando Banking Corporation.

The file directory layout structure is shown in Figure H-1 on page 555. The main subdirectory trees are the following:

- ▶ Base directory (/)
- ▶ Static html and dynamic jsp pages (/html)
- ▶ Images used in html and jsp pages (/html/images)
- ▶ Internal classes (/com/ibm/itso)
- ▶ Enterprise bean subdirectory (/EJB)
- ▶ Backend account code (/EJB/AccountBean)
- ▶ Metadefinitions for the bean (/EJB/AccountBean/META-INF)
- ▶ Frontend account subdirectory (/EJB/frontend)
- ▶ Standard and WebLogic deployment information (EJB/frontend/WEB-INF)
- ▶ Servlet code for account processing (/EJB/frontend/WEB-INF/classes)
- ▶ Application description (/EJB/META-INF)
- ▶ Third-party application integration example (/PDPerm)

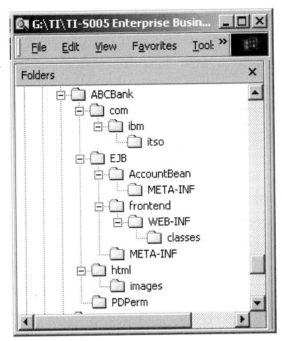

Figure H-1   Application directory structure

This directory layout is the same for all banking projects that we have some code for. The term *base code* refers to the existing application and how they should work as a standard (non-Access Manager) application. The project sections introduce the changes to the base environment in such a way that they modify some of the existing functionality of the application with respect to authentication and authorization. Some of the objects need to be placed in the WebSEAL server. The code is basically stored in WebLogic as a Web application as described in the installation steps in this chapter. Enterprise JavaBean (EJB) deployment instructions for our examples are also available. The enterprise archive (EAR) is the base unit for the sample EJB we deploy.

Application packages

There are basically four packages for our code: The core banking application, two project I packages, and the project II package.

> **Attention:** The existing code implements a method called getHome() to create the fully qualified URL for the jsp pages. This is a hardcoded value that can be changed by opening the file jsp00.java source file and modifying this method to return "" (blank), or something else appropriate, or you can also add the host w2ktst in your /etc/host file.
>
> This is required due to an existing PMR to PD 3.8.0.0 base code when using WebSEAL to connect directly to WebLogic in the standard 7001/7002 ports and the JSP code uses sendRedirect() to send the browser to a new location.
>
> This code is in class file com.ibm.util.jsp00.java. The method forces the application to use HTTPS only and to point to a Web resource ABCBank on machine w2ktst as follows:
>
> ```
> public String getHome()
> {
> return("https://w2ktst/ABCBank/");
> }
> ```

Core banking application

This is the application as it is today, with no Access Manager components or interaction. This is here as a reference to explain how we implemented the security controls and what we modified in the ongoing chapters. This application is made of HTML, JSP, and internal Java classes. This example is very simple so that you can get familiar with the JSP pages and the application flow. You can install the base application and apply any of the two variations of the code (basic/forms-based authentication) to exercise any of the two authentication scenarios.

The core package is named ABCBank_CORE.zip and has the following directory structure:

- ▶ \sg246556\ABCBank_CORE
- ▶ \sg246556\ABCBank_CORE\com
- ▶ \sg246556\ABCBank_CORE\com\ibm
- ▶ \sg246556\ABCBank_CORE\com\ibm\itso
- ▶ \sg246556\ABCBank_CORE\html
- ▶ \sg246556\ABCBank_CORE\html\images

Project I - basic authentication

This is the implementation of basic authentication with Access Manager. Refer to "Approach I - Implementation with basic authentication" on page 345 for details. This code implements a trust check for Access Manager using WebSEAL basic authentication and the junction information to propagate authentication information for the application.

The project I basic authentication package is called *ABCBank_P1_BA.zip* and it has the following directory structure:

- ► \sg246556\ABCBank_P1_BA_Kit
- ► \sg246556\ABCBank_P1_BA_Kit\com
- ► \sg246556\ABCBank_P1_BA_Kit\com\ibm
- ► \sg246556\ABCBank_P1_BA_Kit\com\ibm\itso
- ► \sg246556\ABCBank_P1_BA_Kit\html
- ► \sg246556\ABCBank_P1_BA_Kit\html\images

Project I - Forms-based authentication

This is the implementation for forms-based authentication with Access Manager. Refer to "Approach II - Forms-based authentication" on page 353 for details.

This code modifies the authentication method to now use a customized, user-friendly HTML form for login. The project I forms-based authentication package is called ABCBank_P1_FA.zip and has the following directory structure:

- ► \sg246556\ABCBank_P1_FA_Kit
- ► \sg246556\ABCBank_P1_FA_Kit\com
- ► \sg246556\ABCBank_P1_FA_Kit\com\ibm
- ► \sg246556\ABCBank_P1_FA_Kit\com\ibm\itso
- ► \sg246556\ABCBank_P1_FA_Kit\html
- ► \sg246556\ABCBank_P1_FA_Kit\html\images

Project II - WebLogic and application API integration

This is the implementation of the WebLogic Customer Real allowing shared authentication information between Access Manager and WebLogic and enabling WebLogic to trust Access Manager's authentication process. This section also covers the integration with Java and J2EE applications running the PDPerm API.

The project II package is called ABCBank_P2.zip and it has the following directory structure:

- ► \sg246556\ABCBank_P2
- ► \sg246556\ABCBank_P2\com
- ► \sg246556\ABCBank_P2\com\ibm
- ► \sg246556\ABCBank_P2\com\ibm\itso
- ► \sg246556\ABCBank_P2\EJB
- ► \sg246556\ABCBank_P2\EJB\AccountBean
- ► \sg246556\ABCBank_P2\EJB\frontend
- ► \sg246556\ABCBank_P2\EJB\META-INF
- ► \sg246556\ABCBank_P2\EJB\AccountBean\META-INF
- ► \sg246556\ABCBank_P2\EJB\frontend\WEB-INF
- ► \sg246556\ABCBank_P2\EJB\frontend\WEB-INF\classes

- ► \sg246556\ABCBank_P2\html
- ► \sg246556\ABCBank_P2\html\images
- ► \sg246556\ABCBank_P2\PDPerm

Installation

The installation of the packages is simple. You need to unzip the package with a ZIP utility. The files are all copied to specific WebLogic locations such as the application home directory or the Enterprise archive directory. We assume that you have created a WebLogic Web application called ABCBank in a server called w2ktst.

Depending on the package that you want to test (Core code, Project I - Basic authentication, Project I- Forms-based authentication, or Project II) you may need to move more or less files. We detail each possible installation for each package in the following sections.

Core installation

For core installation:

1. Stop the WebLogic Server using the WebLogic console or a script.

2. Create a directory for the application as *ABCHOME* in your WebLogic Server (for example,
   E:\W2K\BEA\WLSERVER6.1\CONFIG\PFORTSER\ABCBANK).

3. Copy all contents of SG246556\ABCBank_CORE\com\ibm\itso to *ABCHOME*\com\ibm\itso. This writes files jsp00.class and errorlog.class only.

4. Copy all contents of SG246556\ABCBank_CORE\html to *ABCHOME*. This writes all .JSP, .GIF, and .HTML files to your application root directory, following the directory sub-tree for images.

5. Start the WebLogic Server.

Project I with basic authentication features

The installation steps for this package are exactly the same as those of the core installation, as described in "Core installation" on page 558. There is no additional subdirectories or configuration settings other then the modified files in this new package.

For details about the code usage please see "Approach I - Implementation with basic authentication" on page 345.

Project I with forms-based authentication features

The installation steps for this package are exactly the same as of the core installation, as described in "Core installation" on page 558. There are no additional subdirectories or configuration settings other then the modified files in this new package.

For details about the code usage please see "Approach II - Forms-based authentication" on page 353.

Project II with WebLogic integration

The installation steps for this package use the same main items as of the core installation described in "Core installation" on page 558, plus some additional steps covered here. Bare in mind that you should only start WebLogic after completing all the steps including the following:

1. After executing all steps from the core installation (except starting WebLogic), create a directory for the Access Manager files as *PDHOME* (for example, E:\PD).

2. Modify the CLASSPATH variable in weblogic.cmd to include the PDPerm libraries as shown in Example H-1.

Example: H-1   WebLogic CLASSPATH setting

```
...
set CLASSPATH=.;.\lib\j2ee12.jar;.\lib\weblogic_sp.jar;.\lib\weblogic.jar
set
CLASSPATH=%CLASSPATH%;e:\pd\PDPerm.jar;e:\pd\ibmjceprovider.jar;e:\pd\ibmjsse.j
ar;e:\ibmpkcs.jar;e:\pd\jaas.jar;e:\pd\ibmjcefw.jar
...
```

> **Note:** This code uses the PD libraries available in *PD_Install*/example/authzn_demo/java/122/jre/lib/ext if you are using JDK 1.2.2 or *PD_Install*/example/authzn_demo/java/13/jre/lib/ext if you are using JDK 1.3.x. The JAR files were copied to a work directory such as c:\jar for development purposes.

3. Restart the WebLogic Server (in case you have it running).

Additional package information

We document here the XML parameters that we used in the deployment descriptors, the files that changed in each package, and the full list of files that should be present in each package.

EJB XML files

Here we explain the keywords that we use in the sample XML ABCBank application.

File application.xml

The application.xml file is the deployment descriptor for Enterprise application archives. The file is located in the META-INF subdirectory of the application archive.

▶ Application: Application is the root element of the application deployment descriptor.

▶ Display name: Specifies the application display name, a short name that is intended to be displayed by GUI tools.

▶ Description: The description element provides descriptive text about the application.

▶ Module: The application.xml deployment descriptor contains one module element for each module in the Enterprise archive file.

▶ Web: Defines a Web application module in the application file. The Web element contains a Web-uri element and a context-root element.

    – Web-uri: Defines the location of a Web module in the application file. This is the name of the .war file.

    – Context-root: Specifies a context root for the Web application.

    – ejb: Defines the name of the Java archive with the bean code.

File weblogic-ejb-jar.xml

The weblogic-ejb-jar.xml descriptor describes the behavior of your enterprise beans that is specific to WebLogic Server. weblogic-ejb-jar.xml has many unique WebLogic elements. It includes elements for enabling stateful session EJB replication, configuring entity EJB locking behavior, and assigning JMS queue and topic names for message-driven beans.

▶ WebLogic-ejb-jar: Root element of the WebLogic component of the EJB deployment descriptor.

▶ WebLogic-enterprise-bean: Contains the deployment information for a bean that is available in WebLogic Server.

    – ejb-name: Specifies the name of an EJB to which the WebLogic Server applies isolation level properties. This name is assigned by the ejb-jar file's deployment descriptor.

    – jndi-name: Specifies the JNDI name of an actual EJB, resource, or reference available in WebLogic Server.

File weblogic.xml

The key words are:

- weblogic-web-app: The root element for weblogic.xml.

- description: Text description of the Web application.

- security-role-assignment: Declares mapping between a security role and one or more principals in the realm.

  - role-name: Specifies the name of a security role.

  - principal-name: Specifies the name of a principal that is defined in the security realm. You can use multiple *principal-name* elements to map principals to a role.

File web.xml

The key words are:

- display-name: Specifies the Web application display name, a short name that can be displayed by GUI tools.

- servlet: Contains the declarative data of a servlet.

  - servlet-name: Defines the name of the servlet used to reference the servlet definition elsewhere in the deployment descriptor.

  - servlet-class: The fully qualified class name of the servlet.

- servlet-mapping: Defines a mapping between a servlet and a URL pattern.

  - servlet-name: The name of the servlet to which you are mapping a URL pattern. This name corresponds to the name you assigned a servlet in a *servlet* declaration tag.

  - url-pattern: Describes a pattern used to resolve URLs. The portion of the URL after the http://host:port + WebAppName is compared to the *url-pattern* by WebLogic Server. If the patterns match, the servlet mapped in this element will be called.

- security-constraint: Defines the access privileges to a collection of resources defined by the *web-resource-collection* element.

  - web-resource-collection: Defines the components of the Web Application to which this security constraint is applied.

  - auth-constraint: Defines which groups or principals have access to the collection of Web resources defined in this security constraint.

  - role-name: Defines which security roles can access resources defined in this security constraint. Security role names are mapped to principals using the security-role-ref element.

► login-config: Configures how the user is authenticated, the realm name that should be used for this application, and the attributes that are needed by the form login mechanism. The user must be authenticated in order to access any resource that is constrained by a *security-constraint* defined in the Web Application. Once authenticated, the user can be authorized to access other resources with access privileges

Special file notes

Some of the files are changed in each project as the complexity of the migration expands. Some of the code is kept without modifications. We make special notes in this appendix and in the next section about the files that were changed and what the scope of those changes is.

Shared

Files that are the same (SHARED) for all packages (CORE, Project I, and Project II):

► errorlog.java
► error.jsp
► logout.jsp
► /images/*.gif
► query_trn.jsp
► undercon.jsp
► welcome.jsp

Project I

These are the files that have changes in Project I:

► login.html: Used in forms-based authentication package, since basic authentication relies on a browser pop-up dialog box.

► login.jsp: Added Access Manager trust functionality.

► jsp00.java: Class file for wrapper codes. All wrapper code calls are here regardless of the project separation.

Project II

These are the files that have changes in Project II:

► exec_trn.jsp: Support for PDPerm API calls.

► jsp00.java: Class file for wrapper codes. All wrapper code calls are here regardless of the project separation.

► main.jsp: Add PDPerm option to demonstrate J2EE/JAVA calls to PD directly.

► navbar.jsp: Add /TAME reference for EJB tests using the ABCAccountServlet.

Since this is a full package of all changes for project II together, there is new functionality here that is only available in this package (the existing Project I files do not have, for example, the EJB data or the third party example in the directory structure). This is the complete application with forms-based authentication support and all the other application features available such as HTML, JSP, Servlet, EJB, and stand-alone Java utilities or integration code.

Manifest (file list)

Here we show the files that should be present in each package.

Core package

The files that should be present in the core package are:

```
\SG246556\ABCBank_CORE\jsp00.java
\SG246556\ABCBank_CORE\errorlog.java
\SG246556\ABCBank_CORE\filelist.txt
\SG246556\ABCBank_CORE\com\ibm\itso\jsp00.class
\SG246556\ABCBank_CORE\com\ibm\itso\errorlog.class
\SG246556\ABCBank_CORE\html\login.html
\SG246556\ABCBank_CORE\html\exec_trn.jsp
\SG246556\ABCBank_CORE\html\error.jsp
\SG246556\ABCBank_CORE\html\login.jsp
\SG246556\ABCBank_CORE\html\logout.jsp
\SG246556\ABCBank_CORE\html\main.jsp
\SG246556\ABCBank_CORE\html\navbar.jsp
\SG246556\ABCBank_CORE\html\query_trn.jsp
\SG246556\ABCBank_CORE\html\undercon.jsp
\SG246556\ABCBank_CORE\html\welcome.jsp
\SG246556\ABCBank_CORE\html\images\loginbtn.gif
\SG246556\ABCBank_CORE\html\images\products_services.gif
\SG246556\ABCBank_CORE\html\images\lanim.gif
```

Project I - Basic authentication

The files that should be present in the basic authentication package are:

```
\SG246556\ABCBank_P1_BA_Kit\jsp00.java
\SG246556\ABCBank_P1_BA_Kit\errorlog.java
\SG246556\ABCBank_P1_BA_Kit\filelist.txt
\SG246556\ABCBank_P1_BA_Kit\com\ibm\itso\jsp00.class
\SG246556\ABCBank_P1_BA_Kit\com\ibm\itso\errorlog.class
\SG246556\ABCBank_P1_BA_Kit\html\login.html
\SG246556\ABCBank_P1_BA_Kit\html\exec_trn.jsp
\SG246556\ABCBank_P1_BA_Kit\html\login.jsp
\SG246556\ABCBank_P1_BA_Kit\html\error.jsp
\SG246556\ABCBank_P1_BA_Kit\html\logout.jsp
```

\SG246556\ABCBank_P1_BA_Kit\html\main.jsp
\SG246556\ABCBank_P1_BA_Kit\html\navbar.jsp
\SG246556\ABCBank_P1_BA_Kit\html\pdappstatus.jsp
\SG246556\ABCBank_P1_BA_Kit\html\query_trn.jsp
\SG246556\ABCBank_P1_BA_Kit\html\undercon.jsp
\SG246556\ABCBank_P1_BA_Kit\html\welcome.jsp
\SG246556\ABCBank_P1_BA_Kit\html\images\loginbtn.gif
\SG246556\ABCBank_P1_BA_Kit\html\images\products_services.gif
\SG246556\ABCBank_P1_BA_Kit\html\images\lanim.gif

Project I - Forms-based authentication

The files that should be present in the forms-based authentication package are:

\SG246556\ABCBank_P1_FA_Kit\com
\SG246556\ABCBank_P1_FA_Kit\html
\SG246556\ABCBank_P1_FA_Kit\jsp00.java
\SG246556\ABCBank_P1_FA_Kit\errorlog.java
\SG246556\ABCBank_P1_FA_Kit\filelist.txt
\SG246556\ABCBank_P1_FA_Kit\com\ibm
\SG246556\ABCBank_P1_FA_Kit\com\ibm\itso
\SG246556\ABCBank_P1_FA_Kit\com\ibm\itso\jsp00.class
\SG246556\ABCBank_P1_FA_Kit\com\ibm\itso\errorlog.class
\SG246556\ABCBank_P1_FA_Kit\html\images
\SG246556\ABCBank_P1_FA_Kit\html\login.html
\SG246556\ABCBank_P1_FA_Kit\html\exec_trn.jsp
\SG246556\ABCBank_P1_FA_Kit\html\login.jsp
\SG246556\ABCBank_P1_FA_Kit\html\error.jsp
\SG246556\ABCBank_P1_FA_Kit\html\logout.jsp
\SG246556\ABCBank_P1_FA_Kit\html\main.jsp
\SG246556\ABCBank_P1_FA_Kit\html\navbar.jsp
\SG246556\ABCBank_P1_FA_Kit\html\pdappstatus.jsp
\SG246556\ABCBank_P1_FA_Kit\html\query_trn.jsp
\SG246556\ABCBank_P1_FA_Kit\html\undercon.jsp
\SG246556\ABCBank_P1_FA_Kit\html\welcome.jsp
\SG246556\ABCBank_P1_FA_Kit\html\images\loginbtn.gif
\SG246556\ABCBank_P1_FA_Kit\html\images\products_services.gif
\SG246556\ABCBank_P1_FA_Kit\html\images\lanim.gif

Project II - WebLogic and API integration

The files that should be present in the WebLogic and API integration package are:

\SG246556\ABCBank_P2\errorlog.java
\SG246556\ABCBank_P2\jsp00.java
\SG246556\ABCBank_P2\filelist.txt
\SG246556\ABCBank_P2\com\ibm\itso\jsp00.class

```
\SG246556\ABCBank_P2\com\ibm\itso\errorlog.class
\SG246556\ABCBank_P2\EJB\buildear.bat
\SG246556\ABCBank_P2\EJB\buildjar.bat
\SG246556\ABCBank_P2\EJB\buildobj.bat
\SG246556\ABCBank_P2\EJB\buildwar.bat
\SG246556\ABCBank_P2\EJB\ABCDemoApp.ear
\SG246556\ABCBank_P2\EJB\ABCAccountBean.jar
\SG246556\ABCBank_P2\EJB\ABCfrontend.war
\SG246556\ABCBank_P2\EJB\AccountBean\ABCAccount.class
\SG246556\ABCBank_P2\EJB\AccountBean\ABCAccountBean.class
\SG246556\ABCBank_P2\EJB\AccountBean\ABCAccountHome.class
\SG246556\ABCBank_P2\EJB\AccountBean\ABCAccountHome.java
\SG246556\ABCBank_P2\EJB\AccountBean\ABCAccount.java
\SG246556\ABCBank_P2\EJB\AccountBean\ABCAccountBean.java
\SG246556\ABCBank_P2\EJB\AccountBean\META-INF\weblogic-ejb-jar.xml
\SG246556\ABCBank_P2\EJB\AccountBean\META-INF\ejb-jar.xml
\SG246556\ABCBank_P2\EJB\frontend\WEB-INF\weblogic.xml
\SG246556\ABCBank_P2\EJB\frontend\WEB-INF\web.xml
\SG246556\ABCBank_P2\EJB\frontend\WEB-INF\classes\ABCAccountServlet.c
                lass
\SG246556\ABCBank_P2\EJB\frontend\WEB-INF\classes\ABCAccountServlet.j
                ava
\SG246556\ABCBank_P2\EJB\META-INF\application.xml
\SG246556\ABCBank_P2\html\login.html
\SG246556\ABCBank_P2\html\exec_trn.jsp
\SG246556\ABCBank_P2\html\login.jsp
\SG246556\ABCBank_P2\html\error.jsp
\SG246556\ABCBank_P2\html\logout.jsp
\SG246556\ABCBank_P2\html\main.jsp
\SG246556\ABCBank_P2\html\navbar.jsp
\SG246556\ABCBank_P2\html\pdappstatus.jsp
\SG246556\ABCBank_P2\html\query_trn.jsp
\SG246556\ABCBank_P2\html\undercon.jsp
\SG246556\ABCBank_P2\html\welcome.jsp
\SG246556\ABCBank_P2\html\images\loginbtn.gif
\SG246556\ABCBank_P2\html\images\products_services.gif
\SG246556\ABCBank_P2\html\images\lanim.gif
\SG246556\ABCBank_P2\PDPerm\exec.bat
\SG246556\ABCBank_P2\PDPerm\build.bat
\SG246556\ABCBank_P2\PDPerm\pforsterTH.class
\SG246556\ABCBank_P2\PDPerm\pforsterTH.java
```

Additional material

This redbook refers to additional material that can be downloaded from the Internet as described below.

Locating the Web material

The Web material associated with this redbook is available in softcopy on the Internet from the IBM Redbooks Web server. Point your Web browser to:

```
ftp://www.redbooks.ibm.com/redbooks/SG246556
```

Alternatively, you can go to the IBM Redbooks Web site at:

```
ibm.com/redbooks
```

Select the **Additional materials** and open the directory that corresponds with the redbook form number, SG24-6556.

Using the Web material

The additional Web material that accompanies this redbook is described in detail in Appendix H, "Code examples for Armando Brothers Banking Corp." on page 553.

Glossary

ActiveX ActiveX is the name Microsoft has given to a set of strategic, object-oriented programming technologies and tools. The main technology is the Component Object Model (COM). Used in a network with a directory and additional support, COM becomes the Distributed Component Object Model (DCOM). The main thing that you create when writing a program to run in the ActiveX environment is a component, which is a self-sufficient program that can be run anywhere in your ActiveX network (currently a network consisting of Windows and Macintosh systems). This component is known as an ActiveX control. ActiveX is Microsoft's answer to the Java technology from Sun Microsystems. An ActiveX control is roughly equivalent to a Java applet.

BS7799 British Standard 7799, a document describing enterprise security.

CA A Certificate Authority is an authority in a network that issues and manages security credentials and public keys for message encryption. As part of a public key infrastructure (PKI), a CA checks with a Registration Authority (RA) to verify information provided by the requestor of a digital certificate. If the RA verifies the requestor's information, the CA can then issue a certificate.

CORBA Common Object Request Broker Architecture is an architecture and specification for creating, distributing, and managing distributed program objects in a network. It allows programs at different locations and developed by different vendors to communicate in a network through an interface broker. CORBA was developed by a consortium of vendors through the Object Management Group, which currently includes over 500 member companies. Both the International Organization for Standardization (ISO) and X/Open have sanctioned CORBA as the standard architecture for distributed objects (which are also known as components). CORBA 3 is the latest level.

CTCPEC Canadian Trusted Computer Product Evaluation Criteria published by the Canadian government.

DMZ A demilitarized zone is an area of your network that separates it from other areas of the network, including the Internet.

EJB Enterprise JavaBeans is an architecture for setting up program components written in the Java programming language that run in the server parts of a computer network that uses the client/server model. Enterprise JavaBeans is built on the JavaBeans technology for distributing program components to clients in a network. Enterprise JavaBeans offers enterprises the advantage of being able to control change at the server rather than having to update each individual computer with a client whenever a new program component is changed or added. EJB components have the advantage of being reusable in multiple applications. To deploy an EJB Bean or component, it must be part of a specific application, which is called a container.

ITSEC Information Technology Security Evaluation Criteria, published by the European Commission.

J2EE Java 2 Platform Enterprise Edition is a Java platform designed for the mainframe-scale computing typical of large enterprises. Sun Microsystems, together with industry partners such as IBM, designed J2EE to simplify application development in a thin client tiered environment.

JDBC Java Database Connectivity is an application program interface (API) specification for connecting programs written in Java to the data in popular databases. The application program interface lets you encode access request statements in the structured query language (SQL) that is then passed to the program that manages the database. It returns the results through a similar interface. JDBC is very similar to the SQL Access Group's Open Database Connectivity (ODBC) and, with a small bridge program, you can use the JDBC interface to access databases through the ODBC interface.

JNDI Java Naming and Directory Interface enables Java platform-based applications to access multiple naming and directory services. Part of the Java Enterprise application programming interface (API) set, JNDI makes it possible for developers to create portable applications that are enabled for a number of different naming and directory services, including file systems, and directory services, such as Lightweight Directory Access Protocol (LDAP), Novell Directory Services, and Network Information System (NIS), and distributed object systems, such as the Common Object Request Broker Architecture (CORBA), Java Remote Method Invocation (RMI), and Enterprise JavaBeans (EJB).

JSP Java Server Page is a technology for controlling the content or appearance of Web pages through the use of servlets, small programs that are specified in the Web page and run on the Web server to modify the Web page before it is sent to the user who requested it.

LDAP Lightweight Directory Access Protocol is a software protocol for enabling anyone to locate organizations, individuals, and other resources, such as files and devices, in a network, whether on the public Internet or on a corporate intranet. LDAP is a lightweight (smaller amount of code) version of Directory Access Protocol (DAP), which is part of X.500, a standard for directory services in a network.

LTPA Lightweight Third Party Authentication implements an authentication protocol that uses a trusted third-party Lightweight Directory Access Protocol (LDAP) server. LTPA causes a search to be performed against the LDAP directory. LTPA supports both the basic and certificate challenge type.

MASS Method for Architecting Secure Solutions.

NIS Network Information System is a network naming and administration system for smaller networks that was developed by Sun Microsystems. NIS+ is a later version that provides additional security and other facilities. Using NIS, each host client or server computer in the system has knowledge about the entire system. A user at any host can get access to files or applications on any host in the network with a single user identification and password. NIS is similar to the Internet's domain name system (DNS), but somewhat simpler and designed for a smaller network. It is intended for use on local area networks.

OSI Open Systems Interconnection is a standard description or reference model for how messages should be transmitted between any two points in a telecommunication network. Its purpose is to guide product implementors so that their products will consistently work with other products. The reference model defines seven layers of functions that take place at each end of a communication. Although OSI is not always strictly adhered to in terms of keeping related functions together in a well-defined layer, many, if not most, products involved in telecommunication make an attempt to describe themselves in relation to the OSI model. It is also valuable as a single reference view of communication that furnishes everyone a common ground for education and discussion.

PDA Personal digital assistant. A term for any small mobile hand-held device that provides computing and information storage and retrieval capabilities for personal or business use, often for keeping schedule calendars and address book information handy.

PKI A public key infrastructure enables users of a basically unsecure public network such as the Internet, to securely and privately exchange data and money through the use of a public and a private cryptographic key pair that is obtained and shared through a trusted authority.

POP Protected Object Policy.

RA A Registration Authority is an authority in a network that verifies user requests for a digital certificate and tells the certificate authority (CA) to issue it. RAs are part of a public key infrastructure (PKI), a networked system that enables companies and users to exchange information and money safely and securely. The digital certificate contains a public key that is used to encrypt and decrypt messages and digital signatures.

RAS Remote Access Service.

SOAP Simple Object Access Protocol is a way for a program running in one kind of operating system to communicate with a program in the same or another kind of an operating system by using the HTTP Protocol and XML as the mechanisms for information exchange.

SSL The Secure Sockets Layer is a commonly-used protocol for managing the security of a message transmission on the Internet. SSL has recently been succeeded by Transport Layer Security (TLS), which is based on SSL.

UDDI Universal Description, Discovery, and Integration is an XML-based registry for businesses worldwide to list themselves on the Internet. Its ultimate goal is to streamline online transactions by enabling companies to find one another on the Web and make their systems interoperable for e-commerce.

WAP Wireless Application Protocol is a specification for a set of communication protocols to standardize the way that wireless devices, such as cellular telephones and radio transceivers, can be used for Internet access, including e-mail, the World Wide Web, newsgroups, and Internet Relay Chat (IRC). While Internet access has been possible in the past, different manufacturers have used different technologies. In the future, devices and service systems that use WAP will be able to interoperate.

WIM WAP Identity Module. A WIM will support class 3 functionality and have embedded support for public key cryptography. An example of a WIM is a smart card, which you can use in a mobile phone or PDA or it can be part of a Subscriber Identity Module (SIM in the case of GSM networks).

WML Wireless Markup Language, formerly called Handheld Devices Markup Languages (HDML), is a language that allows the text portions of Web pages to be presented on cellular telephones and personal digital assistants (PDAs) via wireless access. WML is part of the Wireless Application Protocol (WAP) that is being proposed by several vendors to standards bodies.

WSDL The Web Services Description Language is an XML-based language used to describe the services a business offers and to provide a way for individuals and other businesses to access those services electronically. WSDL is the cornerstone of the Universal Description, Discovery, and Integration (UDDI) initiative spearheaded by Microsoft, IBM, and Ariba.

WTLS   Wireless Transport Layer Security is the security level for Wireless Application Protocol (WAP) applications. Based on Transport Layer Security (TLS) Version 1.0 (a security layer used in the Internet, equivalent to Secure Socket Layer 3.1), WTLS was developed to address the problematic issues surrounding mobile network devices, such as limited processing power and memory capacity, and low bandwidth, and to provide adequate authentication, data integrity, and privacy protection mechanisms.

XML   eXtensible Markup Language is a flexible way to create common information formats and share both the format and the data on the World Wide Web, intranets, and elsewhere. For example, computer makers might agree on a standard or common way to describe the information about a computer product (processor speed, memory size, and so forth) and then describe the product information format with XML. Such a standard way of describing data would enable a user to send an intelligent agent (a program) to each computer maker's Web site, gather data, and then make a valid comparison. XML can be used by any individual or group of individuals or companies that wants to share information in a consistent way.

XSL   eXtensible Stylesheet Language is a language for creating a style sheet that describes how data sent over the Web using the eXtensible Markup Language (XML) is to be presented to the user.

Abbreviations and acronyms

AAT	Application Assembly Tool
ACL	Access control list
API	Application programming interface
aznAPI	Authorization Application Programming Interface
BA	Basic authentication
CA	Certificate Authority
CDAS	Cross Domain Authentication Service
CDMF	Cross Domain Mapping Framework
CDSSO	Cross Domain Single Sign-On
CLI	Command line interface
DHCP	Dynamic Host Configuration Protocol
DNS	Domain name service
EAS	External Authorization Service
EGW	Everyplace Wireless Gateway
EPAC	Extended Privilege Attribute Certificate
GUI	Graphical user interface
IBM	International Business Machines Corporation
IEFT	Internet Engineering Task Force
ITSO	International Technical Support Organization
J2EE	Java 2 Platform Enterprise Edition
JAAS	Java Authentication and Authorization Service
JsP	Java Server Pages
LTPA	Lightweight third party authentication mechanism
MAS	Master Authentication Server
MASS	Method for Architecting Secure Solutions
MPA	Multiplexing Proxy Agent
MS-ISDN	Mobile Subscriber-Integrated Services Digital Network
MTA	Mail transport agent
NAT	Network Address Translation
NTP	Network Time Protocol
OCSP	Online Certificate Status Protocol
OTA	Over The Air
OU	Organizational unit
PAM	Plug-on Authentication Module
PDA	Personal Digital Assistants
PDC-P	Personal Digital Cellular-Packet
POC	Proof-of-concept
POS	Point-of-sale
RACF	Resource Access Control Facility
RADIUS	Remote Authentication Dial In User Service
RAS	Remote Access Server
RDBMS	Relational database management system
REACT	Realtime Easily Accessible Customer Transactions
SIM	Subscriber Identity Module
SMS	Short messaging services
SPA	Standard Proxy Agent

SSL	Secure Sockets Layer
SWE	Siebel Web Extension
TAI	Trust Association Interceptor
TGSO	Tivoli Global Sign-On
TIM	Tivoli Identity Manager
TLS	Transport Layer Security
TSM	Tivoli Security Manager
WAP	Wireless Application Protocol
WEP	Wired Equivalent Privacy
WIM	WAP Identity Module
wLAN	Wireless Local Area Networks
WLS	WebLogic Server
WML	Wireless Markup Language
wPAN	Wireless Personal Area Networks
WPM	Web Portal Manager
WTLS	Wireless Transport Layer Security

Related publications

The publications listed in this section are considered particularly suitable for a more detailed discussion of the topics covered in this redbook.

IBM Redbooks

For information on ordering these publications, see "How to get IBM Redbooks" on page 579.

▶ *Enterprise Security Architecture using IBM Tivoli Security Solutions*, SG24-6014

▶ *HACMP Enhanced Scalability Handbook*, SG24-5328

▶ *IBM WebSphere Everyplace Server: A Guide for Architects and System Integrators*, SG24-6189

▶ *IBM WebSphere Everyplace Server Service Provider Enable Offerings: Enterprise Wireless Applications*, SG24-6519

▶ *IBM WebSphere Performance Pack Load Balancing with IBM SecureWay Network Dispatcher*, SG24-5858

▶ *IBM WebSphere Version 4.0 Advanced Edition Security*, SG24-6520

▶ *MQSeries Security: Example of Using a Channel Security Exit, Encryption and Decryption*, SG24-5306

▶ *New Capabilities in IBM WebSphere Transcoding Publisher Version 3.5 Extending Web Applications to the Pervasive*, SG24-6233

▶ *WebSphere Edge Server: Working with Web Traffic Express and Network Dispatcher*, SG24-6172

Other resources

These publications are also relevant as further information sources:

▶ *IBM Tivoli Access Manager for e-Business Administration Java Classes Developer's Reference*, SC32-0842

▶ *IBM Tivoli Access Manager for e-Business Administration C API Developer Reference Version 3.9*, GC32-0843

▶ *IBM Tivoli Access for e-Business Manager Authorization C API Developer's Reference Version 3.9*, GC32-0849

- *IBM Tivoli Access Manager for e-Business Authorization Java Classes Developer's Reference Version 3.9, GC23-4688*

- *IBM Tivoli Access Manager for e-Business Base Administration Guide Version 3.9, GC23-4684*

- *IBM Tivoli Access Manager for e-business Base Installation Guide Version 3.9, GC32-0844*

- *IBM Tivoli Access Manager for e-Business Capacity Planning Guide Version 3.9, GC32-0847*

- *IBM Tivoli Access Manager for e-Business Maintenance and Troubleshooting Guide Version 3.9, GC32-0846*

- *IBM Tivoli Access Manager for e-Business WebSEAL Administration Guide Version 3.9, GC23-4682*

- *IBM Tivoli Access Manager for e-Business WebSphere Application Server User's Guide Version 3.9, GC32-0850*

- *IBM Tivoli SecureWay Policy Director WebSEAL Administration Guide, GC32-0684*

- *Network Dispatcher User's Guide Version 3.0 for Multiplatforms, GC31-8496*

- *Tivoli Policy Director for MQSeries Administration Reference Guide 3.8* (provided with the product)

- *Tivoli Policy Director for WebLogic Server User Guide Version 3.8, SC32-0831*

- *Tivoli Policy Director for WebSphere Application Server User Guide Version 3.8, SC32-0832*

- *Tivoli SecureWay Policy Director Authorization ADK Developer Reference Version 3.8, GC32-0810*

- *Tivoli SecureWay Policy Director Error Message Reference Version 3.8, GC32-0815*

- *Tivoli SecureWay Policy Director WebSEAL Administration Guide, GC32-0684*

Referenced Web sites

These Web sites are also relevant as further information sources:

- All sample banking source codes

  ftp://www.redbooks.ibm.com/redbooks/SG246556

- Information about LDAP support in WebSphere 4.0.2

  `http://www-3.ibm.com/software/webservers/appserv/doc/v40/prereqs/ae_v402.htm`

- Information about WebSphere 3.5.3

  `http://www-3.ibm.com/software/webservers/appserv/doc/v35/idx_aas.htm`

- Sun's Web site

  `http://java.sun.com`

- The Open Group security home page

  `http://www.opengroup.org/security/topics.htm`

- Tivoli Customer Support software download site

  `http://www.tivoli.com/secure/support/downloads`

How to get IBM Redbooks

You can order hardcopy Redbooks, as well as view, download, or search for Redbooks at the following Web site:

ibm.com/redbooks

You can also download additional materials (code samples or diskette/CD-ROM images) from that site.

IBM Redbooks collections

Redbooks are also available on CD-ROMs. Click the CD-ROMs button on the Redbooks Web site for information about all the CD-ROMs offered, as well as updates and formats.

Index